D1617242

FULTON J. SHEEN

Fulton J. Sheen

An American Catholic Response to the Twentieth Century

KATHLEEN L. RILEY

ST PAULS

Alba House

Library of Congress Cataloging-in-Publication Data

Riley, Kathleen L.
   Fulton J. Sheen : an American Catholic response to the twentieth
century / Kathleen L. Riley.
      p. cm.
Includes bibliographical references.
   ISBN 0-8189-0915-3
1. Sheen, Fulton J. (Fulton John), 1895-1979. 2. Catholic
Church—United States—Bishops—Biography.   I. Title.

BX4705.S612R55 2003
282'.092—dc21
                                        2002156622

Produced and designed in the United States of America by the
Fathers and Brothers of the Society of St. Paul,
2187 Victory Boulevard, Staten Island, New York 10314-6603,
as part of their communications apostolate.

ISBN: 0-8189-0915-3

Printing Information:

Current Printing - first digit   1   2   3   4   5   6   7   8   9   10

Year of Current Printing - first year shown
2004   2005   2006   2007   2008   2009   2010   2011   2012   2013

Contents

v

Preface

The publication of this book is long overdue. When I originally wrote my dissertation in 1988, it was the first scholarly treatment of Fulton J. Sheen as a major figure in the history of American Catholicism. For a variety of personal reasons, first and foremost my vocation as a mother which began with my daughter's arrival from Korea in 1990, I was never able to find the time and energy necessary to revise it in a timely fashion. For years, the spirit of Bishop Sheen has haunted me — always in a gentle and supportive fashion — so I am most thankful that my long quest has finally been fulfilled.

Despite the fact that others have written about Sheen in the intervening years, I think that my research and work stands up well as a pioneering effort to take Bishop Sheen seriously, above and beyond his status as a television star, too easily dismissed as a nostalgic figure from the past. So, like my subject, I am recycling some "old wine" in a "new bottle," and I am especially grateful to Fr. Edmund Lane, SSP at Alba House for the opportunity to finally publish my work.

During the long and winding road I've traveled to arrive at this point, I've received a good deal of support and encouragement along the way. I have been blessed with many fine teachers and mentors, starting with Rev. Francis Shimscheiner, OSFS, who first taught me how to write at DeSales Catholic High School in Lockport, New York. At Nazareth College of Rochester, Dr. Richard DelVecchio modeled the life of the history professor so well that his example led me to follow in his footsteps. And at the University of Notre Dame, Professors Philip Gleason and the late M.A. Fitzsimons made a world of difference in how I live my life as a student and teacher of American Catholicism.

Family and friends have always been my source of greatest strength, along with my faith. Three long-time friends — Molly, Ann and Molly — deserve special mention, along with my fellow graduate students from my Notre Dame days, especially Fr. Bill Miscamble, CSC. And to two wonderful priests, friends and fellow historians, Fr. Robert F. McNamara and Fr. William Wolkovich-Valkavicius, I owe a profound debt of gratitude, for their regular inquiries about how "the book" was progressing, and persistence in encouraging me to tell my story about Bishop Sheen. My colleagues, at both Ohio Dominican University and Canisius College, have also been a great source of support, both personally and intellectually.

It is to my family, however, that I owe my greatest appreciation: to my parents, John and Patricia, for sacrificing so much for my education; and my siblings (and their families), just for being fellow Riley eccentrics: Peg (and Brent and Katie); J.P. (Rev. John P. Riley, CSC); Tom (and Mary and children); Dr. Dan; and Matt; and finally, to Emily, my pride and joy — I hope that you will be proud of your Mom, and understanding of my preoccupation with "that Bishop."

Over the years, I've always taken special comfort and inspiration in the following quotation from the New Testament, St. Paul's Letter to the Philippians (2:12-13, 16); I offer it here with some sense of closure:

> Work with anxious concern to achieve your salvation.
> It is God who, in His good will toward you, begets in
> you any measure of desire or achievement... you give me
> cause to boast that I did not run the race in vain, or work
> to no purpose.

December 9, 2002   *K.R.*

Introduction

In the years since this book was originally conceived — as a doctoral dissertation at the University of Notre Dame[1] — interest in the life of Archbishop Fulton J. Sheen has grown, on both the popular and scholarly fronts. Presently, the most intriguing aspect of this peaking interest can be found in the canonization process underway in the Diocese of Peoria, Illinois — the home diocese where Sheen was born in 1895. Bishop Daniel R. Jenky, CSC, has taken up the cause originally initiated in 2000, when John Cardinal O'Connor of New York approved a preliminary effort to advance the case for having the greatest twentieth century preacher and evangelist in the United States become a saint, "an American son born in our American heartland."[2]

The case for sainthood, according to Bishop Jenky, is based upon Sheen's personal sanctity and his reputation as a major figure in the history of American Catholicism. For sixty years — from his ordination in 1919 to his death in 1979 — Fulton Sheen was guided by the maxim of working out a "Christian response to the challenge of the times." As Thomistic philosopher and professor at the Catholic University of America, prolific writer, pioneer of the electronic gospel and convert-maker, leader of both the Catholic

---

[1] See Kathleen Riley (Fields), "Bishop Fulton J. Sheen: An American Catholic Response to the Twentieth Century," Ph.D. dissertation, University of Notre Dame, 1988. A complete bibliography and short essay on the Bishop Sheen Archives can be found in that original dissertation.

[2] For examples of news coverage of the Sheen canonization process, see the "special issue" of the *National Catholic Register,* September 22-28, 2002: "Canonization Process Begun for Archbishop Fulton Sheen," based upon the information gathered by the Catholic News Service; and H. Gregory Meyer's "Going for Church's Highest Rating/From Prime Time to a Patron Saint?" in the *Chicago Tribune,* November 3, 2002.

anti-communist crusade and the missionary Society for the Propagation of the Faith, and Bishop of Rochester in the aftermath of
the Second Vatican Council, Sheen lived in the religious spotlight
during the middle years of the American Century. This "life worth
living" was a long-running performance during times of great
growth and change for the Church Sheen served so well.

Now recognized as a "Servant of God" by the Congregation
for the Causes of Saints at the Vatican,[3] Sheen's life continues to
inspire the faithful in the twenty-first century, an example of piety
and singular achievement as a priest and loyal son of the Church.
An image from Sheen's own fertile imagination, taken from the
last book he wrote, *Those Mysterious Priests,* is especially appropriate in this context; Sheen likened the life of a priest to that of a
"sailor in a storm at sea" who "functions best at times of crisis like
ours."[4] Certainly, having weathered the storms of twentieth century American history, times of both peril and promise, Sheen's
personal odyssey mirrored that of the Catholic Church; bearing
witness during times of crisis in his own lifetime, he was a transi-
tional figure whose reputation after his death might now earn him
a place in history as the first American-born male saint.

A spate of recent attention focused on the life of Fulton Sheen,
which has served to recognize the important role he played in the
emergence of a public American Catholicism — above and beyond
that of being a television star during the fifties — began in 1995,
the centennial of his birth. Several representative treatments of
American religious history share a common emphasis and overlap-
ping themes,[5] starting with a commemoration held at the Athe-

---

[3] H. Gregory Meyer, "Going for the Church's Highest Rating."

[4] Fulton J. Sheen, *Those Mysterious Priests* (Garden City, NY: Doubleday and Co., 1974),
p. 11.

[5] In addition to the six more "scholarly" treatments of the life and times of Bishop Sheen
I have chosen to analyze here, there are numerous other works, both academic and popular,
which testify to a renewed interest in Sheen. For examples, see Patricia Kossmann's *From
the Angel's Blackboard: The Best of Fulton J. Sheen, A Centennial Celebration* (Liguori, MO:
Triumph Books, 1995); Christopher Owen Lynch's *Selling Catholicism: Bishop Sheen and
the Power of Television* (Lexington: The University Press of Kentucky, 1998); and Gregory Ladd's *Archbishop Fulton J. Sheen: A Man for All Media* (San Francisco: Ignatius Press,
2001), a "coffee table" book of photographs.

naeum "Regina Apostolorum" in Rome on May 10, 1995.[6] The two conferences of the Program were designed to tie the person of the Archbishop — "The Life and Times of Fulton J. Sheen" by Monsignor (now Bishop) Timothy Dolan — to the larger topic of the "Mass Media and the New Evangelization," by Archbishop John P. Foley. Dolan invoked the memory of Sheen — "the greatest preacher and teacher... the most popular, recognized and influential priest... the Catholic Church in the United States has ever known" — for its inspiration to those who would use "the potential of the media for bringing gospel values to the world."[7] The secret of Sheen's success "...the engine which drove Fulton J. Sheen was the intense desire to make the Catholic Church known, accepted and appreciated in American society, and in doing so, to move Catholics in America from an outsider to an insider status... without compromising essential Catholic identity."[8] Sheen was able to accomplish this feat because of three trends which gave him the "providential opportunity" to prove the compatibility of Catholicism and the American spirit: the popularity of Thomistic philosophy in academia following World War I, when Sheen launched his public career; the crusade against Communism; and the religious revival which followed in the wake of World War II, when Sheen reached the apex of his popularity and influence.[9] Placing Sheen in the context of the mass media because of his "knowledge, skill, spirituality and dynamic appeal," Archbishop Foley saw him as "representing Catholicism to the nation with the intellectual clarity and eloquence of speech which the true faith demanded... no one figure in the history of the U.S... touched as many lives as did Archbishop Sheen":

[6] I am indebted to Fr. Mark Williams of the North American College for sending me a printed copy of the two conferences presented at the commemoration; Fr. Williams is at work on a dissertation on Sheen and his views of the priest as "victim."

[7] See Monsignor Timothy Dolan's "Archbishop Fulton J. Sheen, 1895-1995" in the pamphlet printed in Rome in 1995, pp. 9-17.

[8] *Ibid.*, pp. 12-13.

[9] *Ibid.*, pp. 13-16.

...he would have relished the approach of the year
2000.... Sheen was a man who appreciated the dramatic
touch and symbolic event... he knew how to use the
media. He was a master of the written word, the spoken word, and of the special needs of a television appearance.[10]

These words, underscoring Pope John Paul II's calls for a "new
evangelization," are evocative of the advocates of Sheen's canonization, who see him as the "eventual patron saint of the modern
media."[11]

Historian Martin Marty devoted his attention to Bishop
Sheen in the third volume of his masterful synthesis on *Modern
American Religion: Under God, Indivisible, 1941-1960*.[12] Writing
about his topic in light of Henry Luce's characterization of the
twentieth century as the "American Century," Marty analyzed
Sheen in terms of his value as a symbol of popular culture during
the national search for unity and harmony in the post-war religious
revival. Fulton Sheen was truly one of the Catholic Church's most
vital assets during this critical period, and the full measure of his
contribution should be appreciated and recognized. Bishop Sheen
played an important role in the forging of an American Catholic
identity, and the Church was a vital institution representing order
and unity as an alternative to the chaos of the secular world. In fact,
no one exceeded Sheen, in terms of his "popularity, eloquence, rep-
resentativeness and reach beyond Catholicism," in "making the case
for Catholicism to the American public."[13]

This same recognition of Sheen's unique contribution in cre-

---

[10] Archbishop John P. Foley, "Mass Media and the New Evangelization," in the commemo-
rative pamphlet printed in Rome, 1995.

[11] Gregg Ladd, co-founder of the Archbishop Fulton John Sheen Foundation; quoted in
the *Chicago Tribune* article by H. Gregory Meyer.

[12] Martin E. Marty, *Modern American Religion, Volume 3: Under God, Indivisible, 1941-1960*
(Chicago: The University of Chicago Press, 1996).

[13] *Ibid.*, p. 89. This author is struck by how neatly Marty's criteria match up with those in
the conclusion to my dissertation and this book.

ating an American Catholic identity can be found in *American Catholic: The Saints and Sinners Who Built America's Most Powerful Church* by Charles R. Morris. Calling Sheen the "most successful public lecturer in the history of television," Morris noted that the "public image of the Catholic Church in the forties and fifties was nothing short of spectacular"[14] — in no small measure due to Sheen:

> If there was a public face of Catholicism in the 1950's, it was a distinguished one with silver hair, arresting black eyes and a gentle smile... {on "Life Is Worth Living"}... he was elegant, elevated, relaxed, often very funny... he pulled it off without a hint of sectarianism.... All at the same time he managed to be religious, undogmatic, humane and unthreatening... week after week, the performances were simply brilliant.[15]

Sheen's featured role in the post-Vatican II drama of American Catholicism was updated by the Rev. Robert F. McNamara in the second edition of his history, *The Diocese of Rochester in America, 1868-1993*. Characterizing Sheen as a "bright meteor" as the sixth bishop of Rochester, New York, Fr. McNamara saw Sheen as an innovator and a reconciler, despite the fact that he "burned out" toward the end of his administration.[16] The Bishop's overall record was a positive one, as a man whose earlier career was one of "arresting, innovative insights, calculated to reconcile the Church to the secular world... speaking for a point of view that was non-partisan, cosmopolitan rather than nationalist, eternal rather than temporal, Fulton Sheen came to be regarded as a prophetic voice."[17] With the passage of time, Sheen's contributions to the Church of

---

[14] Charles R. Morris, *American Catholic: The Saints and Sinners Who Built America's Most Powerful Church* (New York: Times Books/Random House, 1997), p. ix.

[15] *Ibid.*, pp. 225-227.

[16] Robert F. McNamara, *The Diocese of Rochester in America, 1868-1993* (The Roman Catholic Diocese of Rochester, NY, 1998), p. 538.

[17] *Ibid.*, p. 539.

Rochester have become more evident; his legacy is not so much a bequest of achievements, though there were many, but one of focus. In the final analysis, Fulton Sheen should be remembered as a "catalytic agent."[18]

In *Catholics and American Culture: Fulton Sheen, Dorothy Day and the Notre Dame Football Team,* Mark Massa, SJ, argues that "irony" provides the best lens for understanding the religious meaning of America, and gives Sheen his due by including him in the "trinity" of popular American Catholic cultural icons which comprise the sub-title of his book. On a more serious analytical level, Massa depicts Sheen as a "paradox," who hardly fit the simplistic profile of either a "television celebrity or a peace of mind peddler"; he "announced the somewhat ironic arrival of Catholics into the American cultural mainstream in the decade after World War II" and "played a singularly important role in mediating" this "Catholic emergence."[19] The Bishop's "Life Is Worth Living" television show represented the "first sustained exposure to Catholic beliefs and practices for millions of Americans," and it "assured American Catholics that their faith was 'safe' for America, an assurance that became something of a two-edged sword"[20] as Sheen built a bridge which helped American Catholics make the transition from the "pre" to the "post" Vatican II Church. The irony of Sheen's achievement can be found in the fact that he recognized the ambiguities inherent in Catholics being accepted into American society, for he would have distrusted the gospel being used for purposes of "accommodation." This analysis meshes well with Sheen's perception of himself as one who always tried to maintain a sense of balance, theologically orthodox yet progressive and open to new ideas as he dedicated his life as an American Catholic priest and spokesman to "reading the signs of the times," and responding with boldness and creativity to the challenges he encountered.

---

[18] *Ibid.,* p. 540.

[19] Mark J. Massa, *Catholics and American Culture: Fulton Sheen, Dorothy Day and the Notre Dame Football Team* (New York: The Crossroad Publishing Company, 1999), pp. 84-85.

[20] *Ibid.,* p. 16.

Not until the new millennium was a formal biography of Sheen written — *America's Bishop: The Life and Times of Fulton J. Sheen* by Thomas C. Reeves.[21] According to Professor Reeves, Sheen was the most popular and influential American Catholic of the twentieth century.[22] Despite the controversies that often swirled around his outspokenness on public issues, and his personal failings — secrets, ambition, vanity, and a luxurious lifestyle — he was "ever the defender of the Catholic faith."[23] And he remains influential today, in terms of his books which remain in print, re-issued audio and video recordings, numerous anthologies of his works published since his death, and the initiation of the canonization process.

The lengthy investigation required by the Church's canonization procedure will determine how well Fulton Sheen weathers the challenge of this final act in his dramatic odyssey through the history of American Catholicism. Historians have frequently written of the phenomenon of a "sea change" which occurred during the twentieth century, regarding the Church's standing in American society, and the image of Sheen as a "sailor in a storm at sea" remains relevant in the aftermath of his life. Surviving the many demands of one who dedicated his life to an active engagement with the modern world as he fashioned a prominent public Catholicism, he was anchored by a calm and steady sense of spirituality and holiness. The more private Fulton Sheen faithfully made a daily "Holy Hour," and credited this practice with sustaining him through the difficult trials and tribulations of his life.

While reflecting on the subject of holiness during one of his television shows, Sheen said that a false conception of a saint is that

---

[21] Thomas C. Reeves, *America's Bishop* (San Francisco: Encounter Books, 2001). Fr. McNamara noted in his diocesan history in 1998 that despite my academic dissertation, Sheen "awaited" a biographer; Reeves responded judiciously to that call. His book offers many new details on Sheen's family and life — see my review in the *Catholic Historical Review*, Vol. LXXXVII, No. 2 (April, 2002).

[22] Reeves, p. 1.

[23] *Ibid.*, p. 6.

he is one who is "completely separated from the world."[24] Rather, three basic principles constitute a more positive conception of what type of human being God might "weave" into a "beautiful tapestry of sanctity or holiness": a divine rather than a human standard of judgment; the fact that a saint "diffuses goodness"; and "total surrender" to the will of God.[25] Sheen's own ideas make for an interesting basis of determining his own prospects for sainthood; toward the end of his life, he often simplified things by telling his audience that he had been trying for years to get "a little closer to the Lord." He also noted that:

> Saints diffuse holiness because they reflect the life of Christ as color reflects light… it takes an infinite variety of saints shot through the prism of love and penance to reflect the holiness of the Son of God… saints are always different. They break up the monotony of life.[26]

According to these criteria, Sheen is a worthy candidate. Monsignor John Tracy Ellis, writing as both a friend of Sheen and as a more objective Church historian, offered this assessment in the entry he wrote for the *New Catholic Encyclopedia*:

> It is owed to the memory of this remarkable churchman to state that in his hey-day almost literally millions called his name blessed for the religious inspiration, the kindling of renewed hope, and the spiritual enrichment that he brought to their lives.[27]

---

[24] Fulton Sheen, "Saints and Atheists," in *Life Is Worth Living*, Fourth Series (New York: The McGraw-Hill Book Co., 1956), p. 207.

[25] *Ibid.,* pp. 210-212.

[26] *Ibid.,* p. 211.

[27] John Tracy Ellis, "Sheen, Fulton J.," *The New Catholic Encyclopedia*, second edition, Vol. 13 (Washington, DC: Thomson Gale for the Catholic University of America Press, 2002), p. 75.

Another metaphor for the priestly life, fashioned by Sheen during his final decade on earth,[28] can serve as context for the challenge ahead. For the twenty-first century, perhaps a "new kind of saint is needed,"[29] a man ahead of his time in some respects, forging a path for future generations to follow. Acknowledging the unique contribution of Fulton Sheen, as one who consistently "broke up the monotony of life," a fitting and inspiring image of him might be one he conceived of himself — that of the "trapeze artist,"[30] who, in anticipation of what is to come, is "swinging between time and eternity."

[28] For a more detailed analysis of Sheen's view on the vocation of the priest, see my article entitled "A Life of Mystery and Adventure: Fulton Sheen's Reflections on the Priesthood" in the *U.S. Catholic Historian* 11:1 (1993), 63-82.

[29] Kenneth Woodward, *Making Saints: How the Catholic Church Determines Who Becomes a Saint, Who Doesn't, and Why* (New York: Simon & Schuster, 1990), p. 406.

[30] Fulton Sheen, *Those Mysterious Priests*, p. 11.

FULTON J. SHEEN

CHAPTER ONE

Thomistic Philosopher and Catholic Educator:

The Formative Years, 1919-1935

> I should like to know two things — first, what the modern
> world is thinking about; second, how to answer the errors of
> modern philosophy in the light of the philosophy of St. Thomas.
> *Fulton Sheen to Rector Thomas Shahan,*
> *Catholic University of America, 1920*

> Each succeeding day will bring to a world drunk with the
> anarchy of ideas, the necessity of the philosophy
> of St. Thomas as the path to intellectual sobriety.
> *Fulton Sheen, "Mercier and Thomism," 1926*

On September 20, 1919, Fulton J. Sheen was ordained a priest at
St. Mary's Cathedral in Peoria, Illinois. Joining the ranks of the
priesthood was the fulfillment of the young Sheen's lifelong ambition, and it marked the beginning of a public career destined to
make him one of the Catholic Church's most famous sons. Over
the next sixty years, Fulton Sheen would serve the Church in a variety of capacities, always rising to meet the challenge of his times.
At the time of his ordination, American Catholicism was characterized by two main currents of thought: the Scholastic revival,
which heralded the Thomistic synthesis as the official philosophy
of the Catholic Church; and a growing commitment to social justice and reform. Both currents had been championed by Pope Leo
XIII, and both would profoundly influence Sheen during his formative years, and for the rest of his life. On the immediate horizon in 1919, though, was the continuation of his education, a foun-

dation waiting to be constructed at the Catholic University of America and the University of Louvain. Sheen saw much of the shape of his early life as being determined by the decision of his parents that each of their children should be well educated,[1] and so his family background merits some attention.

Sheen was born on May 8, 1895, in El Paso, Illinois. The first of four boys born to Newton and Delia Sheen, he was christened Peter John Sheen. Fulton, the family name of his maternal grandparents, replaced Peter sometime during his childhood when he was enrolled in school,[2] and he was known thereafter as Fulton John Sheen. The boy benefitted from a strong Catholic family tradition and a parochial school education. At St. Mary's School in Peoria he soon emerged as an "extremely bright pupil,"[3] and served Mass as an altar boy at the adjoining cathedral. In his autobiography, Sheen recalled fondly the time he served the "great Bishop John L. Spalding," who told him: "You go home and tell your mother that I said when you get big, you are to go to Louvain, and someday you will be just as I am."[4] This "prophecy," colored by the vagaries of a recollection late in life, was no doubt enhanced by the benefit of hindsight; in fact, Sheen would study at Louvain, and become a bishop as well.

After graduating from St. Mary's Grammar School, Sheen was entrusted to the care of the Brothers of Mary at the Spalding Institute. Here too he excelled at his studies[5] and was the class vale-

---

1   Fulton Sheen, *Treasure in Clay* (Garden City: Doubleday & Co., 1980), p. 7. Many of the details of Sheen's early life are contained in this autobiography, published posthumously.

2   How and when the name "Fulton" was adopted is not entirely clear; it was either given to him by his grandfather Fulton when he was enrolled at St. Mary's parochial school in Peoria in 1900, or initiated later by Sheen himself when he enrolled at the Spalding Institute (a sign of Sheen's closeness to and affection for his maternal grandparents). See Ken Crotty's series of articles, published in the *Boston Post* (May 7-May 18, 1953); a copy of the twelve part series is found in the Fulton J. Sheen Archives, Diocese of Rochester, New York.

3   Crotty, "Bishop Sheen's Devotion Recalled," *Boston Post*, May 9, 1953.

4   Sheen, *Treasure in Clay*, p. 12.

5   Crotty, "Spike, Nickname for Bishop Sheen," *Boston Post*, May 10, 1953.

dictorian when he graduated in 1913. For his higher education, Sheen went first to St. Viator's College and Seminary at Bourbonnais, Illinois, and then on to St. Paul's Seminary in Minnesota. St. Viator's was well-suited to Sheen's needs because of its course in theology; already he knew that he wanted his life's work to be the priesthood.[6] His literary skills were refined in *The Viatorian*, the students' monthly publication. Sheen served as the personals editor and wrote articles on drama from a religious and philosophical perspective, including one on "Hamlet's Moral Nature."[7] In addition, he refined his talents as an orator by joining the debate team. One of his favorite and frequently told stories was on the valuable lesson he learned from his coach, Fr. William J. Bergan, before the annual debate with Notre Dame. Sheen spoke of his shock and dismay at being told that he was one of the worst speakers that Fr. Bergan had ever heard. Nonetheless he persisted, and found the key to success in the simple adage: "be natural."[8] It was a lesson he learned well, for St. Viator's won the debate against Notre Dame in 1915, and Sheen's natural style as a public speaker in later years was one of his greatest strengths.

After receiving his B.A. and A.M. degrees from St. Viator's, Sheen completed his seminary training at St. Paul's, and then went on to the Catholic University of America, after his ordination, to work for a doctorate. He had been recognized as an especially gifted student by his superiors, particularly by Bishop Edward Michael Dunne of Peoria, who gave Father Sheen his blessing and sent him off to Washington.[9] During his studies at the Catholic University of America, his devotion to Thomistic philosophy and social justice was conceived and nurtured by excellent teachers such as Dr.

---

[6] Crotty, "Bishop Sheen Star as College Debater" and "Bishop Sheen Recalled as Top Scholar in Class," *Boston Post*, May 11 and May 14, 1953.

[7] Fulton Sheen, "Hamlet the Man" and "The Abraham Isaac Miracle Play"; articles from *The Viatorian,* Memorabilia Files, Fulton Sheen Archives.

[8] The story about the debate was reported often; in addition to the *Boston Post* series, see *The Bishop Sheen Story* by James C.G. Conniff (Greenwich, CT: Fawcett Publications, 1953), p. 24, and "Microphone Missionary," *Time,* April 14, 1952, p. 73.

[9] Crotty, "Opportunity Comes to Bishop Sheen."

Edward Pace and the famous Dr. John A. Ryan, a leader in the
field of social ethics.[10] It was also during these student years in
Washington, D.C., that Sheen was introduced to the pulpit; invited to give a Lenten course at St. Paul's Church, he was at first
mistaken for an altar boy. He delivered a fine sermon, and was invited back to preach many times thereafter.[11]

After receiving his J.C.B. (Canon Law) degree in 1920, the
young scholar from Catholic University set his sights higher, although he would one day return as a faculty member to his alma
mater.[12] Thus far, his educational experience had been molded by
the legacy of Pope Leo XIII. Fulton Sheen would eventually adopt
the crusade for social reform inspired by the Pope's historic encyclical *Rerum Novarum* and root it firmly in the philosophy of St. Thomas Aquinas. This Neo-Thomism, institutionalized by the Church
as the only proper mode of Catholic thought and a safe intellectual route to orthodoxy, provided Sheen with the anchor of his own
spiritual and intellectual life. Sheen summed up the meaning of his
life's journey when he articulated what he wanted of his education:
"…first, to know what the modern world is thinking about; and
second, how to answer the errors of modern philosophy in the light
of the philosophy of St. Thomas."[13] On the recommendation of
one of his professors, he left for Europe in search of this knowledge, and continued his studies at the University of Louvain in
Belgium. Again, with Bishop Dunne's blessing and support, Fulton
Sheen left for Europe in September of 1921, accompanied by his
brother Tom, who was to study medicine at Louvain.[14]

The experience at the University of Louvain was to be a critical
one in the formation of Fulton Sheen, especially instrumental in
his decision to make Thomism the cornerstone of his scholarly life.
Louvain was founded in 1425, the oldest remaining Catholic Uni-

[10] Sheen, *Treasure in Clay*, p. 22.
[11] Crotty, "Opportunity Comes to Bishop Sheen" and Sheen's autobiography.
[12] Sheen, *Treasure in Clay*, p. 3.
[13] Sheen, *Treasure in Clay*, p. 23.
[14] *Ibid.*

versity in the world.[15] In 1882 the university created the chair of Thomistic philosophy at the specific request of Pope Leo XIII, and Cardinal Désiré Joseph Mercier was commissioned to set up the Institut Superieur de Philosophie[16]:

> Mercier endeavored to realize the program formulated in the encyclical *Aeterni Patris*: to restore the philosophy of St. Thomas Aquinas, harmonize it with the progress of modern science and thought, and extend its influence to the scientific and social disciplines.[17]

It was in this Superior Institute of Philosophy that Fulton Sheen enrolled, and he received a "license in the philosophy of St. Thomas" on July 11, 1922.[18] The following year, he was awarded his doctor of philosophy degree, and it was as a disciple of Cardinal Mercier and Dr. Léon Noel, another eminent Neo-Scholastic leader at Louvain, that he emerged from his formal studies as a scholar and a Thomist. The training at Louvain was intellectually rigorous and broad in scope; among the courses Sheen took were Logic, Pragmatism, Metaphysics, Cosmology, Aristotle and Psychology.[19] Psychology, which would remain a special interest, was considered to be the favorite discipline of Cardinal Mercier. There was a direct link between Sheen's education under Mercier's direction and his first scholarly publications in the field of philosophy. A major emphasis of the Cardinal's program at the Institute, according to Sheen, was to "concentrate his revival of Thomistic philosophy as

---

[15] For information on the University of Louvain, and its place in the Scholastic revival, see *The New Catholic Encyclopedia* (New York: McGraw-Hill, 1967): "Louvain, Catholic University of" by V. Denis; and "Mercier, Désiré Joseph" by A.L. Wylleman.

[16] "Mercier, Désiré Joseph," *New Catholic Encyclopedia* (Vol. 9), p. 671.

[17] "Mercier," p. 671.

[18] A copy of this certificate, in French, is located in the Memorabilia Files at the Sheen Archives.

[19] This list combines Sheen's recollections in the autobiography (p. 23), and seven notebooks written in his student days at Louvain; these notebooks were donated to the Archives of the Catholic University of America in 1946, and comprise the "Fulton Sheen Collection," ACUA.

a solution to false science."[20] In keeping with the ideal of adapting St. Thomas to modern times, an ideal which Sheen adopted as his own, Cardinal Mercier laid down the keynote of the school in his inaugural address of 1894: "Philosophy does not precede the sciences, but follows them to synthesize their results under the direction of the first principles of the human intellect."[21]

Accordingly, the core of the curriculum at the University of Louvain was Thomism. In the philosophy of St. Thomas Aquinas, Sheen discovered the rock upon which to build his priestly vocation, a secure refuge and point of origin for the multiple roads he would later follow. All the areas of knowledge that he studied at the university stressed the contemporary, and the application of the universal truths of Catholicism to any situation or challenge which might arise. This became the pattern of his subsequent work as teacher and orator. Sheen acknowledged that he was "immersed in the philosophy of St. Thomas,"[22] and recorded in his diary: "the more I study St. Thomas, the more I feel drawn to God."[23] As Sheen was drawn closer to God — keeping up the practice of his daily Holy Hour, winning the first of many converts to the Catholic faith, and practicing many acts of charity toward the poor[24] — he was excelling at his primary task of scholarship. He was also winning a fine reputation as a gifted orator on both sides of the Atlantic. He preached in London at Westminster Cathedral and St. Patrick's Church in Soho Square, and also lectured at the University of Cambridge Summer School.[25]

---

[20] Fulton Sheen, "Mercier and Thomism," *Commonweal,* III (February 10, 1926), p. 372. This was one of Sheen's first articles after the publication of his dissertation; *Commonweal* described him as "the only American Fellow at the University of Louvain."

[21] Cited by Sheen in "Mercier and Thomism," p. 372.

[22] Sheen, *Treasure in Clay,* p. 25.

[23] Sheen, entry for March 6, 1922, in a Diary found in the collection at the Fulton Sheen Archives.

[24] The archives collection contains only two diaries kept by Sheen: for the year 1922, when he was a student at Louvain; and for the year 1948, when Sheen accompanied Cardinal Spellman on an extensive tour of the "Orient and the Pacific."

[25] See Ken Crotty's articles in the *Boston Post* and the numerous publicity announcements issued by the National Council of Catholic Men when Sheen became the premier speaker on the "Catholic Hour" radio broadcasts.

On the academic front, he passed the examinations for his doctorate easily, after having resolved to "read through every single line that St. Thomas wrote."[26] He was then invited to pursue a higher degree, the "agrégé in philosophy." The agrégé degree was a high honor, and there were several conditions to receiving it: the university had to extend the invitation, a book had to be written to qualify, and the candidate had to pass a public examination before professors of other universities. Upon successful completion of these requirements, the candidate became a fellow of the University of Louvain, aggregated to the faculty.[27] While pursuing this degree, Sheen also studied at the Sorbonne and the Collegio Angelico in Rome. In 1925, when the time to take the examination for the agrégé arrived, Sheen returned to Louvain, and performed brilliantly. It was customary after the exams to be invited to dinner and formally inducted into the faculty; according to tradition, the beverage served with dinner indicated the quality of the exam. As Sheen liked to recall, "the champagne tasted so good that night," the night he passed with the "Very Highest Distinction."[28]

With his degree in hand and some teaching experience gained at St. Edmund's College in ware, England, Fulton Sheen now entertained thoughts of where to begin his career as a university professor. His growing reputation brought him several promising offers. Even before he completed the requirements for his degree, he was offered a position at the Detroit Seminary, and noted in his diary that he would have liked to accept it.[29] In 1925, though, his real choice was between two offers: one from Cardinal Bourne in London, asking that he go to Oxford with Father Ronald Knox, a colleague from St. Edmund's, to teach philosophy and theology, and the other from Nicholas Murray Butler, President of Columbia University, who invited him to start a course in Scholastic phi-

---

[26] Sheen, *Treasure in Clay*, p. 27.

[27] Sheen, *Treasure in Clay*, p. 27. Sheen was extremely proud of having earned the "agrégé" degree. Popular characterizations of his achievement referred to a "Super Ph.D." (Conniff) and a "souped up doctor's degree" (Crotty).

[28] Sheen, *Treasure in Clay*, p. 28.

[29] Sheen, 1922 Diary, entry for March 29.

losophy there.[30] Sheen asked his bishop which job he should accept, and was instead called home to serve as a parish priest at St. Patrick's Church in Peoria. Disappointed but obedient, he accepted the decision as the will of God, forgetting his desire to follow a more intellectual career and resigning himself to being a curate.[31] After about a year, Sheen was sent to the Catholic University of America; his bishop had promised his services to the rector as a new faculty member. The brief interlude in Peoria had been a test, to see whether Sheen would remain obedient and humble after the success and prominence he had achieved. Remaining always a loyal son of the Church, he went on to Washington to begin the work which would occupy him for the next twenty-four years.

This appointment in 1926 to the School of Theology at Catholic University followed in the wake of the acclaim which had arisen over the publication of his first book, *God and Intelligence in Modern Philosophy*.[32] Written originally as his dissertation for the agrégé degree, it was praised in Europe and America as a substantial intellectual achievement. It won the prestigious Cardinal Mercier Prize in Philosophy, making Fulton Sheen the first American to be so honored. The Mercier Prize was awarded by the University of Louvain once every ten years for the best dissertation in Thomistic philosophy. It was conferred upon Sheen in 1926 by Dr. Léon Noel, who had replaced Mercier as the President of the Institut Superieur de Philosophie.[33] The book *God and Intelligence* received a good deal of favorable attention in the academic com-

---

[30] Sheen's own recollections of these offers to teach can be found in his autobiography (p. 28), the articles by Conniff and Crotty, and in a further elaboration during the course of an interview he granted to William Hanford; the interview was incorporated into Hanford's "A Rhetorical Study of the Radio and Television Speaking of Bishop Fulton Sheen," Ph.D. dissertation, Wayne State University, 1965, p. 44.

[31] Sheen, *Treasure in Clay,* p. 42.

[32] *God and Intelligence in Modern Philosophy: A Critical Study in the Light of the Philosophy of St. Thomas Aquinas,* was published originally in 1925, in both New York and London, by Longmans, Green and Co.

[33] Contained in the Memorabilia Files at the Fulton Sheen Archives is a document which records the awarding of the agrégé degree and "le prix de Philosophie fondé par le Cardinal Mercier," dated July 5, 1928 — noting that both had been officially conferred in 1926.

munity. The recently established Catholic journal of opinion, *Commonweal*, devoted an article to the subject of Fulton Sheen's arrival on the scene of international philosophy. In "A Champion of Reason," Ernest Sutherland Bates, a regular contributor of book reviews, said that Sheen's *God and Intelligence* "may safely be called one of the most important contributions to philosophy which has appeared in the present century."[34] Among the book's greatest strengths were Sheen's fairness and impressive research; he allowed the modern philosophers, such as Alfred North Whitehead, William James, and Henri Bergson and Samuel Alexander to speak for themselves. According to Sheen, modern philosophy revealed itself to be in flight from reason, and the Church alone championed reason and the intellect. Scholastic philosophy, particularly Thomism, could refute the errors of modern philosophy and prove the existence of God.

Other reviews of this initial effort of Fulton Sheen were equally glowing. The Jesuit magazine *America* called it "an examination of what the wise men of our day think of God… in the light of the philosophy of St. Thomas. And the examination is not merely critical and scholarly, but brilliant."[35] On the other side of the Atlantic, the *London Universe* described Dr. Sheen as the "new Catholic philosopher of the age."[36] And *The Month*, a publication of the English Jesuits, said that "no work then could possibly have been more timely… and we may say at once that no praise bestowed upon it could be too great":

> No book published in recent years does more credit to Catholic philosophy than this. It is masterly from the first page to the last, masterly in exposition and masterly in criticism. Then again (rarest of virtues in philo-

---

[34] *Commonweal*, III (January 13, 1926), pp. 264-265.

[35] *America*, 35 (June 19, 1926), p. 238.

[36] Cited by Edward Heffron in "Contemporary Catholic Authors: Monsignor Fulton Sheen, Theologian, Philosopher, Orator," *Catholic Library World* (Vols. 12-13, 1940-1941), p. 203.

sophic tomes) it is written in a fresh, crisp style... any
Catholic who knows this book and can use its treasure
will be able to hold his own in the cleverest of modern
company. We all owe a great debt of gratitude to Dr.
Sheen for the splendid service he has done us.[37]

In an introduction by G.K. Chesterton, the book was put forth as
a critical study of the modern world in light of Scholastic philosophy. As Chesterton observed, Fulton Sheen was clearly a product
of the prevailing atmosphere of his times, and would use the
Thomistic synthesis to illumine a host of modern issues. *God and
Intelligence* was well suited to the Church's task of combating the
rising tide of secularism: "The Catholic Church comes forward as
the one and only champion of Reason."[38] This first in a long line
of books by Sheen offers a vivid insight into several of the recur-
ring themes dominant in the multiple dimensions of his later life.

As envisioned by Sheen himself, the book was essentially an
exercise in Thomism applied to the world: "It seeks to make St.
Thomas functional, not for a school, but for a world... to suggest
solutions of modern problems in the light of the philosophy of St.
Thomas."[39] Sheen often said that St. Thomas belonged to the thir-
teenth century only by accident, for his wisdom was relevant to all
ages:

> If need makes actuality, then St. Thomas was never more
> actual than he is today. If actuality makes modernity,
> then St. Thomas is the prince of modern philosophers.
> If a progressive universe is a contemporary ideal, then
> the philosophy of St. Thomas is its greatest realization.[40]

---

[37] *The Month*, 147 (February, 1926), p. 177.
[38] Sheen, *God and Intelligence in Modern Philosophy* (Image Books Edition: Garden City,
1958), p. 7.
[39] *Ibid.*, pp. 11-12.
[40] *Ibid.*, p. 12.

And the need at present was especially pressing, given the "self-confessed bankruptcy of modern thought."[41] Thus recognizing modern thought's inadequacies, and the fact that man's faith in secular values had failed him, Sheen was determined to champion religion as the fundamental solution to contemporary problems. A restoration of religious values offered the best hope for the future. And to promote such a solution, Fulton Sheen resolved to bridge the gap separating the Church from the modern world.

Teaching the truth about the Catholic Church presented him with the best means of bridging that gap. Consequently, Sheen set out to demonstrate the Church's relevance to the modern world, her willingness and ability to serve the times in which she lived. Citing the French philosopher Jacques Maritain, Sheen stated that Thomism was "ultra-modern": preeminently suitable to modern times because of its spirituality and universality.[42] To correct a common misconception, Sheen argued that faith was not contrary to reason; in fact, one of the Church's greatest strengths was its rich intellectual heritage, especially Thomism. Standing on the firm ground of reason, the Scholastic philosopher insisted that the primary element in religious experience was the rational or the intellectual.[43] And in 1926, in keeping with his defensive posture, Sheen stood ready to turn the weapons of genuine intellectualism against the adversaries of the Catholic Church: "each succeeding day will bring to a world drunk with the anarchy of ideas, the necessity of the philosophy of St. Thomas as the path to intellectual sobriety."[44]

Following the favorable reception of *God and Intelligence*, Sheen embarked upon his career as a professor at the Catholic University of America. He was appointed to the faculty as an Instructor of Theology, to teach apologetics in the School of Sacred

---

[41] *Ibid.*, p. 22.

[42] *Ibid.*, p. 23. Sheen's reference is to Maritain's *Antimoderne* (1922): "Antimodern against the errors of the present time, [the philosophy of St. Thomas] is ultra-modern for all truths enveloped in the time to come."

[43] *Ibid*, p. 178.

[44] Sheen, "Mercier and Thomism," p. 373.

Sciences, in April of 1926. Almost from the beginning, his position was a troubled one; within a year, he requested a transfer to
the Department of Philosophy, although he would continue to be
listed as a member of the Theology Faculty until 1931. Dr. Sheen's
exact status at Catholic University from 1927 to 1932 is difficult
to pin down; an examination of the official records of the university reveals several inconsistencies.[45] According to the "Minutes of
the Faculty of Theology," a special meeting of full professors on
April 6, 1927, "approved of and expressed its willingness to agree
to the suggested transfer of Dr. Sheen from the School of Sacred
Sciences to the School of Philosophy." Yet Sheen continued to attend the meetings, on an irregular basis, until May of 1930. During these years the Faculty of Theology was involved in a bitter
dispute with the newly appointed Rector of the University, James
H. Ryan. According to H. Warren Willis, in his study of "The
Reorganization of the Catholic University of America During the
Rectorship of James H. Ryan":

> The School of the Sacred Sciences was the foundation
> stone of the Catholic University of America, but became
> its stumbling block. The school was in a poor condition
> when James H. Ryan became Rector, and was to become
> worse before becoming better.[46]

Fulton Sheen was caught up in the maelstrom of these administrative difficulties and contributed to several conflicts during
his short tenure on the Faculty of Theology as well. The first source
of trouble was the proposed establishment of a seminary course, to

[45] The Archives of the Catholic University of American (ACUA) contain several valuable
sources on Sheen's status and standing as a faculty member; the published "Reports of
the Rector," the CUA Announcements/Catalogues, the papers of the Archbishop Nicholas Investigating Committees, and the "Minutes of The Faculty of Theology" notebook
were all consulted. The best overall source on these years of controversy is H. Warren
Willis: "The Reorganization of the Catholic University of America During the Rectorship
of James H. Ryan, 1928-1935" (Ph.D. dissertation, Catholic University of America, 1972).
[46] Willis, "The Reorganization of the Catholic University of America During the Rectorship
of James H. Ryan, 1928-1935," p. 228.

help bolster the sagging enrollment figures, in January of 1927.[47] Sheen, along with John A. Ryan, Peter Guilday, Heinrich Schumacher, and John M. Cooper, was selected to serve on the committee to draw up the program of studies. From the start, there was opposition and a lack of cooperation regarding the seminary, and the program was never successful.[48] In October of 1928, Sheen applied for a promotion to the rank of Associate Professor, but his application was denied, as "there was not sufficient reason to deviate from the standard rules regarding promotion."[49] The disappointment over the refused promotion was compounded by further difficulties in the Theology Department. One controversy arose over John A. Ryan's suggestion that Fr. Francis Haas be appointed as an Instructor of Moral Theology. The suggestion was turned down by the rector because Fr. Haas lacked the necessary academic credentials in theology,[50] and the position was left vacant for some time. In addition, the turmoil over the scope and responsibilities of the seminary course remained unabated. The full professors suggested that the work in philosophy and apologetics should be divided among three available professors — Fr. Barron, Fr. Cooper, and Fr. Sheen.[51] Sheen immediately objected, saying he was unprepared to take over the regular course in undergraduate and graduate apologetics, as that subject "was outside of his preparatory studies." He stated that the second year philosophy subjects — metaphysics and cosmology — were more in line with his background, an indication that he might be happier and better utilized in the Department of Philosophy. Several months later, noting that "a few new difficulties have arisen," the Dean of the School of Sacred Sciences, Dr. Coln, said that according to the wishes of the

---

[47] See the "Minutes of the Meetings of the Faculty of Theology," January 10, 1927, ACUA.

[48] Sheen did teach in the Seminary — philosophy and apologetics courses — for two years, 1931 and 1932.

[49] "Minutes of the Meetings of the Faculty of Theology," October 28, 1928.

[50] See the "Minutes of the Meetings of the Faculty of Theology," June 1, 1929, and Sheen's *Treasure in Clay*, p. 45. The circumstances surrounding Sheen's transfer were very complex.

[51] "Minutes of the Meetings of the Faculty of Theology," April 8, 1929.

rector, with which he fully concurred, "Dr. Sheen should be used in the Seminary as little as possible."[52]

Even after the satisfactory solution to this problem, though, Sheen became embroiled in one last, and more serious, controversy in the Faculty of Theology. In a special meeting called on May 30, 1930, the subject of the rejection of a dissertation by the Rev. Lambert Victor Brockmann, a student of Sheen's, was discussed at great length. After his essay was not accepted, Fr. Brockmann went to the Rector and accused the faculty of failing him "out of jealousy against Fr. Sheen."[53] The Rector had reported that he was aware of the "unfair attitude" in the faculty against "himself and Dr. Sheen," and that certain members "try everything, even accusing Dr. Sheen of heresy, in order to have him removed from the faculty."[54] The seriousness of these charges, and the personal accusations, indicated the explosiveness of the situation both within the Faculty of Theology, and between the faculty and the Rector. The other members denied the charges of jealousy and prejudice against Sheen; they argued that the Brockmann dissertation deserved to fail on its own merits, for it was "a hopeless mass of confusion and superficiality,"[55] and abounded in "wild and meaningless statements."[56]

Dr. Sheen testified that "there were two angles to the case: the objective merit of the thesis, which must ultimately be determined by the readers; and the personal element which touched on jealousy." He went on to assure his fellow faculty members that he neither asked nor encouraged Fr. Brockmann to visit the Rector. Ultimately this academic battle was settled when the faculty voted to allow Fr. Brockmann to take his exams again after he apologized for "his unfounded accusations of injustice and jealousy." But the evidence of personal rivalries and difficulties surrounding Fulton

[52] "Minutes of the Meetings of the Faculty of Theology," October 24, 1929.
[53] "Minutes of the Meetings of the Faculty of Theology," May 30, 1930.
[54] *Ibid.*
[55] This description came from Dr. Schumacher.
[56] This assessment was offered by Dr. Healy.

Sheen continued, and he was eventually transferred to the Philosophy Department in 1931, and to the newly created School of Scholastic Philosophy in 1936, where he served out the rest of his years at the Catholic University of America. In the immediate aftermath of the Brockmann case, however, charges and countercharges of jealousy and personal accusations were revived, and Sheen remained a source of contention. The Rector said that one faculty member informed him that another had stated that "he would use every means, no matter how crooked it was, in order to have Dr. Sheen removed."[57]

Later, during the course of the investigations launched by the two special committees, other references to Sheen's status and personality conflicts emerged. In 1931, Fr. John A. Ryan told the committee that Dr. Sheen was transferred because he was unhappy; he seemed to feel that he was not fitted for the work in theology and was academically unprepared to teach the classes he was asked to teach.[58] In reference to the Brockmann case, it was Ryan's opinion that "the charges of jealousy, etc. all emanated from Dr. Sheen's very vivid imagination," and that "he made them quite generally known around the university and off campus."[59] In a letter from Rector Ryan to Archbishop McNicholas on the topic of Sheen's status and standing, in the Theology Department and the Seminary, the Rector saw the greatest difficulty as making Sheen realize that he could do the type of work he was asked to do. Ryan kept insisting that Sheen should devote practically all of his time to his work at the university, which would be of "a permanent character":

> Dr. Sheen has the best will in the world but has become so accustomed to the feverish life of a public speaker that it is going to be extremely difficult to tie him down to the more or less drudgery of preparing men for the kind of work he is doing.[60]

---

[57] "Minutes of the Meetings of the Faculty of Theology," May 30, 1930.
[58] Ryan to the Visiting Committee, May 13, 1931 — McNicholas Papers, ACHA.
[59] *Ibid.*
[60] Ryan to McNicholas, letter dated September 25, 1931 — McNicholas Papers.

Similar concerns over Sheen's spending too much time outside the university were raised later during the visit of the Episcopal Committee in 1934. Sheen had opted for things other than the
"more or less drudgery" of life at the university, including frequent
public appearances and radio broadcasts. Church historian Peter
Guilday, in reviewing the reasons for the failure of the Faculty of
Theology, talked about the lethargy and failure to produce on the
part of certain members — F.J.S., J.A.R. — who spent too much
time in outside activity. Although this activity brought prestige to
the university, Guilday believed that these men were consequently
lost as "teachers and trainers of men." Finally, Guilday added that
he had personally turned down "over 500 invitations" to lecture or
preach, preferring to devote himself to his duties within the university.[61]

Sheen's own remarks before the committee concentrated on
his personal preference for teaching Apologetics, whether it be in
the School of Philosophy or Theology. He had been changed to
Philosophy, "partly at his own request, and partly out of some
difficulty arising." Sheen also said that he had been called by the
Rector to set up an Institute of Apologetics, but that they differed
over the specifics. The plan for the Institute was devised after the
bigotry unleashed by Al Smith's presidential campaign in 1928. The
aim of the proposed Institute, according to a document in the Archives of the Catholic University of America, was:

> ...to provide such instruction and training as will en-
> able priests and laymen to make known more fully and
> accurately, the doctrine and practice of the Church, her
> attitude with regard to various movements — religious,
> moral and social — of the present day, and thereby to
> remove the obstacles of ignorance, misunderstanding,
> or prejudice which hinder the spread of the Catholic
> faith among our people.[62]

---

[61] Rev. Dr. Peter Guilday to McNicholas, letter dated April 20, 1935, in the Episcopal
Visiting Committee File, McNicholas Papers.

[62] See Sheen's statement/interrogation to the Episcopal Visiting Committee, McNicholas
Papers, and Sheen's *Treasure in Clay*, pp. 52-53.

Fulton Sheen would have been a wise and logical choice for work in the Institute of Apologetics, given his talents as an orator, and his own interest in and devotion to the cause. In the official report of the Episcopal Visiting Committee, Bishop Gerald P. O'Hara spoke of "one outstanding professor of Apologetics, who was transferred" to the Graduate School of Arts and Sciences, a clear reference to Sheen. It was suggested that his return to Theology would strengthen the faculty, and that he would make the Department of Apologetics a "powerful instrument for good in the university."[63] But Sheen never did get the chance to devote himself to Apologetics at the university. From the Department of Philosophy he moved on to the School of Philosophy; in light of the School's emphasis on Scholasticism, the move was a good one. Yet the devotion to Apologetics, from the perspective of the Thomist method of adaptation, would be taken by Sheen to new heights in his capacity as a public speaker outside of the university community.

The time Sheen spent in Philosophy, from 1931 to 1950, when he left Catholic University to become the National Director of the Society for the Propagation of the Faith, was uneventful, and seemingly satisfying to both Sheen and the university administration. Dr. Ignatius Smith, O.P., Sheen's dean, seemed favorably impressed with Sheen's work from the start. In his report before the Episcopal Visiting Committee, Smith lamented that the "quality of teaching was not up to the proper standards," but pointed to Dr. Sheen as an exception: "Monsignor Sheen knows the matter he is teaching very well, namely Theodicy."[64]

For twenty years Sheen taught a regular rotation of courses in the Graduate School of Philosophy. In his own "Interrogations for Faculties of Theology, Canon Law and Philosophy" form, submitted to the Episcopal Committee in 1934, Sheen listed three courses: "Modern Idea of God in the Light of St. Thomas," "Mod-

---

[63] O'Hara's statement in the Episcopal Visiting Committee Report, August 19-24, 1935, in the McNicholas Papers.

[64] Statement by Dr. Ignatius Smith, OP, to the Episcopal Visiting Committee, December, 1934, McNicholas Papers.

ern Idea of Religion in the Light of St. Thomas," and "Philosophy of Science and Religion." These courses were his standard offerings, reflected in his scholarly publications. The book *God and Intelligence in Modern Philosophy* was followed by *Religion Without God* (1928), *The Life of All Living* (1929), and after some more popular volumes, *Philosophy of Science* (1934). In addition, Sheen published a series of articles in the journal *New Scholasticism*, from 1927 to 1929; these were all excerpts from his books, or were later incorporated into his books.[65] Also on the academic front, Sheen was a charter member of the American Catholic Philosophical Association, founded at the Catholic University of America in 1926, "to promote study and research in the field of philosophy, with special emphasis on scholastic philosophy."[66] He delivered a paper at the second annual meeting of the association in 1927, entitled "Contemporary Concepts of Religion." In it, Sheen argued along the same lines as he had in *God and Intelligence*, that "intellectual restoration is the condition of the restoration of traditional religion."[67] In 1929, he was elected to the position of Secretary-Treasurer, and became the President of the American Catholic Philosophical Association in 1941.

By 1941, Monsignor Sheen was investing a good deal of his time and energy outside the university as well. Almost from the beginning of his tenure at Catholic University, Sheen spent a considerable amount of time away, lecturing and giving retreats, and preaching regular sermons at both the Paulist Church and St. Patrick's Cathedral in New York City.[68] Also, he was a regular

---

[65] In *New Scholasticism*, Sheen published "Professor Whitehead and the Making of Religion" 1 (April, 1927); "Religion and Values" 2 (January, 1928); and "New Physics and New Scholasticism" 3 (July, 1929). He also contributed a scholarly article to the first volume of *Thought* (March, 1927), entitled "God in Evolution."

[66] *Proceedings of the American Catholic Philosophical Association* 1 (1926), p. 4.

[67] Fulton Sheen, "Contemporary Concepts of Religion," *Proceedings of the A.C.P.A.* 2 (December, 1927), p. 79.

[68] As early as 1927, Sheen was traveling around the country — and overseas — quite frequently; according to the annual reports he submitted to the Rector, he preached Lenten sermons, conducted retreats, and preached radio broadcasts regularly — in 1928, he listed thirty-one appearances.

speaker on the "Catholic Hour" radio broadcasts, becoming one of American Catholicism's most famous and sought-after speakers.

A change in the type of book coming from the pen of Fulton Sheen was also becoming apparent; the academic treatises were being replaced by books written for a much wider audience, in a simpler, straightforward style. The intellectual was being transformed into a popularizer. Many of these books were slightly revised versions of his radio talks and public lectures: *The Divine Romance* (1930); *Old Errors and New Labels* (1931); *Moods and Truths* (1933); and *The Eternal Galilean* (1934). Sheen was especially adept at getting maximum mileage out of his work. Often, in a single year, he would produce a pamphlet from the radio series; a book, oftentimes of a different title, but essentially the same material; and his lectures and sermons, devoted to the same subject, and covered widely in the press as he traveled from coast to coast.

Throughout these years Sheen managed to maintain a balance between his responsibilities at the university and his frequent forays into the public arena. From 1932 to 1950, he usually taught two courses in the graduate school and an occasional seminar.[69] Basically, he rotated the following courses: "God and the Universe," "God and Theology," and "God and Modern Philosophy"; on a few occasions, he branched out in new directions. In 1939, for example, his "Modern Idea of God" placed special emphasis on the Marxist critique of God; in 1948, after being promoted to the rank of Professor, he taught a course on "Humanism and Religion."[70] During the late thirties and early forties, when it was estimated that Sheen filled over "150 speaking dates a year,"[71] he had a tendency to fall back on the same courses, offered in alternate years, and a seminar in Natural Theology. Clearly, the main focus of Sheen's life was outside of the university. He generally took little part in university

---

[69] See the CUA Announcements/Catalogues and the Rectors Reports, ACUA.

[70] *Ibid.*

[71] "Monsignor's Tenth," *Time*, March 11, 1940, p. 60. See also the chronology compiled at the Fulton Sheen Archives.

affairs besides his limited teaching schedule. As his star was on the rise, Fulton Sheen found happiness in the limelight, speaking before the crowds, rather than lecturing in the classroom. But he remained an educator forever; he simply charted an unusual path in his endeavor to educate and enlighten an ever-widening audience, in both traditional and unorthodox ways.

Early in his career, Fulton Sheen issued several public pronouncements on his views regarding education and the concept of a Catholic university and its role in the larger American society. An important address delivered in 1929 on the topic of teaching religion and the "primacy of the spiritual" demonstrates that he was successfully integrating his roles as teacher, intellectual popularizer and apologist. As a leading figure in the Church's Thomistic Revival, he upheld the philosophy of Aquinas as the ideal force needed to restore an organically unified Catholic culture, a synthesis of Catholicism and American culture for the twentieth century. "In these years the underlying quest of American Catholics for a unifying integrating principle on which to build a vision of America and their specific role in it acquired a significant new dimension."[72] In this address to the National Catholic Educational Association, Sheen struck a dynamic evangelical note in calling for an education that would make Catholics apostles to a world in need of the religious vision and human understanding that only the true faith could provide"[73]:

> In these days when philosophy is not only in evolution
> but in revolution, and when false prophets make a reli-
> gion out of their irreligion, it behooves Catholic educa-
> tors, who are charged with the responsibility of a Di-
> vine Mission, to clarify the intellectual atmosphere of

---

[72] James Henessey, SJ, *American Catholics* (New York: Oxford University Press, 1981), p. 255. Along these same lines, see Philip Gleason, "In Search of Unity: American Catholic Thought, 1920-1960," *Catholic Historical Review* LXV (April, 1979), pp. 185-205; and William Halsey's *The Survival of American Innocence* (Notre Dame: University of Notre Dame Press, 1980).

[73] Gleason, "In Search of Unity," p. 197.

our generation, expel the foul miasma of error and scepticism, and by a Christ-like charity lead men to the glorious liberty of the sons of God. It is for this purpose that we are gathered here in solemn convention, that by the corporate council of the members of Christ's Mystical Body, and the guidance of the Holy Spirit, we may be inspired to deliverances which will make for a Catholic Renaissance in the souls and hearts of men.[74]

The thrust of Sheen's subsequent remarks concerned the problem of presenting Catholic truth in view of the contemporary environment. Guided by the advice Cardinal Mercier had given him at Louvain — "always keep current"[75] — and relying upon his training in Scholastic philosophy, he proclaimed the necessity of building a unified system of Catholic religious education, "for unity is the note and character of life."[76] According to Sheen's vision, every educator must ask himself whether or not he is integrating his thought with that of his contemporaries: "our finger must be kept on the pulse of the present day… we are responsible to the times in which we live."[77] His interpretation of that responsibility led him to devise a twofold system of education, for the two worlds of "Peter" (the Church) and "Pan" (the secular society). In accordance with Sheen's double objective of presenting the truth to both believers and non-believers, he proposed two principles of education be utilized: "The Principle of Vitalization for the world of Peter, and the principle of Integration for the world of Pan."[78]

The principle of vitalization meant the presentation of Christian truth as an "organic whole" and a practical adaptation of that truth to make it the "very soul and unifying spirit" of the student's own experiences. Faith was to be a living reality, the vital center of

---

[74] Fulton Sheen, "Educating for a Catholic Renaissance," *N.C.E.A. Bulletin* XXV (August, 1929), p. 6.

[75] Cited in Sheen's *Treasure in Clay*, p. 51.

[76] Sheen, "Educating for a Catholic Renaissance," p. 11.

[77] *Ibid.,* pp. 14-15.

[78] *Ibid.,* p. 7.

life, and Christian doctrine a "living body of truth."[79] Quoting the Rev. John Montgomery Cooper, a colleague at Catholic University, Sheen suggested that religion should "enter into, permeate, and spiritualize life's activities."[80] Catholic educational philosophy, in the final analysis, was to be guided by the Thomistic search for unity. Catholics aimed to educate the whole, rather than merely part of, man. And given the contemporary climate, when the forces of secularism seemed to be gaining strength, Catholic education must take that influence under greater consideration and be prepared to adapt its wisdom to the reality of the modern world. "Christian truth is the soul of our course, but secular courses are its environment," stated Sheen. "In proportion then as we vitalize the presentation of religious doctrine… we will be effective instruments in keeping national life religious, and extending the world of Peter under the glorious Kingship of Christ."[81] This reference to Catholics as primary instruments in the restoration of religion to national life explains a subsidiary motivation behind Sheen's principle of integration. This second, but equally important, principle was designed to lead to the integration of the Catholic religious faith into the American context. In a tone reminiscent of traditional apologetics, Sheen was also anxious to demonstrate the compatibility of Catholicism and Americanism.

As both educator and apologist, Sheen acknowledged that Catholics were called to explain the precepts of their religion not only to those already in the fold, but to those outside it as well: "our mission is also to bring other sheep into the pastures of faith." Moving beyond the standard techniques of convert-making (a task at which he would later excel, gathering many famous sheep into the fold), however, that principle of integration meant that "Catholic doctrine must be presented to the non-Catholic mind not as something foreign to it but as something capable of developing the

---

[79] *Ibid.*, p. 8.
[80] *Ibid.*, p. 10.
[81] *Ibid.*, p. 11.

best that is in their own system."[82] Sheen had specifically addressed the question of apologetics at the beginning of the speech, regretting that the term had become identified with "apologizing, and that tolerance should become identified with indifference to creed."[83] He remained a devotee of apologetics all of his life, emphasizing the practical role of his achievements in advancing the Church's mission and improving her public image. However, his principle of integration, taking as its point of departure the "truth which both Catholics and non-Catholics hold in common,"[84] gave rise to what he would refer to as the "new apologetics." The new apologist perceived that every error had within it some admixture of good, and sought out the common denominator in the adversary's system, and then "elevated, or spiritualized it."[85] The redemptive mission of the Church, after all, was to "convert the world, not condemn it."[86] It was no coincidence that in the same year that Sheen was articulating his philosophy of education, he was also gaining national attention as an apologist: "Sheen does a great service to the Church by his apologetics — he makes the Church less mysterious, more understandable, and breaks down the walls of prejudice."[87] Advancing the course of Americanization as well, Sheen was beginning to persuade a Protestant America that there was a nobility and tolerance in the Catholic cause he espoused.

The example of Sheen's own life offers a striking testimony to the effectiveness of his twin principles of vitalization and integration. Bound by his commitment to the tasks of enlightenment and education, he helped prepare Catholics to meet the problems presented by the age in which they lived. In seeking to restore reli-

---

[82] *Ibid.*

[83] *Ibid.*, p. 6.

[84] *Ibid.* Sheen also quoted G.K. Chesterton, who lamented the verbal degeneration of "Apologia" to a feeble thing called an Apology.

[85] Sheen, as quoted in the *New York Times*, March 9, 1936. Newspaper clipping files, Fulton Sheen Archives.

[86] Sheen, as quoted in the *New York Times*, February 3, 1936. Newspaper clipping files, Fulton Sheen Archives.

[87] *The Baltimore Catholic Review*, October 18, 1929. Newspaper clipping files.

gion as a vital force in modern man's life, he ably defended and vindicated the position of the Catholic Church while building up a harmonious relationship between Catholicism and American culture. This theme of harmony between American society and Catholicism was quite prevalent in Catholic circles during the twenties, so Fulton Sheen was in good company. In *The Catholic Spirit in America,* George N. Shuster, an editor of *Commonweal* and a leading intellectual, attempted to forge a link between the American experience and Catholicism.[88] Although disavowing any "dogmatic or apologetic purpose," Shuster wrote the book "to make it possible for Catholics to go a little farther outside their church circles," to bring about the day when Catholics could participate more actively in American life.[89] Peter Guilday, noted church historian and a colleague of Sheen's at Catholic University, also sought to demonstrate the "perfect harmony that existed between Americanism and Catholicism" in a 1926 "Sesquicentennial" essay.[90] In reviewing recent American Catholic history, Professor Guilday pointed out that Catholics had amply demonstrated their loyalty during the recent World War, fusing religious and patriotic convictions — a development reinforced on the philosophical level by Neo-Scholasticism. In sharing the common ground of natural law, Catholicism and Americanism were in profound harmony.[91] Thus, Sheen's thought was very much in the mainstream of American Catholic sentiment. His reasoning was perfectly in keeping with the Church's decision to give meaning and coherence to the whole of life through a Thomistic revival, and a more active participation of Catholics in American life. Sheen's underlying purpose was "to convey the realization, not merely that Catholic truth constituted a coherent and rationally grounded system, but also that it meshed

---

[88] See Halsey, *The Survival of American Innocence*, p. 97.

[89] George Shuster, *The Catholic Spirit in America* (New York: Dial Press, 1927), pp. ix, x.

[90] Philip Gleason, "The Bicentennial and Earlier Milestones" in *Keeping the Faith: American Catholicism Past and Present* (Notre Dame: University of Notre Dame Press, 1987), pp. 107-109.

[91] *Ibid.*, pp. 109-110.

perfectly with the needs of modern society and fulfilled the inchoate spiritual longings of modern man."[92] Thus fortified with an integrated world view, a generation of Catholics would be inspired to carry this vision out into the world.

Regarding the Catholic vision that should infuse the atmosphere of the university, one corner of that world, Sheen saw the role of the Catholic University of America as "depending in great part upon how it regarded its mission and purposes in relation to the other universities of the nation."[93] According to Sheen, one of the Catholic University's greatest strengths was the organic unity of its curriculum. In the acquisition and dissemination of truth, and its one fundamental idea — the primacy of the spiritual — the Catholic University should be a leader rather than a follower in the field of education. In this way it could make a positive contribution to American life and increase its own prestige, and that of American Catholicism in general, in the nation's eyes:

> The Catholic University is to education what the Catholic Church is to religion, namely, the leaven in the mass. The Church is not one of the sects; it is the unique life of Christ; the Catholic University is not one of American Universities; it is their soul… the best way [a Catholic University] can keep apace with the times is to save the times by emphasizing that religion is not a department, or a portion, but the very condition of knowledge.[94]

The underlying tone of these remarks, stressing the superiority of the Catholic way of life, was one which Sheen often

---

[92] Gleason, "In Search of Unity," pp. 196-197.

[93] Willis, "The Reorganization of the Catholic University of America During the Rectorship of James H. Ryan," p. 256.

[94] Sheen to O'Hara, "Episcopal Visiting Committee Exhibits" (1935). Cited by Willis, pp. 256-257. See also Sheen article, "Organic Fields of Study," *Catholic Educational Review* 28 (March, 1930).

adopted. Whether addressing the relationship between the Church and the modern world in general, or the subject of Catholic education in particular, Fulton Sheen was always a strident defender of Catholic doctrine, but not in a negative sense. Rather, like many in the American Catholic community at this point in history, he sought to bridge the gap that separated Catholics from their fellow Americans in a more positive fashion. And one way of doing that was to bring the unique strengths of the Catholic tradition to bear upon the American situation, revealing the fact that the Catholic Church had something valuable to offer the nation. From the concepts, then, of vitalization, integration, and organic unity — which guided Sheen in the realms of education and philosophy — he next moved on to the pressing questions of social justice and reform. In going out into the larger world, a world increasingly characterized by chaos and disorder, educated Catholics hoped to bring with them the harmony, order and law they perceived in Scholastic philosophy.[95] From this search for unity, undertaken by both Fulton Sheen and the American Catholic Church in the twenties, additional benefits for a world in need of guidance would follow. Sheen's use of the philosophy of St. Thomas, to counter secularization and point out the fundamental weaknesses in modern thought, also served as the basis for the Church's suggested correctives, the more positive program of reform. Some of the concrete results which would accrue from this revival of Catholic thought had first been revealed in the pages of *God and Intelligence in Modern Philosophy*:[96]

> If we look to the foundation, the super-structure will take care of itself. Thomistic Intellectualism is the remedy against anarchy of ideas, riot of philosophical systems, and breakdown of spiritual force.... Intellectual

---

[95] Henessey, *American Catholics*, p. 255.
[96] Halsey, *The Survival of American Innocence*, p. 15.

restoration is the condition of economic and political restoration.[97]

As Catholics passed from the decade of the twenties into the thirties, they were submerged in a new crisis where "anarchy, riot and breakdown"[98] threatened the American nation in the midst of the Great Depression. Catholicism, long embattled without, clung more desperately to the unity within.[99] And Catholic intellectuals continued to insist "emphatically on the organic wholeness of Catholic truth, contrasting it sharply to the prevailing order that was plunging mankind headlong to destruction."[100] It was in the 1930's that the Catholic Church took up the crusade for social justice in earnest, and Fulton Sheen followed suit.

At the beginning of his career, dedicated to a practical application of Thomism to the problems of the modern world, he made a tentative reference to the social nature of religion: "Christianity is the religion of humanity... the only possible service of God must consist in the service of men."[101] So, faced with the challenge presented by the social and economic crisis, it was only fitting that the Church should adopt a program for reform. And Fulton Sheen, America's "most successful representative of everyman's Thomism,"[102] was in a good position to demonstrate the intrinsic relationship between the philosophy of St. Thomas and the Church's proposals for social reconstruction.

Sheen would make the most of the opportunity to influence the larger society and bring it into conformity with the basic principles of justice and Christian ideals. Like the American Church

---

[97] The same theme, and methodology, persisted in many of Sheen's subsequent books, especially *Religion Without God* — wherein St. Thomas becomes a modernist — and *Old Errors and New Labels.*

[98] Sheen, *God and Intelligence in Modern Philosophy,* p. 23.

[99] Halsey, *The Survival of American Innocence,* p. 159.

[100] Gleason, "In Search of Unity," p. 97.

[101] Sheen, *God and Intelligence in Modern Philosophy,* p. 255.

[102] Halsey, p. 156.

in general, Sheen would make religion the basis of his critique of
contemporary society's failures and unjust social conditions. The
central concept of adaptation had always guided Sheen's intellectual growth, and now the university professor responded to the
challenge of his times by becoming the intellectual popularizer.
During the years ahead, Fulton Sheen would dedicate himself to
expounding the gospel of social justice found in the papal encyclicals.

CHAPTER TWO

Intellectual Popularizer and Advocate of Social Justice

1930–1945

> The restoration of social justice is the key to the Kingdom of Heaven.… "Seek ye first the Kingdom of God and His justice and all these things will be added unto you." (Matthew 6:33)
> *Fulton J. Sheen*

> This longed for social reconstruction must be preceded by a profound renewal of the Christian spirit.
> *Pius XI, Quadragesimo Anno*

With the publication of the papal encyclical *Quadragesimo Anno* in 1931, the Catholic Church officially renewed its commitment to social justice. Pope Pius XI's prescription "On Reconstructing the Social Order" commemorated the fortieth anniversary of *Rerum Novarum*, Pope Leo XIII's proposed remedy for the material and spiritual ills of the modern world. Pius XI noted that "*Rerum Novarum* laid down for all mankind unerring rules for the right solution of the difficult problem of human community known as the social question."[1] And given the context of the Great Depression during which this latest papal letter was issued, and persistent calls for social reform, Pius also pointed out that the Church had been "ever careful to adapt its message to the changing conditions of the times."[2] The second of the great social encyclicals, then, not

---

[1] Pope Pius XI, *Quadragesimo Anno* in *Seven Great Encyclicals* (Glen Rock, NJ: Paulist Press, 1963), p. 125.

[2] *Ibid.*, p. 129.

only celebrated the progress of the past, but faced up to the challenge of an uncertain future as the Catholic Church was coming of age in America. During the Depression decade, the challenge was especially great; it was a time of both crisis and opportunity. And Fulton Sheen, along with many other American Catholics of his generation, found the intellectual resources to meet that challenge in the legacy of Pope Leo XIII: the Thomistic synthesis and Catholic social thought.

Pope Leo XIII was the spiritual leader of the Roman Catholic Church from 1878-1903, but his influence persisted beyond his years well into the twentieth century. His effect on Father Sheen was profound, and Sheen frequently acknowledged his debt to Pope Leo's thought during his formative years. It was Leo XIII's encyclical *Aeterni Patris* (1879) which had supported and encouraged the Scholastic revival in Catholic philosophy and thought. Scholasticism in general, and Thomism in particular, was the intellectual environment that nurtured Sheen, and was responsible for his appearance as a promising young Catholic scholar in 1925. In *God and Intelligence in Modern Philosophy* Sheen wrote that "not until the time of Leo XIII and his encyclical *Aeterni Patris* did the defenders of religious truths turn the weapon of genuine intellectualism against their adversaries."[3] Following the papal example in insisting upon a return to the doctrines of St. Thomas Aquinas as the best means of refuting the modern evil of false philosophies, Sheen emerged on the scene of American Catholicism as an ardent defender of religious truths. Like his mentor at Louvain, Cardinal Mercier, "it was just this ideal of adapting Saint Thomas to modern times, in accordance with the wishes of the Vicar of Christ," which summoned forth all the strength and character[4] of Fulton Sheen. Inspired by that ideal of adaptation, and again following the example set by Pope Leo, Sheen found himself caught up in the currents of social reform which flowed through American Catholicism in the aftermath of the First World War.

---

[3]   Fulton Sheen, *God and Intelligence in Modern Philosophy* (Garden City, 1958), p. 77.

[4]   Fulton Sheen, "Mercier and Thomism," *Commonweal* III (February 10, 1926), p. 373.

The year of Fulton Sheen's ordination to the priesthood, 1919, was the same year that the National Catholic Welfare Conference issued the "Bishops' Program of Social Reconstruction," written by Father John A. Ryan, professor of theology at the Catholic University of America. The N.C.W.C. grew logically from its predecessor, the National Catholic War Council, organized during the war years to coordinate American Catholic efforts of support. When the war ended, the N.C.W.C. was maintained as a peacetime organization to represent the hierarchy's views on national affairs, and to heighten the Church's influence on American society. Father Ryan, leader of the Conference's Social Action Department, drew much of his inspiration for the Bishops' Program from the rich heritage of Leo XIII; in fact, Leonine Thomism was "the source of Ryan's method and the basis of his social criticism."[5] At the heart of Leo's lasting contribution to the intellectual awakening of Catholicism were his pronouncements on the "social question" in the modern world. After restoring Thomism as the quintessential Catholic philosophy, the Pope proceeded to "spread it far and wide for the defense and beauty of the Catholic faith, and for the good of society."[6] In the historic encyclical issued in 1891, *Rerum Novarum*, Leo had demonstrated that Thomism offered the soundest means of combating modern errors and solving modern problems, especially in the social order. The message of *Rerum Novarum*, though, did not become widely circulated in the United States until 1919, when the Catholic bishops adapted Leonine thought to the American scene and contemporary problems. And it was not until several years later that Fulton Sheen would be in a position to make the transition from Scholastic philosopher to popularizer and advocate of social justice, taking up the work of social education recommended by the hierarchy in their important pronouncement.

The correlation between the Bishops' Program and the ca-

---

[5] Joseph M. McShane, SJ, *Sufficiently Radical: Catholicism, Progressivism, and the Bishops Program of 1919* (Washington, DC: Catholic University of America Press, 1987), p. 34.

[6] Pope Leo XIII, *Aeterni Patris*, cited in "Scholasticism," *The New Catholic Encyclopedia* (Vol. 12), p. 1167.

reer of Fulton Sheen was indirect, and delayed until Sheen attracted an audience as an orator and writer. Nevertheless, the significance of the document, and its timing, was bound to have an effect on the subsequent history of the American Catholic Church and Sheen's place in it, as he would devote considerable time and energy to spreading the hierarchy's message. The Bishops' Program of Social Reconstruction was a provocative, forward-looking document which advocated measures of reform to uphold the Catholic commitment to social justice, a cornerstone in "the hierarchy's decision at the end of World War I to make social action an integral and positive part of the Church's mission."[7] In his study of "Catholicism, Progressivism and the Bishops' Program of 1919", *Sufficiently Radical*, Joseph McShane, S.J., argued that the Bishops' Program was a "pivotal document in American Catholic history, and a bridge document,"[8] between two traditions, Americanism and Catholicism:

> The Bishops' Program of Social Reconstruction of 1919 was a spectacular public announcement of the American Catholic resolve to effect a rapprochement with American Progressivism and Leonine Social Catholicism.... In the future, a passionate and principled commitment to the cause of reform would have to direct her every social action. The events of 1919 tested the Church's resolve to redeem the promise of the program and revealed the depth of her commitment to the cause of reform, thereby bearing witness to the impact the program had on the American Church.[9]

The social consciousness of the American Catholic Church would be transformed by the Bishops' Program of Social Recon-

---

[7] Aaron Abell, *American Catholic Thought on Social Questions* (Indianapolis and New York: Bobbs-Merrill Co., 1968), pp. xxix, xxvii.

[8] McShane, p. 188.

[9] *Ibid.*, p. 239.

struction, and the repercussions in the "great work of social education and social welfare"[10] would be felt well into the future, when Sheen would have the opportunity to make his personal contribution of disseminating the Church's message of social justice and reform. The Bishops' Program was truly a "bridge," spanning across the eras of World War I and the crisis of the Great Depression, a period of time when the Church was moving forward in its attempt to enter into the American religious mainstream. The direction of the Catholic Church's course was also determined by a "widespread awareness of the need to counter the rapid secularization of society that was the legacy of war."[11] The Bishops' Program "signaled an American Catholic appropriation" of Leonine thought and Leonine-inspired social action, an appropriation which Fulton Sheen undertook in his own life, a personal commitment to the cause of Catholic social reform. For the American Church, then, the publication of the document in 1919 was merely the "opening salvo in the Church's long struggle to establish her claim to moral leadership."[12] In many respects, Sheen would be a beneficiary of this opening salvo during the years of his intellectual formation. As a philosopher and apologist for the Catholic faith, Sheen evolved into an advocate for social justice as part of his comprehensive effort to educate the American people about the Church and its doctrines. Ever adept at reading the signs of the times, he incorporated the Church's prescriptions for reconstructing the social order into his more traditional religious message aimed at restoring spiritual values to a society troubled by a whole host of modern evils.

When the young Dr. Fulton Sheen first returned from Europe to the United States in 1925, his main concern was to lay the foundations of a career as a scholar and professor of theology at the Catholic University of America. A prolific writer and gifted orator, his early publications were philosophical and theological treatises, and his lectures focused on standard religious themes and

---

[10]   Cardinal Gibbons, "Letter to the Hierarchy," cited in McShane, p. 247.

[11]   James Henessey, SJ, *American Catholics*, p. 240.

[12]   McShane, pp. 279, 281.

refuting atheism and the "new paganism."[13] And from his fundamental premise of "applied Thomism," Sheen would move in several new directions, seeking to make the philosophy of St. Thomas functional for the modern world. From this essential Thomism
flowed many of the major ideas associated with Catholicism over
the next several years. Those especially germane to Fulton Sheen's
role in the history of American Catholicism are: the doctrine of the
Mystical Body of Christ; Catholic Action; and social justice and
reform.[14]

Thomism was a philosophy depicted by many reformers during the decade of the thirties as uniquely modern and American
— "Catholic Action in the sphere of thought" — and it mobilized
the Catholic community to build a structure of security within
which it could safely enter into American life.[15] Sheen, like many
of his contemporaries, was thoroughly immersed in the intellectual waters of his time, a blend of Scholasticism, synthesis, and social
teaching. But it was not until the middle thirties that Sheen began
to address the social question directly, after the impact of the papal encyclical *Quadragesimo Anno* had been felt, and leadership had
been assumed by American Catholicism's foremost social reformer,
Father John A. Ryan.[16] Starting with the publication of *The Mys-*

---

[13] See the newspaper clipping files, Fulton Sheen Archives, Diocese of Rochester. For example, a series of lectures delivered in 1928 on "The New Paganism" received a good
deal of attention in the Catholic Press; Sheen pointed out the fallacies of such modern
ideas as individualism, pragmatism and evolution. These lectures were later incorporated
into the book *Religion Without God.*

[14] These three concepts best explain how, and why, Fulton Sheen, Thomistic philosopher
and theologian, went on to become an eloquent exponent of social justice. Many historians of American Catholicism have perceived the symbiotic relationship existing among
the Mystical Body, Catholic Action, and social reform, all rooted in the Thomistic synthesis with its emphasis on the organic unity which characterized American Catholic
thought during the first half of the twentieth century. See James Henessey, SJ, *American
Catholics;* Jay P. Dolan, *The American Catholic Experience* (Garden City, NY: Doubleday
and Company, 1985); and David O'Brien's *American Catholics and Social Reform* (New
York: Oxford University Press, 1968).

[15] William Halsey, *The Survival of American Innocence,* pp. 156, 166.

[16] For details of Monsignor Ryan's leadership in the field of social ethics and reform, see
O'Brien's *American Catholics and Social Reform* and Francis Broderick's biography of Ryan,
Right Reverend New Dealer (New York: The Macmillan Co., 1963).

tical Body of Christ in 1935, and culminating with *Liberty, Equality and Fraternity* and *Freedom Under God* at the end of the decade, Fulton Sheen became a leading popularizer of Catholic social teachings. In his earlier work, though, he ventured into the social realm only occasionally and tentatively. Taking his lead from Pope Leo XIII — "Society can be healed in no other way than by a return to Christian life and Christian institutions"[17] — Sheen adapted traditional Catholic doctrines to the problems of the modern world, an adaptation which required a discussion of social and economic issues, but always from a religious point of view. Thus Sheen became associated with social reform by an indirect route, as a secondary concern, for the "primacy of the spiritual" was uppermost in his mind and public pronouncements.[18]

In *The Life of All Living*, published in 1929 and advertised as a "Supernatural Biology and Treatise on the Divine Life," Sheen stated that "the Catholic contends that man is not only an individual, but also a member of society hence, religion is social as well as individual."[19] In *The Divine Romance*, compiled from his first regular series on the "Catholic Hour" radio broadcasts in 1930, Sheen started from the premise that man, in his search for God, sought answers to both universal problems and pressing contemporary problems. In 1930, the nation was mired in the depths of the Great Depression; in discussing the life of Christ, then, Sheen emphasized Christ's identification with the poor, hungry, persecuted members of the Church, His Mystical Body.[20] *Old Errors and New Labels*, one of Sheen's most popular early works, was devoted

---

[17] Pope Leo XIII, quoted in the Bishops' Pastoral Letter of 1919, cited in *Pastoral Letters of the U.S. Catholic Bishops,* edited by Hugh Nolan (Washington, DC: United States Catholic Conference, 1984), Vol. I, p. 270.

[18] The "primacy of the spiritual" was one of Sheen's favorite concepts/phrases. For example, he used it as the title of Chapter II in *The Cross and the Crisis* (Milwaukee: The Bruce Publishing Co., 1938).

[19] Fulton Sheen, *The Life of All Living* (New York: Garden City Books, 1951 reprint), p. 69.

[20] Fulton Sheen, *The Divine Romance* (New York: Garden City Books, 1951 reprint), pp. 83-103. This work has gone through five reprints since 1982 (New York: Alba House, 1982, 1983, 1988, 1992 and 1997) and continues to appeal to audiences in 2002.

to refuting many modern beliefs in a traditional apologetical mode. Determined to offer resistance to the growing sway of secularism in American life, Sheen belonged to a "very influential strain" of Catholic apologetics which took the "form of a critique of modern culture."[21] In *Old Errors and New Labels*, Sheen challenged a host of modern errors from the fortress of Catholic orthodoxy. Among the errors he took on were atheism, humanism, evolution, and birth control, which he refuted with his characteristic wit and style.[22] In the chapter on "The Philosophy of Charity," he addresses the topic of social ills directly, but offers only traditional religious answers, a relatively conservative cure for the times. "Social ills," according to Sheen, "must be remedied in order that the life of the soul and the spirit may be free to move on to God... filling empty stomachs is but a prelude to filling empty hearts."[23]

In *The Eternal Galilean*, which appeared in 1934 as a book and a pamphlet of the Catholic Hour Broadcast Series, Sheen presented a very orthodox treatment of the life of Christ. He insisted that religion was primarily divine, and only secondarily social and political:

> The shattering of material illusions during the world war and the present economic recession has made the clear-visioned minds of our day see that apostasy from the principles of the Savior, the abandonment of the spiritual life, and the transgressions of the commandments of God, have led of necessity to our ruin, and our confusion worse confounded.[24]

So, even in the midst of the crisis of the Depression, Sheen offered his listeners and readers a very old-fashioned message: return to

[21] Avery Dulles, *A History of Apologetics* (Hutchinson of London, Corpus of New York, 1971), p. 218. Dulles mentions Sheen as a "high apostolic priest who swelled the volume of Catholic apologetical writing" (p. 218).

[22] Fulton Sheen, *Old Errors and New Labels* (New York: The Century Co., 1931).

[23] *Ibid.*, pp. 250-251.

[24] Fulton Sheen, *The Eternal Galilean* (New York: Garden City Books, 1950 reprint), p. 65. This work was brought back into print in 1997 (New York: Alba House).

religion. Beginning in the middle of that decade, though, he began to absorb some of the more innovative developments taking place in Catholic social thought and to disseminate the good news to his American audience.

Because of several developments in Fulton Sheen's career during the 1930's — his elevation to the rank of Monsignor, the publication of a multiplicity of books and articles, and his reputation as an orator and radio preacher — his growing fame made him one of American Catholicism's best known spokesmen. Consequently, Monsignor Sheen was in a unique position to render an invaluable service to his Church, to spread the Catholic message across the United States. The American hierarchy was dedicated to promoting papal social teachings in a variety of ways: carrying on its educational tradition; venturing into the political arena to advocate legislative solutions to current social problems; and supporting the formation of reform communities, such as the Catholic Worker movement. The Catholic Church embraced a wide spectrum of reformers during these years, and Fulton Sheen assumed a position in the middle of that spectrum.

Monsignor Sheen's contribution during these critical years was to publicize, interpret, and adapt the social teachings of the Catholic Church. His was a timely response to the papal call for action contained in the great social encyclicals, and he consistently relied upon them — *Rerum Novarum* and *Quadragesimo Anno* — for his support. He seldom deviated from the papal prescriptions, and clung to the safety of the middle ground. It was Sheen's prerogative to accommodate the Church to its present social and political conditions, without sacrificing any of its essential truths. Following the methods employed by Popes Leo XIII and Pius XI, he first refuted the false teachings of the current age — particularly socialism and communism — and then went on to explain the Church's plan for setting things right. His lectures, radio addresses, and books were often long on rhetoric and repetition, and short on specifics. His task was simply to enlighten and educate, to convey the traditional wisdom of the Catholic Church, which had survived for centuries, to a new age in need of its guidance. After a careful study of the encyclicals, and the work of many contemporary social reformers, he came to the conclusion that there was no incompatibility between the Church's social teachings and the modern world, only a lack of knowledge. And he proceeded to correct it.

Perhaps the best example of how Sheen took the eternal wisdom of the Church and tried to apply it to the practical needs of his times can be found in *The Mystical Body of Christ*, published in 1935.[25] Sheen's was a popular exposition on a subject which enjoyed a renewed emphasis among Catholic theologians during the thirties.[26] In the preface, Monsignor Sheen noted that his "modest contribution" was born of a study of St. Thomas' treatise on the Mystical Body, and influenced by the "profound historical study" of Fr. Emil Mersch.[27] Rather than being "dangerous or novel," Sheen said that he was simply reviving, or restoring, a traditional doctrine of the Church:

> …a thorough knowledge of the Mystical Body is the condition of not only a fruitful apostolate, but also a spiritual priesthood and laity… it will make Catholicism operative in our lives, which is only another name for Catholic Action.[28]

This revival of the concept of the Church as the Mystical Body of Christ during the Depression decade seemed almost "providential,"[29] given the current social crisis.

In his writings on the doctrine of the Mystical Body, Sheen was well aware of the need to make the Church's message heard in

---

[25] Fulton Sheen, *The Mystical Body of Christ* (New York: Sheed and Ward, 1935), was based upon Sheen's "Catholic Hour" broadcasts of the same year, "The Fullness of Christ."

[26] One example of the general renewed interest can be found in the review article written by W.J. McGarry, SJ, in *Thought* 12 (March, 1937), pp. 169-170. McGarry noted a common theme in Sheen's book and that of Daniel A. Lord, *Our Part in the Mystical Body*: both were popularizations of profound dogmas, designed at the present time to "stir up Catholic Action."

[27] Sheen, *The Mystical Body of Christ*, pp. 6, 11.

[28] *Ibid.*, p. 12.

the modern world. He sought to link the Mystical Body, therefore, with the resounding call of Pius XI — the Pope of Catholic Action — for a dynamic lay participation in the historic mission of the Church. In fact, Monsignor Sheen repeatedly equated "Mystical Body" and "Catholic Action" in an attempt to clarify his purpose. The term "Catholic Action" was in and of itself a very controversial one, an ambiguous concept which led to considerable misunderstanding between Catholic and non-Catholic Americans.[30] Though aware of the ambiguities inherent in the term "Catholic Action," which he openly acknowledged, he chose not to dwell on them specifically and to avoid becoming embroiled in the heated arguments occurring between some Catholics and several notable American liberals.[31] Sheen's aim, in employing "Catholic Action," was simply to enhance the influence of the Catholic Church in America and to create enthusiasm among his followers, not to stir up resentment and anti-Catholic sentiments.[32] Fulton Sheen's conception of Catholic Action and the Mystical Body relied on the more orthodox religious notion of having Catholic laymen participate in the redemptive mission of the Church, infusing the world with Christ's spirit. His writings and lectures were designed to inspire the members of his audience to do good works in

---

[29] E.S. Berry, in a review in *The Catholic Historical Review* XXII (October, 1936), p. 373, praises Sheen's book, noting that it offers the "same clear, logical presentation" and "striking comparisons" which characterized the Monsignor's radio addresses.

[30] For a succinct explanation of this "ambiguity of concept," see D.J. Geaney's "Catholic Action" article in the *New Catholic Encyclopedia*, Vol. 3, pp. 262-263.

[31] For examples of the American liberals' case against Catholic Action, see George Seldes' *The Catholic Crisis* (New York: Julian Messner Inc., 1939) and D.A. Saunders' "Liberals and Catholic Action," in the Protestant journal *Christian Century* 54 (October 20, 1937), pp. 1293-1295.

[32] Sheen's best intentions, however, were not always realized. He was prone to rhetorical excess. Many of his most excessive statements were made on the subject of communism; like other American Catholics he employed terms like "army," "mobilization" and "waging war." This rhetoric did nothing to quell non-Catholics' fears about Catholic Action. Historian David O'Brien, in *American Catholics and Social Reform*, refers to "men like Fr. Coughlin and Msgr. Fulton Sheen" who spoke of a "struggle between the Mystical Body of Christ and anti-Christ" (p. 181). This comparison is not entirely fair, since it fails to note the differences between the two men; Sheen never subscribed to Coughlin's anti-Semitism, or supported fascism.

the secular world, and he relied on such images of the members of Christ's Church as spiritual "leaven"; "Missionaries" who would "extend the frontiers of Christ's kingdom"; and spiritual "plasma"[33]. In "Catholic Action and the Mystical Body,"[34] Sheen stated his purpose clearly:

> ...to define Catholic Action in terms of the Church, or the Mystical Body of Christ.... There is probably no term used in the Church more vague and obscure than Catholic Action. This is not because it lacks either meaning or content, but rather because some of its exponents have too often dissociated it from the doctrine of the Church. As in all things else, parts are intelligible only in the light of the whole. The term is bound to be vague when made synonymous with the activity of Catholics, just as it is bound to be clear when identified with the action of Catholicism.[35]

The actions of the Catholic Church, enlightened through the theology of the Mystical Body, were described as the "prolongation of the Incarnation." To be understood properly, Sheen told his American audience, the Church should be regarded as an "organism," not an organization.[36] Following the lessons of the encyclicals, Sheen depicted the work of the Catholic Church as "the adaptation of Christian principles to the needs and circumstances of the age."[37] And presently, Christ was using the Church as "the social instrument of His teaching."[38] Social action was a contemporary focus of the Catholic Church and would be guided by the

---

[33] Sheen, *The Mystical Body of Christ*, pp. 25, 307, 360.

[34] "Catholic Action and the Mystical Body" was printed as an article in *The Homiletic and Pastoral Review* 35 (1935), pp. 866-873.

[35] *Ibid.*, p. 366.

[36] Sheen, *The Mystical Body of Christ*, pp. 70-72.

[37] *Ibid.*, p. 116.

[38] *Ibid.*, p. 171.

Catholic emphasis on the Brotherhood of Man and Fatherhood of God. Serving as an example to the rest of the world, "this brotherhood, through the Eucharist, was intended by our Lord to be the basis of all international agreements, as well as the relations between Capital and Labor."[39] Quoting the Holy Father's definition of Catholic Action as "organic to the Church," as a hand and a foot are to a body, Sheen underscored Pius XI's directive to Catholics to become actively involved in society:

> Catholic Action is the participation of the laity in the hierarchical apostolate, for the defense of religious and moral principles, for the development of a healthy and helpful social action under the leadership of the Ecclesiastical hierarchy, but outside and above all political parties, in order that Catholic life might be restored to the family and society.[40]

Again, he invoked the image of the activity of the Mystical Body in the world as the activity of a "leaven in the mass." It was not a "rival political system or economic policy or international code set up in contrast with the world, but rather the very soul of those activities."[41] Catholic Action, though designed to be "outside and beyond all political parties"[42], must not be indifferent to economics or politics. Members of Christ's Body were directed "to seek first the Kingdom of God and His justice" by becoming active participants in the social arena, assured by Sheen that "Catholic Action keeps the Mystical Body alive, healthy and growing."[43]

In the same year that Monsignor Sheen was expounding on the relevance of the Mystical Body for American Catholics, he

---

[39] *Ibid.*, p. 369.

[40] Sheen, "Catholic Action and the Mystical Body," *The Homiletic and Pastoral Review*, p. 868.

[41] *Ibid.*, p. 871.

[42] Pius XI, *Qua Nobis*, cited by Sheen in "Catholic Action and the Mystical Body," p. 871.

[43] *Ibid.*, p. 873.

delivered an address to the National Conference of Catholic Charities, entitled "A Changed Outlook on Social Work."[44] Viewing Catholic social workers as involved in the endeavor to keep the Mystical Body healthy and growing, and praising them for responding to the challenge of the times, Sheen also explained his own growing interest in the social question: "Never before have your opportunities been greater... because apologetics has shifted to the social realm."[45]

Just as Sheen's apologetics would increasingly begin to focus on defending the Church against communism, his emphasis on social justice and reform was irrevocably linked with anti-communism. He seldom discussed one subject without alluding to the other.[46] This address, like his explanations on the relationship between the Mystical Body and Catholic Action, brings the subject of communism prominently into the discussion. It also demonstrates why it is virtually impossible to separate Sheen the "advocate of social justice," from Sheen the "foe of communism." In the present age, Sheen informed the social workers, "civilization was no longer being molded from above, but from below," and the communists were going directly to the masses. Catholics, too, should recognize that the future was in the hands of the masses, the collective, the unemployed, who were eager for direction and guidance as well as bread. Therefore, he advised the Catholic social workers to go down to the masses, for they held the keys to the future of the state and the Church:

> Go down to them and build just as strong and vigorous
> a Christian proletariat among them as communists must
> build a communist proletariat. Down to the masses we

---

[44] This address was published in *The Catholic Charities Review* XX (March, 1936), pp. 69-75.

[45] *Ibid.*, p. 74.

[46] See Kathleen Riley Fields, "Anti-Communism and Social Justice: The Double-Edged Sword of Fulton Sheen," *Records of the American Catholic Historical Society of Philadelphia* 96 (March-December, 1986), pp. 83-91.

> must go, infusing them with a Christian conscience...
> for the conflict of the present day will be settled in the
> realm of social philosophy and social action.[47]

This realization that the conflict of the present day would be
settled in the realm of social philosophy and action — and that the
communists were already active in the social arena — was certainly
not unique to Fulton Sheen. Many Catholic social reformers were
cognizant of the fact; consequently, the American Catholic
Church's "opposition to communism was coupled with a radical
program of social justice."[48] A major concern of the American
Catholic Church during these years, intrinsically related to its espousal of social reform and its condemnation of communism, was
to demonstrate its loyalty to the nation, to become more fully
Americanized. Thus, the motives and concerns of Catholic social
reformers during the New Deal years "covered a wide spectrum,
from an anxiety to prove that the Catholic Church was loyal and
patriotic, to an equally intense passion to remake America as a truly
Christian society."[49] Monsignor Fulton Sheen's passion to make
America more Christian took the form of a double-edged sword:
crusading against the threat of communism, and for the Catholic
vision of social justice.

Fulton Sheen's version of social reform, like that of many of
his contemporaries, was based upon the papal prescription outlined
in *Quadragesimo Anno*. Like its predecessor, this second social encyclical highlighted the Church's response to modern civilization
in order to counter the spread of radicalism and restore the Church
to a position of power, prestige, and influence.[50] And given the crisis
mentality precipitated by the Depression, Pius XI's pronouncement
was "greeted with the confident expectation that the confusion and
adversity of the contemporary situation would provide fertile soil

---

[47] Sheen, "A Changed Outlook on Social Work," p. 75.

[48] Henessey, p. 291.

[49] O'Brien, p. ix.

[50] *Ibid.*, p. 29.

for the Pope's message."[51] The papal program "On Reconstructing
the Social Order" was built upon many of the Church's traditional
beliefs: the necessity for both individual and social reform, with an
emphasis on the primacy of moral reform; the belief that society
requires two virtues of its members, justice as well as charity; and a
definition of the "common good" as the standard by which all social activity must be judged.[52] In addition, this encyclical moved
beyond the traditional gospel in its advocacy of an increased role
for the state, and practical suggestions for reform and legislation,
such as the concept of the guild system, or occupational groups,
and the concept of a just, or living wage for the laborer and his family. Inspired by the Pope's message, Sheen set out to bring that
message to the masses through his popular books, sermons, and
radio broadcasts.

When Sheen read the social encyclicals, it was often with an
eye towards how he could best explain them, in a simplified manner, to his audience. Hoping to correct the misconception prevailing in the minds of many Americans — that the Church was a
bastion of conservatism, and opposed to any type of change or reform — Sheen had a tendency to stress what he saw as the revolutionary potential of the Catholic message (to steal the thunder from
the communists) and its practical application to contemporary
America. Consequently, he failed to consider and evaluate those
aspects of the encyclicals which did not lend support to his aim of
popularization — making the contents understandable for his followers, who were not always capable of subtle intellectual discrimi-
nations.[53] Some of the language used in the encyclicals — "corporate" and "corporatism" being a good example — made Catholicism suspect in the eyes of some Americans, for the same language
was found in fascist ideology. In the context of the Spanish Civil

---

[51] *Ibid.*, p. 47.

[52] *Ibid.*, especially Chapter 1, which provides a summary of the history of Catholic social
thought.

[53] For historical perspective on the encyclical *Quadragesimo Anno*, see the essays contained
in *Readings in Moral Theology, #5: Official Catholic Social Teaching,* edited by Charles
Curran and Richard McCormick, SJ (New York: The Paulist Press, 1986).

War, and the papal concordat with the government of Mussolini, some Americans perceived the Church as a friend of fascism, and the red-baiting campaign waged against communism by some Catholics lent credence to this view.[54] The very idea of a papal directive raised the issue of the authoritarian nature of the Church and the supposed political power of the Pope. These problematic issues and nuance in interpretation escaped Sheen's attention for the most part. Instead, he highlighted those aspects of the papal teachings that would most likely appeal to his listeners and readers, and that would be most relevant to the concerns of the times.

Since much of Sheen's purpose in publicizing the social teachings of the Catholic Church was to resist the growth of secularism in American life, while undermining the appeal communism seemed to have for the common man, he often presented the Church's views from the most positive perspective possible. He sought to demonstrate the superiority of Catholicism over all other prevailing philosophies, and attracted the attention of the press with both his flamboyant rhetoric and pious slogans — the stuff of headlines.

An example of Sheen's ability to garner attention in the press was a story in the Chicago newspapers about an address in which Sheen called for the creation of a workers school, sponsored by the Catholic Church, to "combat the campaign of lies and deceit waged by communism in its drive against the American government and religion."[55] *Catholic Action*, the official publication of the National Catholic Welfare Conference, printed an excerpt of "Ideals of Catholic Social Work," an address by Sheen which offered a "most enlightening comparison of the ideals of Catholic and non-Catholic social teaching" and was delivered at the Washington May Day Party for the National Catholic School of Social Service.[56] Another indication of Sheen's growing prominence as an advocate of social

---

[54] The topics of fascism and communism, raised here, will be discussed in subsequent chapters.

[55] *Chicago Herald Tribune,* November 15, 1936, and *Chicago Herald Examiner,* November 16, 1936, which featured the dramatic headline: "Sheen Proposes Workers School to Battle Red Deceit." Newspaper clipping files, Fulton Sheen Archives.

[56] *Catholic Action* XX (June, 1938), p. 27.

justice was the fact that he joined Monsignor Francis J. Haas and John F. Cronin (figures more readily acknowledged by Church historians as social reformers) on the faculty of a special session of the School of Social Action in Washington, D.C.[57]

Monsignor Sheen had also made headlines when he accompanied Al Smith, former governor of New York and the first Catholic presidential candidate in United States history, on a goodwill trip to Europe. The trip was praised as an example of Catholic Action: "these two gentlemen... serve as fine living examples of the coordination of the clergy and laity in the Church."[58] Several years later, Sheen and Smith teamed up again and *The New York World Telegram* reported that they had been "summoned by the Vatican to discuss with the Pope the fight of the Catholic Church against communism, and the economic conditions that have led to labor unrest here."[59]

In addressing the issue of labor unrest directly, Sheen had argued that too many religious people "forget that in these days the poor demand more than good advice, rebuke for their sins, or praise of the resignation to poverty."[60] He upheld the rights of labor unions, and at a lecture series at St. John's University in 1937, he advocated the formation of workers' guilds, as outlined by the Holy Father: "workers should be given a share in management and ownership."[61] Arguing that it was simply not true that the Catholic religion preaches passivity to unjust conditions, he reminded his audience that Popes Leo XIII and Pius XI both wrote encyclical letters in defense of the workingmen and that the working population had options other than socialism: "the practical approach for Catholics in combating the arguments of socialists is through the

[57] *The Baltimore Catholic Review,* 1938; Newspaper clipping file, Fulton Sheen Archives.
[58] *The Tower* (Catholic University of America), May 11, 1933; Newspaper clipping files, Fulton Sheen Archives.
[59] *The New York World Telegram,* May 10, 1937; Newspaper clipping files, Fulton Sheen Archives.
[60] See the Newspaper clipping files, Fulton Sheen Archives; clipping dated October 8, 1936.
[61] Entry dated December 13, 1937; Scrapbook of newspaper clippings collected by "Joseph F. Sheen of Chicago," Fulton Sheen Archives.

encyclicals of the Popes, for no communist has ever found a better plan for social justice than is to be found in the encyclicals... the Catholic Church was recruited from the poor, and we must recruit them again."[62]

Presenting the Church's case to the poor and to the American public at large during the Depression decade became a major preoccupation of Fulton Sheen. His mature version of the social gospel, formulated throughout the decade in lectures and sermons, was summarized in two of his books: *Liberty, Equality and Fraternity* (1938), and *Freedom Under God* (1940).[63] These books incorporated many of Sheen's early ideas about the social question, and contained his personal interpretation and application of the principles outlined in *Quadragesimo Anno* — the books are dense with quotations from that papal encyclical. In that document, Pius XI, not wishing to place the Catholic Church in the camp of any particular ideology — liberal or reactionary — called for the establishment of a Christian social order as a "middle way" between capitalism and communism. This was the essential premise of Sheen's work: he also chose to occupy the middle ground, or golden mean, in advocating social action. Repeatedly, he pointed out the connection between the rise of communism and the failings of monopolistic capitalism. Catholicism offered the only answer to modern man's search for order and justice, a viable alternative between extremes.[64] The Catholic Church alone proposed a reconstruction of society on the basis of "mutual cooperation, joint effort, harmonious organization, justice, charity, and a love of the common good."[65] Presented in Sheen's style, this was a prescription which most Americans would find acceptable.

---

[62] *New York Wisdom*, November, 1936; Newspaper clipping files, Fulton Sheen Archives.

[63] These two books appeared in essentially the same form as pamphlets in the Catholic Hour Broadcast Series, *Justice* and *Charity* and *Freedom*.

[64] Sheen continuously seized the middle ground in his arguments, a position which can be traced back to his intellectual foundation. In *God and Intelligence in Modern Philosophy*, for example, he noted that the philosophy of St. Thomas "stands between extremes" (p. 142).

[65] Fulton Sheen, *Liberty, Equality and Fraternity*, p. 54.

In the introduction to *Liberty, Equality and Fraternity*, Sheen states his case: "The world today stands in need of two virtues: justice and charity. These two virtues are the only effective cure for two evils, one the accidental evil of capitalism, the other the essential evil of communism."[66] This is the fundamental tenet of Sheen's position on social reform and communism. His views on how to achieve justice contrast sharply with the communists' plan of creating turmoil, bitterness and class conflict in an effort to hasten the revolution, a plan which Sheen saw as proof of the communists' selfish interests. Sheen proposes instead that "social justice means seeking and loving the common good. No one class is always right, whether it be Capital or Labor, because society is not founded upon antagonistic classes, but upon their mutual functioning and correlation for the good of all."[67] To traditional Catholic doctrine, Sheen adds a more enlightened view of the Church, as much opposed to the abuses of capitalism as it is to the evils of communism:

> For the Catholic, then, the defense of the present system of capitalism in which wealth is in the hands of a few, is almost as wrong as the communist solution which would destroy that wealth and appropriate it all in the hands of the red leaders.[68]

This balanced viewpoint, simple and straightforward, was designed to correct some misconceptions about the Church — that it always sided with the wealthy, for example — while it maintained the Church's traditional opposition to communism: "we believe that justice is a better remedy than reaction, and that charity is a better solvent than revolution."[69]

Sheen's construction in *Liberty, Equality and Fraternity* presents a quick historical review of how the Church came to occupy

---

[66] *Ibid.*, p. vii.

[67] *Ibid.*, p. viii.

[68] *Ibid.*, pp. 74-75.

[69] *Ibid.*, p. xiii.

the safe, and correct, middle ground, and why its advice ought to be followed. Liberty, the solution posed by liberalism; Equality, the ideal advocated by communism; and Fraternity, the answer according to Catholicism, were currently under discussion as remedies for the malaise of the modern world. Historically, liberalism, or individualism, had failed, destroying true Liberty in the process by dispensing the individual from his social responsibilities. As far back as 1891 the Pope had warned against the dangers of this false view of liberty, stating that man could enjoy liberty only when it was based upon natural law. Arguing that the Pope's warning was correct, Sheen goes on to suggest that this historic failure of liberalism in turn "begot capitalism." And it is the inequalities of capitalism that the communist proposes to cure,[70] illustrating the intrinsic relationship between the faults of capitalism and the growth of communism.

Capitalism is found wanting, in Sheen's judgment, and the judgment of the Church, precisely because of its abuses: concentrating wealth in the hands of a few; and its search for dominance (in politics, economics, and in the international sphere). The present system of "monopolistic capitalism" is consequently in conflict with the Church's advocacy of the poor and the workers, who found themselves dependent on (and neglected by) a class of wealthy capitalists.[71] The most grievous fault of capitalism is that, because of its abuses and its failure to respond to legitimate cries for reform and social justice, it has given rise to the greater evil of communism: "capitalism gone mad" or "rotted capitalism."[72] Declaring communism to be the most pressing threat of the times, he nevertheless conceded that its protests against the injustices of capitalism were correct, and this explained its appeal to the downtrodden workers. But the Church was equally critical of capitalism's faults.[73]

---

[70] *Ibid.*, pp. 11-12. The underlying message here is that society was in its present desperate state precisely because the Church's message was being ignored.

[71] *Ibid.*, p. 15.

[72] *Ibid.*, pp. 19, 49.

[73] *Ibid.*, p. 19.

Although the Church defends the right to private property, it is careful to condemn its abuse, and "denies against capitalism that its right to profit is prior to the human right to a living wage. The virtue of justice, championed and defended by the Church, intervenes against both capitalism and communism."[74]

In taking up the explanation of Equality, the supposed ideal of the communists, Sheen demonstrated that the Catholic Church was capable of some advanced thinking. The Church was not blind to the fact that evil was present in both camps, and unequivocally opposed a rampant capitalism as well as a raging communism — its protests against the injustices begotten by liberalism — while immediately warning that "we must not be fooled by believing that because the protests of communism are right, therefore their reforms are right."[75] Employing an oversimplified analogy, as he often did, Sheen added: "Communism, finding rats in the barn, burns the barn. The Church drives out the rats."[76] By this route, he finally arrives at the Catholic position of the golden mean between extremes. The solutions proposed by communism and Catholicism, to correct the problems of inequality produced by capitalism and its abuses, are completely different: while communism proposes to solve inequalities by confiscation, collectivism and violence, the Church proposes legislation and distribution.[77]

The Catholic Church alone is the true advocate of reform — practical yet enlightened — and guided by the spirit of Fraternity, or Brotherhood. The world need not be forced to choose between capitalism's individual selfishness and communism's collective selfishness. The Church insists that there is a third choice — a golden mean — the more equitable distribution of property: "the Church has made the wide distribution of property the cornerstone of her social program."[78] Offering more concrete suggestions, the

---

[74] *Ibid.*, p. 20.
[75] *Ibid.*, p. 26.
[76] *Ibid.*, p. 21.
[77] *Ibid.*, p. 22.
[78] *Ibid.*, p. 42.

Church would follow two steps in securing greater economic freedom for the worker by distribution. The first was the payment of a living wage, specifically mentioned in the encyclical, and the second was securing for the worker, when possible, a "share in the ownership, profits and management of industry."[79] For many of his readers and listeners, this was no doubt a progressive stance for a priest, or the Church, to take. And given its proposed legislative remedies, the Church would necessarily have to cooperate with the state in an effort to secure the common good. Supporting an increased role for the state might be viewed as suspicious, or dangerous. But once again, safety was to be found in the virtuous mean, between the extremes of state indifference and state control.[80]

The book *Liberty, Equality and Fraternity* would prove to be the most elaborate and carefully balanced compendium of Sheen's opinions on the social question,[81] written at a time when this subject was paramount on the agenda of the American Catholic Church. All things considered, it was a thoughtful rationale for the Church's position that a realization of social justice would provide a practical solution to the pressing problems of communism as well:

> The Church believes that one of the greatest obstacles in the way of effectively combating the evils of communism is the "foolhardiness of those who neglect to remove or modify unjust conditions which are exasperating the minds of people and preparing for the overthrow and ruin of the social order." Remove the environment in which communism grows, and you do much to remove the menace of communism.[82]

---

[79] *Ibid.*, p. 69.

[80] *Ibid.*, p. 62.

[81] This book received many favorable reviews; one of the most impressive is contained in a letter to Sheen, dated December 22, 1938 (found in the Fulton Sheen Archives): "Thanks for the copy of *Liberty, Equality and Fraternity.* I am confident that it will contribute substantially to that reawakening of Christian conscience in the field of civics and sociology, which is so much needed for the health of contemporary society." The letter was written by Cardinal Pacelli, who became Pope Pius XII the following year.

[82] Sheen, *Liberty, Equality and Fraternity,* pp. 80-81.

Succinctly put, peace would be the "fruit of social justice, coming through a process of spiritual regeneration."[83]

Tilling the soil of social justice so that the fruit of peace might grow was the focus in Sheen's following volume on social reform, *Freedom Under God*. It was published in 1940, at the beginning of a decade which would bring the storm clouds of the Second World War to American shores. In many respects, this book is one of transition, wherein Sheen's emphasis shifts from the social reform of the New Deal years to a greater concern for the restoration of peace — social and international — in the aftermath of war. One of Sheen's better performances as an intellectual popularizer was given in the accompanying radio broadcasts. He continued to combine Catholic orthodoxy and social reform in a pragmatic application of the principles of justice to the pressing situation. In addition, he began to infuse his talks with more "Americanism," setting the stage for American Catholics to demonstrate their patriotism and loyalty to the nation:

> Americanism is the political expression of the Catholic doctrine concerning man. Firstly, his rights come from God and therefore cannot be taken away; secondly, the state exists to preserve them… the Declaration of Independence and the Gospel affirms the dignity of man… such is the traditional concept which is today the essence of Catholic social teaching and the basis of Americanism.[84]

Sheen's objective in this equation of Catholicism and Americanism was to prove the "relevance" of religion to public affairs, religion being defined as "the sum of virtues which condition justice and peace."[85] The present state of violence, disorder and blood-

---

[83] This idea was reiterated again and again by Sheen, in slightly different versions: "Justice is the foundation of world peace, coming through a process of spiritual regeneration."

[84] Fulton Sheen, *Freedom Under God* (Milwaukee: The Bruce Publishing Company, 1940), p. 167.

[85] *Ibid.*, p. 5.

shed was the direct consequence of the belief that justice is irrelevant to the social and economic order, according to Sheen. He argued that to leave religion out of society was not merely to create a "secular civilization, but chaos."[86] Lamenting the fact that the Church's efforts to restore order and harmony to the world by a re-infusion of Christian principles had not come to fruition, he described the results:

> Never before has man had so much power, and never before has that Power been so amassed for the destruction of human life; never before has there been so much education, and never before so little coming to the knowledge of the Truth; never before has there been so much wealth and never before so much poverty; never before did we have so much food, and never before so many hungry men.[87]

The whole world had gone awry without religion. Reiterating his contention that the Catholic Church was the last bastion of freedom in the world, he resounded the dire warning from *Quadragesimo Anno*: "unless serious attempts are made… to put (our ideas) into practice, let nobody persuade himself that the peace and tranquility of human society can be effectively defended against the forces of revolution."[88] Coming back to his original point of departure, that society was in need of the twin virtues traditionally upheld by the Catholic Church, Monsignor Fulton Sheen admonished: "There will never be a radical transformation of society unless there is a spiritual generation of persons through a rebirth of justice and charity… only when justice and charity are rooted in the souls of men can we expect any measure of social peace."[89]

Working out a creative response to the challenge of the times

---

[86] *Ibid.*, p. 4.
[87] *Ibid.*, p. 10.
[88] Cited in *Freedom Under God*, p. 120.
[89] *Ibid.*, pp. 74, 239.

was the hallmark of Fulton Sheen's life. Like the Church he served, he discerned a certain wisdom in trying to shape the great changes wrought by the twentieth century, rather than simply resisting them. During these early years in his career many of the changes revolved around the questions of social justice and reform. Rooted in the wisdom of the ages, the American Catholic Church created a program of social reform that offered "more space, more depth, and more freedom than Americans, including Catholics, had suspected."[90] And Fulton Sheen played an important role in making the basics of the program known through his books and radio broadcasts.

In evaluating Sheen's role during these years of advancement for the American Church, it should be noted that he measures up well to the standards invoked by the historians of American Catholic social reform: Aaron Abell, in *American Catholicism and Social Action: A Search for Social Justice, 1865-1950*[91]; and David O'Brien, in *American Catholics and Social Reform: The New Deal Years*. Sheen crusaded for the cause of social justice effectively through his interpretation of the encyclicals for the masses who followed him. Abell's book discusses the Church's record of charity and social service in the context of Americanization in Catholic thought, noting that the Church was faced with a dilemma: "how, on the one hand, to champion the cause of the poor without endangering the public interest or the common good, and, on the other, how to oppose socialism without negating or ignoring the claims of social reform."[92] This dilemma caused the Church to cling to the safety of the "middle ground," or as Sheen sometimes phrased it, the "golden or virtuous mean" between the abuses of a liberal capitalism and communism.[93] In league with the Americanizing element

---

[90] O'Brien, p. 227.

[91] Aaron Abell, *American Catholicism and Social Action: A Search for Social Justice, 1865-1950* (New York: Doubleday and Company, 1960).

[92] Abell, *American Catholicism and Social Action*, p. 7.

[93] Another study of Catholic social thought by Michael Novak, *Freedom With Justice* (San Francisco: Harper and Row, 1984), also makes reference to the ideal of the "Catholic Middle Way," p. 22.

in the Church, Sheen sought to construct a bridge between Catholics and non-Catholics, making the Church both more acceptable, and more influential, in American life. Americanizers steered a middle course in driving the two major vehicles of Americanization — social reform and anti-communism; in both cases, Sheen was part of the Catholic consensus. In *American Catholics and Social Reform*, O'Brien also noted the official Church position as occupying the middle ground between the "abuses of liberal capitalism and the irreligious tyranny of red revolution."[94] He also decried the fact that "many Catholics appeared to ignore the bishops' ambiguous demand for reform to concentrate on the clearly defined issue of anti-communism."[95] Although Fulton Sheen is perhaps better remembered as a leading foe of communism — the "prophet and philosopher" of Catholic anti-communism[96] — he was certainly not remiss regarding social reform, persistently linking the two issues when speaking from the prominent national pulpit he enjoyed. The initial efforts of the American hierarchy to effect justice and reform revolved around two means: social education and the promotion of legislation. The legislative option was exercised with considerable success during the New Deal years by men like Monsignors John A. Ryan and Francis Haas. When Sheen was faced with a choice, he rose to the occasion with the talents God gave him and became a teacher, on the popular level, of the Church's social doctrine. Particularly through his radio broadcasts, he was able to take the message to the masses; unlike the other radio priest, Fr. Charles Coughlin,[97] Sheen's was a more enlightened and balanced presentation. Many American Catholics urged the formation of a united Catholic front to promote Church interests and teachings, to spread acceptance of Christian moral principles and defend democratic ideas and institutions against communism and

---

[94] O'Brien, p. 227.

[95] *Ibid.*, p. 227.

[96] Donald F. Crosby, *God, Church and Flag: Senator Joseph R. McCarthy and the Catholic Church, 1950-1957* (Chapel Hill, NC: The University of North Carolina Press, 1978), p. 5.

[97] A comparison of Sheen and Coughlin will be discussed in following chapters.

secularism.[98] On the crucial battlefield of education, Fulton Sheen,
a pragmatic popularizer, carried on the good fight.

The effectiveness of Sheen's educational efforts during these
years, on the subjects of the world crisis and the threat of communism, as well as on behalf of the Church's social program, was due
to his radio apostolate. More than any other single factor, his ability to pioneer in the use of the electronic gospel led to his success
as a spokesman for the American Catholic Church. As the principal speaker on the "Catholic Hour" broadcasts for over two decades
(1930-1952), he was hailed as the "greatest evangelist" of the day,
and won fame as a convert-maker as well.[99] His radio pulpit would
become a "spiritual meeting place" for many,[100] and he would exceed the expectations of the National Council of Catholic Men
when they chose him as the premier speaker for their radio program:

> ...to undertake an exposition of the Catholic faith... by
> employment of the radio as a means of promoting a
> better understanding of the Catholic Church, and more
> friendly relations among the several religious groups in
> America.[101]

This was the hope expressed by the National Council of Catholic
Men in their historic undertaking, and the performance of Fulton
Sheen more than fulfilled that hope.

---

98 O'Brien, p. 218.

99 Typescript produced by the National Council of Catholic Men, in the collection of the
Fulton Sheen Archives, entitled "Right Reverend Monsignor Fulton J. Sheen and the
Nation-wide Catholic Hour."

100 See the pamphlet published by Our Sunday Visitor entitled "Memories, 1930-1940,"
which reprinted the addresses delivered on the tenth anniversary broadcast of the "Catholic
Hour" on March 3, 1940, Fulton Sheen Archives.

101 *National Catholic Welfare Conference Review* 12 (March, 1930) p. 15.

CHAPTER THREE

Electronic Evangelist and Convert-maker

1930-1952

> Radio has made it possible to address more souls in the space
> of thirty minutes than St. Paul did in all his missionary journeys....
> Broadcasting and television are the distant echoes of the Gospel.
>
> *Fulton J. Sheen*

> Priests do not convert. The Grace of God converts....
> We are merely the gardeners, hoeing the earth a bit and
> watering the roots. It is God who drops the seed.
>
> *Fulton J. Sheen*

When the National Broadcasting Company offered the American Catholic Church the opportunity to broadcast a weekly Sunday program on national radio in 1930, Fulton J. Sheen was chosen as the first regular speaker on the "Catholic Hour." For the next twenty-two years, Sheen delivered a series of broadcasts which would establish his reputation as the most popular Catholic preacher in the United States. The young professor at the Catholic University of America was a logical choice to pioneer in the new radio apostolate; his interests and background meshed with those of the National Council of Catholic Men, the sponsor of the "Catholic Hour" broadcasts. At its annual convention in 1928, the Catholic laymen had decided to undertake an exposition of the Catholic faith in the apologetical mode. It was a timely decision, one which enjoyed the support of the hierarchy, especially in light of the renewed wave of anti-Catholic sentiment which had accompanied the presi-

dential campaign of Al Smith.[1] Sheen's skill as an apologist, and
his growing reputation as a brilliant orator, thus made his selection a natural one, with the promise of success. Also, Sheen had
some experience preaching on the radio, having made his broadcasting debut in 1927 when the Paulist Fathers of New York invited him to give a series of Lenten sermons which were carried on
the local station WLWL.[2] Here, too, his talents coincided with the
needs of his sponsor, for Sheen ably carried out the Paulists' mission of teaching the truth about the Catholic faith and exerting a
greater influence on American society. In many respects, then,
Fulton Sheen was "the right man in the right place at the right
time," well-equipped to make the most of the historic opportunities presented to the American religious community at the dawn-
ing of the radio age.

   The rise of the electronic media would have a great impact
on many churches in the twentieth century, as organized religion
recognized the tremendous potential of reaching a vast audience
through the new technology. The first religious broadcast in history originated from the facilities of station KDA in Pittsburgh on
January 2, 1921: the vesper services conducted by the Rev. Edwin
J. Van Etten at the Calvary Episcopal Church.[3] In this historic
broadcast, according to an analyst of the wedding of religion and
radio, "an ancient quest of the human spirit had in fact been linked
with the most modern and most amazing of man's instruments of
communication."[4] The field of religious broadcasting would grow
rapidly over the next two decades. And although it would not be

---

[1]   In the *National Catholic Welfare Conference Bulletin* 11 (November, 1929), Archbishop
     McNicholas commended the apologetical program of the N.C.C.M., defending
     apologetics as "the science which states the Catholic position, and defends the Church
     against those who malign, misrepresent and misinterpret her," p. 7.

[2]   Two letters in the Fulton Sheen Archives (Diocese of Rochester), written by Sheen to
     the Very Rev. Fr. McSorley, CSP, indicate that the broadcasts delivered over WLWL
     occurred in 1927; this conflicts with Sheen's autobiography, which gives the date 1928
     (*Treasure in Clay*, p. 63).

[3]   See "Radio and Religion" by Spencer Miller, Jr., in the *Annals of the American Academy of
     Political and Social Science* 177 (January, 1935), p. 135.

[4]   Miller, p. 135.

long before an ecumenical quality was apparent, with Catholics and Jews taking the message of their respective faiths to the air waves, it was the Protestants who were the first on the scene.[5]

Mainline Protestantism took full advantage of the medium of radio from the start; in 1925, the Greater New York Federation of Churches began the "National Radio Pulpit" on station WEAF, and the Federal Council of Churches of Christ in America created the National Religious Radio Committee to set standards and regulations.[6] But perhaps the greatest Protestant success story was the radio revivalism adopted by the fundamentalists. Dr. Joel A. Carpenter's study, "The Renewal of American Fundamentalism, 1930-1945,"[7] explores the fundamentalist movement's contribution to the resurgence of Christianity following the Second World War, made possible by the creation of a thriving network of institutions founded during the thirties. It was radio broadcasting which presented the fundamentalists with the most powerful new measure to assist them in staying alive and healthy during the Depression decade:

> ...enterprising urban pastors were the first to adapt it to the task of reaching the unchurched, building and nurturing their own constituencies, and convincing the world that their message was a timely one... between 1930 and 1935, radio broadcasting became a movement-wide force of tested success.[8]

---

[5] Fr. Coughlin, the original "radio priest," broadcast his first "Golden Hour of the Little Flower" in 1926; see Charles J. Tuli's *Father Coughlin and the New Deal* (Syracuse, NY: Syracuse University Press, 1965). Among numerous other studies of the famous Fr. Coughlin, see Alan Brinkley's *Voices of Protest: Huey Long, Fr. Coughlin and the Great Depression* (New York: Alfred A. Knopf, 1982) and Chapter VII, "Father Coughlin and American Catholicism" in David O'Brien's *American Catholics and Social Reform.*

[6] Peter Elvy, *Buying Time: The Foundations of the Electronic Church* (Mystic, CT: Twenty-Third Publications, 1984), p. 35; and Miller, p. 136.

[7] Joel A. Carpenter, "The Renewal of American Fundamentalism, 1930-1945" (Ph.D. dissertation, Johns Hopkins University, 1984).

[8] *Ibid.*, pp. 145, 147.

Those fundamentalists who employed the radio most successfully included Paul Rader, who began broadcasting from his Chicago Gospel Tabernacle in 1922,[9] J. Elwin Wright and his New
England Fellowship, and President Will Houghton of the Moody
Bible Institute.[10] In all three cases, radio broadcasting served as the
base for creating a wider ministry of revivalism. The rising commercial radio industry of the 1930's "provided the fundamentalists
with a new medium with which to send out their message to the
rest of the nation," at a time when the radio was the first leisure
time entertainment in America, and the number of radio receiving
sets had doubled from 1930-1935 to a high of 18 million.[11] But
the greatest legend in the history of American fundamentalism was
Charles E. Fuller, whose "Old Fashioned Revival Hour," a weekly
broadcast based in Los Angeles, became "the most popular religious
program in the country." In 1939, Fuller's program was broadcast
coast to coast, and overseas, to an estimated 15-20 million listeners over 152 stations, "the largest single release of any prime time
radio broadcast in America."[12] It is clear then, that the decision to
employ the radio to advance the cause of religion was largely responsible for the survival of American fundamentalism during
troubled times:

> Fundamentalists were well-suited for the medium —
> both their evangelistic messages and their gospel music
> were designed for mass appeal, and they presented them-
> selves as promoters of widely shared American tradi-
> tions… radio reached out and bypassed denominational
> barriers.[13]

Along other denominational lines, Fr. Charles Coughlin became the first to demonstrate that the radio was well-suited to use

---

[9] *Ibid.*, p. 145.
[10] *Ibid.*, p. 151.
[11] *Ibid.*, p. 25.
[12] *Ibid.*, pp. 28-29.
[13] *Ibid.*, p. 147.

by American Catholics. In addition to being the first "radio priest," Fr. Coughlin also attracted the largest audience of any priest in American history — estimated as high as 40 million — "a national popularity of bewildering proportions."[14] It should be noted, however, that although Fr. Coughlin had the largest following, he became so mired in political controversy that he lost his effectiveness as a spokesman for Catholicism. His popularity, compared with that of Fulton Sheen, was relatively short-lived.[15] Eventually, he became such a source of embarrassment to the Church that he was silenced by Archbishop Edward F. Mooney of Detroit, and after 1942 lived in obscurity as a simple parish priest.

During his heyday, however, Father Coughlin was probably the best-known priest in America. When he first started his radio career — on October 3, 1926 — Coughlin rapidly gained in popularity; within four years, he had secured time on the Columbia Broadcasting System, one of the two major networks of the day. Within a year after that, however, he was eased off the network, in 1931, because his subject matter was increasingly political and less religious.[16] When his efforts to buy time from the competing network, N.B.C., proved futile, he was forced to create his own broadcasting set-up. His popularity continued to increase steadily over the next few years, but the controversial, and often offensive, nature of his broadcasts soon placed him outside the mainstream of religious radio.[17] This status he shared with the Protestant funda-

---

[14] Alan Brinkley, *Voices of Protest*, p. 83.

[15] Invariably, the idea of a comparison between Coughlin and Sheen arises when one considers the subject of the radio. Fr. Coughlin was most famous for his extremism and political views, whereas Sheen was a much more balanced representative of the Church who never became politically involved. The common features in the careers of the two radio priests include their motivations for going on the air — to enhance the image of the Church in America and combat anti-Catholicism; reputations as anti-communists; and magnificent speaking voices. In the final analysis, Sheen enjoys and deserves a more favorable historical reputation, while Coughlin, according to Professor Brinkley, is remembered as a "man of hysterical passion and hatred, a harsh and embittered bigot" (p. x).

[16] Tull, pp. 3-5.

[17] *Ibid.*, pp. 5-8.

mentalists, who were also considered "outsiders," and were required to maintain their own radio networks at their own expense.

According to Professor Carpenter, this financial consideration raised some problems in the fundamentalist community; as the leaders discovered "how to use the radio profitably for publicity and fund-raising," they were often guilty of "self-serving boosterism."[18] The problems associated with the fundamentalist gospel, and, to a greater degree, "Fr. Coughlin's controversial radio blasts over the C.B.S. chain,"[19] led the networks to adopt a new policy of regulation in 1930.

In the new spirit of regulation, both networks decided to donate free time to the three major religious denominations — Protestant, Catholic, Jewish — as a public service.[20] C.B.S. rotated the representative national religious bodies on a program called "Church of the Air"; by donating the time rather than selling it, the network could lay down the principle that all programs "must be of a constructive character" and that "no time shall be allotted for attacks on the clergy or lay members of any denomination."[21] The National Broadcasting Company adopted a similar set of principles: only the central or national agencies of great religious faiths would be served; all programs were to be non-sectarian, with the widest popular appeal; and only the "recognized outstanding leaders" of the several faiths would be chosen to "interpret religion at its highest and best," responsible to both organized churches and the larger American society.[22] N.B.C. directed its offer to the Catholic Church through the National Catholic Welfare Conference and the National Council of Catholic Men. In announcing the inauguration of the "Catholic Hour," the *N.C.W.C. Review* stated that the program would make its debut on March 2, 1930 on station WEAF

---

[18] Carpenter, pp. 165-167.

[19] *Ibid.*, p. 27.

[20] Elvy, p. 36. Both networks developed good working relationships with the Federal Council of Churches, the Jewish Seminary of America, and the National Council of Catholic Men.

[21] Miller, p. 137.

[22] See Miller, p. 137, for a complete summary of N.B.C.'s fivefold statement of principles.

in New York City; the program was scheduled to air every Sunday evening from 6 p.m. to 7 p.m.[23] The talks would be given by "priests noted for their scholarship and eloquence" and "laymen of distinction," and would cover a "wide range of religious subjects."[24] The initial broadcast was delivered by Patrick Cardinal Hayes of the Archdiocese of New York, who simultaneously gave the "Catholic Hour" his approval and blessing, and stated its purpose:

> This radio hour is one of service to America, which certainly will listen in interestedly and even sympathetically... to the voice of the ancient Church... [T]o voice before a vast public the Catholic Church is no light task.... We feel certain that it will have both the good will and the good wishes of the great majority of our countrymen. Surely, there is no true lover of our country who does not eagerly hope for a less worldly, a less material, and a more spiritual standard among our people.[25]

After Cardinal Hayes, the first priest chosen to speak on the "Catholic Hour" was Father Fulton J. Sheen, who premiered on March 9, 1930.

Once Sheen's broadcasting career was launched by the National Council of Catholic Men, he became the focus of much of the publicity surrounding the "Catholic Hour." He would regularly deliver a series of talks which extended from Christmas or the first of the year, through the Lenten season, for the next twenty-two years. Sheen's addresses were the most frequently quoted in the pages of *Catholic Action*, the official journal of the N.C.W.C., which

---

[23] *N.C.W.C. Review* 12 (March, 1930), p. 15.

[24] *Ibid.*

[25] Cardinal Hayes, in an extract of his address, reprinted in the pamphlet containing the eulogy delivered by Monsignor Sheen for Cardinal Hayes on October 5, 1936. The pamphlet was printed and distributed by Our Sunday Visitor in conjunction with the N.C.C.M., and is contained in the collection at the Sheen Archives.

actively promoted the radio program. And the volume of Sheen's mail would be used to gauge the impact and popularity of the broadcasts.[26] Within two years, there were so many requests for reprints of the "Catholic Hour" broadcasts that the N.C.C.M. and Our Sunday Visitor cooperated in a joint effort to print and distribute copies of the address transcripts in pamphlet form.[27] Since Father Sheen was also widely-known as an author, the power of his words over the radio would be enhanced by offering them in written form, a tactic first employed by Sheen at the suggestion of the Paulists. In a letter to Joseph McSorley, C.S.P. of the Church of St. Paul the Apostle, Fr. Sheen wrote:

> I had almost abandoned the idea of printing the sermons I preached last year, but your kindly thought that they might be worthwhile revived such an idea... I am sending you... the sermons I preached last Lent from WLWL.... I believe there is much repetition in them, so I give you an absolute right to "cut here and burn there, but spare for eternity," as St. Augustine said.[28]

Most of Fulton Sheen's radio talks would be "spared for eternity," due to the amount of attention they received. His first broadcast, "Man's Quest for God," was indicative of the spirit that would guide Sheen's apostolate throughout his life — man's search for God and for satisfying answers to the problems of human life. It was a spirit which seemed to spark an interest, as this first "Catholic Hour" address evoked a widespread response in the form of

---

[26] For the purposes of this study, the incomplete and sparse materials on Sheen's radio broadcasts in the Sheen Archives were supplemented by a review of the contents of *Catholic Action* from 1929 through 1952. *Catholic Action* consistently highlighted Sheen as the "star" of the "Catholic Hour" broadcasts, for he was the most popular speaker on the program.

[27] See *Catholic Action* 14 (April, 1932), p. 17, for the first notice that Sheen's addresses would be available in pamphlet form.

[28] Two letters from Sheen to McSorley, dated October 2 and November 18, 1927, can be found in the administrative files of the Sheen Archives. Sheen's admission that there was a repetition in his talks was an understatement.

hundreds of letters. This first response was indicative of many of the qualities which would come to characterize Sheen's return performances. At the end of the first series, which ran from March 9 to April 30, 1930, the National Council of Catholic Men had received 1,026 commentaries, overwhelmingly favorable, and many from non-Catholics.[29] After one year on the air, it seemed apparent that the "Catholic Hour" was moving in the right direction, fulfilling the N.C.C.M.'s apologetic goals:

> ...to use all resources to cause the Church, its doctrines and its teachings to be better known to America in order that she may be better understood in places where there is misunderstanding and prejudice.[30]

Commonweal referred to the "Catholic Hour" as "the outstanding achievement of Catholic Action in the United States."[31] As Sheen's role in the success of the "Catholic Hour" was considerable, the spotlight of publicity was often centered on him. In a notice in 1934 — "Dr. Sheen Now on the Catholic Hour in Fourth Annual Series: The Eternal Galilean" — he was described as "an outstanding figure in the religious life of the nation... known by millions of listeners for his highly popular Catholic Hour addresses... upwards of one million copies of his radio talks have been requested and distributed."[32] Later that year, *Catholic Action* reported:

> The Holy Father, recognizing Dr. Sheen's notable service as a pulpit and radio orator, has elevated him to the dignity of Papal Chamberlain, with the title of Very Rev. Monsignor... the news came when Sheen was on his

---

[29] *N.C.W.C. Review* 12 (May, 1930), pp. 12-13.

[30] Charles A. McMahon, in "The First Year of the Catholic Hour," *N.C.W.C. Review* 13 (March, 1931), p. 9, cites this statement. After only one year on the air, the broadcast was being carried on more stations, having increased from 33 to 45 stations.

[31] Cited in *Catholic Action* 15 (May, 1933), p. 9; *Commonweal,* October 1, 1930.

[32] *Catholic Action* 16 (January, 1934), p. 16.

way to England to lecture; at Rome, he was received in a special audience, and received a special blessing on the "Catholic Hour" and his own apostolic work.[33]

Clearly a "rising star" in the Catholic Church's galaxy, Monsignor Sheen had been responsible for drawing the Holy Father's attention to the apostolate of the radio. Over the next few years, Sheen's apostolic endeavors continued to revolve around his affiliation with the "Catholic Hour." The relationship forged by Fulton Sheen and the National Council of Catholic Men was proving to be a mutually beneficial one.[34] The Executive Secretary of the National Council of Catholic Men, Edward J. Heffron, attempted to measure the success of the "Catholic Hour" in an address entitled "The Contribution of the Catholic Church Through Radio to the Religious Life of the American People."[35] By 1937, the broadcast was being carried over 57 stations and elicited an average response of 2,000 letters a month. This mail contained a number written by "fine, fair-minded non-Catholic listeners cordial to Catholicism." According to Heffron, these letters were especially heartening, for they "give hope that the lingering bitterness and misunderstanding of another day may yet be completely dissipated... the 'Catholic Hour' is therefore serving not only the cause of religion, but the cause of democracy... and education."[36] This service in the causes of religion, democracy and education was an underlying purpose of Sheen's apostolate as well; the following month, it was reported that Monsignor Sheen's pamphlet "Communism Answers the Questions of a Communist" was being made available by the N.C.W.C. News Service, part of the effort of the Catholic press to be the nation's bulwark against communism, and defender of the American gov-

[33] *Catholic Action* 16 (August, 1934), p. 13.

[34] The details of the relationship can be found in a copy of the contract which survives in the Memorabilia Files of the Sheen Archives.

[35] Excerpts of this address were printed in *Catholic Action* 19 (January, 1937).

[36] *Ibid.*, p. 17. *Catholic Action* frequently reported that the mail sent by non-Catholics — 20-30% of the total — proved that many Americans were becoming more favorably disposed toward the Catholic Church.

ernment and its democratic institutions.[37] As Monsignor Sheen continued to speak out on the social and political issues of the day, from a religious perspective, his popularity soared. His series for 1938, "Justice and Charity" (The Social Problem and the Church) elicited record receipts of mail. At a time when letters to the N.C.C.M. were averaging 2,000 a month, Sheen's talks brought in 6,007 letters for January and 8,590 letters for February.[38] And in 1940, Sheen's tenth series on the "Catholic Hour" was hailed as "the most popular religious series ever given on radio."[39] Entitled "Peace: The Fruit of Justice," it was a commentary on *Summi Pontificatus*, the first encyclical of Pope Pius XII[40]; heard over 106 stations, the National Council of Catholic Men estimated that it reached an audience of 17 million listeners.[41]

The tenth anniversary of the "Catholic Hour" was the occasion for celebration, a celebration which took the form of a special radio program broadcast on March 3, 1940.[42] After a blessing by Archbishop Spellman, who stated that the hope of Cardinal Hayes — "that the 'Catholic Hour', with the charity of Christ, might come to make better known our Faith"[43] — had been realized, the major address was delivered by Monsignor Sheen. In "Memories," Sheen told his listeners that the "Catholic Hour" had broadcast its "messages on eternal life" over five hundred and twenty times, which he

---

[37] *Catholic Action* 19 (February, 1937), p. 4.

[38] *Catholic Action* 20 (April, 1938), p. 13. This series was later published as the book *Liberty, Equality and Fraternity*.

[39] *Catholic Action* 22 (March, 1940), p. 23. The N.C.C.M. reported that 28,000 letters a week were sent in response to Sheen's broadcasts.

[40] This series was published as the book *Whence Comes War?* (New York: Sheed and Ward, 1940).

[41] *Catholic Action* 22 (November, 1940), p. 17.

[42] A special pamphlet entitled "Memories: 1930-1940" was prepared to commemorate the occasion. Although the pamphlet is very laudatory — containing messages of congratulations from Pope Pius XII and the Most Rev. Amleto Giovanni Cicognani, Apostolic Delegate to the U.S. — it offers good insight into the significance of the "Catholic Hour" as appreciated by the American Catholic community. A copy of the pamphlet can be found in the Sheen Archives.

[43] Spellman, in "Memories," p. 12. Spellman also praised the radio as an instrument which sent out the word of God "in new ways, striving to bring men together."

characterized as repetitious in a positive sense, "the thrill of monotony" on the "Catholic Hour."[44] Stepping out of character, Sheen proceeded to offer a retrospective look at a decade of broadcasting, and the "changes in the religious frontiers of America" that had occurred. As Sheen perceived it, there were two major changes: "a decrease of bigotry, but an increase of hate," and "a re-awakened interest in the spiritual."[45] The first change was apparent in the thousands of letters Sheen had received, which revealed a general decline in bigotry — intellectual opposition to the Church — a result of the increased enlightenment regarding religion achieved by the "Catholic Hour." However, he had also received a small number of "hateful" letters, which expressed negative emotions and a general hostility to God rather than a particular hostility towards Catholicism. These hateful letters always elicited a kindly response from Sheen, "for these souls may be like Saul who hated ignorantly."[46]

Regarding the second change, Sheen stated that "America was never more ripe for a genuine spiritual rebirth." Disenchanted with secularized religion, the hearts of modern men nevertheless sought deliverance and guidance in a revitalized sense of religion:

> The Catholic Hour has satisfied this need in the hearts
> of millions; it has never dabbled in politics; never once
> attacked any religion; never stirred up hatred against any
> person; but with scrupulous precision has had and will
> have only one purpose: the salvation of souls.[47]

This singular purpose of saving souls, said Sheen, was evident in the number who had converted to Catholicism as a result of listening to the "Catholic Hour." Sheen was receiving a good deal of attention from the press for his responsibility in many of those con-

---

[44] Sheen, "Memories," pp. 13-14.
[45] *Ibid.*, pp. 14-15.
[46] *Ibid.*, pp. 14-15.
[47] *Ibid.*, p. 15.

versions. On this occasion, and on every other occasion when he was asked to discuss his success as a convert-maker, he refused to take the credit, reserving all of it for God: "No priest can give the Faith to anyone; Faith is God's gift. A priest is a spiritual agriculturalist. He tills the soil; it is God who drops the seed."[48]

In his capacities as both spiritual agriculturalist and radio preacher, Monsignor Sheen was the focus of much of the praise accorded to the "Catholic Hour." The diocesan newspaper of New Orleans, *Catholic Action of the South*, referred to Sheen as "the John Chrysostom of the U.S. air waves" who deserved special commendation as a veteran of the broadcast.[49] The *Catholic Review* of Baltimore lauded the "Catholic Hour" for its "Catholic Truth, Catholic eloquence, and Catholic scholarship," and added that "there is... little cause to doubt that Monsignor Sheen is the most eloquent and most effective Catholic speaker on the radio in this country."[50] "One of the country's best known and best loved orators," in the eyes of the *Denver Catholic Register*, Sheen had spoken on the outstanding radio program "more times than any other man."[51] And looking ahead to the future, the *St. Louis University News* suggested that "if the next ten years of the work of Monsignor Sheen and the Catholic Hour are as fruitful as the last, we may have a much changed country."[52]

An article on the "Catholic Hour" in *Radio Varieties* recognized the changes that had already occurred in the industry as a result of the union between radio and religion. According to David Sarnoff, president of the Radio Corporation of America, the "great benefit" of the "Catholic Hour" was that it preached "understand-

---

[48] These self-deprecating comments by Sheen were undoubtedly sincere, but they generally caused more attention to be focused on him.

[49] February 29, 1940, cited in "Memories," pp. 48-49. Sheen was also described as "more feared for his scholarly and irrefutable defense of principles than any other American priest."

[50] February 23, 1940, cited in "Memories," p. 53.

[51] March 7, 1940, cited in "Memories," p. 59.

[52] March 8, 1940, cited in "Memories," p. 69.

ing and tolerance."[53] The program's addresses were credited with
"contributing their share in resisting bigotry and destroying prejudice": "America's leading Catholic preachers, typified by the well-
loved and inspiring figure, Rt. Rev. Msgr. Fulton J. Sheen, present
a message of dignity and simple sincerity."[54] The national news-
weekly *Time* headlined its coverage of the "Catholic Hour"'s anniversary with "Monsignor's Tenth," and used the occasion to draw
a sharp and timely distinction between Fulton Sheen and the other
"radio priest":

> ...her nearest equivalent to a great preacher is the
> Radiorating Father Coughlin. Last week a son of
> Mother Church in whom she can take greater pride
> celebrated his tenth anniversary as a radio preacher....
> Monsignor Sheen is a persuasive, lucid speaker, with a
> well-cultivated voice, who can make religion sensible and
> attractive to great masses of people.... Take away Fr.
> Coughlin's microphone and *Social Justice* and there
> would be little left but a parish priest. But Monsignor
> Sheen is much more than a pulpiteer — he is one of the
> Church's ablest converters.[55]

Sheen remained as a speaker on the "Catholic Hour" for another twelve years; in 1952 he delivered his final series of radio
broadcasts on the "Life of Christ," leaving to devote himself to television and the missions. During these last years, the effects of
Sheen's radio ministry remained much the same. The publicity
surrounding the "Catholic Hour" continued to promote the idea
that anti-Catholic prejudice was abating, and that Catholics were
proving themselves as good American citizens. This was an especially important theme as the World War predominated as the sub-

---

[53] *Radio Varieties* (January, 1940), p. 3. A copy of this article, written by Aileen Soares, can
be found in the Memorabilia Files, Sheen Archives.

[54] *Ibid.*

[55] *Time,* March 11, 1940.

ject of many of Sheen's broadcasts. *Catholic Action* made a point of quoting from an article in *The Living Church*, an Episcopalian journal, which called Sheen "salutary and inspiring," and welcomed his "spirited and enlightened defense of the Taylor appointment to the Vatican against the foolish Protestant assertion that the separation of Church and state is endangered thereby."[56] Mindful that most of the Protestant reaction to Myron Taylor's appointment as the president's representative at the Vatican was very negative, this official publication of the American hierarchy was determined to draw attention to the positive:

> When a semi-official spokesman, and an official organ of the Protestant Church can be led to such statements, the "Catholic Hour" has indeed achieved its purpose: in the words of Frank J. Sheed, "not to prove other people wrong, nor even to prove Catholicism right, but simply to render it intelligible."[57]

In his own personal reflections on the radio ministry and the art of preaching, Fulton Sheen often made reference to this same point — that one of the greatest effects of his efforts was the improved image and reputation enjoyed by the Catholic Church in the United States, and the greater religious understanding that prevailed among Catholics, Protestants and Jews.[58] He appreciated the fact that the radio afforded him the opportunity to correct many misconceptions about the Catholic Church at a time when it was still viewed with suspicion by many Americans:

> the bigoted... think that we are antiquated, medieval, shallow. It will be my purpose to present our picture and

---

[56] Cited in *Catholic Action* 22 (December, 1940), p. 25.

[57] *Ibid.*

[58] For example, on the eve of the Second World War, Sheen observed that in his years of broadcasting, he had witnessed the "gradual diminishing of hatred and bigotry, and a growing interest in religion." *Catholic Herald* (of London), August 11, 1939. Newspaper clipping files, Sheen Archives.

our program in such a way as to brush aside their pre-
conceived ideas.[59]

Whether preaching on the radio or from the pulpit, Sheen
could remain true to his original calling as an educator.[60] If, as he
suspected, the misunderstandings about the Church were founded
on erroneous beliefs, it followed that the basic need of the day was
instruction; on the radio, Fulton Sheen could be an instructor for
the entire nation. He insisted that not proselytizing, but "Christian witness" and education was the thrust of his preaching. Feeling "called by God to reach the masses,"[61] he simply adapted a traditional preaching style, inspired by St. Paul, to the challenges of a
new day. Sheen had taken to heart two valuable lessons of St. Paul,
lessons which were responsible for his success. From a literary perspective, Sheen learned that a preacher had to be universal in study,
widely informed about the world and the interests and needs of his
audience: "In talking to wise men, men must be wise." At the same
time, from a psychological viewpoint, a preacher must also "establish a common denominator with the masses."[62] This combination
of scholarship and the common touch was the key to Sheen's great
success, a fact recognized by his contemporaries and by historians.
In his popular history of American Catholicism written in 1941,
Theodore Maynard called Sheen "an exceptionally profound philosopher" who had been "deflected from speculation to the pulpit
and the radio" where he is "unquestionably performing a notable
service."[63] This service was due to his almost universal appeal, which

---

[59] Fulton Sheen, quoted in the newspaper article "Lives of Great People" in the *Boston Post*,
sometime in 1940, preserved in the Scrapbook kept by "Joseph F. Sheen of Chicago,"
Sheen Archives.

[60] In his autobiography, Sheen stated that "lecturing had been good preparation for radio,
and evangelism was inseparable from professional teaching" (pp. 55, 105).

[61] Sheen, in a reflective conversation he had with the Rev. John Brady, of the Ministr-O-
Media Company (which produced audio cassettes by Sheen), in 1974. Sheen's quote is
found in a letter from Fr. Brady in the administrative files, Sheen Archives.

[62] Sheen, "Preaching as a Saving Event," a 1972 typescript in the personal papers collection, Sheen Archives.

[63] Theodore Maynard, *The Story of American Catholicism* (New York: The Macmillan Co.,
1941), p. 580.

extended beyond traditional Catholic doctrine, and his talent as an orator with a great speaking voice. Combined with the technology of the radio, it was possible for Fulton Sheen to lend a whole new dimension to the biblical injunction to "go forth and teach." Sheen's performance of such a notable service on behalf of his Church led him to be assessed as "the most listened to American Catholic preacher of all time" who "mingled his obvious learning and scholarship with a common touch that appealed to millions."[64]

It was this great appeal, and the personal magnetism of Fulton Sheen, which led many potential converts to the Catholic faith to seek him out. Although proselytization was not his primary motive, it was his popularity on the radio which explains his success as a convert-maker. He achieved his greatest notoriety (thus far in his career) during the forties, when his radio apostolate and reputation for leading souls to God went hand in hand. Never averse to making headlines, he attracted widespread attention when famous people came to him in their quest for salvation.[65] Although it was the famous converts who created the most publicity, Sheen had enjoyed a quiet measure of success as a convert-maker for years.[66] In 1942, for example, Sheen reported that he had baptized ten persons on Good Friday; all "influenced in their decision by the Catholic Hour."[67] Later that summer, Sheen conducted a three day mission in Sanford, North Carolina; helping to establish the Church of Our Lady of Lourdes there.[68] For many in his audience it was impossible to separate the Monsignor and his message from the Church he represented, so he could not help attracting souls drawn

---

[64] See John Delaney's *Dictionary of American Catholic Biography* (Garden City, NY: Doubleday and Co., 1984), p. 527.

[65] This phenomenon of Sheen's "star" quality had been noted by Wilfrid Sheed; in *Clare Booth Luce* (New York: E.P. Dutton, 1982), he noted that "she had to go and get converted by Fulton Sheen, official priest to the celebrities" (p. 10). In *Frank and Maisie* (New York: Simon and Schuster, 1985), he spoke of the "World War II Catholic boom — the march of the converts was on, with Fulton Sheen ushering in the big fish" (p. 204).

[66] Sheen's reflections on a lifetime of making converts are found in Chapter 16 of *Treasure in Clay*. See also "Fulton J. Sheen: Unprofitable Servant," by George Frazier in *Catholic Digest* 14 (October, 1950), p. 25.

[67] *Catholic Action* 24 (May, 1942), p. 25.

[68] *Catholic Action* 24 (August, 1942), p. 25.

to Catholicism. His fan mail contained numerous inquiries about instructions in the Catholic faith, and throughout the years that he preached on radio and television, and taught classes at the Catholic University of America and directed the offices of the Society for the Propagation of the Faith, he conducted convert classes for serious inquirers. These classes met in both Washington D.C. and New York City as Sheen commuted between them. At times, the classes had to be conducted in large school halls to accommodate the number of students, and they lasted from four to six months, or the equivalent of eighty to one hundred hours of instruction.[69]

Some of the most prominent Americans to be counted in the company of Monsignor Sheen's converts were Horace Mann, of the Republican National Committee; Henry Ford II, heir to the fortune of the automobile industry's Ford Motor Co.; Fritz Kreisler, the musician; and Heywood Broun, the journalist/columnist.[70] But by far, the two conversions which attracted the most attention were those of Clare Boothe Luce and Louis F. Budenz; the Budenz conversion was of a special publicity value because he was a leader in the American Communist Party.[71] In the cases of Mr. Budenz and Mrs. Luce, both remained newsmakers in their own right, and wrote about the circumstances surrounding their conversions to Catholicism, contributing to the growing genre of Catholic apologetical literature written by converts. Both figures also maintained contact with Sheen throughout their later years, and continued to be identified in the press as "one of Msgr. Sheen's converts."[72]

---

[69] Details about these classes are not readily available, because Sheen kept no accurate or complete records about them. Several stories written about Sheen and his famous converts mention the classes, however; see John Jay Daly's "The Man Behind the Mike" in *The Sign* 24 (May 10, 1945), and Stanley High's "Catholic Converts" in *Current History and Forum* 52 (September, 1940).

[70] These two converts were chosen for analysis because they are the ones most frequently mentioned in the media stories about Sheen and his converts.

[71] After Budenz joined the Catholic Church in 1945, he helped to usher in other communists, such as Elizabeth Bentley and Bella V. Dodd.

[72] Both Sheen and his famous converts, Budenz and Luce, benefitted from the publicity following their very public conversions. For an anecdotal reference to Sheen's legendary status as a convert-maker, see J.F. Powers' short story, "The Valiant Woman," in the *Prince of Darkness and Other Stories* (New York: Doubleday and Co., Image Books Edition, 1958), p. 120.

When Louis F. Budenz, the editor of the Communist *Daily Worker* in New York City, was received into the Catholic Church by Monsignor Fulton Sheen on October 10, 1945, the announcement of his conversion was considered a major news story. Sheen, realizing the dramatic value of winning over such a prominent communist, had sent word to the Associated Press of the conversion of the entire Budenz family. The announcement was delayed until after the fact had been accomplished, and the entire conversion story had been kept a secret, the instructions "conducted by stealth," according to Sheen. When the time was right, however, Sheen provided the details to the press — on the day after, when Budenz was publicly welcomed into the Church at St. Patrick's Cathedral. The Communist Party had been so surprised that on the very day of the public announcement, the masthead of the *Daily Worker* still carried the name of Louis Budenz as Editor-in-Chief, quite a public relations coup in Sheen's mind.[73]

Budenz' story was the stuff of melodrama, told in 1947 in his confessional autobiography, *This Is My Story*. Raised a Catholic, Mr. Budenz had renounced his faith on the occasion of his marriage. Joining the Communist Party in 1935, he worked his way up through the ranks to the influential position of editor of the *Daily Worker*. In an editorial published on Christmas day in 1936, Mr. Budenz issued a direct challenge to Monsignor Sheen, one of American Catholicism's leading anti-communists, and offered him the outstretched hand of good will. Sheen replied to the gesture in a pamphlet entitled "Communism Answers the Questions of a Communist." It was this initial confrontation, according to Budenz, which "led to the jolt that changed my life after many years, and made me see the Red cause in its proper colors and brought me back to Christ." However, it would take Budenz nine years to make his way back to the Church.[74]

---

[73] Details about the conversion of Louis Budenz can be found in the press notices found in the Sheen Archives, and *This Is My Story* by Louis Francis Budenz (New York: Whittlesey House, The McGraw-Hill Book Co., 1947).

[74] Budenz, p. 157.

Bringing his wife and three daughters with him when he finally returned to the Church in 1945, Budenz made headlines. The *New York Times* announced "Daily Worker Editor Renounces Communism for Catholic Faith."[75] Giving credit to Monsignor Sheen for "engineering" the conversion, the *Times* explained that through Sheen's intervention, Budenz would be joining the Economics Department at the University of Notre Dame. The following day, another story, with an equally dramatic headline, appeared: "Foster Calls Budenz Deserter from Labor: Sheen Tells How Editor Rejoined the Church."[76] Contrasting the communists' disavowal by William Z. Foster, a party leader, with Monsignor Sheen's welcome, most of the story focused on Sheen's explanation of his own role in the conversion, which he told in a broadcast over the Mutual Radio Network. Simplifying, Sheen reported that he had invited Budenz to dinner, "and talked to him about God, grace and Our Blessed Mother":

> ...Herein is the answer to the question: How can I reconcile my opposition to communism with the Christianity I profess? The answer is simple: I hate communism, but I love communists.[77]

Sheen's other "most famous" convert, Mrs. Luce, followed in Budenz' path and became a Catholic in the following year, on February 16, 1946.

Clare Boothe Luce was a distinguished author-playwright, Congresswoman from the state of Connecticut, and the wife of Henry Luce, editor and owner of the *Time-Life* magazine empire[78] — and one of the most well-known and respected women of her day. She converted to Catholicism after a lifelong search for truth, and was received into the Church by Monsignor Sheen at St.

---

[75] *New York Times*, October 11, 1945.

[76] *New York Times*, October 12, 1945.

[77] *Ibid.*

[78] For details on Mrs. Luce's life, and her conversion, see Wilfrid Sheed's *Clare Boothe Luce*.

Patrick's Cathedral. A year after her baptism, she wrote a three-part series of articles in an attempt to answer all the questions raised by her conversion. "The Real Reason" was published in *McCall's* magazine, and launched Mrs. Luce in yet another career — convert-apologist for the Catholic faith.[79]

In her public testimonial, Mrs. Luce discussed at some length the reasons behind her attraction to Catholicism, and how Monsignor Sheen came to be the instrument of her conversion. Briefly, she stated that the "real reason" behind her decision to become a Catholic was that "upon careful examination, Catholic doctrine seemed to me the solid objective Truth."[80] She was led to examine Catholicism for two reasons: disappointment at not finding the meaning she sought in life, and the tragic death of her only child, Ann, in an automobile accident in 1944. In the autumn of 1945, finding herself at the edge of despair in a hotel room, she phoned a Jesuit priest who had maintained a correspondence with her since writing her a letter about one of her newspaper stories. Upon hearing from Mrs. Luce, the priest, Fr. Edward Wiatriack, felt that someone like Mrs. Luce would encounter intellectual difficulties in her search for faith. So he recommended Monsignor Sheen as the priest most capable of persuading her. In response to all the questions about Sheen which had been directed toward her, Mrs. Luce had this to say:

> ...it always pleases me to talk about him. He was so great a friend, and a teacher at once so unyielding and so patient, so poetic and so practical, so inventive and so orthodox.... God intended me to be a Catholic, or He would not have sent me to see Fr. Sheen, the one best-equipped to rid my mind of nonsense and fill it with the sense of the Lord.[81]

---

[79] Clare Boothe Luce, "The Real Reason," *McCall's*, February, March and April, 1947.

[80] *McCall's*, February, 1947, p. 118.

[81] *McCall's*, April, 1947, p. 87.

This conversion of Clare Boothe Luce enlisted her and Monsignor Sheen in a common endeavor over the next several years. Increasing attention was paid in the American Catholic community to the task of winning converts, and Sheen was frequently hailed as the best convert-maker, with Mrs. Luce substantiating that claim. For example, the Rev. John A. O'Brien, research professor of philosophy and author-in-residence at the University of Notre Dame, featured Sheen and Luce in the books and pamphlets he edited about the necessity of winning American souls for Christ — the great crusade of the twentieth century. In *Winning Converts*, Fr. O'Brien published a collection of articles which grew out of a 1948 symposium on "Methods of Convert-Making for Priests and Lay People."[82] In the Introduction to a revised edition, O'Brien listed Bishop Sheen, Clare Boothe Luce and the Paulist Fathers as "leading authorities" in the field. The book contains essays by both Sheen and Luce.[83] Although Sheen was unable to fulfill O'Brien's request and attend the symposium at Notre Dame, being constrained by the demands on his time, he nevertheless offered his thoughts on "Methods of Convert-Making." In a letter Sheen wrote to Fr. O'Brien on September 12, 1947, he said:

> What I am saying now is not for publication, but it seems to me that we are about fifty years behind the times on the subject of apologetics.
>
> First of all, we give entirely too much concern to Protestantism, which no longer exists as an organized system of belief; secondly, people today are not going from nature to God, hence the proofs for the existence of God are metaphysically sound but have very little appeal.... Furthermore, there has to be greater charity on the part

---

[82] John A. O'Brien, ed., *Winning Converts* (Notre Dame: University of Notre Dame Press, 1957).

[83] Mrs. Luce's essay in O'Brien's book, "The Right Approach," was a version of a talk she had given to clerical students and priests at the Catholic University of America; it was also circulated by the Paulists in *Techniques for Convert-Making*, a monthly newsletter.

of those who instruct, for many non-Catholics are basically timid as they come to us with many prejudices, and there is great need of us manifesting a deep spirit of Christ.[84]

Many of Sheen's thoughts on his method of instructing converts were published, both by Sheen and in the course of the interviews he gave to the press on the subject. In "Instructing Converts," Sheen advised that instructors should talk in an "intensely interesting and inspiring manner for thirty minutes without interruption," giving the inquirer the opportunity to ask questions afterwards.[85] He advised, too, that the potential convert should be given "considerable reading matter" — all free of charge. All books and pamphlets should be given away, and no gratuity should ever be accepted from a convert.[86] Sheen's recommended reading list for converts included Frank J. Sheed's *Map of Life;* G.K. Chesterton's *Everlasting Man* and *Orthodoxy;* and his own *Preface to Religion* (1946), a popular presentation of some essential Christian truths.[87] Most importantly, Sheen warned against "winning an argument and losing a soul": rather than proving the opposition wrong, "we are sent to be witnesses to the truth." According to Sheen, there were three rules for dealing with converts: "Kindness, Kindness, Kindness!"[88] In "Spreading the Faith,"[89] taken from his "The Love That Waits for You" broadcast series in 1949, Sheen advised that "the Christian vision of truth must never be separated from the Christian love of the adversary." Those giving instructions should be mindful of the fact that there is "some truth everywhere" and numerous paths to faith; others who do not see it our way should never

[84] Sheen to O'Brien, September 17, 1947, in the John A. O'Brien papers, Archives of the University of Notre Dame.

[85] Sheen, "Instructing Converts," in *Techniques for Convert-Making,* September, 1949, Sheen Archives.

[86] *Ibid.*

[87] See Sheen's personal papers in the "Converts" collection, Sheen Archives.

[88] Sheen, "Instructing Converts."

[89] Printed in *Techniques for Convert-Making,* September, 1949.

be dismissed as "stupid or perverse."[90] The basic assumption guiding all convert-makers, said Sheen, is that "there are only two classes of souls in the world: those who have found the Faith and those who are still looking for it."[91]

As Monsignor Sheen continued to lead a parade of souls into the Church, interest in the leader increased. In 1940, even before the conversions of Budenz and Mrs. Luce, *Newsweek* magazine called Sheen the "Convert Specialist."[92] Sheen was "as skilled an instructor as the American Church can offer," for he had long ranked as its foremost apologist and orator; *Newsweek* credited him with engineering "three of the most notable Roman Catholic conversions of the decade: Horace Mann, Heywood Broun, and Henry Ford II."[93] In "Catholic Converts," a more all-encompassing view of the subject, Stanley High, a Protestant journalist, took note of the fact that in 1939, there were more converts to Catholicism than ever before in America — 73,677.[94] Those responsible for such impressive gains were the Paulists, and Monsignor Fulton J. Sheen, "the best known exponent of Catholicism to non-Catholic Americans." High also reported that Sheen had been largely freed from his academic teaching responsibilities at the Catholic University, in order to carry on this wider ministry, and informed his readers that for those who prefer "demagoguery, Sheen has nothing to offer."[95]

"Why All These Converts? The Story of Monsignor Fulton Sheen" appeared in *Look* magazine in 1947.[96] It was written by Gretta Palmer, a free-lance journalist who became a convert herself after meeting Sheen in 1942.[97] In answering her own question,

---

90 *Ibid.*

91 *Ibid.*

92 *Newsweek*, February 26, 1940.

93 *Ibid.*

94 Stanley High, "Catholic Converts"; see also the notice of High's article in *Catholic Action* 22 (November, 1940), pp. 29-31.

95 *Ibid.*, p. 31.

96 *Look* (June 24, 1947). Reprint in *Techniques for Convert-Making*, July-August, 1947. Sheen Archives.

97 See Gretta Palmer's "Escape from an Atheist's Cell," in *The Road to Damascus*, John A. O'Brien, ed. (Notre Dame: University of Notre Dame Press, 1949).

Miss Palmer spoke of Sheen's "zeal and energy, and his magnificent speaking voice," stating that when he preached at St. Patrick's Cathedral, it was often necessary to put loudspeakers out in the street to accommodate the overflow crowd.[98] In addition to re-telling the stories about Sheen's most famous conversions, she also allowed him to describe the types most likely to become converts: sinners, who desire forgiveness; "mixed-up modern intellectuals"; troubled souls unhappy about personal problems; and bigots. Sheen had successfully drawn converts from all of these categories, so he spoke from personal experience. Adding one more final note of flattery to her glowing report on Sheen, Miss Palmer reported that he was noted for his generosity; he gave away most of his earnings, in a somewhat reckless style that troubled his staff. But a wonderful monument to this generosity, a real work of charity, was a maternity hospital for Negro mothers in Mobile, Alabama, which had been founded and funded by Sheen.[99]

In spite of all this favorable attention that was showered on Monsignor Sheen, not every account of his success as a convert-maker was so glowing. In fact, several articles about Sheen were very critical, and indicated that anti-Catholic sentiment was alive and well in the United States. In some circles, Sheen was misunderstood, ridiculed and resented, and even vilified. Side by side with Clare Boothe Luce, Sheen was vigorously criticized in the pages of *The American Scholar*. Fanny Sedgwick Colby, in "Monsignor Sheen and Mrs. Luce,"[100] announced that many Americans were troubled by the "utterances of these leading Catholics," which were labeled as "inaccurate, misleading and combustible." It was regrettable that Catholics were being given a "platform by which they can justify intolerance and arrogance towards the sincere efforts towards good will on the part of the non-Catholic world."[101]

A group of former Catholics, according to the *Converted*

---

[98] Palmer, "Why All These Converts?", p. 1.
[99] *Ibid.*
[100] *The American Scholar* 17 (Winter, 1947-1948), pp. 35-44.
[101] *Ibid.*, p. 44.

Catholic Magazine (associated with Christ's Mission, an organization for people who had converted from Catholicism to Protestantism), had sponsored a prayer crusade for Monsignor Sheen's conversion in November of 1947.[102] This crusade to win Sheen over to Protestantism was endorsed by several eminent conservatives, including President Dean G. McKee of the Bible Seminary in New York City and William Ward Ayer of the International Marching Truth Broadcast, an evangelical radio preacher.[103]

Pastor Ayer, also of the Calvary Baptist Church in New York, penned the most extreme attack on Sheen: "Romanism's Pied Piper: a Gospel-eye View of the Roman Catholic Church's Top Propagandist."[104] An eight page frontal assault on Sheen and Catholicism, the tone of this pamphlet borders on the hysterical, and is filled with bitterness and invective, the type of hatred that Sheen had perceived as growing in America. At first, Ayer granted Sheen his strengths: his popularity, his prodigious work schedule, his scholarly credentials. Another point in Sheen's favor was the fact that he sounded like a genuine evangelical. But Ayer also quoted L.H. Lehmann, an ex-priest turned fundamentalist, who attributed Sheen's "spiritual foolishness" to the fact that he was "either blinded by the devil's deceit, or a conscious hypocrite."[105] Also, Sheen had an unfair advantage in "the power of the world's most intricately organized institution behind him."[106] Ayer also claimed that Sheen's success was "over-estimated and over-publicized by the press."[107]

In moving on to question the value of Sheen's converts — who were formerly "religious nothings" — Ayer posed the question, "To what are they converted?":

---

[102] See Ralph Lloyd Roy's *Apostles of Discord: A Study of Organized Bigotry and Disruption on the Fringes of Protestantism* (Boston: The Beacon Press, 1955), p. 159.

[103] *Ibid.*

[104] A copy of Ayer's pamphlet can be found in the Sheen Archives.

[105] L.H. Lehmann's *Out of the Labyrinth.* Sheen Archives. Lehmann was associated with Christ's Mission, a group of former priests.

[106] Ayer, pp. 3, 4.

[107] *Ibid.,* p. 6.

This is not Christian salvation, but a Satanic system of religion based upon the false premise of Mary's priority. This is not the faith of the New Testament.... Millions of Americans are being deceived.... Monsignor Sheen and the priests who labor with him are badgering and frightening a good many Protestants into the Roman fold.... In reality, they are planning complete religious totalitarianism that will destroy our religious liberty, bring about collusion between Church and state, and turn America into the chaos which has blighted Europe for hundreds of years.[108]

Dr. Ayer concluded his diatribe with a call to Protestants to awake and propagate their faith with a zeal greater than Sheen's: until we do awake, man our ramparts and consolidate our scattered positions preparatory to a heroic stand, we may expect that Rome will "go marching on."[109]

As revealed in the pages of "Romanism's Pied Piper," and according to Sheen's own standards, Dr. Ayer was an example of both hatred and bigotry — emotional and dogmatic hostility toward Catholicism. Choosing to ignore the likes of Ayer, Sheen had argued in 1947 that it was "no longer Protestantism from which we must convert souls, but Confusionism."[110] Under the pressures of that confusion, and "war, insecurity, revolution and chaos," people were coming back to a "consciousness of guilt and sin."[111] In their search for faith and stability, Sheen's converts would come to find it in the Catholic Church. But from a broader perspective, Sheen felt responsible for bringing more than individual souls to

---

[108] Ayer disparaged the character of many of Sheen's converts, implying that Mrs. Luce was basically unstable and had an unhealthy attachment to Sheen; he said that she should be advised to read the New Testament, which would turn her from semi-pagan Romanism to the truth of evangelical Christianity.

[109] Ayer, p. 8.

[110] Sheen, "Instructing Converts."

[111] *Ibid.*

God. He also tried to "convert" the American nation to a greater understanding and open-mindedness toward Catholicism, at a period when American Catholics were also eager to prove their loyalty to the nation. This feat was attempted by way of the radio, at a time when more and more people were beginning to rely on the radio to keep in touch with the world.

During all his years on the "Catholic Hour," Sheen sought to address himself to the pressing problems of the world — international crisis and later the war. In addition to disseminating the social teachings of the Church, and opposing communism and secularism, he resolved to explain the meaning of the World War and the Vatican's plans for peace, an agenda defined by the American hierarchy. Monsignor Sheen, as spokesman, maintained his integrated world view that only a return to religion would secure world peace, a point made by Pius XI back in 1931: "the longed for social reconstruction must be preceded by a profound renewal of the Christian spirit; otherwise, our social edifice will be built not upon a rock, but upon shifting sand."[112] In the thirties and early forties, the sands were shifting, and Monsignor Fulton Sheen was a witness to America's growing entanglement in the world's crisis.

---

[112] Pope Pius XI, *Quadragesimo Anno*, in *Seven Great Encyclicals*, p. 160.

CHAPTER FOUR

American Catholic Spokesman in Crisis Times:
International Conflict and the Second World War, 1930-1950

> Nothing in all the world is as relentless in unmasking a false way
> of life as war.... This war is a judgment of God on the entire world...
> not an arbitrary action, but an execution of the law of justice.
> *Fulton J. Sheen, "War and Guilt" (1941)*

> We cannot avoid the repercussions of a world cataclysm.
> Our faith in a Divine Providence ruling the universe
> should inspire us to have confidence in the benevolent designs
> of a loving God who permits suffering to correct evil and to
> bring forth the fruits of justice, charity and peace.
> *"The Crisis of Christianity" Pastoral Letter of the
> Catholic Bishops of the United States, 1941*

In his first radio broadcast after the United States' entry into the
Second World War, Monsignor Fulton J. Sheen chose to address
himself to the subject of "peace." The first talk of this series on the
"Catholic Hour," entitled "Salvation," was broadcast on December 21, 1941, and Sheen used the opportunity to make a plea for
"an hour of prayer... for a righteous peace, the preservation of
America, and the salvation of our souls":[1]

> ...if Divine Providence decrees days of trial for us, we
> shall accept them patiently, as we received gratefully His

---

[1] Fulton J. Sheen, "Peace," Catholic Hour Broadcast Series, 1942; published by Our Sunday Visitor, p. 10.

> bounteous prosperity... we pledge to our President a
> daily prayer that God may bless, direct and guide him
> in all that is righteous and holy and just... the "Catho-
> lic Hour" consecrates itself to the re-capitalization of
> spiritual energy.[2]

Sheen's energies as an American Catholic spokesman during these
times of crisis were dedicated to explaining the real meaning behind the war, which he saw as religious and theological. In the years
leading up to, during, and after World War II, he tried to bring
about that "profound renewal of the Christian spirit" that the Holy
Father had called for as the only guarantee of a lasting peace. Fulton
Sheen's version of the wartime gospel — preached to a vast audience over the radio — was a mixture of traditional religion, patriotism, and a hopeful optimism about the future, offered to a nation
that longed for the restoration of peace. In the style of the biblical
prophets, he called for men and nations to return to God, insisting
that the goal in fighting this war was not merely victory, but salvation.[3] Secure in the conviction that the war was part of the Divine
plan, and that God's purposes would prevail, Sheen entreated his
countrymen to "worry about getting on God's side" through prayer.
Leading the nation's citizens in prayer, as both Christians and
Americans,[4] Monsignor Sheen espoused a simple, but effective,
message of piety and patriotism.

In preaching this combination of piety and patriotism, both
Fulton Sheen and the Church he served were able to support the
United States with enthusiasm, and demonstrate the loyalty of
American Catholics. Historians have recognized the importance
of World War II as a water-shed in the Church's Americanization
process, a "rite of passage"[5] for the Catholic community. Several

[2]   *Ibid.*, pp. 3, 12.
[3]   *Ibid.*, p. 8.
[4]   *Ibid.*, pp. 129-134.
[5]   James Henessey, SJ, *American Catholics*, p. 280.

controversies which had divided American Catholics, and separated them from their fellow citizens, were abruptly settled by the Japanese attack at Pearl Harbor, and American Catholic patriotism was beyond question. United with all Americans in the crucible of war, American Catholics found strength and security in that unity, and the Church won a greater measure of acceptance in American society. Sheen, and many other leaders of American Catholicism, were determined to demonstrate the compatibility of Americanism and Catholicism during the war, hopeful that the harmony that had prevailed might endure into the post-war years.

That harmony that existed during the experience of war, however, had not always prevailed in the foreign policy debate that raged in the United States throughout the previous decade. The mounting tensions and hostilities that accompanied the rise of fascism and the growth of communism in Europe were reflected in American circles, where the discussion over conflicting ideologies became quite acrimonious. As Americans chose up sides, Catholics often found themselves opposed by a majority of their countrymen, charged with being on the "wrong" side because of their religion. This was especially true in the case of the Spanish Civil War, but American Catholics were also vulnerable to accusations that their Church was sympathetic toward, if not openly supportive of, fascism in general. Many in the American liberal community believed that because of the authoritarian nature of the Roman Catholic Church, many Catholics found it difficult, if not impossible, to be good democratic Americans.

The American liberal case against the Catholic Church was presented in 1939 by George Seldes in *The Catholic Crisis*. Mr. Seldes was a well-known journalist who perceived an alarming trend toward reaction and fascism in the Church, most apparent in Catholicism's active support of Franco in the Spanish Civil War. A summary of additional evidence to support the charge of a Catholic-Fascist "liaison" focused on Vatican sympathies towards Mussolini, the anti-Semitic ravings of Fr. Charles Coughlin in the United States, and the pressure tactics employed by "Catholic Ac-

tion."[6] Seldes claimed to speak for the "progressive and democratic
majority" in America, and said that his words were intended not as
an "attack or an indictment" against Catholicism, but rather were
offered in the spirit of constructive criticism, as a warning to the
Church to choose democracy over fascism:

> The Catholic Church is not only the oldest existing in-
> stitution, but it is also the most powerful, and its deci-
> sion in the present international crisis is a vital one....
> it cannot be denied that the American voice today is loud
> at the Vatican.... Pius XII is aware of the prophecy of
> Cardinal Manning that "the future of Catholicism is in
> America."[7]

Although Seldes' polemic was never aimed directly at Fulton
Sheen, his was a prominent American Catholic voice on the contemporary scene in 1939.[8] And because his message so closely mirrored that of the official Catholic Church — papal encyclicals and
the statements of the American hierarchy — Sheen was vulnerable
on some of the charges leveled against Catholics in this emotion-
ally-charged atmosphere.[9] No doubt it was his awareness of this
fact,[10] coupled with his desire to reach the masses, which led Sheen
to present his ideas on current affairs and the world crisis in the

---

[6] George Seldes, *The Catholic Crisis* (New York: Julian Messner Inc., 1939). Seldes noted
that "Catholic Action" was a loaded term, and viewed it as almost synonymous with fascism, a political arm of the Vatican. He also drew a distinction between the laity and the
official structure of the Church, noting that many American Catholics disagreed with
the hierarchy, and had democratic sympathies.

[7] *Ibid.*, pp. 4-6, 345-349.

[8] Seldes discussed the power of radio in regards to Coughlin and anti-Semitism, noting
that "the "sowers of hate have big funds and loud mouths" (p. 45).

[9] Sheen was open to attack on some of the charges — he toed the official Catholic line
during the Civil War in Spain, though his support of Franco waned over time.

[10] During the course of his radio addresses, Sheen was always cognizant of the fact that
Catholics were often misunderstood and viewed with suspicion and hostility. This was
the whole point of his adoption of the apologetical style as he tried to correct misconceptions about the Church in a non-argumentative fashion. He was, however, resentful
of the charge that Catholics were fascists, saying that this was a favorite tactic employed
by the communists (the "bogey" of fascism).

most positive and general light possible. Often, this led Sheen to be simplistic rather than sophisticated, to become overly-reliant on pious platitudes, and to lose sight of some of the complexities inherent in the intellectual discussions of his day — at least as far as his audience was considered. Instead of getting weighed down by the ambiguities surrounding some of the Church's positions in the public arena, Fulton Sheen offered that audience a steady stream of inspiration, moral guidance, and colorful rhetoric.

The substance of Sheen's message was always theologically orthodox, and adapted to the modern world. He steered clear of purely political matters, and accentuated the religious and spiritual aspects of current issues, seeking to permeate the social atmosphere with Christian ideals and precepts of the Catholic faith. With Fulton Sheen, the style was important also; he could be zealous, righteous, and dramatic, but his words were always infused with a genuine spirit of charity. Mindful of the needs of his Church, he was determined to move beyond the tensions and suspicions between Catholics and non-Catholics, and to prove that good Catholics were good Americans. If World War II was a rite of passage for American Catholics, then Fulton Sheen assisted his Church in that coming of age by repeatedly emphasizing the compatibility between American democracy and Catholicism.

Monsignor Sheen rose to prominence as an American Catholic spokesman when clouds of revolution and war were gathering over the world, a world which had been characterized by the progressive breakdown of international stability and equilibrium as Sheen began his career.

During these times of crisis, the concerns of Sheen's formative years as a priest — education and social justice — persisted, but in the context of the World War, they were somewhat transformed by a new emphasis on Americanism, and the moral foundations of peace. Given the climate of the times, Catholic leaders saw a greater need for the Church's guidance, and to a world in need of spiritual regeneration, Sheen's message offered hope. The experience of war provided both an illustration of the perennial theological problem of evil, and a chance for American Catholics to prove their loyalty and have a greater influence on national policy. In a seminal address in "Peace: The Fruit of Justice," Monsignor Sheen suggested that "religion and politics must be brought into closer relationship if democracy is to be saved." From politics and religion, the themes of his broadcast, "are born the two greatest loyalties known to man: the Cross and the flag."[11]

In emphasizing the relationship between the Cross and the flag, Sheen was trying to put to rest the charge that Catholics could not be counted on to defend democracy. Because Catholics had been placed on the defensive about their loyalty to their nation in the past, there was a tendency to overemphasize their patriotism and Americanism. This tendency to baptize patriotism could raise problems as well as settle them, for then Catholics would be accused of being over-zealous flag-wavers.[12] Sheen, however, was able to maintain a balance between piety and patriotism. Since religion was uppermost in his mind and message, he devoted most of his attention to the Cross.[13]

Perceiving that the Cross, the basic symbol of Christianity, had a special relevance to a world torn asunder by war, Sheen characterized the crisis of his day as a moral and religious one. His standard presentation of this idea was contained in the book *The Cross and the Crisis*, an expanded version of an earlier radio series. Entitled originally "The Prodigal World," the series was broadcast in 1936 as the fragile fabric of peace woven after World War I was unraveling. The major indicators of the contemporary world's condition, as he read them, all signaled trouble: politically, in the rise of dictatorships, both communist and fascist; economically, in the

---

[11] The image of the "Cross and the Flag" is often invoked to explain the spirit of American Catholic patriotism during World War II. See George Flynn's *Roosevelt and Romanism* (Westport, CT: Greenwood Press, 1976) and Donald F. Crosby, SJ, *God, Church and Flag: Senator Joseph R. McCarthy and the Catholic Church, 1950-1957.*

[12] Seldes, *The Catholic Crisis*, p. 67. Seldes charged that all fascists were super-patriots, Catholics and non-Catholics alike; they rallied around the flag in the "guise of Americanism."

[13] Throughout his life, Sheen reiterated his devotion to the Cross; his main purpose in life, he often said, was "to preach Christ and Him crucified."

deficiency of social justice and ramifications of the Great Depression; and religiously, in the denial of the true spiritual nature of man.[14] At the root of the world's problems was the fact that Western Civilization, a prodigal world, had exiled itself from Catholicism, the true representative of Christianity. And only a restoration of Christian principles and beliefs would present a solution to the grave crisis facing the world, the "crux of which is the cross: a day is fast coming when Christians will have to unite in real Christianity to preserve it against the anti-Christian forces which would destroy it... what is all important is spiritual regeneration, for our ills will be cured by forces not involved in the crisis itself."[15]

Stressing the primacy of the spiritual in his talks, Sheen noted that "the world, to be saved, must be put back into the environment of religion and morality... the best solution lies in the cross,"[16] Christianity's symbol of redemption.

To avoid having this focus on the Cross being misunderstood, it should be noted that Sheen's ardent Christianity was never perceived as exclusionary toward Jews. In the same year that *The Cross and the Crisis* was published, 1938, Sheen was invited to speak at a rally in New York City, held to protest the Nazi persecution of the Jews. In his opening remarks, he acknowledged, and condemned, the disturbing presence of anti-Semitism in American life:[17]

> I have received a number of letters from individuals protesting against my appearance on this program on the grounds that I was being "taken in" by the Jews. Let me

---

[14] Fulton Sheen, *The Cross and the Crisis* (Milwaukee: The Bruce Publishing Co., 1938), pp. vii-viii. The book was reprinted as part of a series of hard cover Essay Reprints in 1977 (Manchester, NH: Ayer Co. Pubs. Inc.). The original talks entitled *The Prodigal World* have been re-issued in paperback (New York: Alba House, 2003).

[15] *Ibid.*, p. viii.

[16] *Ibid.*, p. 159.

[17] The year 1938 was a time when Fr. Coughlin's anti-Semitism was at its most virulent. Although Sheen never criticized Fr. Coughlin by name, he often rose to the defense of the Jews in speaking out against religious persecution in all of its forms.

begin by repudiating with all the ardor of my soul such
un-Christian sentiments.[18]

Sheen believed that Catholics shared a deep bond with the Jews,
and that throughout these troubled times, all religious men of good
will must work together — there was no place in Christianity for
"cheap, snarling, bigoted anti-Semitism."[19] As a spokesman for the
Catholic Church, however, he continued to focus on the symbol
of redemption, the Cross.

An important part of the Church's historic mission of redemption, especially during these critical times, was social. According
to Sheen, "once the cross is set up again before the eyes of men
and placarded at the crossroads of civilization, as it was centuries
ago, men will realize that redemption is social, that we are our
brothers' keepers, in helping one another to a fresh start, even
though it is a late start."[20] At the immediate crossroads, however,
was the collapse of civilization in World War II. The war was a
"judgment of God," which only served to underscore Sheen's contention that the world was in desperate need of transformation by
the Church. In the dark days ahead, first across Europe and then
as the tides of world conflict swept closer to American shores,
Sheen's message took on an added dimension — that of the flag
— as he professed loyalty to his nation in its hour of need.

Imbued with the crisis mentality that prevailed during the war,
Sheen contributed to the "formation of sound public opinion," a
responsibility acknowledged by the hierarchy in its 1919 Bishops'
Program of Social Reconstruction.[21] On the functions of the Catholic press, the American bishops wrote:

---

[18] A typescript of Sheen's address, delivered in Carnegie Hall on December 6, 1938, can be
found in the Sheen Archives, alongside a copy of the address printed in *Merit*, a monthly
journal "dedicated to tolerance," published by the Ozanam Guild of Catholic Employ-
ees of the New York City Department of Welfare.

[19] Fulton J. Sheen, "Peace: The Fruit of Justice," Catholic Hour Broadcast Series, 1940, p.
49.

[20] Fulton J. Sheen, *The Prodigal World* (New York: Alba House, 2003), p. 59 in the original series of talks.

[21] This, and all future references to the pastoral letters, or official statements of the American hierarchy, are taken from Hugh J. Nolan's edition of *Pastoral Letters of the U.S. Catholic
Bishops* (Vol. I), p. 292.

To widen the interest of our people by acquainting them with the progress of religion throughout the world, to correct false or misleading statements regarding our belief and practice, and, as occasion offers, to present our doctrine in popular form — these are among the excellent aims of Catholic journalism. As a means of forming sound public opinion, it is indispensable.

The vital issues affecting the nation's welfare usually turn upon moral principles... the treatment of such subjects from the Catholic point of view is helpful to all our people. It enables them to look at current events and problems in the light of the experience which the Church has gathered through centuries, and it points the surest way to a solution which will advance our common interests.[22]

From the perspective of these guidelines, Sheen served his Church as an accurate spokesman, and as an American Catholic patriot. He declared, "We Catholics love America... we love its Constitution and its traditions, and we want to see them preserved; we love the flag, which is the symbol of our liberty."[23] Deftly weaving Cross and flag together, then, Sheen stated that real Christian piety implied a love of country as well as love of God.

Sheen's style of flag waving, however, was not unbridled. Unquestionably a patriot — he would receive many awards for his professed Americanism — his patriotism was not blind or uncritical. Rather, his loyalty to America was based upon a carefully considered philosophy, and constructed on the premise that democracy and Christianity had much in common. In *The Cross and the Crisis*, he observed that "democracy is a very Christian doctrine,"[24]

---

[22] *Ibid.*, p. 292.

[23] Fulton Sheen, in a reply to a letter of protest written to N.B.C. and the Federal Communications Commission by a Mr. Eli Miller of Concord, Massachusetts. Mr. Miller objected to Sheen's harsh criticism of communism; Sheen's reply was preserved in the Scrapbook of "Joseph F. Sheen of Chicago," Sheen Archives.

[24] Sheen, *The Cross and the Crisis*, p. 61.

and he believed that the glory of democracy was to be found in the Christian tradition. In the stark contrasts then prevalent in the world, Sheen saw Christianity and democracy united against dictatorship. But America was not perfect; Sheen persistently criticized the failings of America, measuring society against the gospel standard and lamenting its faults. Always, he called the nation to a higher standard, asking America to live up to the Christian ideals embodied in the Declaration of Independence. Although he would later offer prayers to God to assist the Allied war effort, he reminded his listeners that the American way of life was not something to be saved as it was, but something to be amended: "the future of America depends on Americans' attitude toward God and the Cross of His Divine Son."[25] Believing in America's power of regeneration, his analysis came down to a question of spiritual regeneration — the key to advancing the Kingdom of God on earth, and to the restoration of peace and justice, the twin foundations of the social order.

Sheen's emphasis on justice followed a tradition which went back to John Carroll, the first Catholic bishop in the United States. During the War of 1812, Carroll had declared that "patriotism can never be separated from justice."[26] In championing justice, which would be restored only by a real and lasting peace, the current hierarchy had issued the pastoral "Victory and Peace" (1942). Written in the midst of the conflict, the bishops had supported the concept of a just war while looking ahead to peace. Neither secularism, exploitation, nor totalitarianism could write a lasting peace — only the spirit of Christianity could guarantee peace.[27] Following these leads, Sheen linked the ideas of justice, peace, Christianity and democracy with the American Catholic tradition, joining them

[25] Sheen, *For God and Country* (New York: P.J. Kenedy and Sons, 1941), p. 73. Sheen's Catholic Hour Broadcast Series for 1941, "War and Guilt," was published as two separate books: *For God and Country* and *A Declaration of Dependence* (Milwaukee: The Bruce Publishing Co., 1941).

[26] Cited in Gerald P. Fogarty, SJ, "Public Patriotism and Private Politics: The Tradition of American Catholicism," *US Catholic Historian* 4 (1984), p. 5.

[27] "Victory and Peace" in *Pastoral Letters* (Vol. II), p. 39.

all together in an attempt to provide some continuity, guidance and reassurance through the years of war.

In facing the crisis of World War II, said Sheen, the American Church was shifting from a position of isolationism to greater internationalism, part of the universal Church's going out actively into the world. When Fulton Sheen broadcast a worldwide message to celebrate the coronation of Pope Pius XII in 1939, he called the Catholic Church the "only unified moral voice left on the earth," capable of offering guidance in the troubled days ahead:

> The Church... has been gradually moving out of doors, from a chapel to a sanctuary, and from a sanctuary to the world... the coronation of a new pontiff is the beginning of a rapprochement of the Church and the world — a moving of the Church out to the world through a greater comprehension of the gospel lesson that it is the leaven of the mass, the city on the hill, the salt of the earth, a kingdom not of the world, but for it and its salvation.[28]

This rapprochement referred to by Sheen was evident in the common themes sounded throughout the war by the Vatican and the American hierarchy. Sheen's presentations often drew upon these sources, as he sought to explain God's purposes to his audience. He argued that the "Church and the world are gradually drawing closer together"[29] in some respects. With the American entry into the world, Sheen also sought to demonstrate how some of the ideals expressed by the Allied leadership coincided with those of the Church. The Vatican began to recognize the importance of the United States in world affairs at this time as well, and to consult with members of the American hierarchy. Within the United

---

[28] Fulton Sheen, taken from a reprinted copy of his radio broadcast to mark the coronation of Pope Pius XII, preserved in the Scrapbook of "Joseph F. Sheen of Chicago," Sheen Archives.

[29] *Ibid.*

States, many old religious differences were set aside as the nation united behind the war effort, and "among the architects of that unity were the nation's foremost Catholic leaders."[30]

As a leader of American Catholic opinion, Fulton Sheen helped to forge that unity, through prayer and by keeping his audience informed about the Church's philosophy and opinions on the war. In January of 1940, for example, he began his broadcast series by thanking God "that the air of our land can be filled with messages of peace rather than with engines of death,"[31] a prayer that would not be honored for long. Even before the American involvement, however, Sheen sought to answer the more universal question: "Whence Comes War?"[32] Looking back over the past two decades, Sheen wondered if what was called the First World War had ever really ended, since the peace did not last. From God's point of view, there were two reasons for war: "war may be either something to be waged in the name of God, or something to be undergone at the hands of God... either a vindication of Divine Justice or a chastisement from Divine Justice."[33] Focusing on justice, Sheen indicated that the world's irreligious attitude and repudiation of the principles of social justice was the root cause of the "disturbance of the international equilibrium: wars may be generated out of the social order by injustice and the forgetfulness of God."[34] Logically, if the current cycle of violence which engulfed the world arose from a lack of justice, the international order could only be restored by a return to the principles of justice, as historically outlined by the Catholic Church. In "The Papacy and Peace," Sheen argued that the greatest hope for world peace rested in the moral authority of the Papacy. Quoting St. Augustine — "Peace is the tranquility of

[30] Gerald P. Fogarty, SJ, *The Vatican and the American Hierarchy from 1870 to 1965* (Stuttgart: Antonin Hiersemann, 1982), p. 284.
[31] Fulton Sheen, "Peace: The Fruit of Justice," p. 5. These broadcasts were also published in book form as *Whence Comes War?*
[32] "Whence Comes War" was also the title of the initial broadcast in this series, delivered on January 7, 1940.
[33] *Ibid.*, p. 6.
[34] *Ibid.*, p. 5.

order" — he reasoned that "peace was inseparable from justice...
only justice removes the obstacles to peace."[35]

Returning to a characteristic theme of the American Church
— the compatibility of Christianity and American law as a basis
for social reform — Fulton Sheen followed the example of the bishops, who had "moved the issue of social justice onto the international plane."[36] The war was seen as an opportunity to further
Americanize the Catholic Church while simultaneously working
to approximate the Kingdom of God on earth. The ideals of peace
and justice, intertwined, would nurture the growth of a more Christian civilization. From Sheen's perspective, the war was a judgment
of God, but also "an opportunity for a national resurrection."[37]

Looking beyond the immediate calamity of the war was typical
of the official stance of the Papacy and the American bishops, and
Sheen likewise sounded this more hopeful note. Sustained by a faith
in Divine Providence which ruled the world, said Sheen, the Catholic Church was confident that it would survive the crucible of war
to carry on God's work, as it had done in the past. While it addressed the moral issues of the time, the Church was also able to
remain above the fray, universal and timeless. "While the world
outside was torn by war and dissension, it was a period of extraordinary unity and calmness for the Catholic Church in the U.S."[38]
Mindful of the American flag, Sheen looked forward to the national
resurrection which could be aided by the Church, "the salt for the
preservation of the principles of democracy."[39] But before the resurrection loomed the symbol of the Cross: "Christianity is the religion of the Cross, and it sees a meaning in suffering."[40] By appre-

---

[35] Sheen, "The Papacy and Peace," originally broadcast on February 4, 1940; part of the "Peace: The Fruit of Justice" series, pp. 102-104.

[36] Fogarty, *The Vatican and the American Hierarchy*, p. 287.

[37] Sheen, "Peace," the Catholic Hour Broadcast Series for 1941-1942; pamphlet printed by Our Sunday Visitor, Fulton Sheen Archives, p. 29.

[38] David J. O'Brien, *The Renewal of American Catholicism* (New York: The Paulist Press, 1972), p. 88.

[39] Sheen, *Whence Comes War?*, p. 63.

[40] Nicholas Berdyaev, *The Bourgeois Mind*, cited by Sheen in *The Cross and the Crisis*, p. 17.

ciating the value and meaning of the suffering, Sheen could coun-
sel not only endurance, but "the embrace of the Cross: There is no
reason for despair... some are coming back again to God by a trial
of the world."[41] Secure in the conviction that the Cross was the way
to peace, Sheen confronted the multiple trials which immediately
threatened that peace.

Several foreign policy issues of the thirties and forties were
of special importance to American Catholics in general, and Fulton
Sheen in particular: the rise of fascism in Europe, the Spanish Civil
War, the alliance with the Soviet Union, and U.S. relations with
the Vatican.[42] On all of these subjects, Sheen was outspoken, and
often controversial. When the United States entered the war, Sheen
marched in step to the drumbeat of the hierarchy, professing his
patriotism and support of a just war, while also enunciating his
simplified interpretation of the religious meaning of the war for
his audience. In addition, he drew attention to the Church's plans
for the reconstruction of the post-war world along Christian lines,
and spoke out on the issues which would gain in significance after
the war, such as the United Nations, the atomic bomb, and Soviet
aggression. For Fulton Sheen's internationalism matured alongside that of the Church; with increasing frequency, he moved into
the spheres of foreign affairs and politics, guided always by a theological perspective. And he continued to emphasize the same
themes which persisted throughout his long career as a spokesman
for the American Catholic Church. A pervasive stream of anti-
communism was perhaps the most obvious. This strident crusade
against the anti-religious philosophy of Marx was intrinsically related to the other preoccupations of Sheen during the war years: a
condemnation of all forms of religious persecution and totalitari-

---

[41] Sheen, "The Prodigal World," p. 19.

[42] For a general overview of American Catholics and foreign policy during these years, see
     George Flynn's *Roosevelt and Romanism*. A broader review of the historical literature is
     found in Wilson D. Miscamble's "Catholics and American Foreign Policy from McKinley
     to McCarthy," *Diplomatic History* 4 (Summer, 1982), pp. 223-240.

anism, fascist as well as communist, and the harmony between the spirits of Christianity and democracy.

Essentially, Fulton Sheen's contribution was simply to reflect and publicize the teachings of the Papacy and the American bishops; his originality appeared in his style of presentation. He spoke frequently of the moral status of the Papacy in his efforts to make the world listen to the Church, and to restore the Church to its proper place in the modern world as a "bulwark of freedom":

> The chief hope of the world today is the Catholic Church, the only international authority on law and justice left to us... the same people who ask why the Church doesn't do something about stopping the war are the same ones who previously criticized it for trying to have international influence.[43]

By deflecting some of the misconceptions about the Church in this fashion, Sheen hoped to move on to teach the truth about the Church's views and motives. He concentrated on its devotion to the ideals of peace and justice, ideals which Americans of all faiths could agree with. In pointing out the connection between a lack of justice and the loss of peace, he depicted the failures of the past as partially responsible for the chaos of the present. The world had failed to heed the Church's warnings: "Europe reacted to the false liberalism, and created its dictatorships, its tyranny, its persecution of religion."[44] In the face of that persecution, and the threat of war, Sheen advocated a militant stand by the Church along with a militant spirit of democracy, confident that the Church's position would be vindicated, and that good would triumph over evil.

There was plenty of evidence of the presence of evil in the modern world, seen by Sheen as more of a theological problem than

---

[43] Fulton Sheen, statement made in a lecture in 1940, preserved in the Scrapbook of "Joseph F. Sheen of Chicago," Sheen Archives.

[44] Fulton Sheen, "The Seven Last Words and the Seven Virtues," Catholic Hour Broadcast Series, pamphlet published by Our Sunday Visitor, 1940, p. 65.

a political one.[45] The three great manifestations of evil were nazism, fascism, and communism. An effect of the growth of evil which the hierarchy observed was the persecution of religion around the world. "Speaking in the interests of Church and State, as Americans as well as Catholics,"[46] the bishops condemned this persecution. Although Sheen and the bishops objected to the persecution of religion as churchmen, they would also voice their opposition to events in Mexico, Russia, Germany, and Spain as contrary to the spirit of American freedom. In Sheen's broadcasts for the year 1937, "Our Wounded World," he spoke of an alliance between Christianity and democracy to fight religious persecution:

> ...in Mexico, Spain, Germany and Russia, the State is
> a counter-church, crushing religion by sheer force... it
> is not the civilizations of Rome, Athens and Jerusalem,
> but the civilizations of Mexico, Russia, Spain, and Ger-
> many which nail the Church to a modern Cross.[47]

Sheen's analysis essentially came down to a question about communism and fascism. Unlike some current thought on the subject, however, he insisted that the world need not choose between the two philosophies, which posed as rivals.[48] In fact, Sheen argued that communism and fascism were cut from the same cloth, and condemned them both. Communism and fascism were alike, in that "they agreed that the individual exists for the state; they were intolerant of political opposition; they hated minorities and denied

---

[45] This Catholic view toward modern manifestations of evil was a common one. Historian of American Catholicism Thomas T. McAvoy, CSC, wrote that "the Catholic Church fought fascism and communism — in the realm of philosophy and theology — long before they became the modern Frankenstein monsters of machine warfare." "American Catholics and the Second World War," *Review of Politics,* 6 (April, 1944), p. 142.

[46] "Pastoral Letter to Mexico," December 12, 1926, in *Pastoral Letters* (Vol. I), pp. 338-339.

[47] Sheen, "Our Wounded World," pp. 10-12.

[48] George Seldes, in *The Catholic Crisis,* took issue with Sheen's perspective by arguing that the real struggle was not between Christianity and communism; rather, democracy was in grave danger, and the greatest threat to it was in the form of fascism (p. 9).

freedom of the press; and they were anti-religious, hating God."[49]
The real choice was not between fascism and communism, for that
was a false choice. Instead, Sheen advocated a third alternative,
extending his concept of the "golden mean" to international politics. Sheen's choice was Christianity. The underlying world struggle
was between the forces of dictatorship and democracy; the Catholic Church, representative of spirituality and freedom, was more
attuned to democracy, for the "interests of democracy lie neither
in an alliance with fascism or communism."[50]

Fulton Sheen's recitation of balanced condemnations of fascism and communism continued throughout the war years. Simply put, he said that "Communism was Soviet fascism,"[51] and that
"Communism is the Asiatic form of fascism, and fascism is the
European form of communism."[52] It was a concept he would return to over and over again, growing more specific when he attacked
Hitler and Stalin by name. Several leading Catholic publicists considered fascism and communism as equally dangerous, regarding
fascism as effect and communism as cause.[53] Sheen's own explanation grew out of his views on social justice: individualism and monopolistic capitalism led to selfishness, and the world's reaction was
to swing to the opposite error of collectivization — the state control of communism and fascism. In other words, "Fascism arises as
a reaction against communism,"[54] both equally wrong extremes.

These repeated condemnations of communism and fascism
by Sheen were sounded only towards the latter years of the thirties, a decade characterized by considerable confusion about the
Catholic Church's position on fascism.[55] Early in the decade, the

[49] Sheen, "Our Wounded World," p. 7.
[50] Sheen, *Liberty, Equality and Fraternity*, p. 118.
[51] *Ibid.*, p. 116.
[52] Sheen, "Reply to *Izvestia*," printed in the *Catholic World* 152 (March, 1944), p. 590.
[53] For an analysis similar to Sheen's, see John LaFarge, SJ, "Fascism and Communism: Which is the Greater Danger?" *America* 9 (October 10, 1936).
[54] Sheen, *Liberty, Equality and Fraternity*, p. 116.
[55] See F.K. Wentz, "American Catholic Periodicals React to Nazism," *Church History* 3 (December, 1962), pp. 400-420.

American Catholic community had formed a generally favorable impression of fascism, largely because of the Lateran Treaty and Concordat signed by Pope Pius XI and Mussolini in 1929.[56] This reconciliation between Church and State in Italy was welcomed by American Catholics, in the hope that the religious freedom and independence of the Church would be preserved and protected.[57] Contrary to the charges made by American liberals that this was proof positive of an anti-democratic alliance between Catholicism and fascism, not all American Catholics who approved of the Papacy's course of action in signing the Concordat approved of fascism. Fr. John A. Ryan, a "staunch liberal Catholic and vociferous anti-fascist," supported the Concordat, an indication that Catholics could regard it as an "ecclesiastical rather than an ideological affair."[58]

Monsignor Fulton Sheen also expressed support of the Lateran Treaty, but from a purely religious and ecclesiastical perspective. He saw the Concordat as necessary because the Church, through the centuries, had been forced to make agreements with its enemies just to insure its survival. In the eulogy he delivered for Pope Pius XI in 1939, he looked back to the treaty of 1929 as an illustration of two lessons of Pius XI's pontificate: that the Church must enter the world, and that once in the world, it must rely only on the spiritual:

> The Spiritual Shepherd of the world was asking for a pasture of only 120 acres for three million sheep... from the signing of the Lateran Concordat emerged the sec-

---

[56] For a good historical treatment of the background to the Italian situation, see D.A. Binchy's *Church and State in Fascist Italy* (New York and London: Oxford University Press, 1941).

[57] For the best overall summary of "American Catholics and Italian Fascism," see the article by John P. Diggins in *The Journal of Contemporary History* 2 (October, 1967), pp. 51-68. The article was later incorporated as a chapter in Diggins' more comprehensive book, *Mussolini and Fascism: The View From America* (Princeton, NJ: Princeton University Press, 1972).

[58] Diggins, *Mussolini and Fascism*, p. 189.

ond feature of his reign, namely the primacy of the spiritual... Pius asked only for the rock of the Vatican State to spread that redemption and that peace even unto the ends of the world.[59]

This illustration of Sheen's clearly demonstrates how he preferred to avoid the political complexities of an issue when he could approach it instead in terms associated with simple religious parables. His views on Mussolini and the Concordat neglect any discussion of the problematical nature of the American Catholic Church's supposed "apology" and case of "historical amnesia."[60]

The Vatican's accommodation with Mussolini's fascist state would prove unsuccessful in the long term. Two years after the signing of the Lateran Treaty, the government launched a violent and bitter attack on the Pope's beloved "Catholic Action."[61] The Pope responded by issuing the encyclical letter *Non abbiamo bisogno* in June of 1931, taking elaborate precautions to see that it reached the outside world by having the American prelate, Francis Spellman, smuggle it out of Italy.[62] This encyclical was an outspoken attack on Mussolini and his fascist party; the Pope and the Church had learned a bitter lesson about the dangers of the totalitarian state. The Church's disillusionment with the fascist state grew stronger as Mussolini forged an alliance with Hitler in 1936. In March of 1937, the Church would clarify its position; Pius XI released two great encyclicals within a week of one another: *Mit brennender sorge* and *Divini Redemptoris*, condemning both nazi fascism and communism. From this point on, the Catholic Church was on record as being opposed to both forms of totalitarianism,

[59] Sheen, "Pius XI: Two Eulogies," given over the nationwide network of the National Broadcasting Company on February 11 and 12, 1939; pamphlet printed by Our Sunday Visitor — a copy is found in the collection of the Sheen Archives.

[60] See Diggins, *Mussolini and Fascism*, p. 191.

[61] See Binchy, Chapter XVIII: "Azione Cattolica," on the relationship between fascism and Catholic Action in Italy.

[62] See Binchy, p. 522. Spellman's role in smuggling the letter out of Italy is also discussed in Fogarty's *The Vatican and the American Hierarchy*, p. 240.

and it was this form of opposition that was most closely associated with the pronouncements of Fulton Sheen.

Sheen was outspoken on the subjects of fascism and communism from 1936 on; while condemning them both, he tended to direct most of his attack at communism, the greater of the two evils. He generally discussed fascism in terms of religious persecution and its relation to communism. Even as early as 1931, he had spoken of the need for "world Catholic solidarity," and made a dramatic reference to an updated "voice over Damascus," asking "Stalin, Calles, Mussolini — why persecutest thou me?"[63] Most of his references to Mussolini came after the start of World War II, when Mussolini was depicted in league with the other dictators, as well as the devil. In an address in December of 1939, Sheen pointed to Mussolini, Hitler and Stalin as "three dictators who are attempting to justify their actions by ideas which are only weapons to keep themselves in power."[64] In 1941, Sheen soundly denounced Mussolini. Describing all the dictators as manifestations of the spirit of Anti-Christ, Sheen asked: "Do not evil men disguise their evil? Do not the Bolsheviks destroy Christianity in the name of democracy? Does not Hitler destroy Poland in the name of justice? Does not Mussolini invade Albania in the name of protection?"[65] From the perspective of hindsight, Sheen drew a comparison between the "slave states of Russia in 1918, Germany in 1933, and the totalitarian state of Italy in 1922" — all brought on by "want of discipline and morality."[66] Sheen's record, then, reveals that he was not an apologist for fascism. Although some strident anti-communists ran the risk of being perceived as pro-fascist, Sheen avoided this impression by directing his critique at communists and fascists alike, often equating the two ideologies: "Communism was Soviet fas-

[63] Sheen, in a lecture given on August 7, 1931; preserved in the Scrapbook of "Joseph F. Sheen of Chicago," Sheen Archives.
[64] Sheen, lecture given at "Loyola College," summarized in a newspaper article preserved in the Scrapbook of "Joseph F. Sheen of Chicago," Sheen Archives.
[65] Sheen, *For God and Country*, p. 7.
[66] *Ibid.*, p. 72.

cism; communism was fascism gone mad."[67] This equation, however, did not stand up to scrutiny with regard to Sheen's perceptions of the situation in Spain.[68]

Unfortunately, things were not simple in Spain, for Sheen or the American Catholic Church. The Spanish Civil War was surrounded by more controversy than any other single event during the thirties. On this issue, Catholics were divided from many of their fellow Americans, the Americanization process of the Church was temporarily derailed, and the controversy led to more misunderstandings about the Church and fascism, and the Catholic position on the Church-State question. When civil war broke out in Spain in 1936, it assumed symbolic overtones as a struggle between democracy and fascism, with many American liberals supporting the Loyalist government. To Catholics, however, it represented "a duel between the anti-God forces of communism and the forces of Christian Europe… a clash between militant atheists and Christians, an issue of God or anti-God." The trouble with this interpretation was that it put Franco on the side of God and Christianity.[69] The Catholic Church supported Franco's rebels — a group considered fascist — largely because Franco was a Catholic and his forces fought against the killers of priests and nuns, and were against communism.

As a popular public figure, Monsignor Sheen's views on the crisis in Spain received a good deal of attention. Like many other American Catholics, he was caught up in the controversy, and supported the Church's opposition to the Reds in Spain, participating in the outcry against anti-clericalism and religious persecution. However, a careful examination of his record reveals that Sheen was not a deluded supporter of Franco.

Historians have recognized that in the American debate on the Spanish Civil War, both sides were guilty of harboring a sim-

---

[67] Sheen, "Our Wounded World," p. 13.

[68] See Theodore Maynard, "Catholics and the Nazis," *The American Mercury* 53 (October, 1941), pp. 391-400.

[69] George Flynn, *Roosevelt and Romanism*, pp. 29, 37.

plistic world view, overlooking or ignoring the complexities of Spanish history in depicting the other side as inherently evil.[70] A certain amount of naivete, cloudy reasoning, and confused motives[71] prevailed on both sides: the Catholics over-zealous in emphasizing the red menace, and the liberals failing to take the Loyalist persecution of the Church into consideration. Sheen was guilty of the occasional overstatement, and exaggeration. In a talk at the Catholic Summer School of America in New Haven in 1937, he said: "Franco is saving western civilization by keeping the barbarians out of Europe."[72] This misguided characterization of Franco as opposed to the "barbarians" grew out of Sheen's preoccupation with communism; Pope Pius XI had advised Sheen "to speak on communism... at every opportunity, and to warn America of its dangers."[73] But he could also offer a more balanced view, and charged that the U.S. press — some newspapers — distorted the true facts concerning the Spanish Civil War. As the historical record proves, there was distortion enough to go around on all sides. Sheen did, however, gradually mellow his views on Spain, growing uncomfortable with Franco's actions; he acknowledged that the protests of the world against the bombings in Spain were justified.[74] He continued to argue that Americans should strive to keep both communism and fascism from U.S. shores (although he sidestepped the fascist connections with Franco). However, in his most famous statement on the subject of Spain, an address delivered at a mass rally in Washington, D.C., on January 9, 1939, Sheen's most carefully considered viewpoint is apparent.

The National Council of Catholic Men had organized the

---

[70] See J. David Valaik, "American Catholics and the Spanish Civil War," (Ph.D. dissertation, University of Rochester, 1964); and Flynn's *Roosevelt and Romanism*.

[71] Flynn, pp. 38-39.

[72] Sheen, address reprinted in the Scrapbook of "Joseph F. Sheen of Chicago," Sheen Archives.

[73] Sheen, "Eulogies for Pope Pius XI," p. 13.

[74] Sheen spoke about the world's outrage at the bombing in Spain in a broadcast address from January of 1941, "Conditions of a Just War," part of the "War and Guilt" series (Our Sunday Visitor pamphlet, p. 36).

"Keep the Spanish Embargo Committee," with support from the Knights of Columbus, in an attempt to publicize the position of the American Church on the Spanish Civil War and to influence the government's policy. The major American Catholic spokesmen of the time "fell into line,"[75] including Monsignor Fulton J. Sheen. At the rally in Constitution Hall, attended by 4,000 people, "the most effective speaker was the magnetic, popular and respected Sheen."[76] His lengthy address[77] began by defining the purpose of the meeting: not to urge support of Franco, but to plead for the retention of the neutrality act, "to keep us out of someone else's fight."[78] Directing his remarks at two groups interested in lifting the embargo — "international propagandists" and "loyal Americans who believed the Loyalist cause to be just" — he set out "to expose the first and answer the second," vowing to tell the truth.[79] Sheen suggested several good reasons why neutrality was the best policy, including the problems inherent in choosing sides in any civil war — "when the attack comes from inside the nation, it is not always easy to define the aggressor"[80] — and the moral reservations he had about supplying arms and contributing further to the bloodshed: "Let us, instead of lifting the embargo to sell gun powder to Spain, spend that money on the poor."[81] The bottom line of Sheen's case was his definition of Americanism:

> True Americanism means two things — positively, the recognition of the sovereign, inalienable rights of man,

---

[75] For background on the Committee, formed for "patriotic and humanitarian" reasons, see Valaik, "American Catholics and the Spanish Civil War," pp. 345-354; and Flynn's *Roosevelt and Romanism*, Chapter 2.

[76] J. David Valaik, "Catholics, Neutrality and the Spanish Embargo, 1937-1939," *Journal of American History* LIV (June, 1967), p. 78.

[77] The rally addresses were printed and distributed in pamphlet form by the N.C.C.M.; Sheen's remarks at the rally were also widely covered in the press. One of the more colorful examples is a reprint of excerpts in *The Irish Monthly* 67 (March, 1939), entitled "Spain Through Red-Tinted Glasses."

[78] Sheen address, printed in N.C.C.M. pamphlet, p. 37.

[79] *Ibid.*, p. 37.

[80] *Ibid.*, p. 48.

[81] *Ibid.*, p. 53.

and negatively, unqualified opposition to all totalitarian forms — whether they be NAZI, FASCIST, or COMMUNIST — which deny these rights. There is irreconcilable opposition between the regimes of Russia, Germany and Italy.

Over there, the state is the source of rights; here man is the source of rights. Over there, freedom resides in the collectivity: in the race as in Germany, in the nation as in Italy, and in the class as in Russia; over here, freedom resides in man.[82]

Sheen's methodology of basing his entire argument on Americanism was a wise one, in light of the charges leveled against Catholics in the American debate over the Spanish Civil War. His address was designed to defuse the suspicions of those who believed that Catholics could not be good Americans because of their divided loyalties, and to obviate the circumstances which found the Church opposed by American liberals, who supported the Loyalists and claimed to be the true representatives of America and defenders of democracy. Sheen avowed that Catholics deserved credit for equating, and opposing, communists as well as nazis and fascists, pointing out that President Roosevelt himself agreed: "Why are Governor Lehman and President Roosevelt always careful when mentioning anti-American activities to enumerate all three...?"[83] Rattling off numerous statistics, Sheen pointed out the atrocities committed by the Popular Front in Spain during a single year: 20,000 churches and chapels burned, and 11,000 religious murdered.[84] These facts, according to Sheen, might go unreported in the newspapers, but President Roosevelt recognized the threat to democracy and the injustices of such persecution: "Where freedom of religion has been attacked, the attack has come from sources

---

[82] *Ibid.*, pp. 37-38.
[83] *Ibid.*, p. 41.
[84] *Ibid.*, p. 51.

opposed to democracy. Where democracy has been overthrown, the spirit of free worship has disappeared."[85]

Most American Catholics, then, saw the Spanish Civil War first and foremost from the vantage point of religion, arguing that freedom of religion was an American right. Falling back on his central theme, and some favorite metaphors, Sheen voiced his support of the embargo as an American as well as a Catholic:

> No American is interested in the distinction between the three totalitarianisms, for to us they offer the same choice as a choice between theft, burglary and larceny. I can be anti-communist without being pro-nazi just as I can hate caviar without being mad about limburger; but I cannot be pro-communist or pro-nazi or pro-fascist without being anti-American. As Americans we are not concerned with whether a dictator has a long moustache or a short moustache; or whether he invades the soul through the myth of race or the myth of the class; we are concerned only with the fact that there has been an invasion and expropriation of the inalienable liberties of man.[86]

True Americanism required unqualified opposition to all totalitarian regimes — nazi, fascist and communist; therefore, neutrality was the only acceptable policy in Spain, for there were totalitarians supplying arms to both sides.[87] What happened in Spain was of particular importance, for Spain was "an international proving ground."[88] It was also a classic example of Sheen's views on history, and the cause and effect relationship between communism and fascism: the best way to keep down fascism "is to keep down that against which fascism is a reaction. It is a historical fact that fas-

---

[85] *Ibid.*, pp. 51-52.
[86] *Ibid.*, p. 38.
[87] *Ibid.*, p. 44.
[88] *Ibid.*, p. 46.

cism arises wherever there is communism. It was so in Hungary, Belgium, France, Italy, Germany and the South American republics — and it will be true here. First you have the moths, then the moth balls; first the rats, then the rat poison."[89]

This most controversial episode in American Catholic history, and Fulton Sheen's role in it, remains problematic for the historian. Sheen's internationalism seemed sidetracked when he advocated neutrality in Spain, but "the Catholic position was in line with traditional American isolationism."[90] In 1939, many Americans were still hoping to avoid entanglement in another European war. Monsignor Sheen's position was sometimes misrepresented and misunderstood. In a controversy which took place between the liberal and Catholic press, the difficulties with Sheen's position were obvious. Ernest Sutherland Bates wrote an "Open Letter to Monsignor Fulton J. Sheen" in the *New Republic* magazine.[91] A former fan of Sheen, Bates now expressed his "profound shock" that Sheen, a "leader of liberal Catholic thought in America," could support the "anti-democratic and anti-American regime of General Franco in Spain."[92] Charging that neutrality was a "cheap evasion," he went on to declare that Protestants would now be suspicious of Sheen, and coupled the "formerly honored name of Sheen with that of Fr. Coughlin."[93] This letter stirred up quite a debate, though Sheen, following his usual practice, did not respond directly to the charge.

However, Michael Williams of *Commonweal* wrote a reply to Bates, speaking on behalf of Sheen and the American Catholic community.[94] Speaking as one "who had read pretty nearly everything Sheen has written," Williams questioned whether Sheen "ever

---

[89] *Ibid.*, p. 54.

[90] *Ibid.*, p. 55.

[91] The letter was published in *The New Republic* in the issue dated February 1, 1939, right after the "Keep the Spanish Embargo" rally (pp. 371-372). Bates was the same writer who had called Sheen "A Champion of Reason" when he had reviewed *God and Intelligence in Modern Philosophy* for *Commonweal* back in 1926.

[92] *Ibid.*, p. 371.

[93] *Ibid.*, p. 372.

[94] *Commonweal* 30 (February 10, 1939), pp. 435-436.

labeled himself a liberal."[95] Bates had made charges that not only Sheen, but other American Catholics, were "hypocrites and liars,"[96] an indication of how polarized the debate had become. Taking the high ground, Williams concluded that "reasonable Catholics would not and do not say that American liberals who support the Loyalists are all allied with the communists and anarchists, and at heart are dishonest in their lip service to democracy and religious liberty. Charges of that character are usually explosions of emotion, excusable of course, but not helpful to a discussion in which reason should control even righteous emotions."[97]

This episode illustrates the difficulty in drawing conclusions about Sheen, and the American Catholic Church, when it comes to the highly charged and emotional atmosphere surrounding Spain's civil war. Even those who deem Sheen mistaken here, if they examine his complete record, cannot believe that in opposing communism in Spain he was supporting fascism. And it should be remembered that Fulton Sheen was in good company in this instance; certainly John A. Ryan and Dorothy Day, recognized as liberal, even radical, in their social thought, were not construed as apologists for fascism because they supported neutrality in Spain. Father Ryan, while admitting the "sordidness of Franco's fight," nonetheless expressed a preference for his cause over that of the Loyalist government as the "lesser of two evils."[98] Several years after the rally, in an interview in 1946, Sheen summed up his position: "I never defended Franco. I always defended Spain against the attack of the communists. Simply because one is anti-communist, it does not follow that he is a fascist. Franco was the lesser of two evils."[99] In this attempt to set the record straight, Sheen de-

---

[95] *Ibid.*, p. 435.

[96] *Ibid.*, p. 435.

[97] *Ibid.*, p. 436.

[98] See George Flynn, p. 38, who cites Francis Broderick's *Right Reverend New Dealer* as his source.

[99] Sheen, quoted in an interview in the liberal *P.M. Magazine* (June 16, 1946): "An Interview with America's Outstanding Roman Catholic Proselytizer and Philosopher," by Kenneth Stewart; a copy of this article is in the collection at the Sheen Archives.

picted himself as standing on the "middle ground," where he felt
comfortable on most issues. Historian J. David Valaik, author of
the most complete study on "American Catholics and the Spanish
Civil War," referred to public opinion polls, taken in 1938, indicating that "39% of Catholics favored Franco; 30% were pro-Loy-
alist; and 31% were neutral."[100] Sheen, like some of the American
Catholics who actively dissented from the official Church position,
"correctly rejected fascism as well as communism as contrary to the
dictates of Christianity and alien to American democracy."[101]

On every public issue addressed by Fulton Sheen during these
years of crisis, from the Spanish Civil War through the Cold War,
his underlying motive was to defend religion. With Americans of
all religious faiths, he grew increasingly concerned about the multiple threats to religious freedom and American democracy in the
years immediately prior to the outbreak of world war. News of racial and religious persecution across Europe prompted Mayor
Fiorello LaGuardia of New York City to organize a mass meeting
in 1938 to protest those persecutions, a "rally for American Liberty."[102] Before a crowd of thousands, one speaker after another
"warned the citizens of this country to be on guard to protect themselves from the forces of group hatred from any source."[103] The
speakers included Secretary of Agriculture Henry Wallace; William Dodd, former ambassador to Germany; Episcopal Bishop
William Manning; and Monsignor Fulton Sheen. The general
purpose of the rally was to protest nazi persecutions, but many of
the speakers broadened the scope of their remarks to condemn other
fascists and totalitarians. They also reminded Americans, who loved
liberty and democracy, to fight "the unparalleled encroachment on

---

[100] Valaik, "American Catholics and the Spanish Civil War"; polls for 1938 and 1939 cited
on pp. 396-397.

[101] Valaik, "American Catholic Dissenters and the Spanish Civil War," *Catholic Historical
Review* LIII (January, 1968), p. 555.

[102] This rally was the same one where Sheen had spoken out against anti-Semitism. The
following quotations are taken from an article in the *New York Times*, December 10,
1938 ("LaGuardia Rally Warns of Dangers of Hatreds in U.S.").

[103] *New York Times*, December 10, 1938.

world civilization."[104] Sheen, in character as a foe of communism, directed his assault against the Soviets as well, reminding the audience that "we have already been too patient with man's inhumanity to man during the past twenty years. We were silent when 2,000,000 kulaks met death and 60,000 churches were closed by the atheistic government in Russia. Now the secret is out: those who cannot pull God down from heaven are driving his creatures from the face of the earth."[105] And sounding his fundamental premise, he boldly declared that "only those who condemn persecution irrespective of where they find it have any right to be heard."[106]

Determined to be heard, Sheen extended this argument from his condemnation of fascists and nazis to the subject of the Allied friendship with the Soviet Union. His criticisms of the Soviet alliance were frequent, voiced both before and after the U.S. entry into the war. It was an unpopular subject, he admitted, but one which he felt very strongly about. He based his case on ethics and morality rather than politics and pragmatism, and was generally a lonely crusader in this effort. It was, however, a logical conclusion, given his belief that "justice demands the condemnation of evil irrespective of where one finds it."[107] Sheen was persistently bothered by the tendency to be alert to the danger posed by fascism, but not communism, and he accused Americans of picking and choosing the foreign evils they opposed. His suspicions about the Soviet Union were confirmed with the signing of the Nazi-Soviet Non-Aggression Pact in August of 1939. During a radio broadcast, he told his followers to remember that "the Catholic Hour speaker referred to the likelihood of a union between the nazis and Sovi-

---

[104] From the remarks of William Dodd, *ibid.*

[105] *Ibid.*, p. 6.

[106] Sheen repeated the same sentiment, verbatim, at the Spanish embargo rally, prefaced with "I joined the Jews in New York in their protest against the abominable outrages of Hitler against them and their religion. I only ask now that all who believe in freedom, democracy and religion join us in protest against the Reds." "Keep the Spanish Embargo" rally, reprint by N.C.C.M., p. 52.

[107] Sheen, "War and Guilt," p. 55.

ets."[108] Sheen referred to the Nazi-Soviet treaty as the greatest menace on earth, warning that the devil would make the dictators of Germany and Russia friends: "If Russia and Germany do not become allies by themselves, we may be sure that Satan will bring them together."[109] Equating Hitler and Stalin as forces of evil was a favorite tactic of Sheen's; he compared them to "Pilate and Herod — Christ-haters,"[110] and called them "assassins of justice."[111] After the announcement of the Nazi-Soviet Pact, Sheen noticed that "America has suddenly turned against communism… not because of a universal moral judgment based on the intrinsic wickedness of communism, but because of a particular judgment that communism signed a treaty with someone whom most Americans hate, namely Hitler."[112] Sheen spoke for a moral consistency, alluding to the fact that the basis for condemning Stalin only when he allied with Hitler was not a sound one; he would be proven right later. When Hitler broke the treaty, the Allies entered into an alliance with Stalin.

Even while Hitler and Stalin were allied, Sheen was more suspicious about the Soviets, sounding this warning:

> Look out for Russia that walks like a bear and crawls like a snake. Mark these words: the enemy of the world in the near future is going to be Russia, which is playing democracies against dictators, which is using peace when it can and war when it must, and is preparing, when Europe is exhausted from war, to sweep over it like a vulture to drink its blood and make away with the spoils.[113]

Sheen pointed out the hypocrisy of those who called Russia a

---

[108] Sheen, "War and Guilt," address given on January 19, 1941.

[109] Sheen, "The Seven Last Words and the Seven Virtues" (1940), p. 65.

[110] *Ibid.*, p. 66.

[111] Sheen, *Whence Comes War?*, p. 97.

[112] Sheen, "Peace: The Fruit of Justice" (1940), p. 14.

[113] Sheen, "War and Guilt" (1941), p. 55.

"friendly nation, when the facts prove that Russia has been just as destructive of humanity, as hateful of religion, as oppressive of the masses and as cruel to hearts as the nazis" — as damning an indictment as could be made of any nation.[114] He suggested that the Soviets had "revealed their true character when they wantonly attacked little Finland."[115]

In an address entitled "Primacy of Ethics Over Politics," Sheen said that he was shocked by the prospect of an alliance with "Red Russia," believing that it would be the "beginning of the end of America — it may be good politics, but bad ethics."[116] Good politics, in Sheen's view, had caused "Nations which boast that they are defending religion to seek to enter into pacts with anti-religious governments."[117] This policy, in addition to being morally indefensible, was based on "ridiculous statements and inconsistencies: Hitler is an enemy when he invades the left side of Poland, and Stalin is a friend when he invades the right?"[118] Focusing instead on ethics, Sheen resolved to keep up his efforts: "the cause of democracy is not being aided by whitewashing the sad and tragic facts about religion in Russia."[119] He vowed also to continue to speak out, to keep America on guard, lest its generous aid to the allies should aid communism; Sheen began to suggest that "as a condition of aid to Russia, the U.S. should demand a guarantee of religious freedom in the Soviet Union."[120]

Many of the questions of politics and ethics were pushed aside when the Japanese attack on Pearl Harbor settled the debate about

---

[114] Sheen, *For God and Country*, p. 67.

[115] Sheen, remarks reported in the *Boston Sunday Advertiser*, January 7, 1940. Newspaper clipping files, Sheen Archives.

[116] Sheen, remarks reported in the *Boston American*, October 24, 1941. Newspaper clipping files, Sheen Archives.

[117] Sheen, *Whence Comes War?*, p. 4.

[118] Sheen, *For God and Country*, p. 3.

[119] Sheen, remarks reported in the *Village News* of Balling, Arkansas, October, 1941. Newspaper clipping files, Sheen Archives.

[120] Sheen, remarks reported in the *Philadelphia Enquirer*, September 27, 1941. Newspaper clipping files, Sheen Archives.

the American entry into the war. Once the nation joined the war effort, Sheen, like all good American Catholics, renewed his loyalty to the government and the basic ideals of the American Republic. In an earlier Pastoral Letter issued by the U.S. hierarchy, "Peace and War," this patriotism on the part of American Catholics was clearly evident. The bishops asked the members of their flock to stand by the noble Christian ideals embodied in the Declaration of Independence: "By standing fast to these high principles we can best serve our national defense and preserve our national ideals."[121]

Despite this profession of loyalty by the American bishops, lingering doubts about Catholics and the intentions of the Church persisted in the controversy surrounding President Roosevelt's decision to dispatch Myron Taylor as his personal representative to the Vatican in 1939. Taylor's mission — to promote "parallel endeavors for peace and the alleviation of suffering"[122] — stirred up anti-Catholic sentiment again. While Catholics greeted the announcement with great enthusiasm, some other Americans reacted with troubling questions about the old "separation of church and state" issue. Monsignor Sheen sent a telegram to Roosevelt, calling Taylor's assignment "the first concrete recognition any great nation in modern times has given to the spiritual and moral foundations of peace."[123] Aware of the revival of bigotry, Sheen spoke out on several occasions in an attempt to defuse anti-Catholicism. In a broadcast on "The Papacy and Peace" Sheen noted that "the recent appointment of Mr. Taylor has aroused fears groundless enough to be a prejudice," and went on to declare that "neither the pope nor the Church was interested in usurping the rights of nations."[124] He also suggested that the Pope harbored no hidden motives: "If the Pope works for world peace, it is not to force Ca-

---

[121] "Statement on War and Peace," (1939), in *Pastoral Letters* (Vol. I), p. 434.
[122] White House news release, December 23, 1939, cited by Flynn in *Roosevelt and Romanism*, p. 98.
[123] Cited in Flynn, p. 110.
[124] Sheen, *Whence Comes War?*, pp. 82-83.

tholicism down our throats."[125] Scorning the loose talk of Church and State conflicts, he characterized the current charges as "stupid": "the plea that nations invoke spiritual authority for the settlement of international issues is called bringing the Pope to the White House!"[126] In an effort to move beyond the debate over the Taylor appointment, Sheen proceeded to concentrate on the more pressing task at hand: explaining the war to the American people, and pointing out the objectives that Christianity and democracy, the Catholic Church and the American nation, shared in their common quest.

Fulton Sheen's analysis of the Second World War, contained in his broadcasts and books from 1941 to 1945, revolved around three basic ideas: the theology of war, or the religious and spiritual overtones of the conflict; the opportunity the war presented for America to return more fully to God; and the Church's plans for peace and reconstructing the social order. On the eve of Pearl Harbor, in November of 1941, the American bishops issued a statement entitled "The Crisis of Christianity." Recalling that the late Holy Father had issued encyclicals condemning both nazism and communism, they declared that "Christianity faces today its most serious crisis since the Church came out of the catacombs."[127] This same crisis mentality characterized, even dominated, many of Sheen's comments throughout the war. For the next decade, all of the hierarchy's pastorals were concerned with two problems: peace and secularism.[128] The main priority during the war was to secure a just and lasting peace, based upon Christian ideals rather than the false faith in secular values which had contributed to the coming of the war:

> Secularism, or the practical exclusion of God from human thinking and living, is at the root of the world's

[125] Sheen, "Peace: The Fruit of Justice," p. 49.
[126] Sheen, *For God and Country*, p. 5.
[127] "The Crisis of Christianity," in *Pastoral Letters* (Vol. II), p. 28.
[128] Hugh J. Nolan, "Introduction" to *Pastoral Letters* (Vol. II), p. 11.

travail today. It was the fertile soil in which such social monstrosities as fascism, nazism and communism, could germinate and grow.[129]

"War and Guilt" was the title of Sheen's "Catholic Hour" broadcast series for 1941, delivered before the U.S. entry into the war. He characterized war as a "judgment of God," and said that "political and economic upheavals are only symptoms of a more radical evil.[130] Like World War I, this war would "unmask a false way of life and shatter secular illusions."[131] God used war throughout history to "chastise nations and move them to saving amendment";[132] He permitted evil so that good might arise from it. This lesson was evident, stated Sheen, in the "fundamental evil of the day, which was irrational, violent and atheistic."[133] If this war was an instrument of God's justice, then Americans could be assured that they would be fighting for a just cause.

Defining the conditions for a "just war" had always been important in Church history. Sheen set these three criteria: "A morally good end, right intentions, and justifiable methods."[134] The traditional Catholic position avoided the extremes of militarism and pacifism; sometimes, good, peace-loving people were required to go to war for a higher cause, to resist oppression and to defend their God-given rights. According to Sheen the present war was clearly such a case, for "God's goodness cannot be indifferent to evil."[135]

In addition to fighting to defeat the spirit of "Anti-Christ,"[136]

---

[129] "Statement on Secularism," issued by the N.C.W.C. on November 14, 1947, in *Pastoral Letters* (Vol. II) p. 74.

[130] Sheen, "War and Guilt," p. 12.

[131] *Ibid.*, p. 14.

[132] *Ibid.*, p. 60.

[133] *Ibid.*, p. 5.

[134] *Ibid.*, p. 37.

[135] *Ibid.*, p. 73.

[136] This reference to the enemy as "Anti-Christ" was not peculiar to Sheen; he mentioned Hitler and Stalin as modern manifestations, but many Catholic writers employed the term with reference to evil as well.

American Catholics were also advised to be "prepared to build a different and a better world than the one which was collapsing."[137] The guidelines for that better world could be found in the Five-Point Peace Plan of Pope Pius XII. Good would triumph, said Sheen, if the world followed these five principles of justice:

1. to assure all nations of their right to life and independence;
2. to release nations from the slavery imposed upon them by the race for armaments;
3. to erect some juridical institution which shall guarantee the loyal and faithful fulfillment of treaties;
4. to establish strictly legal rights for the real needs and just demands of nations, populations and racial minorities;
5. to restore deep and keen responsibilities which measure and weigh human statutes according to the sacred and inviolable standards of the laws of God.[138]

Although these principles were enunciated by the leader of the Roman Catholic Church, they were in keeping with the spirit of America as well: the nation could fight to preserve the basic fundamental liberties which were the natural foundation of Christianity and democracy. America might even find itself regenerated through the war — hadn't the Founding Fathers, and Abraham Lincoln, called the nation to penance and self-sacrifice in the past, to become "a nation that trusts in God?"[139]

Following the same train of thought in his later broadcasts, Sheen informed his audience that "moments of great catastrophe are often the eves of great spiritual renaissance."[140] There was no escaping the cross, but despite the calamity of war, Americans could look to the future with hope. Sheen opened his series in 1942 with a vow to pray for the President, following the example set by the

---

[137] Sheen, "War and Guilt," p. 86.
[138] *Ibid.*, p. 54.
[139] *Ibid.*, p. 57.
[140] Sheen, *For God and Country*, p. 97.

U.S. bishops, who had pledged their wholehearted cooperation to
President Roosevelt. And the President had responded in kind,
demonstrating again the harmony that existed between the goals
of Catholics and the American nation: "We shall win this war and
in victory we shall seek not vengeance but the establishment of an
international order in which the spirit of Christ shall rule the hearts
of men and of nations."[141] Sheen also spoke to the question of refugees in this series, and reiterated his contention that "persecution
should be condemned irrespective of where it is found and who is
persecuted."[142] But the unifying thread running throughout the addresses was Americanism, and Sheen's calling to the nation to re-
pent and reform.

Citing the U.S. bishops' letter of support to Roosevelt, a
pledge of "all out aid for morality," Sheen underscored the "moral
objectives for which we fight," as defined by the President: "we are
defending a Christian civilization; we are fighting for religious freedom; we are fighting for justice."[143] America, the bastion of Justice, went to war to "re-establish in the world four justices: Divine
Justice, Legal Justice, Distributive Justice, and Commutative Justice."[144] Sheen's was not a blind patriotism, however, but one that
recognized the need for reform: "I love America — not America
right or wrong. If it is wrong, we will make it right."[145] Only in striving to live up to its ideals, and pledging its willingness to sacrifice,
would America receive God's assistance, for God did not take sides
on the basis of geography, but goodness: "With that assurance that
God's moral law is entwined with national ideals, we need never
fear the destiny of the stars and stripes."[146] "To the extent that our

[141] Letter written by Franklin D. Roosevelt to the American Bishops, December 24, 1941;
cited in *Pastoral Letters* (Vol. II), p. 37.
[142] Sheen, "Peace," p. 14.
[143] *Ibid.*, p. 32.
[144] *Ibid.*, p. 38.
[145] *Ibid.*, p. 38.
[146] *Ibid.*, p. 40.

purposes are identical with His, we can never lose.… God's purpose prevails."[147]

From this note of hope and confidence, Sheen swung back to the image of the cross in his 1943 broadcasts: "The Crisis in Christendom."[148] Sheen stated that his purpose was to give the "theologian's view of war rather than the journalist's," and suggested that the intelligent American people wanted to know why the war was happening, and what they were fighting for.[149] In proceeding to tell them, Sheen declared that the war was a theological struggle, resulting from the apostasy of the world. There were two great evils occurring in the modern world: War and Revolution. This distinction was especially useful in Sheen's efforts to explain how America could be allied with the Soviet Union: "Russia is on our side in the war, but not in the revolution,"[150] in the realm of ideas. Sheen went on to say that it was a false assumption that there were only two philosophies of life involved in the revolution: democratic vs. totalitarian, Christian vs. anti-Christian. Sheen saw three world views struggling for mastery of the world: the Totalitarian, the Secularist, and the Christian. The most threatening was the "active barbarism of the anti-Christian totalitarian world view," which existed in four forms: the historical form of fascism (the revival of the imperial traditions of the ancient Roman Empire); the anthropological form of nazism (the glorification of the Nordic race); the theological form of Japanese imperialism (the identification of Divinity with a dynastic house); and the economic form of Marxian socialism (the proclamation of class struggle on the anti-religious basis of dictatorship of the proletariat).[151] Christians were obligated to fight against these manifestations of evil, and the way to begin in

---

[147]   *Ibid.*, p. 124.

[148]   This Catholic Hour Broadcast Series was also published as two books: *Philosophies at War* (New York: Charles Scribner's Sons, 1943) and *The Divine Verdict* (New York: P.J. Kenedy and Sons, 1943).

[149]   Sheen, "The Crisis in Christendom," pamphlet by Our Sunday Visitor, 1943, p. 3.

[150]   *Ibid.*, p. 5.

[151]   *Ibid.*, p. 9.

the present conflict was for America to reform, to set its own house
in order.

The American bishops had given similar advice in their message in 1943, "The Essentials of a Good Peace":

> Let us make ourselves in truth peacemakers... Let us
> recognize the problems in our own social life and cou-
> rageously seek the solution of them. A first principle
> must be the recognition of the sovereignty of God and
> of the moral law in our national life, and in the right
> ordering of a new world born of the sacrifices and hard-
> ships of war.[152]

So, in addition to fighting the active barbarism from without,
Americans had a duty to defeat the "passive barbarism from
within."[153] He then employed the image of the "good ship America"
to illustrate this point; the ship that carried a cargo of rights, liberties and the four freedoms. Currently, there were "barnacles" on
this ship of democracy, which endangered a sound American way
of life.[154] These many barnacles took the form of secular threats,
such as progress, scientism, and materialism, but they also appeared
as the ever-present danger of communism, the "Trojan Horse."[155]
Harkening back to his earlier criticisms of the Soviet-American
alliance, Sheen said that "this grave menace to our country is soft-
pedaled these days because of our alliance with Russia, but for no
good reason. This Trojan Horse might look like a united war effort on the outside, but on the inside, it was the same old anti-
Americanism."[156] Admitting that this might be an unpopular view,

---

[152] "The Essentials of a Good Peace," in *Pastoral Letters* (Vol. II), p. 49.

[153] Sheen, "The Crisis in Christendom," p. 7.

[154] *Ibid.*, pp. 16-21.

[155] The image of the "Trojan Horse" was a common term applied to communism during
this period, by Catholics and non-Catholics alike. Congressman Martin Dies of the
House Un-American Activities Committee, for example, wrote a book entitled *The
Trojan Horse in America* in 1941.

[156] Sheen, "The Crisis in Christendom," pp. 23-24.

he stated that "it is made to appear that anyone who says a word against communism is against Russia, and sabotaging our war effort":

> This is nonsense… the two things are quite distinct, and let no one doubt it. Stalin himself said he was fighting against nazism but not against Germany.
> This gives us the right to say that we are against communism, but not against Russia… we do not want communism in America or Germany or Poland anymore than we want nazism or fascism… We American Catholics are for the Russian Bear, but we are not for the Trojan Horse. We want the Russian Bear to eat the swastika but we do not want the Trojan Horse to eat the American eagle.[157]

Falling back on his earlier references to communism as rotted capitalism, Sheen reiterated his "Christian prescriptions for the ills of capitalism"[18] as one way of fighting the spread of this contagion.

Finally, Sheen concluded "The Crisis in Christendom" with an explanation of the Holy Father's encyclical during the last world crisis, "Darkness Over the Earth." The thesis was that "God permits evil from time to time for the sake of a greater good."[159] History had taught this lesson in the past: as "Nazism was a judgment on Versailles, communism was a judgment on Czarist Russia and capitalism."[160] Perceiving some signs that America was beginning to learn the lesson "that only by living according to God's law can we overcome evil," Sheen illustrated it by quoting two of America's leaders. General MacArthur had issued a communique that said "a merciful Providence has granted us a great victory"; and President Roosevelt had quoted the Sermon on the Mount to remind

---

[157] *Ibid.*, pp. 24-25.
[158] *Ibid.*, p. 34.
[159] *Ibid.*, p. 65.
[160] *Ibid.*, p. 73.

us of "another law than force."[161] In fact, Sheen declared that the
Atlantic Charter of the Allies was a "political counterpart to the
Sermon on the Mount, for it is a defense of the poor and the
weak."[162]

The final years of the war saw Sheen and the American bishops concentrating even more on the peace. Victory was in sight,
and the hierarchy asked: "We have met the challenge of war — shall
we meet the challenge of peace?"[163] Sheen sounded a call to unity
in "One Lord, One World," his radio broadcasts for 1944,[164] and
advised Americans to carry on in the fight for justice by becoming
involved in social causes. Victory in war would not bring an auto-
matic solution to the world's problems, Sheen cautioned. The U.S.
bishops declared in 1945 that "the war is over, but there is no peace
in the world."[165] They expressed their support for the United Nations, and advocated mercy to enemies and private relief for the
casualties of war. Sheen spoke of doing away with old labels, which
were dangerous and threatening to the spirit of peace and unity,
given the "tendency of those who hate the Catholic Church to call
it fascist, or the tendency of many good Christians to call all men
interested in forward social legislation communists."[166]

Above all else, unity was called for; the ideal, in the aftermath
of the war, should be "One World based on One Lord and One
Moral Law."[167] Americans interested in working toward the
fulfillment of that ideal, advised Sheen, should now concentrate on
reforming the capitalist system to make it more just — the economic condition of world peace. Americans should also remain
patriotic, for "patriotism was a form of piety: Love of God, Love
of Neighbor and Love of Country were all grounded in justice"[168]

---

[161] *Ibid.*, p. 70.

[162] *Ibid.*, p. 80.

[163] "A Statement on International Order," 1944, in *Pastoral Letters* (Vol. II), p. 56.

[164] Sheen, "One Lord, One World," pamphlet published by Our Sunday Visitor, 1944.

[165] "Between War and Peace," 1945, in *Pastoral Letters* (Vol. II), p. 62.

[166] Sheen, "One Lord, One World," p. 12.

[167] *Ibid.*, p. 44.

[168] *Ibid.*, p. 30.

— the political condition for world peace. Confirming his allegiance
to the moral law as expressed in the Atlantic Charter and the Four
Freedoms, Sheen closed these preliminary suggestions for the main-
tenance of a post-war peace by saying simply that he remained
"proud to be an American."[169]

The year 1945 witnessed Fulton Sheen, and a more Americanized Catholic Church, gearing up to face a whole new set of
challenges posed by a more complicated world. Historians of
American Catholicism, and American religion in general, have
depicted the experience of World War II as a significant turning
point in the life of the Catholic Church. The dean of American
Catholic history, Monsignor John Tracy Ellis, referred to the
"greater acceptance of Catholics... as part of the national scene,"
contrasted with their "alien status of the past":

> Historically speaking, few aspects of Catholic citizen-
> ship have been more repeatedly urged by the bishops,
> more generally fulfilled by the laity, and more vigilantly
> watched by unfriendly critics than Catholics' participa-
> tion in the wars of the United States.[170]

With specific reference to the Second World War, another historian suggested that "Catholic patriotism in this crusade would be
so shining that never again would anyone dare question their
Americanism."[171] A significant contribution to this nationalizing
process was made by Fulton Sheen. The years of crisis under consideration here, and the message of patriotism and piety aired by
Sheen during those years, underscore Sheen's role in contributing
to the popular image of a more American Church. Historical assessments of this era — "the Golden Age of American Catholi-

---

[169] *Ibid.*, p. 44.
[170] John Tracy Ellis, "Changing Concerns of the American Bishops, 1791-1970," *Catholic
Historical Review* 58 (October, 1972), p. 390.
[171] Flynn, p. 223.

cism"[172]; the period of Catholicism's "Maturation"[173]; the "Postwar Revival Period"[174] — have recognized Sheen's significance from a variety of vantage points. "The eloquence of Fulton Sheen, and the worldwide leadership of Cardinal Spellman, helped make the Church more favorably known."[175] And, "that the situation of the Catholic in American life was changing was indicated by the passing of Coughlin as the nation's great radio priest and the ascent of Monsignor Fulton J. Sheen."[176]

This ascent of Sheen, accomplished over the span of several decades, was propelled by several factors: his great popularity as a Catholic spokesman; his orthodox views on social justice and peace; his fame as a foe of communism; and perhaps most importantly, his patriotism and Americanism. This Americanism was especially important to non-Catholics, for the reassuring voice and image presented by Monsignor Sheen went a long way in convincing many that Catholics could be good citizens. Just one testimonial to the positive effect of Sheen's endeavors is the fact that on several occasions, his broadcasts and lectures were actually read into the *Congressional Record*: his 1938 "Fraternity" broadcast, and lecture at the "Citizens Rally Against Oppression"; and his 1941 broadcast on "Peace" appear there.[177] This was high praise, and a Catholic priest who could safely be quoted in the halls of Congress for his patriotism helped to overcome anti-Catholic prejudice.

Sheen's version of Americanism, his style of patriotism, and his public pronouncements during the war years compare favorably with those of some of his contemporary Catholics. When compared

---

[172] Hugh Nolan in *Pastoral Letters* (Vol. II), p. 7.

[173] Winthrop Hudson, *Religion in America* (New York: Charles Scribner's Sons, 1965).

[174] Sydney E. Ahlstrom, *A Religious History of the American People* (New Haven: Yale University Press, 1972).

[175] Nolan, *Pastoral Letters* (Vol. II), p. 8.

[176] Ahlstrom, p. 1009.

[177] References to these facts are available in the Sheen Archives, both in reports in the newspaper clipping files, and copies of the *Congressional Record* that Sheen kept in his personal papers.

to the anti-Semitic comments made by Fr. Charles Coughlin, for example, the words of Sheen are surely more enlightened and reasonable, and projected a more accurate and favorable image of the Catholic Church. Sheen's purpose, generally successful, was to make a sound Christian contribution to the public debate, rather than to increase the level of hysteria and fear. In many respects, Sheen possessed many of the good qualities of the "other radio priest" without the faults, and Sheen would endure as a popular spokesman long after Coughlin had been forced out of the public arena. This comparison has elicited comment from several observers of American Catholicism. Fr. Andrew Greeley, in *The Catholic Experience* wrote a chapter on "Ryan and Coughlin" in which he said that "the social doctrine tradition represented by John A. Ryan" could not "compete effectively with the splendid rhetoric of Charles Coughlin."[178] In Sheen's presentation for the common man, he combined the best features of both. William Shannon, in his study of *The American Irish*, noted that "Coughlin's appeal was like that of Bishop Sheen twenty-five years later," and the "evil of Father Coughlin might have been avoided if the Church had further spread the teachings of Father Ryan, but few priests had tried to expound Christian doctrine properly."[179] Surely, the example set by Sheen, even during Coughlin's time, refutes that generalization.

And much more was destined to come from Fulton Sheen. On the immediate horizon after the war, however, this representative figure of American Catholicism invested most of his energies in another cause: anti-communism. Of the three anti-American ideologies highlighted by Sheen, communism alone had survived the war, and it now presented the greatest challenge to the American way of life which Sheen continued to champion. The crusade against communism superseded the internationalism of the war years; "by late 1945 internationalism had become a synonym

---

[178] Andrew Greeley, *The Catholic Experience* (Garden City, NY: Doubleday and Co., 1967), p. 250.

[179] William Shannon, *The American Irish* (New York: Collier Books, 1963).

for anti-communism."[180] "A more Catholic America meant an America more conscious of the dangers of communism."[181] The Catholic Church had assumed a position on the forefront of the battle against communism, and this front provided another vehicle for the "simultaneous assertion of loyalty to Church and nation; a way to attain a truly American Catholicism."[182] And on the battlefield of American Catholic anti-communism, there were few better qualified, by knowledge and experience, to lead the crusade than Monsignor Fulton Sheen.

---

[180] Flynn, p. x.

[181] *Ibid.*, p. 224.

[182] David O'Brien, *American Catholics and Social Reform,* pp. 94-95.

CHAPTER FIVE

Ideological Adversary:
The American Catholic Crusade Against Communism, 1930–1960

This all too imminent danger is Bolshevistic and Atheistic
Communism which aims at upsetting the social order and at undermining the very foundation of Christian civilization. In the face of such
a threat, the Catholic Church could not and does not remain silent.
Pope Pius XI, Divini Redemptoris (1937)

The philosophy of communism and to some extent the Revolution of
Communism are on the conscience of the Western world.
Fulton J. Sheen, Communism and the Conscience of the West (1948)

Anticipating the end of the Second World War and the Allied triumph over the forces of "ruthless aggression," the American Catholic hierarchy nevertheless cautioned the faithful against complacency
in victory. The statements of the bishops at the close of the conflict
— "On International Order," "Between War and Peace," and "Man
and the Peace" — all resounded in an atmosphere of continued crisis
as they met the challenges posed by an uncertain peace. In their
efforts to exert their influence in shaping the post-war world, the
bishops warned that only an "alert and informed" public opinion
could secure lasting peace and security.[1] Already in 1945 the long
awaited peace was threatened by a "clash of ideologies." Expressing their grave disappointment, these Church leaders ominously

---

[1] "A Statement on International Order," 1944, Pastoral Letter cited in Hugh J. Nolan,
Pastoral Letters of the U.S. Catholic Bishops (Vol. II), p. 56.

declared, "We are in perhaps the greatest crisis in human history."[2] This new crisis, addressed as the conflict between Russia and the West by the bishops, and christened the "Cold War" by statesmen and politicians, revealed in the aftermath of war a "Soviet totalitarianism no less aggressive against freedom"[3] than the enemy nazi and fascist totalitarianisms of the war years. American Catholicism's suspicions that Soviet Russia would prove to be a "major stumbling block to any 'Pax Christiana'"[4] were being borne out by Stalin's aggressive actions in Eastern Europe. Among the least surprised at this dangerous turn of events was Monsignor Fulton J. Sheen, a leading spokesman for the Church during the war years and a long-time foe of communism. Throughout the thirties, Sheen had been relentless in his criticism of atheistic communism. Years before the Cold War began — in October of 1939, a mere month after the war had commenced — Sheen had foreseen just such a result:

> ...Russia had finally succeeded in turning Europe into a battlefield... the danger to civilization is not the result of a war between Hitler and the Allies. It will be the consequences of that war, when Communism will sweep over Europe. Then the war shall not be between nations, but between philosophies of life.[5]

Fulton Sheen's opposition to communism, voiced early in his career, was a logical outgrowth of both his vocation and the times in which he lived. Anti-communism would become one of his greatest passions. Explaining his own dedication to the cause, he stated that his deep interest was prompted by his training in the "philosophy of St. Thomas Aquinas, which is complete and total

[2]   "Between War and Peace," 1945, *Pastoral Letters* (Vol. II), p. 62.
[3]   "Man and Peace," 1946, *Pastoral Letters* (Vol. II), p. 69.
[4]   George Flynn, *Roosevelt and Romanism*, p. 217.
[5]   Fulton Sheen, "Moscow Makes Confusion for Reds and for Other Nations," *America* (October 28, 1939), p. 61.

in the sense that it embraces God, man and society."[6] Likewise, Sheen viewed communism as a complete philosophy of life, and Sheen's ordination to the priesthood took place just two years after the Bolshevik Revolution, communism's first great triumph. It was only natural that Sheen's interest should be sparked, and he gave himself over to a complete and profound study of communism, eventually reading all of Marx, Lenin and Stalin.[7] When he returned to the United States after studying abroad, he saw and appreciated the danger of communism, especially its appeal to many Americans during the Depression.[8] Thus, while the American nation may have awakened to the full extent of he dangers of communism after the breakdown of the alliance at the end of World War II, Sheen and the Catholic Church had been waging war against the philosophy of communism for years before the advent of the Cold War. Monsignor John Tracy Ellis, in his history of American Catholicism, pointed out the Church's foresight regarding communism: "It is a menace which the Church recognized and denounced far in advance of almost everyone else."[9]

Fulton Sheen's denunciation of communism stemmed from his quest to answer the errors of modern philosophy and bridge the gap separating the Church and the modern world. From the perspective of the Catholic Church in the twentieth century, atheistic communism was the most erroneous and threatening of the modern philosophies. The specter of Marxism had loomed for decades over the course of Catholic history, and fighting the red menace in its various forms had absorbed a good deal of the Church's ener-

---

[6] Fulton Sheen, *Treasure in Clay,* p. 81.

[7] Sheen made this claim in his autobiography, but he often spoke of his intense study of communism in the early days and throughout his career; he spoke of reading all of Lenin, Stalin and the Soviet Constitution, and subscribing to communist publications — believing his best way of combating communism was from a position of strength and being well-informed. See a sensational article written by John F. Cogswell in the *Boston Sunday Post,* April 27, 1937: "Monsignor Sheen Exposes Communism's Threat to the U.S.A."

[8] For the state of American communism during the 1930's, see Harvey Klehr's *The Heyday of American Communism* (New York: Basic Books, Inc., 1984).

[9] John Tracy Ellis, *American Catholicism* (Chicago: University of Chicago Press, 1969), p. 146.

gies. The philosophy of Karl Marx had actually "mesmerized Catholicism... long before the cold war years, Catholics stood in the
vanguard of those dedicated to the eradication of communism."[10]
In America, anti-communism became a dominant impulse of
Catholic life. Beginning in the Depression decade, various Church
leaders advocated the formation of a "united Catholic front to promote Church interests and teachings, to spread acceptance of Christian moral principles, and to defend democratic ideas and institutions against communism and secularism."[11] Consistently on the
front lines of this crusade was Fulton J. Sheen, "the prophet and
philosopher"[12] of American Catholic anti-communism.

  In his study of the Catholic Church and McCarthyism, *God,
Church and Flag*, historian Donald Crosby, S.J., characterized Sheen
as the "prophet and philosopher" of Catholic anti-communism in
contrast to Cardinal Spellman, the "political leader" of the movement: "a super-patriot who pursued a rather thoughtless anti-communism."[13] According to Crosby, Sheen was both "prophetic" and
"philosophical" because "...For nearly twenty years before
McCarthy ever appeared on the scene, Sheen poured forth a gush-
ing stream of books, articles, pamphlets, sermons and speeches
detailing the theory and dynamics of communism, emphasizing its
relation to Roman Catholicism."[14]

  Although Spellman and Sheen are singled out as two of the
best known Catholic prelates of their time, Crosby places them in
the larger context of twentieth century American Catholicism. The
entire American Church mobilized against the forces of communism during the decade of the thirties, when Sheen first emerged
on the national scene as a spokesman for the Church. Fulton
Sheen's anti-communism was part of the general Catholic opposi-

---

[10] Donald Crosby, SJ, *God, Church and Flag*, p. xi.
[11] David J. O'Brien, *American Catholicism and Social Reform*, p. 218.
[12] Crosby, p. 15.
[13] *Ibid.* p. 15.
[14] Crosby confines his references to Sheen to two books, both published in 1948: *Communism and the Conscience of the West* and *Philosophy of Religion*.

tion to Marxism, launched as a religious crusade against a modern manifestation of evil or the spirit of Anti-Christ.[15]

The gospel of anti-communism according to Sheen was always in the mainstream of American Catholicism. Consequently, it featured both good and bad elements of the Church's crusade against communism. Historians have acknowledged that while American Catholics were virtually unanimous in their opposition to communism, there was a wide range of opinions offered as to the reasons for resistance and as to the best means of fighting the communist menace.

On the negative end of the spectrum, Catholic anti-communists could become alarmist, hysterical and even paranoid about their fears of communism. Those who went too far in their crusade — Father Charles Coughlin, the editors of the *Brooklyn Tablet*, and Senator Joseph McCarthy[16] — alienated non-Catholics and created dissension within Catholic ranks. This type of anti-communism would ultimately prove to be counterproductive, damaging the reputation of the Church as Catholics were construed as apologists for fascism, red-baiters and witch hunters. At the opposite end of the spectrum was the more positive brand of Catholic anti-communism, usually associated with the liberal Catholics of *Commonweal* and Father John LaFarge, S.J., an editor of the Jesuit magazine *America*.[17] This type of Catholic anti-communism was always linked with social reform and justice. Rather than merely condemning communism as evil, it advocated the papal program of social reconstruction as the best medicine against communism:

---

[15] Crosby's treatment of the historical background to McCarthyism and the Catholic Church is contained in the first chapter of his book: "The Anti-Communist Impulse in American Catholic Life, 1850-1950." For additional background see David O'Brien's *American Catholics and Social Reform* and James Henessey, SJ's *American Catholics.*

[16] These three examples of negative anti-communism appear often in standard historical assessments.

[17] This "positive" brand is described by David J. O'Brien as representative of the general view of American Catholics during the New Deal years. And Crosby notes that *Commonweal* carried on "warfare" with the conservatives at the *Tablet*, where "far too much of Catholic anti-communism was mindless, hyper-emotional and superpatriotic" (p. 20).

> Throughout the early thirties... anti-communist Catho-
> lics emphasized the need to institute social and economic
> reforms in order to remove the grievances which gave
> communism fruitful soil in which to grow.[18]

Judged by these standards, Fulton Sheen, the popularizer of
American Catholic anti-communism, belongs somewhere in the
middle of this spectrum. Such is the most accurate assessment one
can offer, for Sheen's version of anti-communism defies easy cat-
egorization. As one who crusaded against the communist menace
his public entire life — a period which spanned five decades — he
moved freely across a wide span of what constituted the middle
ground, depending on the times and his audience. The standard
interpretation of Fulton Sheen is that of a zealous and militant anti-
communist, similar to the Knights of Columbus and Cardinal
Spellman:[19]

> Catholicism and America must join together to com-
> bat atheistic communism... the epitome of both
> irreligion and un-Americanism. The good Catholic...
> was one who gave his unstinting support to the efforts
> of both the Church and the nation to the destruction of
> the Communist peril.[20]

But the same Sheen who subscribed to this simple faith could be
charitable and tolerant toward communists, seeking to elevate and
spiritualize their goodness in the spirit of the "new apologetics."
His anti-communism was conventional and extremely repetitive,
but not "mindless." He was appreciated as a worthy adversary by

---

[18] O'Brien, *American Catholics and Social Reform*, p. 83.

[19] Even though Crosby draws a distinction between Spellman as politician and Sheen as
philosopher, he also takes note of the common features of their anti-communism. Fr.
Henessey cites "Catholic War Veterans, the Knights of Columbus, and Fulton Sheen"
as "particularly active anti-communists" (p. 290).

[20] Crosby, pp. 13-16.

leading members of the American Communist Party and demonstrated his thorough mastery of communist philosophy and sources when he entered into public controversies with them.[21]

The same Sheen who "hated communism, but loved the communists" was not above name-calling[22] and was frequently carried away by rhetorical excess or simplistic dualisms. He frequently offered his audience a stark choice between Rome or Moscow; Christianity or Chaos; Christ or Communism; the Cross or the Double-Cross. And in responding to charges that Catholics were fascist sympathizers or red-baiters,[23] he could be fiery, combative, and prone to strident patriotism. Clearly the anti-communist crusade became an overriding passion in Fulton Sheen's life, a passion which bordered on obsession.

Fulton Sheen's preoccupation with communism was essentially ideological. He viewed communism as a complete philosophy of life and sought to refute it with his own ideological beliefs. Because his anti-communist message was ideological, it could be abstract and impractical. He remained consciously detached from most of the political crises that swirled around the subject of domestic communism,[24] and when he did broach an opinion on a political subject, it was often vague and pious. His main goal in speaking out on communism was to educate and inform while alerting America to its dangers, thus obediently following the instructions given him by Pope Pius XI during a private audience in 1935.[25] In bestowing a blessing on Sheen's radio broadcasts, the Pope asked Sheen to speak out on communism "at every opportunity," and

---

[21] This was especially evident in the pamphlets Sheen wrote as direct responses to the statements of Earl Browder and Louis Budenz in 1936 and 1937.

[22] Among Sheen's favorite pejorative images for communists were "dupes," "gangsters," "snakes" and "rats."

[23] See Sheen's pamphlet: "Communism Answers the Questions of a Communist" (1937).

[24] Crosby, pp. 15-16.

[25] The contention that Sheen was asked specifically by Pope Pius XI to speak out against communism appears frequently in the Sheen materials, most notably in Sheen's autobiography and the books written by the Rev. D.P. Noonan: *Missionary with a Mike* and *The Passion of Fulton Sheen.*

Sheen seldom missed one. Throughout his life he tried to maintain a delicate balance between the negative and the positive aspects of the Catholic crusade against communism, although he was not always successful. In *Moods and Truths* (1934), a companion volume to *Old Errors and New Labels*, Sheen made one of his earliest references to the subject of communism:

> Bolshevism, too, is grounded on a very sound Catholic principle, which is the Brotherhood of Man, but it has exaggerated it so far as to leave no room for the Sovereignty of God. And so it is easy to fall into any of these extremes, and to lose one's intellectual balance. The thrill is in keeping it.[26]

As the early reference to communism indicates, maintaining an intellectual balance on the subject was a primary concern. Prior to the Pope's instructions, he occasionally raised the issue of communism from a religious perspective, a logical progression in his refutations of paganism and atheism. In 1933, the *New York Times* reported that Bolshevism was traced to atheism by Sheen: "Communism is the logical extension of a heart and mind that refuse to recognize a God above. There was bound to be this social repercussion."[27] Beginning in 1935, though, communism became one of Sheen's favorite themes, injected into the majority of his radio broadcasts, sermons and books. This anti-communist message was the dominant impulse behind Sheen's public pronouncements from the thirties through the fifties. Although he addressed the subject from many angles, there were several pervasive characteristics of Fulton Sheen's ideological crusade, characteristics which persisted and were sounded repeatedly in his efforts to maintain a balance between extremes while simultaneously offering his own provocative version of American Catholic anti-communism.

---

[26] Fulton Sheen, *Moods and Truths* (Garden City, NY: Garden City Publishing Co., 1950 edition, originally published in 1934 by Appleton-Century Co.), p. 90.

[27] Sheen, cited in the *New York Times*, April 3, 1933.

The first characteristic of Sheen's anti-communist philosophy was that communism's appeal was essentially religious. Even though communism was atheistic, its philosophy fulfilled man's longings for an absolute, especially in the Russian soul. Second, his approach toward communists was charitable, summarized in the dictum, "Hate the sin but love the sinner." Third, Sheen expressed hope and faith that Russia would ultimately be converted back to Christianity (prayers for the return of Russia to Christianity were a staple of Roman Catholic piety). Fourth, Sheen's anti-communism was always linked with his advocacy of social reform and the official Church teaching on social justice. The fifth characteristic was his consistent defense of democratic values and the American way of life, for he perceived communism as equally threatening to the future of the Catholic Church and that of the American nation.

An examination of Sheen's major statements on communism, and how these statements were perceived by the American press — which devoted considerable attention to him — will highlight these characteristics comprising the core of Fulton Sheen's anti-communist gospel.[28] *The Mystical Body of Christ*, published in 1935, contains the first extensive reference to communism. The book, a theological exposition on the doctrine of the Mystical Body, was an attempt to adapt Christian principles to the issues of his age. In the chapter "The Eucharist and the Unity of the Mystical Body," he admonished and encouraged his readers in the spirit of "Catholic Action" to live their faith as a means of halting the spread of communism:

> Catholics have done little so far to be the leaven in the mass... to apply the doctrine of the Eucharistic Brotherhood to their non-Sunday work-a-day lives... it is the failure to live our Communion which is partly respon-

---

[28] The following examination of Sheen's anti-communist views will be constructed around a chronological analysis of his most extensive treatments of communism — supported by materials in the newspaper clipping files, Sheen Archives.

sible for the woes of the day. Communism is a reproach
to our faulty understanding of the Eucharist... a cancer
on society which reminds us of our unfulfilled duty as
Catholics who should be one in economic and social justice.... The communion rail is the most democratic institution on the face of the Earth... the modern world
tries to unite men on the basis of economic equality...
as in Communism.... The Eucharist unites men on the
basis of brotherhood.[29]

Carrying this theme still further, Sheen delivered an address
to the Cleveland Eucharistic Congress in 1935 entitled "The
Church and Communism or the Mystical Body." The main thrust
of his remarks was that only religion could vanquish communism:
"Minds of the future want a complete philosophy of life, and they
find only two: the Church and Communism... and Communism
is a philosophy of life which mobilizes souls for economic and secular ends."[30] This world movement came about as a reaction to the
other extreme error of rugged individualism — the world had swung
too far toward the opposite extreme, which was collectivization and
the forcible organization of chaos which communism provided.
Rather than beginning a new era as it claimed, though, communism was "the dying gasp of a civilization which for 300 years has
forgotten the Kingdom of God and pursued only the things of the
earth."[31] The real danger of communism, then, stemmed not from
its system of economics, but from its status as a religion, the "Ape
of Christianity, like it in all externals but differing in its spirit":

It too has a Bible, which is "Das Kapital" of Karl Marx;
it has its original sin, which is capitalism; it has its Mes-
sianic hope, which is the classless society and the god-

---

[29] Fulton Sheen, *The Mystical Body of Christ*, pp. 373, 367.

[30] Fulton Sheen, "The Mystical Body, or The Church and Communism" printed copy of
Sheen's lecture found in the collection at the Sheen Archives, p. 16.

[31] *Ibid.*, p. 16.

less race; it has its laws of sacrifice, which is class struggle; and it has its priesthood, which is the high commissariat. It is like Christianity in all things save one; it is inspired not by the spirit of Christ but by the spirit of the serpent... the Mystical Body of the Anti-Christ.[32]

Seen in this light, communism could be stopped only by something equally social and communal, the Church: "The Mystical Body of Anti-Christ can be conquered only by the Mystical Body of Christ."[33] Extending this schema of contrast one step further, a standard teaching method employed by Sheen, he called for "Communication over Communism," or "Eucharistic Fellowship over Soviet Comradeship."[34] The Eucharist, Sheen told his audience, makes sacrifice the inspiration of victory. Quoting Matthew 11:12 ("The Kingdom of Heaven suffereth violence and only the violent shall bear it away"), he contrasted the violence of communism toward his neighbor with the violence of Catholicism toward himself and his baser passions.[35] Sheen even claimed that the communists in Russia recognized this weapon of Christianity, quoting "Lunarcharski, the Soviet Commissar of Education":

We hate Christianity and Christians. They preach the love of neighbors and mercy, which is contrary to our principles. Christian love is an obstacle to the development of the Revolution.[36]

In concluding his remarks, Sheen spoke of the future battle between "brotherhood in Christ and comradeship in Anti-Christ." The forces were aligning: "love vs. hate; Moscow and the Kremlin vs. Rome and St. Peter's; the Five Year Plan vs. the Eternal Plan;

---

[32] *Ibid.*, p. 17.
[33] *Ibid.*, p. 27.
[34] *Ibid.*, p. 25.
[35] *Ibid.*, p. 27.
[36] *Ibid.*

the red flag of communism vs. the red sentinel of the Altar; the
Internationale vs. Panis Angelicus." Expressing faith in the power
of Christ and the outcome, he closed with a reminder that "there
will be only one victory, for if Christ wins, we win... and Christ
can't lose!"[37]

The following year Sheen spoke out against communism from
several angles. His "Catholic Hour" broadcast series for 1936, "The
Prodigal World," was filled with references to communism as the
last of the Church's enemies.[38] In this series Sheen joined two premises of his vigilant crusade against communism: the Church's
opposition to communism was balanced by its opposition to the
abuses of monopolistic capitalism; and the Church welcomed the
support of the state in its fight against the communist foe. Communism, said Sheen, was "not a reaction against capitalism, but the
glorification of its worst features, and the ignoring of its better ones":

> The old capitalism made the economic the principal
> basis of civilization. Communism makes it the unique
> basis of civilization. The old capitalism wanted no in-
> terference from the state, but left God and religion alone
> provided they did not interfere. Communism will suf-
> focate the thought of God, extinguish the fires of Di-
> vine love.[39]

Communism grew in popularity, though, because it "satisfied the
need of religion."[40] And because communism was a religion "which
makes the state a god and the factory a place of pilgrimage, it can
only be met by a religion which serves the state by serving God."[41]

---

[37] *Ibid.*, pp. 29, 31.
[38] Fulton Sheen, "The Prodigal World," Catholic Hour Broadcast Series for 1936. Published in pamphlet form by Our Sunday Visitor, Sheen Archives, and in book form by
Alba House (2003). A slightly revised version of this series would be published as the
book *The Cross and the Crisis* (Milwaukee: Bruce Publishing, 1938), and re-released as a
hard bound book in 1977 (Manchester, NH: Ayer Co. Pubs., Inc.).
[39] *Ibid.*, p. 25.
[40] *Ibid.*, p. 26.

The Church was compelled, according to Sheen, to defend man's fundamental liberties, "to be captain of his own fate and destiny, and the right to pray 'Our Father, Who Art in Heaven' instead of 'Soviet Union, which art in Russia'."[42]

Sheen's lectures and sermons, delivered around the nation during 1936, took up another theme as well — that the philosophy of "Americanism" should be enlisted in the opposition to communism, alongside Christianity, because of its insistence on the rights and dignity of man. By thus interjecting patriotism into the discussion, Sheen proposed that a cooperative effort between Catholicism and Americanism would be best equipped to deal with the red menace, and extended his appeal to all Americans:

> I am not begging you to crush communism because it is anti-Catholic. I am speaking as a son of our times.... We oppose communism not only because it is against religion, but because it is opposed to American institutions.... I wonder if America realizes the service we are rendering the Country.[43]

This rhetorical question had elicited one answer — in the affirmative — which commended Sheen for his efforts. The *Catholic News* of New York reported the contents of a letter sent to Sheen by Edward J. Smythe, Executive Secretary of the Protestant Civic Federation: "We are glad to see you take up this issue of communism, for the leaders of the protestant faith are fast asleep to this cancer of the republic... the Catholic Church will be the bulwark against communism in America."[44] The *Scranton Times* also credited Sheen with "performing a great and patriotic service": "the

---

[41] *Ibid.*, p. 28.

[42] *Ibid.*, p. 51.

[43] Sheen lectures cited in *Wisdom*, a publication of the "Trinity League of New York City" (July/August, 1936 and November, 1936), in the newspaper clipping files, Sheen Archives.

[44] New York *Catholic News*, April 6, 1935, in the newspaper clipping files, Sheen Archives.

indictment of the communists by the Rev. gentleman is not too strong. Communists are rats in the American granary."[45]

Sheen's appeal was not limited to the vehement anti-communists who feared the rats in American society, however. A more positive side of Sheen's crusade is evident in a lecture he delivered at the National Catholic School of Social Service. Concentrating on the obvious appeal of communism to the poor, Sheen praised the Catholic effort to counter that appeal by building up a "Christian proletariat." The Catholic strategy was to prove the superiority of the Church's prescriptions for social reform, summarized in the papal encyclicals over the communists' false promises. Citing some success on the part of Catholic social service, he gave the school credit for "keeping back the tides of communism," and suggested that the "whole nation owes them a debt of gratitude for keeping the nation safe."[46]

The indictment of the evils and false promises of communism was balanced by Sheen's charity and open-minded recognition that there was some good in what many communists believed. Despite the fact that "communism has replaced other heresies as the chief enemy of the Church,"[47] Sheen proposed a new attitude in dealing with the communists in his Lenten sermons at St. Patrick's Cathedral. "Instead of constantly haranguing on the evil... let us go out and find what is good in them... then elevate it and spiritualize it."[48] Among communism's good points, he cited "its ideas of justice and service to fellow men," and its recognition that society has a responsibility to provide man's basic needs, and that men were mutually dependent upon one another.[49] This espousal of a greater tolerance for communists generated another favorable impression

[45] *The Scranton Times,* September 21, 1935, in the newspaper clipping files, Sheen Archives.
[46] Fulton Sheen, "The Martyrdom of Man," address delivered to the N.C.S.S.S. on May 4, 1936; a printed copy is located in the Sheen Archives.
[47] *New York Times,* March 30, 1936.
[48] *New York Times,* March 9, 1936.
[49] *New York Times,* March 30 and March 9, 1936.

of Sheen, that his anti-communism could rise above the level of hatred and fear embraced by others. The *New York World Telegram* commented that

> Monsignor Sheen's speeches have not been the customary diatribes, but discussions of the philosophy of communism in which he said that the communists were correct in their protests against social injustice but wrong in their advocacy of violence; right in their idea of service to men, but wrong in their refusal to let individuals call either their souls or their property their own.[50]

Fulton Sheen won his reputation as American Catholicism's most ardent and eloquent adversary of communism during a critical period in the history of the America Communist Party.[51] As a result he became entangled in two public controversies with leaders of the party: Earl Browder and Louis Budenz. Beginning in 1935, the American Communist Party began to change its line in an effort to win new converts by a variety of "front strategies." The "Popular Front" strategy of the international communist structure assumed particular importance in the United States: the "outstretched hand" extended to Catholics. Similarly, the "Democratic Front" tactic sought to form a coalition of reformers opposed to fascism. This was a complete reversal of the Communist Party's attitude toward religion: "no policy better symbolized the idea of the Democratic Front than the Party's attempted reconciliation with Roman Catholics."[52] After years of savagely ridiculing the Catho-

---

[50] *New York World Telegram*, May 10, 1937; newspaper clipping files, Sheen Archives. This same article reported a trip to Europe by Sheen and Al Smith, claiming that they had been "summoned to the Vatican" to discuss the American Catholic crusade against communism.

[51] See Harvey Klehr's *The Heyday of American Communism;* Klehr's book is built upon the premise that the American Communist Party was always controlled by the Soviet Union.

[52] For details, see Klehr, pp. 221-222, and Ralph Lord Roy's *Communism and the Churches* (New York: Harcourt Brace & Co., 1960), especially Chapter 7: "The Outstretched Hand to Roman Catholics."

lic Church and attacking the Vatican's Holy War, the communists launched a vigorous propaganda campaign designed to win the support of Catholic workers. It was in response to this attempted reconciliation and outstretched hand of friendship that Fulton Sheen entered the debate, writing lengthy pamphlets to unveil the communists' lies and deceit. He subjected communism's claims and promises to rigorous scrutiny and found them wanting. He proceeded to reject the false hand of friendship extended by the communists.

In September, 1936, Monsignor Sheen "assailed" Earl Browder, the Executive Secretary of the American Communist Party, during a testimonial dinner sponsored by the Knights of Columbus. Sheen dramatically announced in his talk, "I will now unveil Earl Browder."[53] Sheen attacked Browder and the tactic of the United and Popular Fronts, which he described as a "disguised approach" to trick Americans into the Communist Party. Browder is "offering the kiss of Judas when he says communism is not an enemy of property, the family and religion," and Sheen quoted from the proceedings of the International Congress of the Communist Party in Moscow to reveal the true intent of communism. Communism was bent on revolution and world domination, evident in the civil war raging in Spain: "Sow your Moscow and reap your Spain."[54]

Sheen's attack evoked an immediate reply from Browder in the form of a letter, and the controversy between the two men escalated. The correspondence was made public in the pages of the *Brooklyn Tablet* on September 26.[55] William Z. Foster, the chairman of the Communist National Campaign Committee, entered the fray at Browder's side, protesting Monsignor Sheen's "unjust attack" and requesting that Browder be allowed to reply to Sheen's

---

[53] This incident was reported in the *New York Times*, September 11, 1936. Sheen's speech was also broadcast over the radio station WMCA.

[54] *Ibid.*

[55] *Brooklyn Tablet*, September 28, 1936; newspaper clipping files, Sheen Archives.

charges in a speech at the Catholic University of America. Foster said that Browder was eager to tell students about the tradition of primitive communism during the early centuries of the Catholic Church — "traditions for which the Christian martyrs were crucified by the wealthy Hearsts of that day."[56] Sheen wrote a reply to Mr. Foster stating that he was happy to be noticed by Browder, but he denied that his attack was unjust. He then offered to make arrangements for Browder to speak at the Catholic University under the condition that he make a public statement to the effect that (A) he disapproved absolutely of the communist persecution of Catholics in Spain; (B) that if communism were established in America, it would not close our Catholic Universities, nor our chapels, nor preach that religion is the opium of the people.[57] When Browder did not accept these conditions, the immediate controversy ended, but Monsignor Sheen resolved to continue the struggle and get in the last word. Agreeing that some Catholic workers may have been duped by the new tactics of the communists, he said that this means "I must give this very speech again and warn them they are being deceived."[58]

Not content with merely giving the speech again, Sheen used a lengthy pamphlet — "The Tactics of Communism" — to deliver the next round. The first of several Sheen pamphlets on communism, it employed the question-and-answer format and was filled with communist source material — two qualities which came to characterize the Sheen pamphlet style. "The Tactics of Communism" was originally published in *Sign* magazine in November, 1936, and an editor's note indicated that since Monsignor Sheen's article had more than a "transitory value" it would soon be published in pamphlet form.[59] It was Sheen's hope that by allowing the communists to speak for themselves, they would "hang themselves"

[56] *New York Times*, September 27, 1936.
[57] *Brooklyn Tablet*, September 26, 1936.
[58] *New York Times*, September 27, 1936.
[59] Fulton Sheen, "The Tactics of Communism," *Sign* 16 (November, 1936), pp. 201-204.

when Sheen revealed the inconsistencies, contradictions, trickery and outright lies they employed. In "The Tactics of Communism" Sheen paid special attention to Earl Browder's *What is Communism* and *Lincoln and the Communist.* He quoted directly from communist sources like the Program of the Communist International for 1936, the official organ of the Syndicate of Soviet Workers (Troud), International Correspondence of the Communist Party, and G. Dimitrov's *The Working Class Against Fascism* as he posed, then answered, sixty-one questions.

Sheen concentrated on informing his readers about several facts of communism: that its world goal was a revolution to establish the dictatorship of the proletariat; that its main weapon was violence; that it was against private property and all forms of religion; and that despite Mr. Browder's denials, the American Communist Party took its orders directly from Moscow. Then he proceeded to the more immediate issue of the "United, Common, People's or Popular Front,"[60] which he said was a deceitful ruse. Communism had not changed its essentials, he claimed, only its tactics. The Communist Party would "bore from within" its established fronts to achieve its goal of worldwide revolution. Catholics should be especially sensitive to the communist use of the word "fascism"; it meant "anything that is anti-communist" and was used as a way to disarm and smear their opponents.[61] Here Sheen pointed out that there was no Fascist Party in the United States, but there was indeed a Communist Party, so clearly communism was a greater danger for the country: "the struggle is between communism and anti-communism."[62]

Finally, Sheen declared that communism would be successful in its new tactics only "as long as Americans are gullible enough to be deceived" and let down their guard against "the man who runs a knife in your back." He cautioned his readers to heed the lessons

---

[60] *Ibid.,* p. 203.
[61] *Ibid.,* p. 202.
[62] *Ibid.*

of the Bible — that Judas was the first one in the history of Christianity to use the tactics of the United Front by betraying Christ with a kiss, and, "Our Blessed Lord's warning in Matthew 7:15: 'Beware of false prophets who come to you in the clothing of sheep, but inwardly they are ravening wolves.'"[63]

This pamphlet offers an example of Sheen's tendency to get carried away by his own rhetoric, to lose his intellectual balance and depart from the high road of ideological debate. His name-calling and facile rhetorical points might cause his own credibility to be questioned. In this instance, the "Reverend Gentleman" violated some of his own precepts.

A second Sheen pamphlet, written along similar lines, was "Communism: The Opium of the People,"[64] which appeared first in *The Franciscan* in 1937. In this case Sheen sought to turn the Marxist claim that religion was the opiate of the people on its head to illustrate the fallacy of communism's arguments and claims. In addition to relying on communist sources, this pamphlet is filled with quotations from the social encyclicals of Leo XIII and Pius XI. Sheen's main purpose is to present the Church's social teachings to the workers to undercut the communist appeal. Starting with an historical overview of the origins of communism, Sheen quotes Marx's "Religion is the Opium of the People," the Anti-Religious Institute proceedings of 1934, and *The ABC of Communism* by "N. Bouharin" (Nikolai Bukharin) to demonstrate that communism was grounded in atheism — it was an overtly anti-religious philosophy. According to Sheen, the communists "allege three reasons in support of their contention that religion is the opium of the people": it assists the rich in the exploitation of the poor; it teaches the poor their duties to the rich, thereby assisting the exploitation; and be-

---

[63] *Ibid.*, p. 204.

[64] This two-part article was published in *The Franciscan* 17 (January and February, 1937). A copy of the article is found in the collection at the Sheen Archives. It should also be noted that this article was reprinted and widely distributed, most notably by the Knights of Columbus.

cause religion is passive, it kills any activity whereby man might better his economic lot.[65]

Sheen's methodology in refuting these claims was simply to make counter-assertions of his own: religion was a force of dynamism and activity; the Church never used religion as an opium or to support the status quo. In fact, said Sheen, neither Marx nor Lenin "protested with such justice and with such delicacy and exactness against the exploitation of the poor by the rich as Leo XIII and Pius XI."[66] According to Sheen, communists "accused others of sins in order to cover up their own." Communism was the true "opium of the people because it masks the injustices of Communist exploitation."[67] After gathering his evidence Sheen resorted to some pejorative accusations of his own: the communist was a "capitalist who has greed in his heart but no cash in his pockets."[68] Communism, in addition to creating a form of collective selfishness, then tried to "put the poor to sleep by promising them an earthly paradise."[69] Sheen quoted the communist newspapers in an effort to show that the Soviet worker was worse off than the American — his salary was low, costs were high and he was poorly fed — "the photographs of famine victims alone tell quite a story."[70]

Finally, Sheen offered his readers a contrasting version of the Christian and communist views of man, claiming it was communism, not religion, which destroyed the personality of man, making him subservient to the Party. Relying on a rhetorical question, he asked "which deserves to be called opium, religion or Communism?"[71] and implied that, since he was not convinced by the com-

---

[65] Fulton Sheen, "Communism: The Opium of the People," Part I, *The Franciscan* (January, 1937), pp. 6-7.
[66] *Ibid.*, Part I, p. 8.
[67] *Ibid.*, Part II, p. 8.
[68] *Ibid.*
[69] *Ibid.*
[70] *Ibid.*, Part II, p. 10.
[71] *Ibid.*, Part II, p. 24.

munist war on religion, which was based on force rather than intelligence, neither should the intelligent reader be convinced:

> We have seen their anti-religious museums; we have
> read their anti-God literature; but not all that we have
> seen and heard them do and say against religion has
> convinced us that there is no God. They have only con-
> vinced us that there is a Devil![72]

This pamphlet was also representative of Sheen's style. He
sought to disarm his communist opponents by engaging in ideological jousts. He could be defensive and simplistic even as he displayed his knowledge of communist sources. In the final analysis
he often resorted to platitudes and cliches. It should be remembered, though, that his forte was popularization and that he was
preaching to an audience which was generally predisposed to accept the "wisdom" of the Catholic Church as presented by Monsignor Sheen.[73]

"Communism Answers the Questions of a Communist,"[74]
written in 1937 as a lengthy reply to Louis Budenz, editor of the
Daily Worker in New York City, was the culmination of Sheen's
efforts as an anti-communist pamphleteer. This second public controversy between Sheen and a leader of American Communism
began with an editorial written by Budenz in the *Daily Worker* on
December 25, 1936: "Who Are the Real Fighters for Peace and
Goodwill to Men?"[75] This editorial was a communist message of
peace to the Catholic people: "Communists Hold Out Hand of

---

[72] *Ibid.*

[73] Even though Sheen's pamphlets were designed to appeal to the widest possible audience,
they always appeared under the auspices of the Church — in Catholic magazines and
periodicals, or published by Catholic organizations.

[74] Fulton Sheen's "Communism Answers the Questions of a Communist" was published
by the Paulist Press. The citations which follow are taken from this pamphlet; a copy is
part of the collection at the Sheen Archives. The N.C.W.C. News Service also published
Sheen's reply as a series of six articles. See *Catholic Action* 19 (February, 1937).

[75] A copy of this article from the *Daily Worker* is contained in the newspaper clipping files,
Sheen Archives.

Fellowship to All Enemies of War and Oppression."[76] Budenz took up the matter of the Catholic spokesmen who criticized communists and singled out "Monsignor Fulton J. Sheen of the Catholic University in Washington" as the "most persistent of these spokesmen."[77] The remainder of the message was devoted to replying to Sheen's December 14 sermon in which the Monsignor had recognized communism's good points but went on to repudiate its tactic of calling Catholics anti-communist "fascists."[78] Budenz challenged Sheen to prove his statements and once again proceeded to offer the outstretched hand to American Catholics.[79]

Sheen used the Budenz message as an opportunity to revive a tradition practiced by American Church leaders in the nineteenth century, carrying on public debates and controversies with one's opponents in the interest of publicizing one's views.[80] He wrote a long reply to Budenz entitled "Communism Answers the Questions of a Communist" and sent it along with a request that it be printed in the *Daily Worker* as Sheen's official response.[81] Although Sheen's request was not granted, the pamphlet did receive a wide circulation in Catholic circles. The Paulist Press printed it as a forty-page pamphlet comprising Sheen's detailed responses to eight questions raised by Budenz. A brief review of the highlights of this pamphlet should provide some insight into Sheen's skill as a controversialist and debater. From one important vantage point, Sheen's effort was successful. Louis Budenz was so impressed by it that he renounced communism and returned to the Catholic Church in 1946 — a delayed reaction, to be sure, but one which gave Sheen considerable publicity as a great convert-maker.

---

[76] Budenz, *This is My Story*, p. 154.

[77] *Ibid.*, p. 155.

[78] *Ibid.*, pp. 155-156.

[79] *Ibid.*

[80] For example, Bishop John Hughes of New York engaged in several public debates and controversies with Protestants during the nineteenth century.

[81] See Budenz, p. 158. Budenz referred to Sheen's pamphlet as a "definite and devastating rebuttal to my queries... replete with damaging admissions of Soviet crimes and crudities taken from the official Soviet press."

The method of Sheen's attack in his pamphlet was to allow communism to speak for itself. Among the sources he quoted extensively were *Pravda* and *Izvestia*, Soviet newspapers; International Press Correspondence; and official communist spokesmen, including Dimitrov, Ercoli and Browder. Sheen charged that the article by Mr. Budenz contained "not one single fact, but only exaggerated claims and promises,"[82] and proceeded to review what he saw as the dismal communist record in Russia. Rather than acting as a friend to the downtrodden, the communist government executed peasants, paid its workers starvation wages (as opposed to the "living wage" championed by the Catholic Church), and undermined the efforts of Soviet citizens to "keep the home together."[83] Despite the defects of capitalism, said Sheen, the American worker was better off than the Soviet, enjoying a higher standard of living, and greater freedoms like the right to strike.[84]

Moving on to the subject of foreign policy, Sheen pointed to the Soviet fondness for "double-talk": they might talk peace, but in reality, "Russia was eager for war." As events in Spain had demonstrated, "to say that Communism is for peace is nothing short of nonsense."[85] Posing a familiar rhetorical question, Sheen added:

> Are class struggle, revolution, and destruction the paths to peace? And if it be answered in the language of Dimitrov, that it is a "war for peace," may I ask what kind of peace the world will have after a world revolution?[86]

Sheen suggested that this communist solution of peace "makes me suspect communism, much in the same way that I suspect the love of a husband who immediately after the marriage ceremony begins

---

[82] Sheen, "Communism Answers the Questions of a Communist," p. 8.

[83] *Ibid.*, pp. 9-13.

[84] *Ibid.*, p. 41.

[85] *Ibid.*, pp. 14-15.

[86] *Ibid.*, p. 16.

beating the wife."[87] Although he backed up some of his charges with evidence from communist sources, Sheen also displayed a fondness for these trite analogies, which tended to undercut the value of his polemic and the seriousness of his purpose.

Returning to a familiar theme — that communism was right in its protests but wrong in its reforms — Sheen replied to Budenz: "I can protest social injustice without being a communist,"[88] for communism had no monopoly on protest. As a proponent of Catholic social reform, Sheen implied that he had demonstrated the superiority of the Catholic program, for unlike the communists, the Catholics did not resort to violence. In this regard, he specifically addressed the question of Stalin's violence, purges, and executions to eliminate his rivals:

> It is not at all unlikely that if Stalin continues in power for another five years, either Dimitrov, Litvinoff, or Radek, and possibly all three, will be executed by Stalin the same as Kamenev and Zinoviev, both of whom stood in the way of Stalin's passion for power.[89]

The heart and soul of "Communism Answers the Questions of a Communist" was Sheen's resounding "no" to Budenz' invitation to join the People's Front. In trying to refute the communist charges that he and other Catholics were soft on fascism, Sheen got carried away by his own inflammatory rhetoric, and responded to the communists' name-calling with some slurs of his own. When the communists called fascism a "slimy" movement, Sheen shot back that communism was just as slimy, if not more so. "Because I am not a communist, it does not follow that I am a fascist.... Communism and fascism are fruits of the same tree of the totalitarian state."[90] The communists were guilty of false propaganda, as were

---

[87] *Ibid.*, pp. 16-17.
[88] *Ibid.*, p. 17.
[89] *Ibid.*, p. 19.
[90] *Ibid.*, p. 24.

the fascists, for "the Catholic Church always comes in between the fire of both."[91] The "claptrap of saying that if we do not take sides in the Spanish Civil War we are 'enemies of democracy' must be stopped."[92] He accused the communists of waving the word fascism in front of him "the same way bullfighters wave a communist (red) flag before the bull to enrage him."[93] But Sheen's response indicates that he was becoming outraged at the charges — that "bogey fascism again."[94] The United Front of the communists, he continued, was "a camouflage and a deceit":

> And lest anyone live under an illusion that communism has ceased to be communistic because of a new front, Manuilsky warns — only downright scoundrels... and hopeless idiots can think that by means of the United Front tactics that communism is capitulating to social democracy.[95]

Expressing his surprise that a leading communist like Budenz was not more familiar with communist literature,[96] Sheen smugly implied that his own expert knowledge had enabled him to unmask the communist plot, and he refused the offer of the "outstretched hand":

> We Catholics cannot join your United Front because we have found you out. We know the Front is only a front, and we think the less of communism for insulting our intelligence.[97]

Sheen closed his reply with a mixture of civility and shrill warnings to all Americans to beware of the communist menace.

---

[91] *Ibid.,* p. 25.
[92] *Ibid.,* p. 26.
[93] *Ibid.,* p. 27.
[94] *Ibid.,* p. 33.
[95] *Ibid.,* pp. 35-36.
[96] *Ibid.,* p. 30.
[97] *Ibid.,* p. 38.

Addressing his opponent as "my dear Sir," he said "I believe many communists are in good faith, and here I include you Mr. Budenz." He also added his thanks: "You have done Americans a great service by asking me these questions, and I have done communism a great service by answering them with facts."[98] But then he offered two reasons "why Catholics and all Americans must refuse to join with communists": because the tactic of the United Front was deceitful, and because communism was destructive of all democratic rights which America holds dear "...when they use the word liberty, they mean belly-crawling subservience to the Red leaders."[99] Offering a final suggestion to Catholic workers, who might entertain thoughts of communism in good faith as an answer to their woes, Sheen asked them to be wary of being "dragged into the role of dupes for communism." In an unequivocal, dramatic declaration, he concluded:

> We know your tactics from your documents, we know your purpose from your writings, we know your failures through Mexico, Spain and Russia. No! We will not join with you. We prefer to be loyal to our God and to our Country.[100]

This pamphlet is a classic example of the best and the worst of Fulton Sheen's style of anti-communism; though trying to maintain his intellectual balance, he often lost it and damaged his own credibility when he followed his predilection for extreme language and images. The Catholic press generally praised Sheen's efforts, however, indicating that he was quite successful when preaching to the already converted. *Catholic Action* claimed that Sheen's pamphlet "convicted communism with its own statements"; that his refutation was "brilliant"; and that aside from their great "inherent value" his articles had an added worth because of their timeliness

---

[98] *Ibid.*, pp. 35-36.
[99] *Ibid.*, p. 38.
[100] *Ibid.*, pp. 46-47.

in responding to Moscow's "insidious propaganda."[101] On a more general level, Rev. Dr. George Johnson, Director of the N.C.W.C. Department of Education applauded Sheen's efforts on behalf of social justice and against communism. The Church's conclusions on the social question were acceptable only on the basis of its premises, and those premises were not understood. One who was working to correct that by making the Church's position clear was Sheen: "It is for this reason that I for one believe that the polemic used by Monsignor Fulton Sheen is so promising."[102]

The Monsignor's polemic was part of the Church's larger campaign against communism in 1937. Pius XI issued his encyclical on "Atheistic Communism," *Divini Redemptoris*, in March 1937, and the American Catholic Church enthusiastically participated in the anti-communist crusade. The leading Catholic journals in the United States were obsessed with communism, and the general treatment of the subject was in keeping with Sheen's, and reflected the Pope's sense of urgency and alarm as well.

The Catholic Church had characterized Communism as deceitful, diabolical and godless from the beginning; Pope Leo XIII spoke of the philosophy of communism in terms like satanic, demonic, and a fatal plague upon mankind. Pius XI's presentation in *Divini Redemptoris* echoed the same sentiments:

> ...the communism of today... conceals itself in a false and messianic idea. For the first time in history, we are witnessing a struggle, cold-blooded in purpose and mapped out to the last detail, between man and "all that is called God." Communism is by its nature anti-religious.[103]

The Pope stated that in the face of such a threat, the Church would

[101] *Catholic Action* 19 (February, 1937), pp. 4-5.
[102] Rev. Johnson, "Social Justice and Communism," *Catholic Action* 19 (June, 1937), p. 18. Johnson concluded "He has succeeded in causing a large number of people to divest themselves of their smugness and to re-examine the fundamentals of their position."
[103] Pope Pius XI, *Divini Redemptoris*, cited in *Seven Great Encyclicals*, pp. 180, 185.

not remain silent, and Fulton Sheen heeded this advice without reservation.

There was a significant amount of publicity developing around Sheen in 1937: that he was communism's #1 enemy, and that his revelations about communism's sinister aims were causing consternation among members of the Party in the United States.[104] Always ready to contribute to the public discussion, Sheen himself announced dramatically that he was on the "Reds' death list," and had received several letters warning him to "lay off."[105] Undaunted, however, he vowed to continue his campaign. Pleased that his pamphlets and speeches were having such an effect, he said that he would be "aggrieved if his name were not on the list," for it proved that the communists were taking him seriously. "I'm their greatest propagandist," said Sheen, because "I'm publicizing their entire system, not camouflaging it.... their policy is to conceal the truth until they are ready to strike."[106] Reiterating a spirit of Christian charity, Sheen continued:

> I don't hate them. In fact, I'm rather fond of them. What
> I don't like is their system.... My attitude is like that of
> a physician. He hates the typhoid, but loves the patients,
> and tries to cure them. As a Christian, I'm committed
> to the solemn obligation to love the communists. I'd like
> to make Americans of them.[107]

This metaphor of Sheen as physician, dedicated to preserving the health of the Church and the American nation, was evident in his radio broadcast series for 1937 also: "Our Wounded World." After diagnosing the disease as "the slavery and class

---

[104] For an example of this type of publicity, see the *Boston Sunday Post*, April 25, 1937. Much of this publicity was generated by Sheen himself.

[105] This claim about the death list was made by Sheen at a lecture he gave in Pittsburgh sometime in 1937, after his pamphlet was published. An article with the details of the lecture is preserved in the Scrapbook of "Joseph F. Sheen of Chicago," Sheen Archives.

[106] *Ibid.*

[107] *Ibid.*

struggle consequent upon godlessness and the denial of the spirit,"[108] he expressed his compassion for the afflicted: "I bear no malice toward any communist in the world, though I regard communism as destructive of culture, patriotism and civilization."[109] Communism has thrived on the abuses of capitalism, but their remedy was wrong. Democracy was better medicine, aided by what Sheen called a more revolutionary cure: the Church's program of social reform and the spirit of the Beatitudes.[110]

The two books published by Fulton Sheen in 1938 — *The Cross and the Crisis* and *Liberty, Equality and Fraternity*[111] — were preoccupied with the threat of communism. Although they offered little that was new, because they were printed versions of Sheen's radio broadcasts, they kept his anti-communist crusade alive. He continued to advocate an alliance of Christianity and democracy in the face of the communist peril, encouraging his readers to rally round the Church, God, and the nation's tradition of freedom. Acknowledging the danger posed by nazism and fascism, he stated that his principal concern was communism, since it was "endowed with a missionary activity and was bent on world revolution."[112] Communism's promises were "sheer illusion," for it offered only "forced tranquility"; true peace and redemption would come only through the Church and the Cross.[113]

Liberty, Equality and Fraternity presented a description of the Church's program for social reform, but its main emphasis was communism, which Sheen claimed "had been tried and found wanting."[114] That a refutation of communism was Sheen's main objec-

---

[108] Fulton Sheen, "Our Wounded World" (1937), pamphlet published by Our Sunday Visitor, p. 28.

[109] *Ibid.*, pp. 87-88.

[110] *Ibid.*, p. 42. Sheen contrasted the Church's "revolution of love" with communism's "revolution of violence."

[111] *The Cross and the Crisis* (Milwaukee, 1938) and *Liberty, Equality and Fraternity* (New York, 1938).

[112] Fulton Sheen, *The Cross and the Crisis*, pp. 32-33.

[113] *Ibid.*, p. 145.

[114] Fulton Sheen, *Liberty, Equality and Fraternity*, p. 49.

tive in writing this book is apparent in the bibliography; all sixteen
pages of it were devoted to the subject of communism.[115] This an-
notated bibliography indicated Sheen's broad reading habits, and
ranged from such secular sources as Congressional reports, Elizabeth Dilling's *The Red Network*, and Leon Trotsky, to more philosophical and religious works written by Christopher Dawson,
Waldemar Gurian, Jacques Maritain and Frank Sheed. Chapter VI
on "The Trojan Horse" was a slightly updated version of "Communism Answers the Questions of a Communist." Sheen said that
in Gospel language, the "Democratic Front is the wolf in the clothing of the sheep."[116] The newest tactic employed by the communists was the Trojan Horse, as acknowledged by Dimitrov himself
in a speech to the World Communists at the Moscow Congress.
Continuing in the same strain of rhetoric he had used to disarm
Louis Budenz, Sheen said:

> Communism is urged to wheel the Trojan Horses into
> our labor unions, religious organizations, political par-
> ties… under the guise of a peaceful United Front, until
> it can tear off its mask and turn the country over to a
> barbarous civil war such as they instigated in Spain, so
> that it may emerge victorious and, thus honor their be-
> loved Comrade Stalin.[117]

In place of the old "bogey" fascism, Sheen defended himself against
the charge of red-baiter, by turning the charges around and adding some simple illustrations of his own:

> If it be red-baiting to bring out these facts, then where
> lies America's right to self-preservation? Is the doctor
> who takes out a ruptured appendix an appendix-

[115] *Ibid.*, "Selected Bibliography on Communism," pp. 171-187.
[116] *Ibid.*, p. 88.
[117] *Ibid.*, p. 91.

baiter?... why does no one ever think of calling the communists fascist-baiters?[118]

This type of invective served to demonstrate that Sheen was very defensive about the charges leveled against Catholic anti-communists, and it did nothing to dissuade those who suspected Catholic motives. For good measure, he added a little patriotism and piety to his message, reminding his fellow Catholics "to be conscious of our duty to America, to preserve its freedoms by preserving its faith in God."[119]

This strain of Americanism and patriotism became even more pronounced during the war years. When the United States was allied with the Soviet Union against the Axis powers, Sheen continued his attack against the philosophy of communism unabated, but drew a distinction between the Soviet government and the Russian people. Our ultimate goal, said Sheen, must be the reform of Russia, and he looked forward to a post-war revival of the religious spirit in Russia: "The truly Catholic attitude toward Russia must not be such that it will condemn the sinner as to prevent his conversion."[120] During the war, Sheen balanced his hostility and wariness toward communism's ultimate designs on the free world with his love of the Russian people and prayers for their conversion. In "Moscow: The Second Munich?" he rang his alarmist bell to tell the American nation to be vigilant against communism.

Sheen also rose to the defense of Poland, "the bastion of Christianity in Europe," lest it become a victim once again in the event that Moscow would unleash a "Third World War."[121] No good would ever come from appeasing the Soviets, for the "Hammer might turn out to be the Hammer of Destruction; the Sickle, the Sickle of Death."[122] Seeking to deny the charge that he was anti-

---

[118] *Ibid.,* p. 97-98.

[119] *Ibid.,* p. 135.

[120] Fulton Sheen, "Soviet Russia May Be Helped, But Russia Must Be Reformed," *America* 65 (October, 1941), p. 35.

[121] Fulton Sheen, "Moscow: The Second Munich?" *Sign* 23 (November, 1943), p. 198.

[122] *Ibid.,* p. 200.

Russian, Sheen explained that "the Russian soul is deeply religious. Our bond with Russia is in the people, not in the politics; it is with the nation, not with the state; it is with humanity, not communism."[123]

Sheen's suspicion of Soviet motives and its hostility towards religion was apparent when he rose to the defense of the Vatican against charges in *Izvestia*, the communist government's newspaper.[124] He first turned the pro-fascist charges back upon the Soviets, who "gave the Nazis a green light in the pact of 1939 — to extend fascism all over Europe." In contrast, the Vatican had condemned communism, fascism and nazism in three encyclicals, which was a matter of public record, said Sheen. This attack by *Izvestia* was just another example of the clever misuse of words employed by the Church's enemies. In the past, the Vatican had been called fascist by the communists, communist by the nazis, and anti-fascist by the fascists. Since the Vatican could hardly be all three, this was proof that the Vatican was "opposed to all anti-religious ideology." Issuing a dire warning that the threat posed by communism was imminent, Sheen concluded:

> The time is now five minutes to twelve. America must be prepared for Russia's defection from the common cause and the de-Christianization of Europe: The time is not far distant when the press of America will take from its files the strong, stirring words of the President of the U.S.: "The Soviet Union is a dictatorship as cruel and as absolute as any other dictatorship on the face of the earth."[125]

When the hopes for world peace collapsed in the new rivalry between the superpowers in 1945, Sheen moved into the second

---

[123] *Ibid.*, p. 201.

[124] Sheen's reply to the attack launched by *Izvestia* was covered in the press. The *Tablet* article (from which the following citations are taken) headlined "Attack by *Izvestia* on Vatican Answered by Monsignor Sheen," February 5, 1944.

[125] *Ibid.*

phase of his crusade against communism, defined by the atmosphere of the Cold War. Sheen's philosophy was consistent with his earlier efforts against the menace of communism, but now his cause was more popular with the entire American nation. During the Cold War years, Sheen spoke out on many of the issues of paramount importance to Catholic Americans. Anti-communism became "virtually a way of life," and Catholics "would receive nothing but encouragement from a large part of the American press and electorate," who shared the same obsession.[126] Regarding Poland as a "vivid symbol of the Church's struggle,"[127] Sheen demanded justice, and saw the issue as a test of the "sincerity of the Atlantic Charter."[128] After Poland fell behind the Iron Curtain, Sheen persisted in his calls for Poland's freedom, and that of the other Eastern European nations, although he offered no specific proposals beyond United Nations consideration of the issue. In a Lenten sermon in 1948, he called for "a miracle even greater than Easter… to roll up the Iron Curtain," for "we are driven into the catacombs in Latvia, Estonia, Poland, Romania, Lithuania, Hungary and Czechoslovakia."[129]

Another concern of the American Catholic Church, and Fulton Sheen, was the suffering and persecution of Catholics in the Soviet satellite nations, especially martyrs like Archbishop Alojzije Stepinac of Yugoslavia and Cardinal Joseph Mindszenty in Hungary.[130] Addressing a gathering of the Holy Name Society in 1948, Sheen lauded the "courage of Mindszenty, who knew he was marked for death, but returned willingly to Hungary to be crucified."[131] Later in the fifties, Sheen devoted one of his television shows to this "Dry Martyr of Hungary"; unlike the old wet martyrs, who shed their blood, the Bolsheviks had created "dry

---

[126] Crosby, pp. 8-13.

[127] *Ibid.*, p. 9.

[128] Sheen, cited in the *New York Times,* January 24, 1944.

[129] Sheen, cited in the *New York Times,* March 29, 1948.

[130] See Crosby, pp. 10-13.

[131] Sheen, cited in the *New York Times,* February 14, 1948.

martyrs, who suffer brainwashing and mental torture for their faith."[132]

These Sheen pronouncements on political issues like Poland and the Soviet satellites were confined to protests and platitudes. A good example was his position on the Italian elections of 1948 and the growing strength of the Communist Party there — an issue of particular concern to the Vatican.[133] In a sermon at St. Patrick's Cathedral, Sheen urged American Catholics to write to their friends and relatives in Italy, warning them "not to be deceived by the lies of the communists."[134] If Italy went communist, said Sheen, "the head of the Christian may be beaten with a hammer, and the heart of the Christian pierced by the sickle."[135]

Two issues of special interest to Sheen, which he addressed frequently during the next decade, were the United Nations and the "Voice of America." Even before the U.N. was formally established, Sheen had expressed support for the idea of "an international organization which will respect the rights of God, assure mutual dependence of peoples, impose fidelity to agreements, and safeguard the liberty and dignity of the human person."[136] Sheen suggested that this international organization be composed of three parts: a legislative and executive body; a coercive body; and a judicial body composed exclusively of representatives of religious groups."[137] Sheen said that one international spiritual influence, the Catholic Church, should definitely be represented, but left to his "Jewish and Protestant friends their right to nominate their own representa-

---

[132] This show on Cardinal Mindszenty was broadcast in 1957; a printed transcript of the show can be found in *The Church, Communism and Democracy*, a collection of Sheen's television programs (New York: Dell Publishing Company, 1964), p. 50.

[133] See Fogarty, *The Vatican and the American Hierarchy*, pp. 334-335.

[134] Sheen, cited in the *New York Times*, February 7, 1949.

[135] *Ibid.*

[136] This concept was first expressed by Sheen in an article "Peace, What Shall It Be?" in *PIC* (an entertainment magazine), May 27, 1941. It was a three part article in which representatives of America's religious faiths expressed their views on peace; the other leaders featured were Rabbi Stephen Wise and Methodist Bishop G. Bromley Oxnam. A copy of the article is contained in the collection in the Sheen Archives.

[137] *Ibid.*

tives."[138] Of course, the United Nations never lived up to Sheen's expectations, and although he continued to support the concept of an international peacekeeping body, he was quick to criticize its failings. The United Nations' chief failing, according to Sheen, was the fact that it allowed the Soviet Union to be a member. Sheen had wanted Russia excluded from membership unless she reformed. Calling for action in 1949, he urged America to "wake up, and keep the issue of illegal seizures of nations by the Soviets before the international forum." By coming to the aid of these poor nations, which had fallen from the "frying pan of Nazism into the more terrible fire of communism," America would live up to its ideals as "the defender of the righteous."[139] In his "Bishop Sheen Writes" column, he wrote on the general subject of "The United Nations" and expressed the "good idea of forming a New United Nations, in which no nation would be admitted unless it had by free suffrage elected… its own state. This would, of course, eliminate Russia and its puppets."[140] And in 1957, on the subject "Russia and the Hungarians," he declared that "great moral bodies such as the U.N. have lost the moral integrity to drive buyers and sellers out of the Temple," and suggested that "to show Russia that the deportation of citizens is wrong, Russia should be deported from the United Nations."[141]

Expressing similar doubts about the "Voice of America," Sheen was especially concerned as a broadcaster that the Voice was not as effective as it could be. It would be more effective, he said, if it understood the psychology of the Russian people, and appealed to the "Russian soul," rather than talking about the superiority of the American economy and its prosperity.[142] Because the Russian people were anxious to throw off the yoke of communism, they

---

[138] *Ibid.*
[139] Sheen, cited in the *New York Times*, February 7, 1949.
[140] "Bishop Sheen Writes," December 5, 1954. Copies of Sheen's newspaper columns are found in the collection at the Sheen Archives.
[141] "Bishop Sheen Writes," January 27, 1957.
[142] Sheen, cited in the *New York Times*, June 26, 1949.

could be induced to do so by the "Voice of America," but not "by merely political broadcasts, for politics alone can never fire the souls of men."[143] The "Voice of America" could defeat communism from within Russia, according to Sheen, "If its directors really believed that most people think seriously about God."[144] Sheen's own efforts on behalf of Russia's conversion back to Christianity concentrated on the spiritual aspirations of the Russian people. His faith in the Russian soul, and a real religious renaissance in Russia, colored many of his statements.[145]

Fulton Sheen's best statement on the subject of communism, and the crowning achievement of his efforts as a Catholic anti-communist, was *Communism and the Conscience of the West*, his book published in 1948.[146] One of his more popular and intellectual books, it combined his well-known charitable approach toward Communists with his growing conviction that the errors of the western world were responsible for the rise of communism, and that only a firm resolution to reform would halt its extension. In contrast to the deteriorating national climate of loyalty oaths, charges of subversion, and an anti-intellectual and compulsive super-patriotism, Sheen's views were fair-minded and perceptive. A good example of Fulton Sheen's better side, it is a significant improvement over his statements made during the thirties, relatively free of the pejorative comments and combative style associated with the old "Public Enemy #1" of communism.[147] This modified style is

[143] Fulton Sheen, "Will Russia Survive?" in *Crisis in History*, a pamphlet collection of Sheen essays published by the Catechetical Guild and Educational Society of St. Paul, Minnesota, 1952, p. 60. Copies of this pamphlet are found in the collection at the Sheen Archives.

[144] *Ibid.*

[145] One strange example of Sheen's comments on the possible spiritual renaissance in Russia was reported in the *New York Times*, May 12, 1947. While speaking to an F.B.I. group, Sheen spoke of the communists' fear of the revival of religious feeling in Russia; the communists "attack the mother of us all, because she is the one who crushed the head of the serpent, and can just as well put her foot on the head of the bear."

[146] Sheen, *Communism and the Conscience of the West* (Indianapolis and New York: Bobbs-Merrill Co., 1948).

[147] See Sheen's *Treasure in Clay*, p. 87.

apparent in a passage from his chapter on "How to Meet Communism":

> Toward the deluded people who believe the lies of communism there must be on our part a recognition of their good instincts and passion for social justice. Deluded though they are, they are nevertheless unconscious and involuntary instruments of the Holy Spirit. Our task must be to educate the naïve, for as their attachment to communism grows in ignorance, so will it decrease with education. They must be shown that their basic craving for community and social amelioration are better served within the framework of democracy and the fellowship of a redeemed society where reigns the spirit of Love sent to us by the Father and the Son.[148]

Although there is nothing startling or new here, Sheen's more pastoral side comes through.

Communism and the Conscience of the West received favorable reviews in both the Catholic and the secular press. The *Commonweal*[149] noted that Monsignor Sheen faced communism not as an economic or political concept, but as a philosophy. Though he avoids calling it "anti-Christian," he considers it a "secularization or de-divinization of Christianity."[150] One of the book's strengths was the fact that Sheen did not limit his fight to prayers and meditation, but instead offered "practical moral advice on how to fight communism in the economic, political, educational, moral and religious fields":

> He asks for diffusion of private property, workers share in profits, management and ownership, and perhaps his most interesting notion is for "chaplains" in all types and

---

[148] Sheen, *Communism and the Conscience of the West*, p. 136.

[149] Review of Sheen's book by Max Fischer, *Commonweal* 50 (May 7, 1948), pp. 81-82.

[150] *Ibid.*, p. 81.

sizes of industry with functions like those of army chaplains.[151]

But there was also a weakness in Sheen's book, said the reviewer:
"Monsignor Sheen does not cover the ugly problems of power politics and military decisions in the contents of his book."[152] This
"weakness" was characteristic of Sheen throughout his life, but it
was a conscious omission by a priest who was a popularizer, not a
politician.

Sheen's popularization was appreciated as being more substantial by James A. McWilliams, S.J., who reviewed *Communism
and the Conscience of the West* in *New Scholasticism*, a scholarly journal devoted to philosophy.[153] According to McWilliams, Monsignor Sheen's theme was "genuinely philosophical," and his exposition was "pungent and provocative," designed to "stir the reader
to personal participation in the crusade against the menace."[154] "Not
philosophers alone, but the entire public should be grateful for this
objective picture of the present scene… which expresses the hypocrisy of monopolistic capitalism as well as that of atheistic communism."[155] Sheen's strength here was perceived in his call for religious reform and revival: "the author could not be expected to give
a program and timetable for political, economic and military moves
against Russia." The ideological attack was clearly Sheen's forte,
and the reviewer praised the book as an arsenal of "live ammuni-
tion" in the realm of ideas.[156]

In the book review section of the *New York Times*, Sheen was
praised for an "exceedingly careful and accurate analysis of the philosophy of communism and an equally careful and devastating
analysis of historical liberalism," presented with "a passion which

---

[151] *Ibid.*, p. 82.
[152] *Ibid.*
[153] James A. McWilliams, SJ, review of Sheen's book in *New Scholasticism* 22 (October, 1948), pp. 465-467.
[154] *Ibid.*, p. 466.
[155] *Ibid.*
[156] *Ibid.*

is both refreshing and necessary."[157] In addition, the review stated that "Monsignor Sheen shows here a development into something of the stature of a prophet."[158] Especially impressive was the intellectual foundation of the book, apparent in Sheen's citations and command of the current literature on communism: "the author has read widely and well." To his credit, he read not merely Roman Catholic authorities, but "Protestants like Reinhold Niebuhr and Paul Tillich," and works by Toynbee, Lippmann, and Mumford.[159] This high opinion of Sheen's work was echoed in the New York *Daily News*, where Sheen's views were called "most enlightened" and persuasive: "if anti-communists around the world could bring themselves to follow the Sheen prescription for the next decade, a calamitous Third World War might be sidetracked."[160]

Although much in *Communism and the Conscience of the West* had appeared in Sheen's repertoire before, the central idea "that the philosophy of communism and to some extent the Revolution of Communism are on the conscience of the Western world"[161] was perceived as new. As the reviews indicate, his thesis was seen as a novel idea in an age when many Americans were caught up solely in pointing out the grievous errors of communism. Despite appearances, the ideas expressed in *Communism and the Conscience of the West* were consistent with the evolution of Sheen's philosophy of anti-communism over the previous years, and harkened back to his earlier *The Cross and the Crisis*. Sheen always explained the rise of communism as being related to the growing secularization of the West:

> As Western civilization loses its Christianity it loses its superiority... the ideology of communism rose out of the

---

[157] Bernard Iddings Bell, "Faith versus the Economic Animal," *New York Times Book Review,* April 18, 1948.

[158] *Ibid.*

[159] *Ibid.*

[160] "Monsignor Sheen Views Communism and Capitalism," *New York Daily News,* April 26, 1948; a copy of this review is located in the newspaper clipping files, Sheen Archives.

[161] Sheen, *Communism and the Conscience of the West,* p. 7.

secularized remnants of a Western civilization whose soul was once Christian. Communism is, therefore, as Waldemar Gurian has said, both an "effect and a judgment on the Western world."[162]

Reviewing his theories on history, Sheen traced the decline of liberalism to the new era characterized by "a passion for the absolute" an the ongoing struggle between "Christ and Anti-Christ."[163] Sheen's contention that the rise of communism was proof of the power of the demonic and the persistence of evil in history was buttressed with support from Russian thinkers like Dostoevsky and Nicholas Berdyaev. Despite "the fulfillment of some of these predictions in the present "catastrophe," a "testing of God's power,"[164] Sheen reminded his readers that Christians realize that a "moment of crisis is not a time of despair, but of opportunity."[165] Summoning "all men of good will — Jews, Protestants, and Catholics alike,"[166] Sheen made a plea for unity among all religious people as the most effective means of resisting communism.

Providing an answer to "those inclined to think that the cause of the world's woe is external to our democratic way of life, and is principally due to communism,"[167] Sheen offered this essential truth:

> Communism is related to our material Western civilization as putrefaction is to disease.... every single idea of communism is Western bourgeois in its origin.... because it has never corrected the abuses of our Western World, but only intensified them, communism has made us realize how wrong we were.[168]

---

[162] *Ibid.*, p. 8.
[163] *Ibid.*, p. 22.
[164] *Ibid.*, pp. 38-39.
[165] *Ibid.*, p. 44.
[166] *Ibid.*, p. 46.
[167] *Ibid.*, p. 48.
[168] *Ibid.*, pp. 49, 52.

Therefore, communism might correctly be seen as "God's judgment" upon Western civilization, a last chance for the West to set its own house in order, rather than as an occasion to simply "harangue against the communists."[169] Reexamining his explanation for the historical evolution of communism, through Hegel and Marx, he called attention again to its basic defects. It was right in its protests but wrong in its reforms, and was not revolutionary enough in its attempts to establish a "brotherhood of man without a Fatherhood in God."[170] Reciting a litany of the Church's multiple reasons for opposing communism, he tried to place his emphasis on the positive. In "The Basic Defects of Communism" chapter, he noted that the Church was "embarrassed at being praised as anti-communist, because such praise is for being anti-something rather than pro-something; for a way of thinking that would make the Church admired because it hates an enemy, rather than because its ideals are loved":

> The Catholic Church is sometimes praised for its opposition to communism... for the Church is the only solid moral force in the world that has been consistently opposed to the new barbarism. The Church saw the evils of totalitarianism and condemned each in turn. The Church condemned fascism in the encyclical *Non abbiamo bisogno* which was written in Italian because fascism was a national phenomenon; it condemned nazism in the German language in the encyclical *Mit brennender sorge* because nazism was a racial phenomenon. It condemned communism in the universal language of Latin in the encyclical *Divini Redemptoris* because communism is an international phenomenon.[171]

Regarding more practical advice on how to meet communism, Sheen suggested that the challenge would be best met by multiple

---

[169] *Ibid.*, p. 56.
[170] *Ibid.*, pp. 80, 91-93.
[171] *Ibid.*, pp. 78-79.

fronts of resistance. Politically, Americans should never lose sight
of their national ideals, based on moral and spiritual values. Rather
than choosing candidates on the basis of party affiliation, they
should be chosen on the basis of their "moral worth."[172] Economically, the Church's prescription of a wider diffusion of property,
according to the guidelines in the social encyclicals, should be followed. One means for helping ownership and labor to "coalesce is
worker-ownership of stock in industry."[173] Morally, Sheen called
for the appointment of "chaplains from each of the three faiths to
industry."[174] The value of these chaplains, said Sheen, would be "the
organization of men on a non-competitive spiritual basis"; in due
time, the chaplains could establish "factory reading rooms, discussion clubs... even factory worship where the minor hates of the
working hours could be dissolved in the reminder that all men are
brothers."[175] On the educational front, Sheen advocated "informing the people in a democracy" not only about the errors of communism, but about the "great truths of human nature, history and
religion."[176] This broad-based program of education was Sheen's
own metier as a preacher, writer and popularizer; but the specifics
of his plans were never enumerated. Finally, in the all-important
realm of the spirit, it should be remembered, said Sheen, that communism often appealed to the "disillusioned and frustrated." So the
best spiritual solution was prayer and love. "Communism is to be
hated as a doctor hates pneumonia in a sick child; but the communists are potential children of God, and must be loved as a sick
child."[177] A simple lesson from history was linked with Sheen's faith
in the eventual conversion of Russia as his last word on how to meet
the communist threat:

---

[172]   *Ibid.*, p. 127.

[173]   *Ibid.*, p. 125. This is about as specific as Sheen got, and he backed up his point with a
         simple analogy about the distribution of farmers' eggs: Communists make omelets, but
         Christians distribute hens so that every man can cook his eggs the way he likes them
         (pp. 129-130).

[174]   *Ibid.*, p. 132.

[175]   *Ibid.*

[176]   *Ibid.*, pp. 133-134.

[177]   *Ibid.*, p. 189.

On this farm in the Panther Creek section of El Paso, IL, Sheen spent weekends and vacations with his parents and brothers during his years as a seminarian. (Courtesy, St. Bernard's School of Ministry and Theology)

This 1930's photo of the Sheens shows the close knit family: Mr. and Mrs. Newton Sheen and their four sons (l. to r.) Joseph, Fulton, Aloysius and Thomas. (Courtesy, Fulton J. Sheen Archives)

After graduating as valedictorian of his high school class at Spalding Institute in Peoria, Illinois, Sheen entered St. Viator's College Seminary and was ordained in 1919 at the age of 24. (Courtesy, Fulton J. Sheen Archives)

Sheen was in his early thirties when he began a series of radio broadcasts entitled "The Catholic Hour" sponsored by the National Council of Catholic Men on NBC. (Courtesy, Fulton J. Sheen Archives)

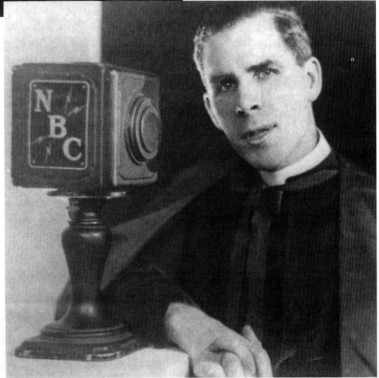

The famous Paulist Choir often provided the music for "The Catholic Hour" during the years 1930-1952 with Sheen as the featured speaker. (Courtesy, St. Bernard's School of Ministry and Theology)

Sheen was a guest street preacher of the Catholic Evidence Guild in Alabama in the 1930's. (Courtesy, Fulton J. Sheen Archives)

Sheen is seen here with participants at a Catholic Summer School in the Adirondacks where he often spent his summers during the 1930's. (Courtesy, St. Bernard's School of Ministry and Theology)

Sheen is seen here in this summer 1935 photo with his niece, Joan Sheen Cunningham, and Alfred E. Smith, the first Catholic presidential candidate at Lake Champlain. (Courtesy, St. Bernard's School of Ministry and Theology)

This photo was taken on the occasion of a visit to the missions in Sasolburg, South Africa on November 27, 1960. (Courtesy, Society for the Propagation of the Faith)

Sheen frequently led a number of pilgrimages to Europe during his summer breaks. Here he is seen with a group in Rome. (Courtesy, St. Bernard's School of Ministry and Theology)

Sheen never visited Europe without paying a special visit to his favorite shrine dedicated to Our Lady in Lourdes. (Courtesy, Society for the Propagation of the Faith)

It was in 1969, during a private audience with Pope Paul VI, that Sheen,approaching the age of seventy-five, offered his resignation as Bishop to the Pope. (Courtesy, Society for the Propagation of the Faith)

Sheen was famous for his use of the blackboard (always kept clean by his unseen angel) during his popular "Life Is Worth Living" television series. (New York News photo)

Sheen often found himself in
the spotlight, and he knew
how to handle it well.
(Courtesy, Society for the
Propagation of the Faith)

Sheen and Ed Sullivan on the occasion of the Look Award, Sunday, December 30, 1956. (Courtesy, Society for the Propagation of the Faith)

Sheen and the Holy Father are noticeably relaxed in this 1960's photo-
graph with good (now Blessed) Pope John XXIII which was taken in the
Pope's study. (G. Felici)

Sheen took an active part in the Second Vatican Council, "one of the great blessings the Lord has bestowed on my life." (Courtesy, Society for the Propagation of the Faith)

Sheen leads concelebrants at a Memorial Mass for drug victim Rafael Cordero at East Harlem's Our Lady Queen of Angels church. (Religious News Service Photo by Chris Sheridan, Courtesy, St. Bernard's School of Ministry and Theology)

St. Patrick's Cathedral in New York City was considered home for much of Sheen's career when he served as Director for the Society for the Propagation of the Faith. (Courtesy, St. Bernard's School of Ministry and Theology)

Sheen directed the Society for the Propagation of the Faith from 1950 to 1966 when he was called to head the diocese of Rochester, NY. Bishop Edward T. O'Meara succeeded him. (Courtesy, St. Bernard's School of Ministry and Theology)

The official portrait of Archbishop Fulton J. Sheen taken shortly after his appointment as Bishop of Rochester, New York on December 16, 1966. (Courtesy, St. Bernard's School of Ministry and Theology)

In 1967, Bishop Sheen was honored as "Rochester Salesman of the Year" by the Rochester Sales Executive Club. (Courtesy, St. Bernard's School of Ministry and Theology)

Celebrating the 25th anniversary of his ordination as bishop, Sheen returned to Rochester in 1969 to dedicate a room in the Seminary library which contained his personal papers, books and tapes. (Courtesy, St. Bernard's School of Ministry and Theology)

Calling him a loyal son of the Church, Pope John Paul II embraces Archbishop Sheen in St. Patrick's Cathedral on October 2, 1979, two months
before his death. (Associated Press Photo)

God's power is more manifested in the conversion than
in destruction.… Rome was the greatest persecutor of
religion until Russia in modern times, but Rome became
the center of Christianity. May God so transfigure Russia that from it one day will radiate a light which will
renew faith in Europe and give it to Asia![178]

The last chapters of the book were dedicated to an explica-
tion of Sheen's fervent faith that Russia would one day return to
God,[179] for "in the spiritual traits of the Russian people is the basis
of hope for world peace."[180] Drawing a clear distinction between
communist ideology and the Russian people, Sheen pointed out
that Russia's true heritage was orthodox Christianity, and closed
his book with his thoughts on the message of Our Lady of Fatima:

But in the end my Immaculate Heart will triumph. The
Holy Father will consecrate Russia to the Immaculate
Heart, and Russia will be converted and an era of peace
will be given to the world.[181]

The publication of *Communism and the Conscience of the West*
marked a period of transition for Fulton Sheen, as the American
Church moved into the decade of the fifties under the shadow of
the Cold War. Appointed National Director of the Society for the
Propagation of the Faith in 1950, much of his time was consumed
by his work for the missions and by his "Life Is Worth Living" television series. He continued to speak out forcefully on the subject
of communism, from an ideological and religious point of view.

---

[178] *Ibid.*, p. 139.

[179] The last four chapters were: "The Attitude Toward the Family in Russia"; "Passion";
Russia and the Faith"; and "Our Lady of Fatima and Russia."

[180] Sheen, *Communism and the Conscience of the West*, p. 184.

[181] *Ibid.*, p. 204. Sheen was a lifelong devotee of the Blessed Virgin; he dedicated his books
to her, and made numerous pilgrimages to Lourdes and Fatima. See "Marian Piety and
the Cold War in the United States," by Thomas Kselman and Steven Avella, *Catholic
Historical Review* LXIII (July, 1986), pp. 403-424, for a comprehensive overview of the
subject and Sheen's place in that context.

Remaining removed from the political conflicts and tensions generated by McCarthyism, Sheen never offered an opinion on Senator McCarthy in public, and he steered clear of the political controversy surrounding him. Both his television shows, which ran from 1952 through 1957, and his popular syndicated newspaper columns, "God Love You" and "Bishop Sheen Writes," were preoccupied with communism. Evoking an even more popularistic style during the fifties, Sheen devoted approximately a third of his public pronouncements to various aspects of communism.[182] His underlying purpose in all of these endeavors was to keep the American people educated and informed about the continuing danger of communism, but as an entertainer he also responded to the popular appeal of the topic. As a result, the intellectual substance of his statements was often sacrificed in favor of flashy rhetoric, simple lessons and stories, and a sense of drama.

Sheen's overriding aim was evident in "The Philosophy of Communism,"[183] from his first season on television. He observed that "there is considerable confusion in our American life about communism; too much emotional hatred of communism and not sufficient reasoning and thinking about it."[184] Hoping to raise the level of the public debate, while also reaching out to the average man in the streets, he focused his attention on several basic ideas, viewed from several angles. Since Marx drew his ideas from the West, communism was western in origin,[185] and Americans had to assume some responsibility for the growth of communism. Rather than advocating military or political solutions, Sheen said that the

---

[182] Sheen's newspaper columns were syndicated by the George Matthews Adams Service, and ran from 1949 through 1979, often recycling the same material found in his books, sermons and television shows. His television series, "Life Is Worth Living," appeared in transcript form as a series of books (five separate volumes). Of the 129 separate shows, about 30 were dedicated to communism; more dealt with communism, interjected in such episodes as "Abraham Lincoln" and "How Traitors are Made."

[183] Fulton Sheen, *Life Is Worth Living* (First Series), (New York: McGraw-Hill Book Co., 1953).

[184] *Ibid.*, p. 62.

[185] Sheen, "The Philosophy of Communism" (1954), cited in *The Church, Communism and Democracy*, p. 19.

real answer to the Cold War conflict was to be found in the ultimate conversion of Russia: "When Russia discovers the Faith, it
will sweep it throughout the entire western world, and then we will
know that Christianity has not failed."[186] In "Russia is Not Communism," he repeated his belief that "Russia, after throwing off the
yoke of communism, will be the spiritual leader of the world."[187]

In addition to talking about Russia's spiritual heritage, Sheen
enjoyed revealing what he called Soviet "lies and double talk," suggesting to his audience that what the communists needed was a
good dictionary, and that their propaganda statements should never
be accepted at face value. In "What the Communists Mean By
Truth," Sheen argued that it was this failure of the West to fully
appreciate the communist vocabulary which was responsible for
some of the Soviet progress on the international scene.[188] There
were three important consequences of this communist position: the
necessity of the Iron Curtain, to shut off those enslaved by the
Soviets from the rest of the world; the fluctuating tactics of diplomacy, to keep Soviet adversaries confused; and the futility of arguing with communists, since they could not be trusted.[189] Regarding the Soviets' devious tactics, Sheen repeatedly warned that the
West should not judge the Soviet Union by its foreign policy slogans, but by its philosophy, which was steady and intrinsically evil.
The foreign policy of Russia was only a "maneuver, a scheme, a
strategy and an imposture" to mask their true goal: worldwide revolution and domination.[190] In "Peace Tactics of the Soviets," Sheen
said that what Russia really wanted was not "peace," but a "piece"
of China or Hungary, and that a peace overture by Russia might
be the beginning of another "Pearl Harbor."[191] "Pax Sovietica"
charged Russia with being an "arsonist in the United Nations,"[192]

---

[186] *Ibid.*, "Russia Is Not Communism" (1956), p. 57.
[187] *Ibid.*, "What the Communists Mean By Truth" (1956), p. 59.
[188] *Ibid.*
[189] *Ibid.*, p. 63.
[190] Sheen, *Life Is Worth Living* (First Series), p. 245.
[191] *Ibid.*, p. 251.
[192] Sheen, *The Church, Communism and Democracy*, p. 103.

and in "The Russian Lullaby of Co-existence," Sheen warned against being taken in by the false promises of the communists, and recited a lengthy list of broken treaties to demonstrate his point.[193]

In stark contrast to these crimes committed by the Soviet Union, Sheen provided his audience with a glowing account of democracy, an American civics lesson. A noticeable thread of patriotism ran through the fabric of Sheen's television shows, reflecting the temper of his times. In the course of his televised civics lessons, Sheen explained the "difference between a democracy and a totalitarian state," offered a "comparison of the Soviet and American constitutions,"[194] and waved the flag in "Three Times in a Nation's History"[195]: "Let America love its stars and stripes," said Sheen, but always appreciate the fact that the nation would conquer communism only with "the stars and stripes of Christ... if God is with us, who can be against us?"[196]

In "Brainwashing," a description of the tortures suffered by Catholic martyrs behind the Iron Curtain, Sheen made a veiled reference to the national debate on communist subversives in the educational system, pleading: "May our educators never wash our brains of true Americanism."[197] Describing America as "at the crossroads of a suffering world, being crucified by communism,"[198] Sheen proposed a stronger alliance of religion and Americanism, for "our fires of patriotism, evangelism and zeal are being reduced to embers." Only such an alliance would fulfill America's role in history, "destined under Providence to be the secondary cause for the restoration of the freedom and liberties of the peoples of the world."[199] One of the immediate tasks of the alliance, suggested Sheen, was

---

[193] *Ibid.*, p. 80.
[194] *Ibid.*, "How a Democracy Differs from a Totalitarian State" (1956); and "A Comparison of the Soviet and American Constitutions" (1956).
[195] Sheen, *Life Is Worth Living* (First Series, 1953).
[196] *Ibid.*, p. 51.
[197] Sheen, "Brainwashing" (1954), in *The Church, Communism and Democracy*, p. 124.
[198] Sheen, "The Role of Communism and the Role of America" (1953), in *Life Is Worth Living* (First Series), p. 270.
[199] *Ibid.*, pp. 267-268.

for "a rabbi, a minister, and a priest to go on the Voice of America" and protest the communist persecution of religion.[200] Finally, a series of fundamental lessons on "great men" in history, like Marx, Lenin, Dostoevsky and Lincoln, rounded out Sheen's lectures on the theme "The Church, Communism and Democracy."[201]

As the preceding overview of Fulton Sheen's opinions on communism, as aired on television, demonstrates, he contributed little of real substance to the national debate in the fifties, and distanced himself from the political controversy engulfing Senator McCarthy and the Catholic Church. Throughout the decade, Bishop Sheen was most closely identified with television and the missions by most Americans. By this time, his fans had come to expect spellbinding oratory from him, not political analysis. It was not Fulton Sheen's province to participate in McCarthy's debate, and he did not. Despite his decision to avoid any personal involvement in the issue, he probably fanned the fires of America's growing obsession with the red menace. Even indirectly, his was not a moderating influence. Although Sheen's strident patriotism was never hidden, he generally preferred to denounce communism on the ideological level.

In an interview he granted to a researcher twenty years after the fact, Archbishop Sheen explained his detachment when he said: "I have no interest in politics… there was no reason that I should have discussed him [Senator McCarthy], and he was not an authority on communism in any case."[202] This justification of his aloofness might seem self-serving, but it did have a validity consistent with his version of American Catholic anti-communism. By saying that McCarthy was not an authority on the subject of communism — as a philosophy or way of life — Sheen could simply dismiss him from consideration, as outside the area of Sheen's inter-

---

[200]   *Ibid.*, "Communism and Russia," pp. 134-135.

[201]   See the book of the same title, Chapters 17-21.

[202]   Fulton Sheen, quoted in an interview given to Sr. Mary Jude Yablonsky, and cited in her Ph.D. dissertation, "A Rhetorical Analysis of Selected Television Speeches of Archbishop Fulton Sheen on Communism, 1952-1956" (Ohio State University, 1974).

ests and responsibility. Sheen always seemed uncomfortable in the political arena, and this was especially true during the heated and highly emotional climate of the McCarthy years. So, Sheen simply withdrew, and confined his comments to vague and passing references to the occasional political topic: Korea, a divided Germany, persistent Soviet propaganda. A brief look at some of those comments, from his newspaper columns and a pamphlet published in 1952, "Crisis in History," will show this to be the case.

"Crisis in History" was published by the Catechetical Guild and Educational Society of St. Paul, Minnesota.[203] A collection of excerpts from earlier Sheen material, its common denominator was a tone of inflammatory hostility towards communism. In "The Eagle and the Carcass" Sheen said that "the key to the future of American life is to be armed at the borders against active barbarism," so that the "eagles may not be at our national carcass, the hammer at our doors, and the sickle at our necks."[204] Sheen drew his inspiration in this piece from the Gospel reference: "Wherever the body is, there shall the eagles be gathered together,"[205] and he spoke in a foreboding tone of communist vultures ready to attack the body of civilization.[206] In posing the question "Will Russia Fight?", Sheen said that the Western world was arming against a communism which didn't bear arms against America, but only in Russian satellites, where the United States would face a "succession of wars":

> Russian communists will resist "American imperialism"
> to the last drop of Chinese, Korean, Indian and Philip-

---

[203] Several copies of this pamphlet can be found in the collection at the Sheen Archives. Its exact origins, or how it was compiled, are unclear. It consists of twenty essays.

[204] *Ibid.*, p. 34.

[205] *Ibid.*, p. 33.

[206] *Ibid.* This essay is typical of Sheen's more colorful images; throughout the pamphlet, he referred to "vultures, cobras, fifth columnists and the demonic." He also rose to a higher level of argument in referring to historian Arnold Toynbee to the same effect — that civilizations were vulnerable to decline from within if they neglected to maintain their moral sense (p. 32).

pine blood. Yet the Koreans are not our enemies, nor are the Chinese: they are our brothers.[207]

In "The Brandenburg Gate," Sheen discussed the plight of the people of East Berlin as symbolized in the little street circle, "where the free air of the West faces the foul miasma of the Soviet, and with that rapid meeting of hot and cold currents, a storm is constantly brewing."[208] And in another essay, Sheen lost his intellectual balance by suggesting that "some fine morning we will be suddenly startled by another Pearl Harbor," if the Soviets were successful in wheeling their third Trojan Horse of "Peace" (following anti-fascism and democracy) into America.[209] Without resorting to such extreme language, Sheen's treatment of the subject of communism in his newspaper columns relied upon the same cliches and images to teach a simple lesson. In "Co-Existence is for Nibbling," Sheen said that Soviets used local wars for "the gradual washing away of free lands into a sea of communist tyranny."[210] "Five Fish for Communist Hooks" singled out those "dupes" who were most gullible to communist bait, including "bored intelligentsia and neurotics."[211] In "Dialogue With Communism is Impossible," Sheen expressed an opinion he would later revise, after the Second Vatican Council. In 1954, however, he viewed compromise with communism as "futile and stupid."[212] Sheen discussed Soviet imperialism and infiltration into the "captive states" of Korea, China and Vietnam in "What Is Happening to Communism."[213] The Soviet Union owed its success to world upheaval: "Communism is a surfboard that rides the waves of historical changes into the shores of a country."[214] "Communism and Tragedy" discussed two different

---

[207] *Ibid.*, p. 40.

[208] *Ibid.*, p. 50.

[209] *Ibid.*, "Three Times in a Nation's History," pp. 36-37.

[210] "Bishop Sheen Writes," April 15, 1955.

[211] "Bishop Sheen Writes," March 28, 1954.

[212] "Bishop Sheen Writes," December 5, 1954.

[213] "Bishop Sheen Writes," August 3, 1958.

[214] *Ibid.*

kinds of reports in circulation about Soviet Russia: those of tour politicians, who found Russia a model of humanity, and the opposite view held by those who knew the truth: labor camp refugees.[215] At the end of the decade, Bishop Sheen offered this prayer: "Please God, not in Latin America," in light of the appearance of the communist "devil" in Cuba.[216]

Aside from this steady stream of popularized pronouncements, Sheen's activities during the height of the Cold War were confined to two areas: momentary appearances in the spotlight hunting for spies, and testimony before the House Committee on Un-American Activities in 1957. Never one to avoid the glare of publicity, Sheen found himself caught up in the melodrama and intrigue of domestic communism and espionage when he sought out headlines. Monsignor Sheen went on one "witch-hunt" in 1946, an unsuccessful foray outside his regular environment.[217] Reporting to a Catholic Institute of the Press Convention that "a Soviet agent had been picked up in a Congressional meeting," Sheen never provided any additional details when questioned, and the F.B.I. denied any knowledge of the alleged Soviet agent.[218] In 1952, while in Rome, Sheen made news at home with a story about "secret orders to American communists to infiltrate the priesthood," which he had learned of almost twenty years ago. These "communist wolves" were planted in religious communities to "destroy them from within"; one man from Moscow had even tried to insert himself in Sheen's own office. This man claimed that "he wanted to fight communism with me," but Sheen was suspicious and called the F.B.I., who told him that the man was a communist agent "traced through China and Mongolia" but subsequently lost. Now, thanks to Sheen's patriotic assistance, the F.B.I. was aware of the agent's dangerous presence in the United States.[219]

---

[215] "Bishop Sheen Writes," July 26, 1959.

[216] "Bishop Sheen Writes" ("The Accuser"), February 26, 1961.

[217] Donald Crosby, SJ, discusses this incident in his book (p. 15), and it was reported in the *New York Times*, March 25, 1946.

[218] *New York Times*, March 25, 1946.

[219] *New York Times*, April 25, 1952.

Sheen recalled these incidents in his autobiography. Once, he claimed, a spy came right to his classroom at Catholic University and said he was a refugee interested in assisting Sheen in his anti-communist crusade.[220] Sheen's guard went up, and he called the Communist Division of the F.B.I.; they reacted quickly and told him, "He is very dangerous. Your life is in danger."[221] But the man then disappeared. One incident turned out better, at least in Sheen's memory. He said that it was perfectly natural for a defector to seek him out, since his anti-communist stance was well-known. In this cloak and dagger style case, Sheen checked out a man with the help of the F.B.I. in a rendezvous at the Plaza Hotel in New York. Agents placed in the adjoining room listened while Sheen interviewed the man, and the F.B.I. report said that he was "absolutely trustworthy."[222] So, Sheen employed him as a source of valuable information; the man reported that Sheen had been christened "Public Enemy # 1" at a meeting of the Communist Party in New York City.[223] Sheen also claimed, some years later, that due to pressure from communists and threats on his life, he was forced to travel with a bodyguard for two years.[224] Exactly what motivated Sheen in the telling of these spy tales, beyond seeking publicity, is open to speculation. He was the only source or authority in each case, and never followed through with additional information. These tales did not seem to damage his credibility with his contemporaries, however.

Bishop Sheen's one venture into the official business of the government during the 1950's was a more positive one, and indicative of his reputation as a leader of American Catholicism's crusade against communism. In the fall of 1957, three prominent clergymen, representatives of the Jewish, Protestant and Catholic faiths, were called into a staff consultation on "The Ideological Fallacies

---

[220] Sheen, *Treasure in Clay,* pp. 84-85.

[221] *Ibid.*

[222] *Ibid.*

[223] *Ibid.*

[224] See Yablonsky, p. 37, in addition to Sheen's autobiography.

of Communism" by the House Un-American Activities Commit-tee.[225] Sheen was chosen for his expertise, and the consultation was held at his offices at the Society for the Propagation of the Faith in New York City on September 25, 1957.[226] Sharing his insights into the principal ideological fallacies of communism, Sheen called com-munism a conglomerate philosophy of Hegel and Feuerbach "united in the brain of Karl Marx."[227] Sheen stated that the "goal of communism is the complete subjection of mankind to a totali-tarian system," and that the underlying conditions for this com-munist form of slavery were "the denial of God and the denial of freedom."[228] Although there was no place for God in communism, Sheen said it was actually a "perversion of Christianity," which at-tempted to fill the spiritual vacuum created in the world."[229]

After offering this diagnosis of the disease of communism, Sheen was asked for his remedy. Noting that remedies could be political, economic, moral and educational, Sheen focused on his specialty, education. "I believe in informing people about the phi-losophy of communism, because that is the only way it will ever be understood and eventually overcome"[230] With reference to the for-eign policy concerns of the administration, Sheen suggested two courses of action to cope with the international communist men-ace: the expulsion of Russia from the United Nations and the in-sistence by the West on the liberation of certain suppressed peoples,[231] particularly those in Poland and Hungary. Sheen con-cluded his remarks with a familiar, but mistaken, idea derived from

---

[225] The texts of the remarks made by the three clergymen were printed in a pamphlet is-sued by the U.S. Government: "The Ideological Fallacies of Communism," for the use of the Committee on Un-American Activities (#97608). The other clergymen consulted were Dr. S. Andhil Fineberg and Dr. Daniel A. Poling.

[226] "The Ideological Fallacies of Communism," p. 9.

[227] *Ibid.*, pp. 9-10.

[228] *Ibid.*, p. 11.

[229] *Ibid.*, p. 13.

[230] *Ibid.* This is the same point of view expressed in *Communism and the Conscience of the West.*

[231] *Ibid.*, p. ix, and pp. 14-15.

the revelation at Fatima in 1917. Sheen believed that communism was on the decline and would be "forgotten in fifty years"; he hoped to witness Russia's reunion with the rest of the civilized world. Sheen believed that Russia would ultimately receive the gift of faith, for "good is self-preserving; evil is always self-defeating."[232] And he told the committee members that there was "no such thing as the liberation of China" until Russia itself disintegrates:[233]

> ...when Russia does disintegrate, Russia will be one of the great spiritual and moral nations of the world, because... communism has restored a sense of discipline and dedication.... Russia is closer to the ultimate reconciliation of the cross and Christ.[234]

In light of this final expression of faith and hope in the reconciliation of Christ and His cross, Sheen's reflections on "The Ideological Fallacies of Communism" before the Congressional Committee can be considered a fitting conclusion to this phase of his crusade against communism.

After this extensive look at Fulton Sheen's views, what conclusions can be drawn about his place in the history of American Catholic anti-communism? To what end did he write and speak out on the subject of communism for over three decades? There is no denying his fame or public prominence as a spokesman for the Catholic Church in the United States, especially from the perspective of his radio and television popularity. His reputation as an uncompromising foe of communism was well-deserved. His zeal for the cause never faltered, and the longevity of Sheen's publicity campaign against the threat of communism was a singular achievement. Although his approach ebbed and flowed with the temper of the times, the Fulton Sheen of the Depression decade was still around after the McCarthy era had passed, preaching the same

---

[232] *Ibid.*
[233] *Ibid.*, p. 16.
[234] *Ibid.*

message (and often using the same material). At all times, Sheen tried to maintain a position in the mainstream of American Catholic anticommunism, and his efforts were generally successful. Consequently, he deserves some credit for the positive results of the Church's crusade, but also bears the burden of responsibility for some of its negative effects.

During the thirties and forties, anti-communism was a vehicle of Americanization for the Catholic Church. According to historian David O'Brien, "in fighting the red peril, the Catholic could dedicate himself to action which was both Catholic and American... demonstrating the compatibility of faith and patriotism."[235] Fulton Sheen was a participant in this dominant impulse in the Church, and although his statements did gravitate to the "clearly defined issue of anti-communism," he did not ignore the bishops' demands for reform in the process.[236] He viewed anti-communism as a worthy form of social action and Catholic action, and as a good forum for his talents as an orator. From the start, he became caught up in the obsessive nature of the campaign. Although this did not prevent him from taking a constructive approach to the problem of communism, Sheen did damage his credibility in some circles when he allowed his combative and overly dramatic style to overwhelm the ideological substance behind his message. As his rhetoric demonstrates, he was aware of and sensitive to the charges aimed at Catholics by liberals and some Protestants. His usual way of dealing with them, however, was to resort to charges of his own, like the "bogey" or red flag of fascism.[237] He also dismissed such charges as absurd, or examples of communist-inspired propaganda. So, Sheen did not always raise the level of the public debate on communism, or the debate on the ability of the Catholic Church to function in a democratic society. Clearly, his position was far removed from the overtly negative one of Fr. Charles

---

[235] O'Brien, *American Catholics and Social Reform*, p. 96.

[236] *Ibid.*, p. 84.

[237] See "Communism Answers the Questions of a Communist" and *Liberty, Equality and Fraternity.*

Coughlin,[238] who was the favorite target of those who saw Catholics as excessive in their opposition to communism before the Cold War. But Fulton Sheen's version of the anti-communist crusade was not entirely positive either, in the eyes of non-Catholics or liberal Catholics.

The anti-communist gospel of Sheen does not lend itself to an easy classification. When measured against the standards of his contemporaries, his record is mixed, but more positive than he is usually given credit for. All too often, he has been summarily dismissed as a media star, but from the perspective of the common man, his message was important, and enjoyed a wider hearing than many of the American Catholic figures whose views on communism have been subjected to critical analysis. For example, liberal Catholics of the *Commonweal* variety were critical of the negative red-baiting aspects of Catholic anti-communism, and Sheen was likely perceived as guilty of this negative style,[239] though he was not singled out for criticism. In 1950, John Cogley of *Commonweal* wrote an editorial entitled "The Failure of Anti-Communism,"[240] lamenting the American Catholic obsession and calling the Church's crusade a failure because it gave "too little time to Christianity itself."[241] He also recognized two schools of thought within the American Catholic framework, the positive and the negative. Measured by these criteria, it would be difficult to place Sheen entirely in one school. On the positive side, he never neglected Christianity, ignored the social encyclicals, or failed to recognize the dynamism and religious power behind the philosophy of communism. On the other hand, Cogley's negative references to "pulpit platitudes" and those who relied on anti-communism as the

---

[238] For Coughlin's views on communism, and his fascist tendencies, see O'Brien's chapter "Father Coughlin and American Catholicism" and Alan Brinkley's *Voices of Protest*.

[239] For an example of this Catholic awareness of the harm done by red-baiters, see the articles on communism in the *Commonweal* for the late thirties and forties — its pages were filled with the subject and the Church's opposition to it.

[240] Cogley, in *Commonweal* 52 (July 21, 1950), pp. 357-358.

[241] *Ibid.*, p. 358.

"unfailing constant" evoke the image of Fulton Sheen.[242] Another
Commonweal journalist, James O'Gara, expressed similar sentiments
in "The Catholic Isolationist."[243] O'Gara spoke of the "predisposi-
tion to the simplistic," which showed up strikingly on the question
of communism, American Catholicism's "magic touchstone."[244]
Simplistic was an accurate description of Fulton Sheen's presentation of the anti-communist message, but when O'Gara continued
that "serious attempts to understand and explain communism have
been rare," the description no longer fits. Mr. O'Gara also faulted
Catholics who failed to convey "an understanding of the dynamism
and appeal of communism," but Sheen conveyed that over a long
period of time, and did it well in *Communism and the Conscience of
the West*. With special reference to Senator McCarthy, a "hero for
the simplistic," O'Gara raised the most controversial issue in the
history of American Catholic anti-communism,[245] and McCarthyism was an issue which Sheen never raised.

Fr. Donald Crosby's *God, Church, and Flag* is the most complete analysis of McCarthyism and American Catholic history. The
Catholic debate on McCarthy was political, not religious, according to Crosby's thesis. Consequently, it should come as no surprise
that Sheen avoided it because he did not get involved in political
debates. If Sheen is to be faulted for his failure to say anything, it
should be noted that the leaders of the American Catholic community were not eager to speak out either. Bishop Bernard Sheil
was the only member of the hierarchy to condemn McCarthy, and
he became embroiled in a heated controversy with Cardinal
Spellman as a result.[246] In one instance, a question about Sheen was
raised. In "A Catholic View of McCarthy," Vincent P. DeSantis
of the University of Notre Dame asked in the pages of the *New*

---

[242] *Ibid.*

[243] James O'Gara, "The Catholic Isolationist," in *Catholicism in America* (New York, 1953).
        The essays in this book were originally published as a series in *Commonweal* during 1953.

[244] O'Gara, p. 115.

[245] *Ibid.*, p. 116.

[246] Crosby, p. 166.

Republic why Catholics did not stand up and criticize Senator McCarthy. "The time is long overdue for those who oppose McCarthy to speak out. If they do not, they run the risk of producing a climate favorable to an anti-Catholic crusade."[247] DeSantis said that Catholics should denounce McCarthy for diverting Americans from the threat of communism abroad by concentrating on subversives at home, real or imagined; DeSantis noted that "even Bishop Fulton J. Sheen argued in a recent television program that the real issue is whether we shall be undermined at home."[248] This was an obvious example of Sheen's role, by abdication of his responsibility to speak out, in the negative repercussions associated with Catholic anti-communism.[249]

In the more recent historical scholarship on the subject of American communism,[250] Sheen would most likely be cast in a negative light if examined. By today's standards, he would appear to be an obsessive Catholic anti-communist, an anachronism. But when judged by the standards of his own times, the only fair standard, Sheen's positive side should be recognized. Fulton Sheen's anti-communism was essentially ideological, not political. And although this ideology was primarily Catholic and Christian, it was also very American. By speaking out as an American citizen, he assisted the Church in making its adjustment into the mainstream of American life, and facilitated its assimilation. During the Cold War years, anti-communism became an integral part of American patriotism, and there occurred a "congruence of the Church's position with the anti-communism of the society at large."[251] "The common fear of communism brought the American people and the American Church closer together," and began to "cancel out the

---

[247] Vincent P. DeSantis, letter in the *New Republic* 130 (June 7, 1954).

[248] *Ibid.*

[249] For the negative repercussions of McCarthyism, see Crosby's chapter on "Protestant-Catholic Tensions."

[250] For a summary of the scholarship, see Theodore Draper's "American Communism Revisited" in the *New York Review*, May 30, 1985.

[251] Wilson D. Miscamble, CSC, "Catholics and American Foreign Policy from McKinley to McCarthy," *Diplomatic History* 4 (Summer, 1980), p. 237.

American prejudices against Catholicism."[252] This was true in the short term, but in the long run, new problems associated with the Church's Americanization and its response to a pluralistic society and the civil religion of the Republic would be raised. These problems would wait until a later time, however.[253] A more immediate result of the crusade against communism would present the Church with opportunities, for it helped to pave the way for the Catholic Church's greater participation in American life. Fulton Sheen's efforts had assisted in that process — the final acceptance of Catholicism as one of the "three great religions of democracy" — and his role as a participant in American life would only grow in the days ahead.

---

[252] Fogarty, *The Vatican and the American Hierarchy,* pp. 345, 341.

[253] See Crosby and David O'Brien's *The Renewal of American Catholicism.* O'Brien noted that "as the anti-communist stance became identified with patriotism and virtue, the prestige of the Church was vastly enhanced and its loyalty to America less and less questioned" (p. 115).

CHAPTER SIX

The Post-war Religious Revival:
A Catholic Version of the "American Way of Life,"
1945–1966

The effect of war and crisis is that… side by side with the growth
of evil you will find the growth of a deep religious spirit.
Fulton Sheen, 1944

Catholicism in America stands today at its highest point of
prestige and power.… In an age when the vacuities of rationalism and
unbelief have become so painfully evident, Catholicism presents the
picture of a dynamic faith sure of itself and capable of preserving its
substance and power despite elaborate institutionalization. In an age of
spiritual chaos and disorientation, Catholicism stands forth as the
keeper of an enduring tradition that has weathered the storms of the
past and stands unshaken amidst the disasters of our time.
Will Herberg, 1953 "A Jew Looks at Catholics"

During the post-war years the United States underwent a religious
revival which flourished in the Eisenhower era. The signs of the
upswing in religious fervor were multidimensional and unmistak-
able. Among the most clearly identifiable were statistics on an increase in church membership and attendance, the acceleration of
new church construction, especially in the suburbs, and the appearance of many religious and inspirational books on the best seller
lists. Also noteworthy was the resurgence of patriotism and piety
which accompanied the Cold War crusade against communism, and
an open profession of a generic brand of religion by President
Eisenhower himself: "Our government makes no sense unless it is
founded on a deeply felt religious faith — and I don't care what it

is."[1] The President, a "prestigious symbol of generalized religiosity and America's self-satisfied patriotic moralism,"[2] demonstrated the nation's favorable disposition toward religion as a means of affirming its Americanism. This tendency toward a national rhetoric linking religion and patriotism, a rhetoric long associated with Fulton Sheen, was perhaps best chronicled during these years in the pages of Will Herberg's "essay in American religious sociology," *Protestant-Catholic-Jew*.[3]

Herberg's essay was published at the height of the religious revival and had a profound influence on subsequent discussions of American religion and ethnicity, particularly in regard to the persistence of his vocabulary: the "triple melting pot"; the "American way of life" as the nation's characteristic religion; and Protestantism, Catholicism and Judaism as the "three great religions of democracy."

Especially perceptive were his observations on American Catholicism, first made in "A Jew Looks at Catholics," as part of *Commonweal* magazine's lengthy series on Catholicism in America in 1953.[4] Billed simply as comments made in the hope that American Catholics will see themselves as a friendly outsider sees them, Herberg's remarks offer vivid testimony to the special significance of the post-war religious revival for the American Catholic Church. For it was during these years that the Church finally "arrived" in America, emerging from its former status as a foreign church to join the national consensus as one of the three versions of the American way of life. This milestone, characterized variously as the golden age of Catholicism, or the maturing of the Church in the United States, was in a "very real sense the climax of American

[1]   Cited in Sydney E. Ahlstrom, *A Religious History of the American People* (New Haven: Yale University Press, 1972), p. 954.

[2]   *Ibid.*

[3]   *Protestant-Catholic-Jew* (Garden City, NY: Doubleday and Co., 1960). Herberg's book was originally published in 1955; subsequent quotations are taken from the revised, Anchor Books edition published in 1960.

[4]   Will Herberg, "A Jew Looks at Catholics," *Commonweal* 57 (May 22, 1953), pp. 174-177.

Catholic history."[5] The post-war years had "strengthened the unity and self-consciousness of the Catholic community in the United States, and marked the fulfillment of its historical goals": growth in numbers, and acceptance as a valued part of American society, with the accompanying rise in its prestige and influence.[6] Not coincidentally, this climax in American Catholic history was also the climax, in terms of popularity, of the career of Fulton Sheen.

In many respects, a leading indicator of the Catholic role in the American religious revival was the phenomenon known simply as "Bishop Sheen." Although he had been a fixture on the American scene for several decades, it was during the fifties that he reached the height of his national prominence and influence. Within the structure of the Church, Sheen became a bishop in 1950, and assumed leadership of the National Society for the Propagation of the Faith, the Catholic Church's organization dedicated to missionary work and evangelization around the world. More important in terms of the Church's integration into the fabric of American life, Sheen's influence extended beyond the traditional confines of the Church into the wider American society. As an author, Sheen penned several more books of the "religious inspirational" type which were runaway best sellers, including *Peace of Soul* (1949) and *Life of Christ* (1958). He also received numerous distinguished awards during this era. Although some were in recognition of his religious achievements, many, including the American Legion of New York's gold medal in 1948 for his exemplary "work on behalf of Americanism," and Notre Dame's second annual Patriot Award (following J. Edgar Hoover, who was first) in 1955 as "an outstanding patriot who exemplifies the American ideals of justice, personal integrity and service to country," were given to commend Sheen for his Americanism and patriotism.[7] Although

[5]   David J. O'Brien, *The Renewal of American Catholicism*, p. 138.

[6]   *Ibid.*

[7]   These two awards were cited, respectively, in the *New York Times,* July 16, 1948, and the Notre Dame *Scholastic* 96 (February 11, 1955). Additional awards presented to Sheen include the Cardinal Gibbons Award (Catholic University of America), the Award of the Catholic War Veterans and the Order of Lafayette Freedom Foundation Award.

difficult to measure accurately, the effect of these awards, and the publicity they generated, were undoubtedly to increase the atmosphere of good will among American citizens of all faiths; for many non-Catholics, Bishop Sheen was the first, or only, association they could make with the Church, and he projected a warm, friendly image. And his projection of that image through the new medium of television, to millions of viewers, does more than any single factor to explain the fifties phenomenon of Bishop Sheen, Catholic "star."

The very fact that a Catholic prelate could preside over one of television's most popular shows — "Life Is Worth Living" — indicates how far the Church had come, to enjoy at last its place in the sun during American religion's "Indian summer."[8] The case of Fulton Sheen and the advent of the new technology of television provided an example of a situation in history when "the man" and "the moment" truly met; the meeting most likely could not have occurred, or been nearly as successful, at any time other than in the middle of the post-war American religious revival. "Life Is Worth Living" was ideally suited to the temper of the times. Bishop Sheen was the show; through the power of his personality and oratory, he dramatically popularized religious philosophy for the viewing audience. His talks were ecumenical in tone and spirit; though he was clearly identifiable as a Roman Catholic bishop, garbed in his purple cape and zucchetto, his message was meant for Americans of all faiths. Sheen reflected American Catholicism's newly found pride and confidence, and also provided reassurance and comfort to the American people in a confusing modern world.

This somewhat ambivalent spirit reflected in Fulton Sheen's performances — optimistic and hopeful, yet cognizant of anxieties and fears — characterized the national mood in the post-war era as well, and helps explain the reasons behind the resurgence of re-

---

[8] The term "Indian summer" to describe the Eisenhower years of religious revival first appeared in Ahlstrom, p. 1088; it was also used in James Henessey, SJ's, *American Catholics*, p. 284. Both authors made reference to Sheen's prominent presence during this season.

ligion. A generalized form of religion helped fulfill the country's need for peace and stability. The horrors of the experience of World War II had ended the "optimistic certitudes of rationality and progress," causing some Americans to "harken back to long obscured notions of sin, evil and guilt."[9] These notions had never been obscured by Fulton Sheen, however; throughout his career, he had been known for cautioning against old errors under the guise of new labels. During the war, the notions of sin, evil and guilt had provided the basis for his explanation of the crisis. Another essential premise of his wartime gospel was a call for a national reawakening, a return to religion and the ideals associated with the American heritage. After the war, Sheen found himself very much in vogue, and his calls were being answered by the American people who returned to religion.[10] Thus, in addition to the spiritual revival, there was a practical reason behind the renewed interest in religion, for it offered consolation in a troubled world, for both individuals and the nation.

From the perspective of patriotism and the religious devotion to the "American way of life," the Catholic Church had something more unique to offer as well. Regarding the threat posed by communism, the most portentous cloud on the American horizon, the Church had a proven record of opposition. And Fulton Sheen was a leader in the struggle against communism. The Church's anticommunist crusade, employed successfully as a means of its Americanization, had prepared it for the contribution it was making as a religion of democracy. Will Herberg, American Catholicism's Jewish friend and critic, had commented on the new position Catholics were in: "the Church's intransigent opposition to communism... has had a profound effect upon the American people, leading them to regard the Church as 'on our side' in a way that would have been unthinkable not so many years ago."[11] Sheen had always invited

---

[9] O'Brien, p. 114.

[10] In his first *Life Is Worth Living* book it was noted that it was due to Sheen's talk on "Reparation" that President Eisenhower issued a proclamation to declare July 4, 1953, as a National Day of Penance and Prayer.

[11] Herberg, "A Jew Looks at Catholics," p. 174.

non-Catholic Americans of good will to join the Church in its fight against communism, an invitation that was more readily accepted in the fifties. His appeal for the creation of an interfaith venture in defense of American ideals was seen more sympathetically in a more pluralistic society.

Now that American Catholics were "no longer aliens and outcasts in America,"[12] the Church stood on a new threshold of participation and responsibility.[13] Poised on that threshold, ready to serve both his Church and his nation in a "common cause" with religious Americans of all faiths, was Fulton Sheen. Herberg had commented that "in contemporary American life Catholicism plays a notably constructive role."[14] In his more detailed analysis of the subject in *Protestant-Catholic-Jew*, he would recognize the role played by Bishop Sheen "leader of the T.V. pack."[15] "Fulton Sheen, though appareled in his bishop's cassock, is followed by a vast audience consisting of many non-Catholics as well as Catholics."[16] Sheen's message, like many of the statements made by the Catholic hierarchy, was "received and discussed by Americans as a general religious pronouncement rather than as a sectarian address." The fortunes of American Catholicism were on the rise, in part due to the efforts of Sheen. As Herberg saw it, "it has become one of the three great religions of democracy, and not because of its claim to speak as the universal Church, that American Catholicism is today listened to with such respect and attention by the American people."[17]

Bishop Sheen commanded this respect and attention, as one of the most widely listened to figures of the American religious revival. But his appeal had a broader and more popular base as well. In an age of fashionable religion, when Billy Graham and Norman

---

[12] *Ibid.*, p. 177.
[13] Ahlstrom, p. 999.
[14] Herberg, "A Jew Looks at Catholics," p. 175.
[15] Herberg, *Protestant-Catholic-Jew*, p. 68.
[16] *Ibid.*, p. 161.
[17] *Ibid.*

Vincent Peale were the popular voices of Protestantism, Sheen demonstrated that Catholicism had become a "live option for many religiously inclined Americans"[18]:

> A congenial public found it could enjoy the soothing ministries of both Catholic Fulton J. Sheen and Protestant Billy Graham, as if there had never been a war between the faiths.[19]

Fulton Sheen played a series of roles on the American stage: television personality, missionary, scholar, writer, patriot and priest. In the fifties, when the renewed interest in religion was prevalent in the American mind, Sheen eagerly accepted his responsibilities as Catholicism's most recognizable figure. Most historical assessments of this period mention Sheen's role, in one capacity or another, as one of the Church's important figures, and place him in the company of Catholicism's other leading lights: Cardinal Spellman, Thomas Merton and John Courtney Murray.[20] Winthrop Hudson, in *Religion in America*, called Fulton Sheen and Thomas Merton the "two major symbols of the post World War II religious revival among Roman Catholics," and noted that "Sheen ranked with Billy Graham and Norman Vincent Peale as the pre-eminent spokesmen of religion during these years."[21] Catholic historian Thomas T. McAvoy, C.S.C., stated that "there was an increasing number of Catholic books published," and that the most popular were Merton's *Seven Storey Mountain* and several by Bishop Sheen.[22] Another survey of American Catholic history by James Henessey, S.J., made the same point about the new popularity of books by

---

[18] Ahlstrom, p. 1099.

[19] Martin Marty, *Pilgrims in Their Own Land* (Boston: Little Brown and Co., 1984), p. 414.

[20] See Marty's Chapter 18, "The American Way of Life," pp. 403-428, in *Pilgrims in Their Own Land.*

[21] Winthrop Hudson, *Religion in America*, p. 403.

[22] Thomas T. McAvoy, CSC, *A History of the Catholic Church in the United States* (Notre Dame: University of Notre Dame Press, 1968), p. 445.

Catholic authors like Merton and Sheen, "television's first significant Catholic star."[23] Of all of the prominent Catholic figures of this era, Fulton Sheen was probably the most successful in terms of attracting the attention of those outside the Church, prefiguring the ecumenical spirit which swept over American Catholicism during the sixties.[24]

The flurry of activities which defined the life of Fulton Sheen during this religious revival mirrored the changes in the national life which caused many Americans to return to religion, or to pledge their allegiance to the "American way of life" as a new civil religion. The crisis mentality which persisted after the war, in light of the threat of the atomic bomb, and the continued aggression by Soviet communists, helps explain the sociological and psychological reasons behind the renewed interest in things religious. Will Herberg spoke of this vague longing for security as one rationale for the religious upswing:

> On every side, insecurity assails us, yet security is becoming more and more the urgent need of our time. In the midst of our prosperity, we... desperately need reassurance and the promise of peace.
>
> In this situation of pervasive crisis, religion appeals to many as synonymous with peace, indeed as offering the best hope of peace in the world today — peace of mind for the individual amid the anxieties and confusions of contemporary existence, peace for the nation in the life and death struggle with communism... religion

---

[23] James Henessey, SJ, *American Catholics,* p. 284. Jay Dolan's *The American Catholic Experience* notes that Sheen was a Catholic media star, a "true Catholic hero" and, in the opinion of Billy Graham, "One of the greatest preachers of our century" (p. 393).

[24] Many general assessments of American history which discuss the religious revival of the fifties single out Sheen (over and above Cardinal Spellman, John Courtney Murray, and Thomas Merton). On a popular level, Sheen was the most representative Catholic prelate in the United States. For representative examples, see Paul Carter's *Another Part of the Fifties* (New York: Columbia University Press, 1983) and Ronald Oakley's *God's Country: America in the Fifties* (New York: Dembner Books, 1986).

commends itself as our greatest resource and most powerful secret weapon.[25]

While Herberg acknowledged the validity of the psychological reasons behind the religious revival, he also warned against the tendency of religion becoming empty, sentimental, and conformist, a "feel good" religion lacking in substance:

> …in the last analysis, it is "peace of mind" that most Americans expect of religion. "Peace of mind" is today easily the most popular gospel that goes under the name of religion; in one way or another it invades and permeates all other forms of contemporary religiosity.… Religion, in short, is a spiritual anodyne designed to allay the pains and vexations of existence.[26]

In addition to the problematic qualities of this shallow type of religion, Herberg was most concerned with what he called the central "perplexing problem" of religion in America: secularism. Ironically, America had become "at once the most religious and the most secular of nations." According to Herberg, "every aspect of contemporary religious life reflects this paradox — pervasive secularism and mounting religiosity… the strengthening of the religious structure in spite of increasing secularization."[27] For Herberg, the ultimate tragedy of this secularized religion was that it falsified the authentic character of the Judeo-Christian tradition in America, "faith itself reduced to the status of an American culture-religion."[28]

This paradox of becoming accepted as one of the three religions of democracy in a framework of secularism was potentially dangerous for the Catholic Church in general, and Fulton Sheen in particular. As Catholicism's popular representative during this

---

[25] Herberg, *Protestant-Catholic-Jew*, p. 60.

[26] *Ibid.*, p. 267.

[27] *Ibid.*, pp. 2-3.

[28] *Ibid.*, p. 262.

religious revival, Sheen became closely identified with an Americanized version of the Catholic faith, but was always careful about maintaining his image as a religious cleric. Fulton Sheen would never be mistaken for a secularist in any sense. His entire career — as educator, Thomistic philosopher, and radio preacher — had been characterized by a persistent and harsh critique of the secularization of modern culture. At various times, Sheen had attacked secularism as the greatest threat to the American educational system; a "barnacle on the ship of democracy"; and the ultimate reason behind the rise of communism.[29]

In *Protestant-Catholic-Jew*, Herberg had commented on the "over-average religiousness of American Catholics,"[30] and judged Catholicism to be the least likely of the three American religions to accommodate in any way with secularism. So, although Fulton Sheen sometimes appeared to be walking a fine line between a sentimentalized "peace of mind" type of religion, and a more orthodox Catholic theology, he never compromised his religious beliefs or lost sight of his Catholic soul. Rather than following the trend toward turning the American way of life into some form of civil religion, Sheen crafted an adaptation of Catholicism to the American situation to meet the challenge of the times. On a narrow scale, it was part of the effort he had made as a young priest to make the philosophy of St. Thomas "functional" for the modern world.[31] Throughout the fifties, he concentrated on the ideas and values shared by Catholics and Americans, hopeful of restoring religion to a place of prominence in the nation's life. This insistence on the continued relevance of religion in American life was reflected in the official pronouncements of the Catholic hierarchy as well.

From the perspective of the Catholic "world view," the great

---

[29] For example, see Sheen's "Educating for a Catholic Renaissance," *N.C.E.A. Bulletin* (August, 1929); "The Crisis in Christendom," "Catholic Hour" broadcasts delivered in 1943; and *Communism and the Conscience of the West*.

[30] Herberg, *Protestant-Catholic-Jew*, p. 221.

[31] See Sheen's dissertation, *God and Intelligence in Modern Philosophy*.

[32] See Philip Gleason, "Pluralism, Democracy and Catholicism in the Era of World War II," *The Review of Politics* 49 (Spring, 1987), p. 210.

evil of the day during the post-war religious revival was secularism.[32] The American bishops issued a "Statement on Secularism" in 1947 which stated that "Secularism, or the practical exclusion of God from human thinking and living, is at the root of the world's travail today... the ideals of Christianity have never been fully realized just as the ideals of the Declaration of Independence and our Constitution have never been fully realized in American political life."[33] This was a theme that would be sounded repeatedly by Fulton Sheen; like the American bishops, he had identified atheistic communism as a "social monstrosity" obstructing the establishment of a "right juridical order in the international community."[34] The hierarchy had argued that "in exiling God from life, secularism had cleared the way for the acceptance of godless ideologies," and the bishops "begged Americans to be true to their historic Christian culture and to reject secularism, which offered no valid promise of better things for the country or for the world."[35]

Several years later, in 1952, the bishops followed this up with a pastoral letter on "Religion, Our Most Vital National Asset." It warned against the danger of regarding religion as simply the "fruit of pious sentiment."[36] So, the Catholic Church was clearly on record as disavowing any secularized forms of religious expression, even as it took pride in its more Americanized status. When Fulton Sheen ventured into the realm of the popularized and peaceful form of religion, he made no concessions to the atmosphere of prevailing secularism, maintaining his essential Catholicism even when addressing troubled souls of any religious persuasion.

The soothing ministries of Fulton Sheen were directed towards the contemporary American's feelings of unease and uncertainty. Sheen served his readers (and television viewers) a palatable brew of traditional religion, Americanism, morality, and a hopeful optimism which many found sustaining. From the end of the war

---

[33] "Statement on Secularism," in Nolan's *Pastoral Letters* (Vol. II), p. 74.
[34] *Ibid.*, p. 79.
[35] *Ibid.*, p. 25.
[36] *Ibid.*, p. 111.

through the Eisenhower era, he wrote many books of a popular and inspirational nature, in keeping with the positive thinking mentality of the age, but without succumbing to it.[37] A simple gleaning of the titles sheds light on Sheen's attempt to respond to the public's need for guidance and reassurance: *Love One Another* (1944); *Preface to Religion* (1946); *Peace of Soul* (1949); *Lift Up Your Heart* (1950); *The Way to Happiness* (1954); *The Way to Inner Peace* (1955); and *Go to Heaven* (1960).[38] Several of these books were immensely popular: the five volume series based on Sheen's television show, *Life Is Worth Living*, climbed to the top of the best seller lists, as did *Peace of Soul.*[39]

Sheen's *Peace of Soul*, in addition to being the Catholic answer to the "peace of mind" genre of religious books, was written for another reason: to set the record straight on his very public controversy with the psychiatric profession, which made headlines for over six months in 1947. Because of the stresses of modern life, psychoanalysis was enjoying a boom period of popularity and prosperity. Concerned that some desperate people might be led astray or even harmed by current techniques he regarded as potentially dangerous, Sheen gave a sermon on the subject of "Psychoanalysis and Confession" at St. Patrick's Cathedral on March 9, 1947.[40] His remarks were reported in the press as an "assault" on psychoanalysis, though Sheen reserved his harshest comments for the particulars of Freudian theory, which he saw as especially hazardous: "Freudianism is based on materialism, hedonism, infantilism and

---

[37] See references to Sheen in Donald Meyer, *The Positive Thinkers: Religion as Pop Psychology from Mary Baker Eddy to Oral Roberts* (New York: Pantheon Books, 1980; originally published in 1965).

[38] Two other Sheen volumes bear mentioning here: *Three To Get Married* (New York: Appleton-Century-Crofts, Inc., 1951), which was an inspirational guide to love and marriage; and *The World's First Love* (New York: McGraw-Hill Book Co., 1952), an up-to-date reflection on the Blessed Virgin.

[39] See Louis Schneider and Sanford Dunbusch, *Popular Religion: Inspiration Books in America* (Chicago: University of Chicago Press, 1958), for statistics on book sales and a contemporary analysis of this phenomenon; the authors singled Sheen out as a truly religious author who was exceptionally well-educated.

[40] Reported in the *New York Times*, March 10, 1947.

eroticism… there were no more disintegrated people in the world than the victims of Freudian psychoanalysis." The main problem with this form of therapy, said Sheen, was that it "failed to relieve the unresolved sense of guilt and sin." Those truly in need of help, he advised, should look instead to "confession," which he called "the key to happiness in the modern world."[41]

Needless to say, these remarks by a leading Catholic figure offended many professionals, and provoked a good deal of controversy and misunderstanding. Several leading psychiatrists spoke up, expressing their shock at Sheen's attitude, questioning his knowledge of psychoanalysis, and wondering whether he spoke on behalf of his Church.[42] As the controversy continued, accusations abounded, and a Catholic psychiatrist, Dr. Frank Curran, quit his post at St. Vincent's Hospital because of the failure of the archdiocese to clarify or repudiate Sheen's attack.[43] Temporarily trying to remove himself from the fray he had set off, Sheen remained silent for several months, perhaps hoping that the furor would blow over. When it didn't, Sheen finally sent a letter to the *New York Times*. It was an attempt to clarify his position, but it added to the confusion. Demonstrating his own lack of knowledge about scientific nuances, he drew a distinction between Freudian psychoanalysis, which he had attacked, and psychoanalysis in general, and described "psychiatry as a perfectly valid science."[44] Laying some of his errors on press reports which distorted his remarks, Sheen compounded his difficulties, saying that he never spoke from a prepared text, and couldn't verify the accuracy of all the press reports. He also called for an end to this "grave distortion."[45] Negative publicity on this issue continued to follow him, so he wrote *Peace of*

[41] *Ibid.*

[42] *New York Times,* July 2, 1947.

[43] *New York Times,* July 20, 1947.

[44] Reported in the *New York Times,* July 21, 1947.

[45] *Ibid.* See also the *New York Times,* July 22, 1947, which reported the remarks of a Dr. Lawrence Kubis, who made a legitimate criticism of Sheen's behavior, suggesting that one who "represents the search for the good life" should be more scrupulous in terms of complete honesty and humility.

Soul in 1949, to clarify his views and to provide a more comprehensive Catholic answer to two philosophies he found objectionable: those of Freud and Marx.

The scope of *Peace of Soul* was wider than this, however, and helps explain its tremendous popularity.[46] Sheen opened this volume by saying that his interest was in "postwar frustrated man, or the modern soul." Of course, Sheen had always been interested in the modern soul, but from this particular angle, his interest had been sparked by Pope Pius XII's prediction that "postwar man would be more changed than the map of postwar Europe":

> Unless souls are saved, nothing is saved; there can be no world peace unless there is soul peace. World wars are only projections of the conflicts waged inside the souls of modern men, for nothing happens in the external world that has not first happened within a soul.[47]

Noting that the "parallel between modern theories of the inner and outer world is striking," Sheen said that there were two systems of thought which emphasized "tension and upheaval." Marx, the prophet of the outer world, centered his philosophy in social conflict. Freud, the prophet of the inner world, was mainly concerned with individual conflicts.[48] Since Sheen had dealt extensively with Marxian philosophy elsewhere, *Peace of Soul* was devoted to Freud and psychological matters, though he did call Marx and Freud "children of the same age who expressed the same basic attitudes."[49]

Speaking as a man of God and an apologist for the Catholic Church, Sheen expressed a desire to rely on tradition, and the philosophy of St. Thomas, but he realized that this was not always possible:

---

[46] Among the indications of the book's popularity are the fact that it was chosen as a selection for four Catholic book clubs, and was published in several foreign languages.

[47] Sheen, *Peace of Soul* (Garden City, NY: Doubleday and Co., 1951 edition), p. 1.

[48] *Ibid.*, p. 5.

[49] *Ibid.*, p. 6.

> It is the point of this book that we must make a start
> with modern man as he is, not as we should like to find
> him. Because our apologetic literature has missed this
> point, it is about fifty years behind the times.[50]

As Sheen found modern man, he was characterized by three alien-
ations, divided from himself, his fellow man and from his God.[51]
Concerned with healing that sense of alienation, with a special
emphasis on man's alienation from God, he addressed himself in
successive chapters of the book to problems like frustration, anxiety, repression, sex and fear of death. Underlying Sheen's entire
discussion, however, were several important themes: the denial of
guilt as the root cause of modern chaos and frustration; the superiority of confession over psychoanalysis; and the primacy of the spiritual over the secular.

The denial of guilt, said Sheen, was the basic flaw of Freudian analysis. No single influence did more to prevent man from
finding God and rebuilding his character, or to lower the moral tone
of society, than "the denial of personal guilt."[52] The Christian view
of man was preferable, for it recognized the reality of sin: "to be a
sinner is our distress, but to know it is our hope."[53] Trying to mend
fences with those in the professional community, Sheen admitted
the validity of both psychiatry and psychoanalysis. Psychiatry, a
science which treated mental ills, was not only valid, said Sheen,
but "a real necessity today."[54] Psychoanalysis he described as a
method of treating mental ills which was based upon the examination of the unconscious. Sheen suggested that rather than pretend-
ing to be a philosophy, psychoanalysis might be viewed as "an application of the Christian doctrine of the examination of conscience"
to the examination of the unconscious.[55] Carried one step further,

---

[50] *Ibid.*

[51] *Ibid.*, p. 7.

[52] *Ibid.*, p. 62.

[53] *Ibid.*, p. 76.

[54] *Ibid.*, p. 79.

[55] *Ibid.*, p. 80.

he compared psychoanalysis to confession, stating an obvious preference for the confessional box over the psychoanalyst's couch. Confession, or the sacrament of Penance, came first in time, and the popularity of psychoanalysis arose from the same desire to confess as a means of achieving peace. To Sheen, this was yet another instance of how "...the world, which threw Christian truths into the wastebasket in the nineteenth century, is pulling them out in isolated, secularized form in the twentieth century, meanwhile deluding itself into believing that it has made a great discovery."[56] The bottom line of Sheen's argument, as usual, was the necessity of restoring religion to modern life: returning to God was the secret of "peace of soul":

> ...to combine detachment from evil with attachment to God, to abandon egotism as the ruling, determining element in living and to substitute our Divine Lord as the regent of our actions. What is anti-God must be repressed; what is Godly must be expressed.[57]

Conversion, one of Sheen's favorite tasks, was the subject of the final chapters of *Peace of Soul*. The subject was viewed from three perspectives: the psychology of conversion; the theology of conversion; and the effects of conversion. This was Sheen's chance to speak as an expert, and when the book was first published, these three chapters were recommended to any readers who wondered about Sheen's great success as a convert-maker. The product of "rich experience accumulated during Sheen's long and fruitful work" with converts to the Catholic faith, they provided an "interesting reflection of his persuasion."[58] Because he wrote during the age of the atomic bomb, Sheen granted that his own persuasive powers were heightened, "for the very thought of an atomic war with a

[56] *Ibid.*, p. 112.
[57] *Ibid.*, p. 177.
[58] See the review by J. Donceel of Fordham University in *Thought* 25 (March, 1950), pp. 183-186.

cosmic catastrophe will make many men hasten the crisis, anticipate the tension, and begin their conversion now."[59] Acknowledging that "everyone in the world is looking for certitude, peace of soul, and freedom of spirit," Sheen suggested that "most men today seek them in the wrong places."[60] The right place could be found by following Sheen's guidelines, for he would lead them to the Catholic Church.

The convert to Catholicism received many benefits, but the most important were certitude and peace of soul.[61] "There is a world of difference between peace of mind and peace of soul,"[62] said Sheen, separating himself and his Church from the false sense of peace offered by psychoanalysis. To support this contention, Sheen relied on a quotation from Scripture:

> Conversion brings the soul out of either chaos or this false peace of mind to true peace of soul. "Peace I leave with you, my peace I give unto you. Let not your heart be troubled, nor let it be afraid" (John 14:27). This true peace is born of the tranquility of order, wherein the senses are subject to the reason, the reason to faith, and the whole personality to the will of God.... This true peace can never come from adjustment to the world, for if the world is wicked, adjustment to wickedness makes us worse. It comes only from identification of one's own will with the Will of God.[63]

Closing his book with a comforting and reassuring tone, Sheen advised his readers to "cease asking what God will give you if you

---

[59] Sheen, *Peace of Soul,* p. 225.

[60] *Ibid.*, p. 263.

[61] In the chapter on the effects of conversion, Sheen also discussed many other benefits, more practical in nature: a re-centered life and a revolution in all of its values: a change in behavior and conduct; and improved health, perseverance, and a sense of harmony with the universe.

[62] *Ibid.*, p. 258.

[63] *Ibid.*, p. 259.

come to Him, and begin to ask what you will give God. It is not the sacrifice it sounds, for, in having Him, you will have everything besides."[64] Essentially, a simple "trust in God" was the foundation of *Peace of Soul.*

Sheen's book was reviewed quite favorably in both the Catholic and secular press, and was even called one of Sheen's "heavier" volumes, directed at the more intelligent reader.[65] It was also seen as the latest contribution to the growing body of work which comprised the "Apologetics of Fulton J. Sheen," assembled over the past two decades.

The subject of Sheen's Catholic apologetic attracted a new wave of interest during the post-war revival. To many Catholics, Fulton Sheen was a faithful and successful champion of the faith, and his growing popularity augured well for the future fortunes of the American Church. In *Extension* magazine, John C. O'Brien called Sheen an "alert apologist for the Catholic faith" who insisted upon knowing the position of his opponents: Marxists, Freudians and secularists. It was this mastery of the other side of the argument which made him such an "effective expositor of Catholic doctrine" and an "instrument of conversion" — "clerical dynamite."[66] Robert E. Brennan, O.P., reviewed *Peace of Soul* in the more scholarly journal, *New Scholasticism*, noting that Sheen's was "not an easy task — this groping for light, this effort to achieve a peaceful compact with a world full of strife, doubt and confusion":

> For more than a quarter of a century, the stream of a solid Catholic apologetic has been flowing from the pen of Fulton Sheen. The sources of his inspiration have been mainly two: Holy Writ and the teaching of St.

---

[64] *Ibid.*, p. 264.

[65] See Joseph McSorley, CSP, in *Catholic World* 169 (May, 1949). A different viewpoint was expressed by George Shuster in the *New York Tribune*, May 29, 1949. Shuster called *Peace of Soul* "interesting reading" and even guesed that "physicians would not dissent from a great deal that is said" by Sheen.

[66] John C. O'Brien, "Monsignor Sheen Will Preach," *Extension* 40 (February, 1946), pp. 8-9.

Thomas Aquinas. In his books and sermons, Sheen has stood as a bulwark against paganism of every sort, as a friend of those in search of truth, a guide for the bewildered who are looking for a way of life that will lead to happiness and ultimate salvation.[67]

In "Bishop Sheen's Threshold Apologetics," Donald Shine, S.J., discussed Sheen's unique appeal to non-Catholics. Sheen integrated popular problems with Scholastic philosophy, speaking a "language that is intelligible to the modern man, digging out of his treasures new things and old."[68] His success, according to Shine, was due to the fact that he met all manifestations of evil with "a brilliant adaptation of St. Thomas' truths."[69] Another Catholic analysis pointed out that not all of Sheen's reviews were favorable. To some, said John J. Keating, C.S.P., the "new kind of Mr. Television" was "too modern," sounding like a liberal minister in a fashionable church, and not relying enough upon "classical apologetics."[70] To others, Sheen was a bishop who simply used the talents God gave him in a new medium. Although his methods were unorthodox, Sheen was presenting a "preface or preamble to the logic of classical apologetics."[71] This was especially important, according to Keating, because Sheen reached out to a large audience of Christians and Jews:

> Sheen has been the Roman Catholic conclusion to the more general Judeo-Christian principles he has taught... he is the purple passage in every telecast by which some are brought into the vestibule of the Church, and then, through the medium of classical apologetics and the Grace of God, into the Church itself.[72]

---

[67] *New Scholasticism* 24 (January, 1950), p. 86.
[68] *American Ecclesiastical Review* 125 (October, 1951), p. 276.
[69] *Ibid.*, p. 279.
[70] John J. Keating, CSP, "Bishop Sheen: Purple Passage to the Church," *Catholic World* 179 (April, 1954), pp. 6-11.
[71] *Ibid.*, p. 9.
[72] *Ibid.*, p. 11.

Sheen's success made it difficult to be overly critical of his methods, and Keating's assessment was one with which Sheen himself could agree, as he frequently spoke of being an instrument of God, a channel of His grace.

Among fellow Catholics, then, Sheen was perceived kindly, but not uncritically. An illustration of the old maxim that "you can't please all of the people all of the time," Sheen could be praised and criticized for the same traits. He had taken this fact to heart when he pointed out a "less pleasant and final effect of conversion" — that "one becomes the target of opposition and hate."[73] The postwar religious revival in American history was also a time of increased tension and hostility between Protestants and Catholics, and Fulton Sheen was the object of his fair share of criticism, and some that was not so fair. Through it all, he maintained his distance from the more heated political controversies of the day, following the practice he employed with respect to McCarthyism. Although Sheen avoided direct responses to the criticisms leveled against him, he played a supporting role in the bitter controversies between Catholics and Protestants/liberals, which reached its climax in the years 1947-1954.[74] Answering the critics of Catholicism indirectly through lectures and sermons, Fulton Sheen never let up on his simple message that good Catholics were good Americans; because of his popularity, he often occupied center stage in the public arena, and his message enjoyed a wide circulation.

One steady opponent of Fulton Sheen during these years of the American religious revival was the *Christian Century*, a leading Protestant journal of opinion which criticized him at every opportunity.[75] In 1956, for example, an editorial — "Bishop Cloys as

---

[73] Sheen, *Peace of Soul,* p. 261.

[74] See Philip Gleason's "Pluralism, Democracy and Catholicism in the Era of World War II," pp. 208-230, for a good, comprehensive source on the post-war religious controversies.

[75] During the years under consideration here, 1945-1966, Sheen was the subject of commentary — much of it negative — on at least a dozen occasions. For some examples, consult the *Christian Century*.

Critic" — charged Sheen with coming "close to blasphemy" in remarks he made on television as a "spiritual symbol of the truth by
which we are saved."[76] "Roman Catholicism's most gifted television performer," continued the editorial, was guilty of cynical exaggeration in likening television to the incarnation of Christ. This
editorial concluded by asking, "Is this the way in which Catholic
discipline guards the purity of Christian doctrine?"[77] In this case,
Sheen was caught in the cross-fire of Catholic-Protestant hostilities, and the *Christian Century* was guilty of some exaggeration of
its own in placing so much importance on a metaphor frequently
employed by Sheen, with no real connotations of blasphemy. Surely,
not even Sheen took his every word this seriously.

In a more extended and fair-minded manner, the Rev. A. Roy
Eckhardt, a professor at Lehigh University, wrote a critical analysis of "Bishop Fulton J. Sheen Tells the Story of the Birth of Christ"
(*Colliers*, December 25, 1953). In "The Christ Child and Bishop
Sheen,"[78] Eckhardt admitted that unlike many of his contemporaries, he had never seen the famous bishop on television in his role
as "popular interpreter." He was familiar with Sheen's reputation
as a Scholastic philosopher, though, and noted that this article, like
most of Sheen's work, followed the Scholastic approach of "beginning with reason and working up to faith."[79] Overall, Eckhardt's
analysis was perceptive, sympathetic to Sheen's strengths and accomplishments, and justly critical of his weaknesses. He focused
on Sheen as an apologist for Catholicism, and posed several intelligent questions.

"In the crucial work of apologetics," asked Eckhardt, "are not
official spokesmen required to use careful language and a sufficiently
profound logic?"[80] Noting that Roman Catholic priests were well-

---

[76] *Christian Century* 73 (December 5, 1956), p. 1413.

[77] *Ibid.*

[78] *Christian Century* 71 (January 20, 1954), pp. 78-80.

[79] *Ibid.*, p. 78.

[80] *Ibid.*

trained in logic, he said that it was "especially incumbent upon them to employ valid reasoning and to bring in all relevant facts."[81] In Sheen's case, he found the reasoning too simplistic and watered down, saying that Sheen carelessly interchanged "Christ" and "Jesus." To Professor Eckhardt, Bishop Sheen exemplified "both the appeal and the shortcomings of the Roman Catholic apologetic":

> Obviously, the bishop is a man keenly and rightly aware that we have to meet people where they are. But unless our strategy pays serious attention not only to reason, and history as such, but to the perplexities reason and history raise, it builds on sand.[82]

This accurate and balanced critique of Bishop Sheen was written at the close of the period of Protestant-Catholic antagonism, as tensions were relaxing. Eckhardt's criticism was of a constructive nature, and expressed a point of view consistent with some of Sheen's fellow Catholics who found the bishop too popularized at times. It was a perspective which contrasted sharply with that of another critic of Fulton Sheen, a man whose name became synonymous with a new wave of anti-Catholicism prevalent during the early fifties — Paul Blanshard.

Blanshard, a journalist and former official in the State Department, made his appearance as a leading proponent of anti-Catholic sentiment in 1949, when his very popular *American Freedom and Catholic Power* was published.[83] Initially, the book was praised in the secular and Protestant press as a thought-provoking critique of the Catholic Church; it was immediately condemned

---

[81] *Ibid.*, p. 79.

[82] *Ibid.*

[83] Paul Blanshard, *American Freedom and Catholic Power* (Boston: The Beacon Press, 1949). This book was followed by a companion volume entitled *Communism, Democracy and Catholic Power* in 1951.

by Catholics as an example of the old nativism in a new guise.[84] Blanshard became associated with a group called Protestants and Other Americans United for the Separation of Church and State, founded in 1948. POAU was founded by several prominent Protestant leaders, such as Methodist Bishop G. Bromley Oxnam and John A. Mackay, president of the Princeton Theological Seminary, who viewed the Roman Catholic Church as a threat to American values and institutions.[85] The formation of such a group was symptomatic of the growing hostility between Catholics and Protestants in America, a hostility exacerbated by Blanshard, who spoke as a secular liberal rather than as a Protestant.

The attack against Catholicism launched by Blanshard focused on the hierarchy of the Church, which he viewed as authoritarian, anti-American, and posing a dangerous threat to the nation's democratic ideals. Other issues dividing Catholics and non-Catholics discussed in Blanshard's books were education, "Catholic Action" political pressure, censorship, moral issues like divorce and birth control, and the Church's anti-communist campaign.[86]

In *American Freedom and Catholic Power*, Blanshard aimed several shots at Monsignor Fulton J. Sheen, an open admission on his part of Sheen's popularity and influence as a leader of American Catholic opinion. On the subject of censorship, Blanshard said that "radio orators like Fulton J. Sheen are freely permitted to indulge in violent attacks on religious liberalism."[87] Sheen had always

---

[84] For the Catholic response to Blanshard, see John Courtney Murray's review of *American Freedom and Catholic Power* in the *Catholic World* 169 (June, 1949), pp. 233-234; Murray's "The Catholic Position — A Reply" in *American Mercury* (reprinted in the October, 1949 issue of the Paulist Fathers' *Techniques for Convert-Making* under the title "Protestant Concern Over Catholicism"); and Murray's "Paul Blanshard and the New Nativism" in *The Month* 5 (April, 1951), pp. 214-225.

[85] For details on the founding of POAU, see Ralph Lloyd Roy's *Apostles of Discord: A Study of Organized Bigotry and Disruption on the Fringes of Protestantism*, pp. 146-152.

[86] For a broad discussion of Catholic-Protestant tensions, see "Issues Between Catholics and Protestants at Mid-Century," in *Religion in Life* 23 (Spring, 1954), written by three prominent and enlightened Protestants: George H. Williams, Waldo Beach, and H. Richard Niebuhr.

[87] Blanshard, *American Freedom and Catholic Power*, p. 206.

opposed the doctrine of historic liberalism, but Blanshard's characterization of Sheen's attacks as "violent" was exaggerated and
inaccurate. He also said that Sheen delivered the hierarchy's official
line on the "Catholic Hour," and said that his broadcasts were "interlarded with political and partisan propaganda."[88] Again,
Blanshard's tone was vitriolic and exaggerated. While Sheen did
act as a spokesman for the hierarchy, his broadcasts were not political, and partisan only in the sense that they reflected official
Catholic beliefs and teachings.

Quoting a lengthy passage from Sheen's *Communism and the
Conscience of the West*, Blanshard continued in the same vein, questioning Sheen's "reliance on necromancy or astrology," and stating
that Monsignor Sheen's position as "a Professor of Philosophy at
America's leading Catholic institution of learning" was a telling indicator of the weakness of Catholic philosophy.[89] This charge was
absurd, and indicated that Blanshard's knowledge of Fulton Sheen
and Thomism was in itself quite limited, and that he was clearly
biased. Finally, quoting the *New York Times*, Blanshard noted that
the "House of Representatives voted to include Franco's government in the Marshall Plan 'less than an hour after the session had
been opened with prayer by Monsignor Fulton J. Sheen of the
Catholic University of America.'"[90]

It was not Fulton Sheen's style to dignify Blanshard's accusations with a direct reply, but a good deal of Sheen's patriotic rhetoric can be perceived as an attempt to counteract just this type of
intolerance. During this period of heightened religious tension,
Sheen was mindful of his prominence as a representative of Catholicism, and was as intense in his Americanism in his public statements as he was in his devotion to moral principles. The soundness of his patriotism and loyalty to his country were powerful rebukes to the suspicions about the divided allegiances of Catholics.
Blanshard's popularity indicated that the Church still had to con

[88] *Ibid.*, p. 209.
[89] *Ibid.*, pp. 233-234.
[90] *Ibid.*, p. 256; quoting from the *New York Times*, March 31, 1948.

tend with the hostility and prejudice remaining in American society; Sheen's method of alleviating it was to replay his familiar themes, hoping that his message would sink in if he repeated it often enough.

An exemplary summary of Sheen's views on Catholicism and Americanism was contained in the speech he gave to the National Confraternity of Christian Doctrine convention, at the Chicago stadium in the fall of 1951. Entitled simply "God and Country,"[91] it was a stirring paean to religion and patriotism, a powerful rejoinder to the Blanshard mentality, designed to blunt the attacks on the loyalty of the nation's Catholics. Declaring that he was pleased to be assigned "one of the choicest topics — loyalty to God and country," Sheen explained that the two loyalties were intrinsically "bound together."

Reviewing the course of American history, Sheen said that the loyalties to God and country were joined in two ways. First, regarding the common assumptions about the "origins of man's rights and duties": the Founding Fathers, in writing the Declaration of Independence which had given birth to the American nation, recognized the "Creator" as the true source of American freedoms. Harking back to an earlier theme, Sheen called for a new "Declaration of Dependence," wherein Americans would once again profess their dependence upon God. Second was the lesson, evident throughout our history, that "prosperity and peace were associated with obedience to God's laws." Invoking the memory of Abraham Lincoln, Sheen reminded his audience that during the "calamity of the Civil War," the President had appreciated the validity of this association in declaring that it would "behoove us to confess our national sins and ask for God's mercy and forgiveness."

After this initial construct, designed to point out the compatibility of Catholic and American beliefs, Sheen proceeded to "answer the false accusations of disloyalty" against Catholics. He

---

[91] This speech, given on November 11, 1951, was recorded as an RCA phonograph record; a copy is part of the collection at the Sheen Archives, and is the source for the quotations from the speech.

said that he was deeply hurt by the charge that Catholics were dis-
loyal to their country just because they loved their God and Church,
and said that there was really no contradiction here. He added: "too
long have we been silent, hoping that time would overcome this
prejudice." Unequivocally avowing that Catholics were good American citizens, he declared their loyalty to, and acceptance of, the First
Amendment, which guaranteed freedom of religion. Then Sheen
asked for "no more lies against us," no "further stirring up of hatred for citizen against citizen." Appealing to any associated with
these lies, Sheen asked them to remember that "we are all Americans," and recited an impressive record of Catholic contributions
to the nation in time of war. Since Revolutionary War times, Catholic soldiers had loyally defended their country: "Catholics are dying on the fields of Korea even now!"

In a heartfelt plea for unity, Sheen called upon his "fellow
citizens" to defend their Catholic brethren in the face of attacks on
their loyalty. In an effort to undermine the credibility of the accusations, Sheen proclaimed: "Let them attack us in the name of bigotry, intolerance or Communism — but not in the name of America
or in the name of God." "We are all living in trying times," said
Sheen, and rather than concentrating on religious differences, "all
good Americans — following the lead of our American eagle, which
flies onward and upward — should seek to draw everyone closer to
God."

Ave Maria was one Catholic magazine that appreciated the
underlying purpose of Sheen's message, informing its readers that
"anti-Catholic bigots received a sound lesson" in American history
and Catholic patriotism from the Bishop in his address.[92] The thun-
derous applause which interrupted Bishop Sheen was more than
admiration for his eloquence:

> It was the mass agreement with a speaker who justly re-
> sented any unjust reflection on the loyalty of American
> Catholics to their country. The bishop was a spokesman

[92] *Ave Maria* 74 (December 1, 1951), pp. 674-675.

for all Catholics… the Blanshards perhaps will not be stopped in their bigoted attacks on Catholics by the Bishop's address, but all fair-minded men now know that the bigots have been cut down to size by it.[93]

Although Sheen's response to Blanshardism might be considered simplistic and defensive, characteristic of his role as a popularizer, it was in tune with the more direct responses of other angry Catholic spokesmen. Father James M. Gillis, C.S.P., a colleague of Sheen's on the "Catholic Hour," wrote an "Open Letter to Anti-Catholic Agitators" in *Catholic World*. Addressing the "Oxnams and Blanshards," Gillis offered few apologies for his choice of epithet, arguing that "agitator" was kinder than "totalitarian," the charge most frequently directed at Catholics.[94] After criticizing the logic of the agitators, Fr. Gillis concluded his letter with a plea for unity and tolerance, and a dose of sarcasm which could just as easily have come from the pen of Fulton Sheen:

If you are really knights in shining armor and not ridiculous Don Quixotes, you can find plenty to fight besides windmills.… Don't fight those who are out in the front line of battle contending against communism and atheism; don't shoot at us from the rear. It isn't good sport, it isn't good sense, and it isn't good religion.[95]

Even John Courtney Murray, who composed the most sophisticated and extended response to the "New Nativism" dismissed much of Blanshard's invective as "nonsense."[96] Murray called Blanshard the "undiluted secularist who has just been co-opted into

---

[93] *Ibid.*

[94] Gillis, letter reprinted in *Techniques for Convert-Making* (June, 1950), in the collection at the Sheen Archives.

[95] *Ibid.*

[96] Murray, "Protestant Concern Over Catholicism," in *Techniques for Convert-Making* (October, 1949), p. 1.

the ranks of the Fathers of the Protestant Church,"[97] and also stated
that Blanshard's book achieved a "closure of mind and an edge of
antagonism that would be the envy of a Bible-belt circuit rider."[98]
To Murray, Blanshardism was the same old article, "anti-Roman
bias" resurrected as a new nativism, more naturalistic than Protestant.[99] Along lines similar to the apologetic of Sheen, Murray argued that

> ...it was over these sacred things, and the Church's
> rights in their regard, that the nineteenth century battle
> between the Church and the Liberal society chiefly
> raged. The issue is still undecided... the fact that the
> state is democratic does not settle the question but rather
> gives it special pertinence, if the State's theory of itself
> is naturalist and secularist.[100]

Murray also saw Blanshard's theories as the "contemporary enemy,"
which "reminds us that, if we lived at the height of our faith and
gave its native dynamism full scope, others might not take so low
and narrow a view," for Catholics possessed the "Power of the Most
High."[101]

    This Catholic response to accusations that the Church had
no place in American society was strengthened by its new sense of
confidence, for the Catholic Church enjoyed its greatest ascendancy
as a major religious force in America at the precise moment that it
came under attack. According to Lerond Curry, whose analysis of
Protestant-Catholic relations encompassed the period from World
War I through Vatican II:

> Blanshard mainly gathered up and reflected fears and
> anxieties of the non-Catholic American which had be-

---

[97] *Ibid.*, p. 2.
[98] See Murray's review in the *Catholic World* 169 (June, 1949), p. 233.
[99] Murray, "Paul Blanshard and the New Nativism."
[100] *Ibid.*, pp. 224-225.
[101] *Ibid.*, p. 225.

come overwhelmed by the new power of the Catholic Church in the nation, and which was the first time affected in all phases of life by that Church.[102]

Fulton Sheen's maturation process occurred alongside that of his Church, which had become an influential force in American society after the Second World War. The prevalent theme of Americanization which carried him through the war years continued into the fifties, but was supported by his ecumenical calls for cooperation among all men of good will, made in the interest of religious harmony. This personal appeal, which predated the official Church pronouncements on ecumenism during the Second Vatican Council, was ecumenical in the sense that Sheen had counted Protestants and Jews among his followers, as evidenced by his books, and in his performances on the electronic media. For example, *Love One Another*,[103] written just as the American religious revival was getting underway, dealt with the general topic of love of neighbor and brotherhood. Like many Sheen books, it was filled with pious platitudes, but these platitudes needed to be heard in 1944. In successive chapters of the book, Sheen spoke of "friendship": between "Christians and Jews," "Catholics with Protestants," and among "all peoples, races, classes and colors."[104] His book was billed as an inspiring solution to the problems of intolerance; Monsignor Sheen was not only making a practical contribution to the growing universal movement for greater tolerance, but set a fine example himself.[105] As a man of God, Sheen exemplified the premise that the "necessary basis of love of neighbor is love of God."[106] This basic "love of God" was the foundation of two of

---

[102] Lerond Curry, *Protestant-Catholic Relations in America* (Lexington, KY: The University Press of Kentucky, 1972), p. 59.

[103] Sheen, *Love One Another* (New York: Garden City Books, 1953; originally published in 1944).

[104] *Ibid.,* Chapters 9-13.

[105] *Ibid.* Press releases and publication information found in the collection at the Sheen Archives.

[106] *Ibid.,* Chapter 14.

Sheen's most popular books to come out of the spirit of the American religious revival: *Preface to Religion* (1946) and *Life of Christ* (1958). Along with *Peace of Soul*, Sheen considered them to be his best books.[107] *Preface to Religion*, which Sheen wrote for converts, and regularly assigned as required reading in his convert classes, was simply a popular presentation of some essential Christian truths. From the love of God, Sheen moved tangentially to discuss topics like "love of neighbor," "righting social wrongs," and zeal for "political justice and equality" for all; according to Sheen, they were "products of something higher."[108] In simple, understandable language, Sheen was able to provide his readers with a practical and relevant form of religion, attractive features in an age when this style of religion was highly valued.

Sheen's *Life of Christ*, a modern retelling of the story of Christ from the New Testament, was geared toward the same audience, and was probably Sheen's single most successful book.[109] His purpose in writing it was clearly inspirational:

> It is hoped that sweet intimacy with the Crucified Christ, which trial brought, will break through these pages, giving to the reader that peace which God alone can bring to souls and enlightening them to see that sorrow is really the "Shade of his Hand outstretched caressingly."[110]

His preface stated that his was not a work of biblical criticism, but a popularization, and he even recommended Giuseppe Ricciotti's

---

[107] Sheen, in an interview conducted by William Hanford on February 15, 1965; transcript is contained in the collection at the Sheen Archives. Sheen saw these three popular books, along with *God and Intelligence in Modern Philosophy*, as his best books.

[108] Sheen, *Preface to Religion* (New York: P.J. Kenedy and Sons, 1946), p. 205.

[109] Sheen, *Life of Christ* (New York: McGraw-Hill Books, 1958). This book was an instant hit, and it remains in print today, still quite popular.

[110] See *Life of Christ* (Popular Library edition, 1960), p. x, from which the subsequent quotations are taken.

The Life of Christ for those readers who wanted something more technical and critical.[111]

Above all, Sheen emphasized that the real and unique purpose of Christ's coming — the Incarnation — was the Cross: "Every other person who came into this world came to live. He came to die."[112] In his preface, Bishop Sheen explained it in these words:

> Christianity, unlike any other religion in the world, begins with catastrophe and defeat. Sunshine religions and psychological inspirations collapse in calamity and wither in adversity. But the life of the Founder of Christianity, having begun with the Cross, ends with the empty tomb and victory.... The Cross was at the end of His life in time, but at the beginning of it in the intent and purpose of his coming.[113]

Sheen's underlying goal, appreciated by the reviewers, was to write a modern version of Christ's life, relevant to the contemporary era. His emphasis on the Cross was also tied in with his preoccupation with communism, which he discussed at length throughout the book. The *New York Times* review, "The Meaning for Our Day," took note of Sheen's practical application of biblical lessons to current issues: the "Devil's tempting of Jesus to become a kind of communist commissar bent on social and economic amelioration without spiritual regeneration."[114]

Reflecting the "temper of the age," Sheen directed the "bulk of his attention to practical issues"; as expressed through his vivid illustrations and little homilies, there was something in Christ's message for everyone.[115] He discussed Christ from a myriad of

---

[111] *Ibid.*, p. ix.

[112] Sheen made this same point in an article in *Colliers* (December 25, 1953), "Bishop Fulton J. Sheen Tells the Story of the Birth of Christ": "Every other person came into the world to live; He came to die."

[113] Sheen, *Life of Christ*, p. vii.

[114] Harold C. Gardiner, "The Meaning for Our Day," *New York Times*, October 19, 1958.

[115] *Ibid.*

angles, as the "Lamb of God," the "Good Shepherd," and, replaying an old theme from *The Divine Romance* and *The Eternal Galilean* radio broadcasts, Christ as "Teacher, King, and Priest." Much of the *Life of Christ* was simply a new format presentation of familiar Sheen material, "designed to foster one's spiritual growth rather than deepen intellectual enrichment."[116] As a popularization, Sheen's *Life of Christ* was bound to enjoy one very significant advantage:

> ...no one will fail to hear in this synthesis an eloquent voice which is saying again for our times, and in contemporary rhetoric, what the great Fathers of the early Church said for their flocks. Bishop Sheen has one advantage over a St. Augustine — the "flock" that will read this book will undoubtedly be many times larger than that which heard or read the Bishop of Hippo.[117]

Combining an awareness of this advantage with his emphasis on Christ's Cross, Sheen concentrated on the redemptive quality of Christ's death in *Life of Christ*, noting that "redemption was as wide as humanity itself."[118] Taking a personal, practical lead from his own story of Christ's life, Fulton Sheen took advantage of a unique opportunity which presented itself in 1952, the chance to reach out to more souls than any previous preacher in history through the new technology of television.

Bishop Sheen's association with television during the fifties marked the pinnacle of his popularity. Nothing he did before or after these years attracted quite as much attention, or generated so much publicity for Bishop Sheen or the American Catholic Church he represented. The height of Sheen's success as a television star was reached in his "Life Is Worth Living" series, which ran as a weekly show for five consecutive seasons from 1952 through

---

[116] *Ibid.*

[117] *Ibid.*

[118] Sheen, *Life of Christ*, p. 269.

1957.[119] Bishop Sheen was originally approached by the DuMont network in 1952, which offered to feature him in his own television program as a public service.[120] He premiered on Tuesday, February 12, 1952, at 8 p.m. over three television stations, and was an instant success. The DuMont network was swamped with phone calls and fan letters, and overwhelmed at the positive response. The popularity of Sheen's program surpassed all reasonable expectations, and any doubts about the viability of a Catholic bishop playing to the American public on a television screen were quickly laid to rest.[121]

The key to Fulton Sheen's success rested on the personality and talent of the Bishop, for the entire half hour was given over to a popular lecture format — Sheen's powerful presence dominated the screen. The "Life Is Worth Living" show was broadcast from the Adelphi Theatre on West 54th Street, near Broadway, on a specially built set which resembled a study, filled with books. Sheen's only props were a blackboard and a statue of the Blessed Virgin Mary, which Sheen called "Our Lady of Television."[122] At the outset Sheen had a clearly defined purpose in mind when he went on television. In using the new technology, Sheen's purpose meshed with the national mood during the religious revival, and met the needs of potential viewers:

> To supply the spiritual, moral and intellectual demands
> of the American people, to the end that they may be

---

[119] For the facts and figures on "Life Is Worth Living" and Sheen's other television appearances, see Les Brown's *The New York Times Encyclopedia of Television* (New York: The New York Times Book Co., 1977), pp. 393-394; and Tim Brooks and Earl Marsh, *The Complete Dictionary to Prime Time Network T.V. Shows* (New York: Ballantine Books, 1979), p. 350.

[120] See *Time* (February 25, 1952), "Video Debut," p. 72.

[121] In the press coverage surrounding Sheen's stardom, it was often noted that network programmers assigned him to an "obituary spot," opposite Frank Sinatra and Milton Berle. Much was made of the rivalry between "Uncle Miltie" and "Uncle Fultie." See *Time* (November 1, 1954) for the effect of Sheen's show on Sinatra's and Berle's ratings.

[122] For details on Sheen's television set, see *The Bishop Sheen Story* by James Conniff (Greenwich, CT, 1953), *Time* magazine's cover story on "The Microphone Missionary" (April 19, 1952) and interviews in *Look* (January 27, 1953) and *Cue* (November 22, 1952).

unified by that "Pietas" which embraces love of God,
love of neighbor and love of country... we offer these
telecasts to the public in the fervent hope that they may
draw at least one soul closer to God; if they do that, the
author will feel he is fulfilling, in a small way, the vocation to which the good Lord has called him.[123]

This statement illustrates an important feature of the show, noted
by the press from the very beginning: its consciously ecumenical
spirit and style. The fact that a Catholic prelate should be so appealing to Americans of all religious persuasions was a pleasant
surprise to many, who perhaps tuned in expecting to find a more
traditional Catholic sermon. Obviously, this style and purpose
proved to be a formula for success.[124]

Immediate reviews and assessments of the "Bishop Sheen
Show" were highly favorable, even glowing. Jack Gould, of the *New
York Times*, wrote after three weeks that "Life Is Worth Living"
was a "remarkably absorbing half hour of television... the viewer,
regardless of his individual faith, finds himself not only paying attention, but doing some serious thinking as well. Sheen not only
has something to say, he has the gift of saying it well."[125] He added
that "while Bishop Sheen's point of view reflects the doctrines of
the Catholic Church, he is not using television for proselytizing or
sectarian ends. A member of the Protestant or Jewish faiths can
draw strength and inspiration from his words just as easily as a
Catholic."[126]

Within a year's time after his television debut, Fulton Sheen
had become something of a celebrity, and "Life Is Worth Living"

---

[123] Sheen, in the Preface to *Life Is Worth Living* (First Series, 1953), p. viii.

[124] Exact facts and figures regarding Sheen's success as a television star are problematic,
because both contemporary reviews and historical assessments offer different reports and
statistics. One gauge of success was audience mail — but it was variously reported that
he received 6,000 per day or 10,000 per week.

[125] Jack Gould, "Bishop Fulton J. Sheen Preaches Absorbing Sermons in LIWL Series,"
New York Times, February, 1952.

[126] *Ibid.*

something of a national pastime. Bishop Sheen was the subject of several interviews in the popular press, and in October of 1952, "Life Is Worth Living" became the first program of a religious character to be financed by a commercial sponsor or advertiser.[127] The Admiral Corporation reportedly paid the expenses of buying the air time, a figure which ranged in the neighborhood of $1 million, and paid Sheen a salary of $26,000 per show, all of which the Bishop donated to charity.[128] In the course of several interviews, Sheen gave his own assessment of his television ministry, and reflected on his methods, style and goals. In April of 1952, at the beginning of his second season on the air, Bishop Sheen claimed, simply: "I went on television to help my sponsor, the good Lord.... I'm just trying to satisfy the decent aspirations in people."[129] He purposely generalized in a philosophical vein, rather than emphasizing pure religious teachings, because he wanted to appeal to the largest possible audience. In response to criticisms about his corny sense of humor, and the fact that he interspersed serious talks with little witticisms, Sheen denied that he was being theatrical: "I've always been inclined to strike a light note," a practice he used while he was a professor at the Catholic University of America.[130] In "Bishop Sheen and the T.V. Camera," the writer reported that Sheen's half hour show had the "same easy dignity and polished simplicity" of his pulpit talks.[131] Essentially, Sheen was a great teacher, said Larry Newman, an opinion which Sheen shared. This fact was illustrated

---

[127] See the *New York Times*, October 26, 1952. This was a controversial decision in the eyes of Mr. Gould, who lamented the fact that religious programs had to be financed by commercial sponsors. Sheen was able to earn money to support the work of the missions, however; all of Sheen's television dealings and negotiations were independent of official Church structures.

[128] See "Bishop Sheen's Sponsor" by Lawrence H. Hughes, *Catholic Digest* 20 (May, 1956), pp. 17-21. Most of the stories about Sheen and television made a point about his great generosity, and the fact that his earnings were donated to charities such as the Society for the Propagation of the Faith, the Blessed Martin de Porres Hospital in Mobile, and Mission Humanity, a member of the voluntary associations of the United Nations.

[129] Cited in Val Adams, "The Bishop Looks at Television," *New York Times*, April 6, 1952.

[130] *Ibid.*

[131] *Catholic Digest* 16 (May, 1952), pp. 115-117.

by a simple drawing Sheen made on his blackboard of the hub of a wheel: "That's what I'm trying to do," said Sheen by way of explanation, "draw the American people closer together."[132] Another interview conducted by Gretta Palmer, a convert of Sheen's, gave him the opportunity to express his views in "Bishop Sheen on Television."[133] Palmer reported that "few speakers would have dared to trust American audiences to find the movement of the reasoning mind exciting enough to compete" on television. Sheen, however, did; he was a popularizer who respected the intelligence of the common man he so obviously played to. In Sheen's own words, his program was not preaching, but teaching: "You preach to those who already share your convictions, you teach those who do not.... my talks are meant to bring enlightenment."[134]

One of the best examples of Sheen's style as a television personality is found in an article which appeared in the popular national magazine, *Look*, in January 1953.[135] It offers some insight into the ambivalent quality of Sheen's status: a Catholic bishop who said that his show was not religious; a man who craved the attention showered upon him, but who also denied that there was anything that special about him. In the course of this interview with Joseph Roddy, Bishop Sheen revealed one of his secrets which many people found surprising: the fact that he never used a script, text, or notes of any kind. He was remarkably well-rehearsed, and had a perfect sense of timing. Striving for spontaneity and freshness, Sheen admitted that although he spent hours preparing for each television show, "I have never written out a speech and I have never memorized a speech in my life.... why should this living mind be made subject to a dead piece of paper? ...to be an orator, you have to use

---

[132] *Ibid.* See also "And now a word with his sponsor" by James Brieg, *US Catholic* 45 (February, 1980), p. 26. This article, written after Sheen's death, recalled the vivid impression this drawing had left on the writer from *Variety:* "God was the hub and we were the spokes; the nearer we came to God, the closer we came to each other.... It was a very effective visualization of a concept."

[133] *Catholic Digest* 17 (February, 1953), pp. 75-80.

[134] *Ibid.*, p. 76.

[135] "A Talk With Bishop Sheen," Joseph Roddy, *Look* 17 (January 27, 1953).

your own words and be on fire with them."[136] When asked to comment on another television preacher, Billy Graham, Sheen surprised Mr. Roddy, saying that although Graham's program was specifically religious, his was not:

> I am talking as a university lecturer on these programs. I was a university professor for twenty five years, and on television, I am discussing subjects in a university sort of way. But I'm bringing them down to the level of the people.[137]

To those who objected to the fact that Sheen's program was commercially sponsored, Sheen once again denied that his was a religious program. It wasn't religion that was being sponsored, said Sheen, but the poor — "the lepers, the ill-fed and the starving" served by missionaries.[138] And to those who might have suggested that it was unbecoming for a Roman Catholic bishop to become a television star, Sheen smugly suggested that if Christ were on earth today, He might even consider appearing on television as a perfectly acceptable practice: "It would be just as acceptable as his entrance into Jerusalem on a donkey. He used the best means available."[139] After that analogy, Sheen closed the interview with his familiar television sign-off: "God Love You."

After this initial burst of publicity, Sheen settled into the television scene as the attention surrounding him continued, and "Life Is Worth Living" continued to gain new viewers. In 1955, Sheen moved over to the ABC network,[140] and it was here that he peaked

[136] *Ibid.*

[137] *Ibid.*

[138] *Ibid.* It was probably the complaints about being commercially sponsored that led Sheen to claim that his was not a religious show — a rather incongruous and uncharacteristic position for him to take.

[139] *Ibid.*

[140] See the *New York Herald Tribune*, April 22, 1955, in the newspaper clipping files, Sheen Archives.

with an audience estimated at 30 million.[141] In addition to Sheen's unique style, the content of his show also had something to do with his success. The subjects covered in Sheen's television shows were an unusually eclectic assortment, ranging from "informal discussions of common, everyday problems to provocative lectures on world events."[142] Few topics escaped Sheen's consideration. Although communism and missions were top priorities which permeated many of his talks, other subjects which came under his scrutiny were: love, death, education, marriage, science, public speaking, psychology and art. "Life Is Worth Living" had something for everyone, though Sheen generally gave his viewers a standard "mixture of common sense, logic and Christian ethics."[143] Sheen's single most newsworthy telecast was delivered on February 24, 1953, and was entitled "The Death of Stalin."[144] A dramatic reading of the burial scene from Shakespeare's *Julius Caesar*, Sheen intended it as a lesson on Soviet power struggles, a comparison of what happened after Lenin's death to what might happen when Stalin died. In reciting Shakespeare, he interjected the characters of Stalin, Malenkov, Vishinsky and Beria. It seemed remarkably prophetic, for the death of Stalin was announced to the world on March 5, 1953. This "dramatic incident" was reported in the press, but it was just a coincidence, and never elicited any official comment from Sheen's office.[145] Perhaps the best insight into the real impact Sheen had on his times can be gained by looking at two contemporary assessments: *Time* magazine's "Microphone Missionary" and James Conniff's *The Bishop Sheen Story*.

Over the course of recent American history, one gauge of a person's popularity and fame is the attention showered upon him

---

[141] This all-time high figure is one generally reported in historical assessments of the Sheen television show. When Sheen left television in 1957, however, rumors circulated that his ratings had been falling. At the height of "Life Is Worth Living"'s popularity, it was carried on 123 television stations — see John Delaney's entry on Sheen in *The Dictionary of American Catholic Biography*.

[142] *New York Times*, October 25, 1953.

[143] *Time* (April 14, 1952), p. 78.

[144] See *Life Is Worth Living* (First Series, 1953), pp. 149-158.

by the national press. In the case of Bishop Sheen, his status as a celebrity was assured when he made the cover of *Time*. The accompanying article, "Microphone Missionary," contributed in no small measure to the growing personality cult of Bishop Sheen. He was introduced as "perhaps the most famous preacher in the United States, certainly America's best known Roman Catholic priest and the newest star of television."[146] The product of two unique forces — the Roman Catholic Church and the United States of America — Sheen was described as a "dedicated man of God and a go-getter, who could be truly moving as well as thoroughly corny."[147] His claim to fame also included his title as "the most successful missionary of them all,"[148] a reference to his position as the National Director of the Society for the Propagation of the Faith, and his reputation as a convert-maker. Most significant, however, were the references to the real and lasting effects of Bishop Sheen. Contributing to the legend, a Vatican official told *Time*: "He is our right arm in the United States," and the article also stated that "his influence as a preacher is incalculably great."[149]

This last reference points to the difficulties inherent in trying to measure, with any real accuracy, the impact of Fulton Sheen. From popular indications, however, Sheen's efforts produced a fruitful harvest. As early as 1953, a Catholic journalist presumed to write *The Bishop Sheen Story*,[150] filled with praise, bordering on adulation, and many superlatives for one he considered to be a "living legend." After only a year on television, Sheen's audience had risen to 10 million, and he was "preaching to more Protestants than any priest ever has,"[151] according to James Conniff. Covering the full saga of Sheen's life story, from his birth over a hardware store

---

[145] See the account in Brooks and Marsh, p. 350.

[146] *Time* (April 14, 1952), p. 72.

[147] *Ibid.*

[148] *Ibid.*, p. 73.

[149] *Ibid.*, pp. 72-78.

[150] James C.G. Conniff, *The Bishop Sheen Story* (Greenwich, CT: Fawcett Publications, 1953).

[151] *Ibid.*

in El Paso, Illinois, to his current run as television's "Man of the Year," the account almost drips with sentimentality and admiration: "There can be hardly any question that the most influential voice in Christendom, next to that of Pope Pius XII, is being raised inside a TV tube by a fifty-eight year old ex-farm boy from Peoria."[152]

Conniff depicted Sheen as a foe of communism, performer extraordinaire, missionary to the world, and a harsh critic of many current "isms," including the selfishness of some capitalists. Sheen was acclaimed as a provocateur, sometimes acting as the moral conscience of the nation. By reading between the lines and flattery, however, one can discover some of the facts about Sheen's television show, his generosity to charities, devotion to Mary, and success with converts. One indication of Sheen's effect on his contemporaries was the fact that he was well respected and admired in the entertainment industry, voted the "most outstanding personality in television." The Advertising Club awarded him a Plaque of Achievement for his efforts to "strengthen the fiber of America through the higher moral standards of its people by the inspirational message carried on 'Life Is Worth Living.'"[153]

Sheen's meteoric rise to television stardom ended just as quickly when he announced his retirement from television in October 1957.[154] Sheen said that the decision was dictated by spiritual considerations: "to devote more time to my first duty, which is to be a beggar with a tin cup in my hand for the poor of the world.... one must occasionally retire from the lights of television to the shades and shadows of the Cross, where the soul is refreshed and strengthened."[155] Speculation swirled around allegations that there were other reasons for his departure, centering on unprovable suspicions that Sheen was being punished by Cardinal Spellman, who was jealous of the Sheen charisma, and because of a falling out be-

---

[152] *Ibid.*, p. 1.
[153] *Ibid.*, p. 8.
[154] *New York Times*, October 19, 1957.
[155] *Ibid.*

tween the two churchmen over mission funds.[156] Whatever the reasons, Sheen never made a real comeback to television, but his legend lived on in memories, and survives in many historical evaluations written decades later.

Included in a study on *Models of Religious Broadcasting*, Sheen was described as the "most memorable and most admired" of all religious broadcasters, who saw himself as a "thoughtful and persuasive conversationalist with America."[157] Bishop Sheen was also hailed as a pioneer of the electronic gospel, a man who deserved the gratitude of all those who followed in his footsteps in television: "Sheen showed all would-be religious broadcasters that a powerful preacher could make it on television."[158] In a discussion of Fulton Sheen as an "Angel of the Airwaves," he was astutely described as a "religious broadcaster who did not easily fit into any category."[159] Perhaps the highest compliment was paid when the author stated that "no other religious program has ever drawn the consistently high audience which Sheen attracted during his five years."[160] Another account of *The Foundations of the Electronic Church* also sings Sheen's praises, calling him a "bright star in a Protestant firmament; thirty years later, there are still no imitators or successors to compare to Fulton Sheen."[161]

After he left television in 1957, Sheen devoted most of his time to his responsibilities at the Society for the Propagation of the Faith. He continued to address a wide range of topics, however, in

---

[156] The sources of these allegations about the Sheen-Spellman feud are problematic; many are based upon unsubstantiated rumor. For examples, see D.P. Noonan's *The Passion of Fulton Sheen*, Paul Murphy's *La Popessa* (New York: Warner Books, 1983), and John Cooney's biography of Cardinal Spellman, *The American Pope* (New York: Times Books, 1984). For a more reliable allusion to the feud, see Monsignor John Tracy Ellis, *Catholic Bishops: A Memoir* (Wilmington, DE: Michael Glazier, Inc., 1983), pp. 76-84.

[157] J. Harold Ellens, *Models of Religious Broadcasting* (Grand Rapids, MI: William B. Eerdmans Publishing Co., 1974), pp. 38, 43.

[158] Jeffrey Hadden and Charles Swann, *Prime-Time Preachers* (Reading, MA: Addison-Wesley Publishing Co., 1981), p. 30.

[159] Peter Horsefield, *Religious Television: The American Experience* (New York, Longman, 1984), p. 7.

[160] *Ibid.*, p. 8.

[161] Peter Elvy, *Buying Time: The Foundations of the Electronic Church* (Mystic, CT: Twenty-Third Publications, 1987), p. 96.

his syndicated newspaper column, "Bishop Sheen Writes."[162] Like his television shows, these weekly columns covered a variety of favorite Sheen themes, such as the nuclear threat and the morality of the atomic bomb, world hunger, and communism. Consistent with Sheen's desire to remain relevant and current, one issue he addressed in this forum and in lectures and sermons was the issue of education. Sheen had always been outspoken on this subject, and he continued to offer his views during the years of the American religious revival, when the issue was a divisive one between Protestants and Catholics.[163]

In 1952, the *New York Times* reported that Sheen devoted one of his Lenten sermons to the issue of religious tensions and education.[164] Sheen declared that Catholics believed in the First Amendment, and did not want an established church in the United States.[165] The most complete summary of Sheen's views on education during this era was contained in "Education in America," an address he gave to the National Catholic Educational Association in 1954.[166] This address was vintage Sheen material, filled with references to communism and the patriotism of American Catholics, part of his effort to "correlate" education with our times.[167] He concentrated on the three tasks facing Catholic educators, with an eye towards responding to critics: "to save our civilization from authoritarianism; to preserve it from straightjacket uniformity; and to keep the foundations of our rights and liberties."[168] Sheen reached a conclusion that "education is related to culture as a rose is related

---

[162] "Bishop Sheen Writes" was syndicated by the George Matthew Adams service starting in 1949. It ran in the secular press for thirty years — through 1979, the year of Sheen's death.

[163] See the *New York Times*, October 21, 1950. Sheen spoke on the theme "Education as the Guardian of the American Heritage" before the 84th convocation of the New York State Board of Regents.

[164] *New York Times*, March 17, 1952.

[165] This sermon, "God and Country" was devoted to a five point declaration of Catholic faith in the U.S.

[166] Sheen, "Education in America," published in the *N.C.E.A. Bulletin* (August, 1954), pp. 50-56.

[167] *Ibid.*, p. 50.

[168] *Ibid.*, p. 51.

to soil," and said that for Catholics, "education must grow out of the soil and ground of morality, religion and faith"[169] — a lesson he sought to apply to the American educational system ten years later.

When the Supreme Court declared school prayer unconstitutional during the sixties, Sheen deviated from his policy of avoiding political conflicts and went before the House Judiciary Committee to state his views on a proposed constitutional amendment to protect the right to pray in school.[170] From Sheen's perspective, the Court's decision had damaged the roots of American religion, freedom and education, and he had devoted several newspaper columns to criticizing the Court's action in 1964.[171] Speaking before the Congressional Committee in May, Sheen said that he disagreed with the ruling, but admonished Congress from overriding the decision lest it disturb the disestablishment clause of the First Amendment.[172]

The hearings were on the amendment proposed by Congressman Frank J. Becker, and Sheen's appearance was harshly criticized by the *Christian Century*.[173] When asked by Congressman Rodino to suggest an acceptable prayer for a pluralistic society, the best Sheen could come up with was: "I would suggest the prayer that every member carries with him in his pocket: 'In God We Trust'… I am asking only for a recognition."[174] This episode demonstrates that Sheen's policy of trying to avoid such controversies was a wise one. The style that worked so well on television was not as successful in an arena such as this, and he could undermine his own

---

[169] *Ibid.*, p. 55.

[170] See the *New York Times*, May 1, 1964: "Sheen Criticizes Court Prayer Ban," by C.P. Trussel.

[171] "Bishop Sheen Writes": "The Eleventh Commandment," March 1, 1964; "Praying for the President," June 28, 1964; and "Black Monday," July 22, 1964.

[172] Sheen, cited in the *New York Times*, May 1, 1964.

[173] See the *Christian Century*, Vol. 81; three separate articles were devoted to Sheen's conduct, who testified at the same time as Gov. George Wallace of Alabama, and was linked with him in all of the accounts. Sheen's testimony didn't receive any comparable coverage from the Catholic press.

[174] Sheen, cited in the *New York Times*, May 1, 1964.

credibility with his simplistic answers. Sheen did try to clarify his position, both before the Committee and in a letter to Congressman Becker.[175] When viewed in its entirety, his statements seem more reasonable. As a matter of principle, he supported the premise that children in public schools should be allowed to pray on a voluntary basis. But he did have reservations about the necessity and wisdom of a constitutional amendment, believing that First Amendment protection should be sufficient.[176] As usual, Sheen was merely trying to demonstrate that one could be a good Catholic and a good American simultaneously, sticking to the safety of the middle ground that had served him so well in the past. He used his prominence as a spokesman for American Catholicism to prove that loyalty to God and loyalty to country need not be in conflict, teaching a timely lesson to a nation which was more receptive to this message during the sixties.

Fulton Sheen passed through the years of America's religious revival strengthened and well-prepared to face the challenges arising from the Second Vatican Council. Having weathered the storms of Protestant-Catholic hostility, he would continue to serve his Church in an age of greater ecumenical harmony. His talents had been ideally suited to making a significant contribution to the Catholic Church in its drive toward internal unity, and exercising a greater influence over American society. Sheen's stellar performance on television had greatly enhanced his own image, and the image of the American Catholic Church.

Finally, the "emerging middle ground of critical pluralism," expressed as a hope by an enlightened Protestant in 1954,[177] was becoming a reality in the sixties. Fulton Sheen had constructed a very successful career by clinging to that middle ground, and his place in it was now secured. As the hostility which had characterized interfaith relations gave way to a spirit of amity, American

---

[175] Sheen, to the Honorable Frank J. Becker, July 9, 1964; contained in the Correspondence file at the Sheen Archives.

[176] *Ibid.*

[177] George Hunston Williams, in "Issues Between Catholics and Protestants at Mid-Century," *Religion in Life* 23 (Spring, 1954).

Catholics, though still cautious, could look forward to the future with greater confidence. John Courtney Murray would produce the "most successful efforts to reconcile Catholicism and Americanism,"[178] expressed in *We Hold These Truths*, and brought to fruition in the "Declaration on Religious Freedom" issued from the Second Vatican Council. Murray believed that the "heart of the American system was consensus,"[179] and it was in the midst of this consensus that Fulton Sheen had established himself as Catholicism's greatest popularizer.

In an age when pluralism was accepted by most as part of the American condition, Sheen was able to navigate that fine line between complete assimilation into the culture, and standing outside it, maintaining a Catholic distinctiveness. A source of Catholic pride, Bishop Sheen not only participated in many of the movements of his time — anti-communism, a defense of traditional American values like education and family, and ecumenism — he provided leadership as well. For Catholics and non-Catholics alike, Sheen supplied an eloquent expression of their unease toward the modern world and its complexities; he offered many a renewed sense of purpose as a counterbalance to their aimlessness and uncertainty. Assuring his audience that life was indeed worth living, he lifted the spirits of a generation.

At a time when the American Catholic bishops declared that religion was not only the "individual's most precious possession, but the nation's most vital asset,"[180] Bishop Sheen was proving himself to be a valuable asset to America and the Catholic Church. Although it is difficult to measure his impact, his influence was certainly profound. One index was a survey conducted by the National Opinion Council in 1956, which cited Sheen for his "major role in raising church attendance,"[181] an indicator of the nation's spiritual health. Charting a course on the frontier of American Catholicism,

---

[178] See David O'Brien's *The Renewal of American Catholicism*, p. 68.

[179] *Ibid.*, p. 67.

[180] "Religion, Our Most Vital National Asset," 1952 Pastoral, cited in Nolan's *Pastoral Letters*, p. 149.

[181] *New York Times*, February 6, 1956.

Sheen shared in the sense of American nationalism and Catholic triumphalism in 1960. That triumph, however, would be short-lived, as both the nation and the Church would be rocked to their foundations in the tumultuous atmosphere which characterized the sixties. Historian David J. O'Brien, in *The Renewal of American Catholicism*, spoke of the early sixties as "years of promise and hope," yet fraught with "great danger."[182] "...Never was the ambiguity of success more evident than in the agonies of mind and spirit that beset American Catholicism in the years that followed."[183]

This "ambiguity of success" would prove to be an all too accurate description of Sheen's fortunes during the late sixties as well. But even though the Church's confidence would be shaken, and it would be troubled by divisions and searching criticisms, Vatican II held out the promise of renewal, reconciliation and reform. Fulton Sheen would go to the Council as a leader of the Church's missionary efforts, his horizons greatly expanded by his experience as National Director of the Society for the Propagation of the Faith. His statements during the sessions of the Council reaffirmed his commitment to the missions, and he urged a new sense of mission upon the universal Church.

In many respects, having crossed the threshold of participation and responsibility at the beginning of the post-war religious revival, he stood poised on a new threshold during the Council, and would be appointed as the sixth Bishop of Rochester. Sheen would remain a power in American Catholic life, even as the Church's confidence gave way to doubt, its consensus to conflict. Having become part of the American religious landscape during the previous decade, the Catholic Church would be subject to the tremors of the "spiritual earthquake"[184] which struck the nation and the Church during the sixties. What final effect that earthquake would have on the life of Fulton Sheen remained to be seen, in the aftermath of his performance as a "missionary to the world."

---

[182] O'Brien, p. 150.

[183] *Ibid.*, p. 139.

[184] The phrase is taken from Philip Gleason's "In Search of Unity: American Catholic Thought, 1920-1960," *Catholic Historical Review* (April, 1979), p. 185.

CHAPTER SEVEN

Missionary to the World
and the Second Vatican Council:
Years of Transition, 1950-1966

Because the vision of Fulton Sheen was never narrow or
provincial, he found a challenge in the Missions. He now thought and
wrote and spoke to the whole world.... The modern missionary, he
maintained, "holds the key to the future union of the East and the
West, at least as much as God ever intended them to be united."
Worldmission, 1980

As chastity was the fruit of the Council of Trent and obedience
the fruit of the First Vatican Council, so may the spirit of
poverty be the fruit of the Second Vatican Council.
Fulton Sheen, 1964

In September of 1950, while the American nation was undergoing
a religious revival, Fulton Sheen received a summons to assume a
wider responsibility within the administrative structure of the Roman Catholic Church. Appointed to the office of National Director of the Society for the Propagation of the Faith, he invested most
of his time and energy over the next sixteen years in furthering the
work of the missions. The historic task of the Church's missionaries — to preach the Gospel and plant the seeds for the future growth
of the Church around the world — was readily adopted by Sheen
in his new role as the primary American spokesman for the mission cause. Although Sheen had no direct experience as a missionary, he welcomed this opportunity to expand his spiritual horizons,
adding another dimension to his already diversified career. With
"great reluctance" he surrendered his Professorship of Philosophy

233

at the Catholic University of America, in order to concentrate on
his new responsibilities: "the four walls of the classroom are now
pushed outward to the four corners of the earth, as a school becomes a continent, and the university a world."[1] In directing his
talents toward a more universal mission, Sheen's earlier success as
an evangelist would serve him, and the Catholic Church, well. He
saw the central charge of the Sacred Congregation for the Propagation of the Faith as "the evangelization of a great part of the
world," and noted that his past service to the Church had taken
various forms of evangelization: preaching, the instruction of converts, and the building of several churches in Alabama designed to
reach out to blacks.[2] And Sheen would prove over time that he
possessed the appropriate qualifications to represent the American
Church's missionary operation, for he quickly made a "remarkable
success of his office with the Society for the Propagation of the
Faith."[3]

Fulton Sheen's success as American Catholicism's missionary leader was measurable from a variety of perspectives. The United
States branch of the Propagation Society, at the time Sheen took
over, was responsible for providing the major share of the funds
collected to support the Church's efforts to spread the gospel message. Financially, the fortunes of the missions flourished during
Sheen's tenure; he was instrumental in raising more than $100
million to support the vast network of 300,000 missionaries,
150,000 schools, 26,000 hospitals, 400 leper colonies and 5,000
orphanages.[4] This achievement stemmed largely from Sheen's
popularization and publicization of the work of the Church's missionaries, a task at which he excelled: "Sheen showed an imagina-

[1] *The Catholic Week* (Birmingham, Alabama), September 23, 1950; Newspaper clipping
     files, Sheen Archives.
[2] Fulton J. Sheen, *Treasure in Clay*, pp. 105-106.
[3] John Tracy Ellis, *Catholic Bishops: A Memoir*, p. 82.
[4] *New York Times*, November 8, 1966. For detailed financial figures on Sheen's sixteen year
     term as National Director, see the editorial by the Most Rev. Sergio Pignedoli, Presi-
     dent, Secretariat, Sacred Congregation for the Evangelization of Peoples, in *Worldmission*
     20 (Fall, 1969), pp. 4-5.

tive awareness of the value of public relations techniques, even in sacred causes."[5] In fact, it was probably Sheen's high public profile, his fame as American Catholicism's most persuasive speaker, which made him such a good choice to promote the work of the missions. His personal popularity would draw more attention to a worthy cause; by simply identifying himself more closely with the missions, Sheen assisted the Church's efforts in this all-important task. His skills as a fund-raiser gained international respect, and with Sheen personally doing the asking, financial contributions to the Propagation office rose significantly. To his large audiences, Sheen described the Society for the Propagation of the Faith as "the greatest philanthropic and charitable organization in the world"[6]; he assured the faithful that their monetary sacrifices were in keeping with the wishes of the Holy Father, who declared that this charity "surpassed all others."[7] The sterling reputation of Fulton Sheen, then, enabled him to ably assist the missionary endeavors of the Catholic Church, a fact recognized in one notice in the Catholic press on "Monsignor Sheen's New Post":

> The Monsignor is well-qualified for the important work of heading the Propagation of the Faith in this country. His many and outstanding talents of heart and mind will henceforth be directed to an all-embracing apostolate. Missionaries in the far-flung outposts of the Catholic Church will find in him a zeal that matches their own. In a sense, the Monsignor's parish is the world and his parishioners the peoples of the earth. Many souls have been enlightened and strengthened by Monsignor Sheen's zealous apostolate within the limits of the United States. His ardor will now have wider horizons

---

[5] Robert F. McNamara, *The Diocese of Rochester, 1868-1968* (Rochester: The Diocese of Rochester, 1968), p. 524.

[6] Daniel P. Noonan, *Missionary With a Mike*, p. 49.

[7] Fulton Sheen's Vita, composed in conjunction with his duties at the Society for the Propagation of the Faith. A copy of this document can be found in Sheen's personal papers at the Sheen Archives.

to pursue in missionary work at a time when the Church will depend more and more upon Catholics in the United States for the support of her missions in foreign lands.[8]

If the Church's missions benefited from the effectiveness of Sheen in his new position, it can also be argued that Sheen benefited from his work on behalf of the missions; it was a mutually beneficial experience at a propitious time in the Church's history. The years of Sheen's service as National Director of the Society for the Propagation of the Faith, from 1950-1966, were marked by a tremendous amount of personal growth on Sheen's part, a real awakening to the realities of world poverty and hunger. As Sheen traveled around the globe to represent the Catholic missions, his awareness regarding the worldwide socioeconomic crisis developed, as did his realization that the Church would have to assume a leadership role in providing solutions to that crisis. He recalled in his autobiography that travel "merely confirmed the teachings of theology that humanity is one"; while his travels in the older civilizations provoked these theological musings, his trips to the Third World "shifted my emphasis from ideology to economics, politics and the social order."[9] This shift in emphasis which occurred in Fulton Sheen's personal odyssey from the fifties to the sixties was reflected in the history of the Catholic Church as well. This was an era characterized above all else by changes, the greatest changes associated with the calling of the Second Vatican Council. Pope John XXIII's decision to convene an ecumenical council arose from his conviction that the time had come to throw open the windows of the Vatican to contemporary currents of change. For Sheen, these currents had been set in motion at the time that he took over as director of the Church's missionary efforts in the United States; over the next several years, they would carry him to the Vatican Council sessions in Rome, and eventually to yet another challenging po-

8   *Ave Maria* 72 (October 7, 1950), p. 452.
9   Sheen, *Treasure in Clay*, pp. 152, 149.

sition as Bishop of Rochester in 1966. These years of transition in the life of Fulton Sheen would also find the American Catholic Church poised on the edge of an era of profound change and transition.

This period has been widely discussed by historians of American Catholicism, and generally depicted as a time when the confidence, security and optimism of "fifties Catholicism" gave way to the controversies and upheaval of the sixties. Along with the possibilities for renewal and reform invoked by the spirit of Vatican II came the turbulence and disarray which followed in the Council's aftermath. From the perspective of hindsight, it can be seen that the consensus achieved and celebrated by American Catholics during the post-war religious revival collapsed in the years following the Vatican Council; the new reality was one of diversity, dissent and conflict. The changes wrought by the Council sent shock waves throughout the Roman Catholic Church. In the United States, however, Catholics had to come to grips with changes on two levels: those unleashed by the reforms resulting from the universal Church's deliberations in Rome, and the revolutionary atmosphere prevailing within American society during the tumultuous sixties. According to Jay P. Dolan's historical assessment in *The American Catholic Experience*, the American Church was passing through the most turbulent period in its short history: "it was a time of both disillusionment and hope, of conflict and harmony, of crisis and growth."[10] Another judgment along similar lines was offered by Philip Gleason, who stressed the interaction of Catholicism with the American environment: "the religious earthquake coincided with the social and political storms" which affected American history in general "...the Catholic revolution both influenced the general American cultural crisis and was influenced by it."[11] Despite the mixed results destined to arise from the spirit of "aggiornamento" which defined the Second Vatican Council, the

---

[10] Jay P. Dolan, *The American Catholic Experience*, p. 426.

[11] Philip Gleason, "Catholicism and Cultural Change in the 1960's," in Ronald Weber's *America in Change* (Notre Dame: University of Notre Dame Press, 1972), p. 91.

general attitude at the beginning of the Council was one of hopeful anticipation, as American Catholics were "predisposed to respond actively" to this historical new departure of "updating the Church, bringing it into closer touch with the modern world, opening the windows and letting in some fresh air."[12] In 1960, two years before the first session, Catholics in America had heard a call to adopt a "realistic and constructive" approach to their responsibilities "within a pluralistic society";[13] in his capacity as America's spokesman for the missions and champion of the poor, Bishop Fulton Sheen had fashioned his own realistic and constructive approach to the pressing problems not just within American society, but around the world.

Actively moving out into the world had been a hallmark of Sheen's distinguished career, an activity which engaged him quite literally in his frequent journeys to the far corners of the globe as an ambassador to mission territories. Reaching out to the modern world had been defined as one of the primary duties of the Catholic Church as well. The *Pastoral Constitution on the Church in the Modern World* — *Gaudium et Spes* — was the most comprehensive document to be issued by the community of bishops in attendance at the ecumenical council. Among the significant conclusions contained in the historic statement, the most resonant echoed forth as a challenge to the Church in the modern world: "to scrutinize the signs of the times and interpret them in the light of the gospel."[14] From 1950-1966, the signs of the times which most attracted Fulton Sheen's scrutiny were precisely those associated with his work on behalf of the missions: the gap between the developed and the undeveloped nations of the world, measured in terms of poverty and hunger; the ever present threat of nuclear war between the West and the East; an ecumenical openness to people of different

---

[12] *Ibid.*, pp. 93-94.

[13] John Tracy Ellis, "American Catholicism in 1960: An Historical Perspective," *American Benedictine Review* 11 (March-June, 1960), pp. 1-20.

[14] *Pastoral Constitution on the Church in the Modern World*, in Walter M. Abbott, SJ, *The Documents of Vatican Council II* (London: Geoffrey Chapman, 1966), pp. 201, 202.

faiths; and the special urgency regarding two issues — peace and social justice — which had long been matters of vital importance in Sheen's ministry. These same concerns would become evident in the encyclicals of Popes John XXIII and Paul VI, and would naturally infuse the whole atmosphere associated with the Second Vatican Council presided over by these two Popes. In many respects, then, Sheen's experiences at the helm of the American Church's missionary organization provided him with the necessary intellectual and spiritual equipment to make the transition required of him by the calling of the Council, and to chart his course into the future.

The prelude to Sheen's years of transition, and the immediate juncture which preceded his appointment as National Director of the Society for the Propagation of the Faith, was a trip he took to the Orient and Pacific with Cardinal Spellman in the spring of 1948. The importance of this tour, and his subsequent travels in connection with his duties at the mission office, cannot be overemphasized. In terms of his personal awakening to the realities of life around the world, and the long-lasting effects of the education he gained on these trips, these experiences had a genuine formative influence on his life. It was the first time that Fulton Sheen had come directly into contact with the extent of poverty and human suffering in the undeveloped nations, and it would forever change his outlook. The change was reflected in all aspects of his work during these years: the books and columns that he wrote; the subject matter for his television shows, and the shift in emphasis he frequently alluded to later in his personal memoirs. Sheen's travels greatly expanded his horizons, and the seeds which would blossom for him at the Vatican Council were first planted during these journeys. Although he had always been an evangelist, his efforts for the missions brought a new dimension to his career. Now, he was taking the light of the gospel into areas of real darkness, and this light carried over into his own growing awareness that the Church lived not in a vacuum, but in the real world. It was not the Gospel that changed, but Sheen's broadened understanding of its implications; in recognizing the signs of his times, he was able to seize the opportunity to not only bring spiritual salvation to hungry souls, but to use the public platform he occupied to draw attention to, and help alleviate, the pressing problem of poverty, both abroad and at home.

Sheen was invited to go on the tour in 1948 by Cardinal Spellman. According to Spellman's official biographer, the Cardinal's duties as Vicar General to the Armed Forces had taken him around the world during the war. And once the war was over, he wanted to travel again because of his "interest in missonaries."[15] The Archbishop of Melbourne, Australia, issued an invitation to Cardinal Spellman to come and help him celebrate the centenary of his archdiocese. Gathering a retinue of associates to accompany him — including Bishop James Walsh of Maryknoll, who would later become a prisoner of the Communists in China, and Monsignor Fulton Sheen — the fifteen member party left for Australia on April 23, 1948.[16] Sheen was taken along for several reasons; it was thought that he was "being groomed for higher things" by Spellman,[17] and Spellman acknowledged that he wanted to give the rising star "some recognition" and "pay back a debt."[18] Most likely, Sheen's eloquence and reputation as an avid and effective foe of communism was the main reason for his being asked to accompany Spellman's entourage; he spent much of his time during the trip speaking to enormous crowds on that subject. His expertise regarding the threat of communism made him an especially valuable member of the party, for he would take his message to areas currently under pressure from the communists, and serve as a spokesman for both the Catholic Church and the United States of America. During the course of his travels, the "latent missionary"

[15] Robert I. Gannon, SJ, *The Cardinal Spellman Story* (Garden City, NY: Doubleday and Co., 1963), p. 471.

[16] *Ibid.*, p. 472.

[17] *Ibid.*

[18] These words were contained in a speech given by Spellman in Australia; it is recounted by Sheen in his autobiography, *Treasure in Clay* (pp. 135-136), and is also contained in the personal diary kept by Sheen on the trip, part of the collection of the Sheen Archives: "Diary of the Orient and Pacific, 1948."

in Sheen "emerged."[19] In the years of his tenure as head of the National Propagation Society, this initial connection between the threat posed by communism and the valuable service performed by the Church's missionaries would be underscored again and again.

From the outset of his trip, thoughts of the mission impinged upon Sheen's whole perspective. One of the first things which came to his attention was the fact that "missionaries used some of his sermons" when preaching to the natives; Sheen expressed "great surprise" at this, and was also "amazed at how well known my name is in Australia."[20] This initial impression was just one indication of the extent of Sheen's influence beyond America's shores. His ability to serve as an ambassador of Christ, and a messenger of good will on behalf of the American Catholic Church, would be evidenced in various manifestations throughout the trip. The following week, he recorded this statement in his diary, in reference to the people of Australia: "They have taken me to their hearts, and I am so happy to have an influence for good over them."[21] Many times, Sheen noted his reactions to the plight of the poor, gaining his first direct exposure to the realities of poverty. Expressing a genuine sympathy for the "have-nots" of the world, a sympathy which would serve him well when he took over the business of begging for the poor, requesting alms for the missions, he applied a familiar biblical story to his new experiences. "I always feel so sorry for these great uninvited," said Sheen. "At times I believe I feel their exclusion more than they do."[22] Before one of his many public addresses in Australia, Sheen was introduced by Cardinal Spellman in these glowing words:

> I want to say a word about Monsignor Sheen, who in America is doing more than any Cardinal, Archbishop

---

[19] Although the phrase was used by Father Gannon in reference to Spellman in *The Cardinal Spellman Story*, p. 471, it is equally applicable to Sheen, a fact made evident by reading through his diary.

[20] Sheen, 1948 Diary, entries for April 26 and April 28.

[21] *Ibid.*, entry for May 6.

[22] *Ibid.*, entry for May 4.

or Bishop to make the faith known and loved. He is one
of the truly apostolic souls of our times. He has the ear
of Catholics, and he has the ear of non-Catholics, and
I rejoice to know that you love him as much as we do.[23]

In light of the fact that Sheen would be elevated to the rank of
Bishop shortly after taking command of the U.S. branch of the Society for the Propagation of the Faith — partially through the "good
graces" of Cardinal Spellman[24] — this introduction was along the
lines of a rehearsal for the official announcement of Sheen's appointment two years later. As administrator of the Church's missionary
efforts in America, Monsignor Sheen would make an even greater
contribution toward making the faith known and loved among the
previously "great uninvited."

Propagating the faith had been a specialty of Fulton Sheen's
in his capacity as pioneer of the electronic gospel and convert-
maker; he would be equally productive as a spokesman for the missions. During his stay in China in 1948, Sheen noted that the missionaries were given credit by the Apostolic Delegate for being
"good for the apostolate of charity and the masses," but were seen
as "ineffectual in their mission to the intelligentsia."[25] Sheen's reputation and credentials would prove to be a way of correcting this
deficiency when he took up the cause, for he would become an intelligent theoretician of missionary ideology as well as the missions'
most famous representative. One of Sheen's frequently voiced ideas
regarding the missions was the necessity for all Catholics to become "mission-minded." He recorded this thought in his diary,
while he was en route from Java to Singapore, sometime in the
middle of his trip. In a reflective mood, he wrote: "a visit like ours…
enlarges a point of view, develops sympathy for others, and makes
one mission-minded."[26] This statement serves as a concise summary

[23] *Ibid.*, entry for May 10.
[24] Sheen, *Treasure in Clay*, p. 92.
[25] Sheen, 1948 Diary, entry for June 4.
[26] *Ibid.*, entry for May 20.

of Sheen's readiness to take on the challenge which would arise in two years; now thoroughly "mission-minded," he would be given the opportunity to put his ideas into practice, and to learn more, when he was appointed to the post of National Director of the Society for the Propagation of the Faith.

As one of the truly apostolic souls of his time, Fulton Sheen would follow the example of Christ's apostles, using his talents to teach all nations and spread the good news of the gospel message. The Society for the Propagation of the Faith, the Catholic Church's principal missionary organization, had been founded in 1822 for the purpose of "furthering the evangelization of the world by united prayer and the collection of alms for distribution among Catholic missionaries throughout the world."[27] Sheen's appointment as missionary leader in America came "at a time when the world has suddenly become mission-minded; two great movements campaign for mankind: Communism and Christianity."[28] Communism was very much on the mind of Sheen and the entire Church in 1950, and evidently influenced his conduct in the office: "as communism swept across the face of the earth and Catholic missions went up in flames, the burdens of the Propagation of the Faith became heavier, and the Holy Father turned his eyes and hope once more to the U.S. for help."[29] Looking to Fulton Sheen for help was a logical choice in this struggle, but over the course of sixteen years, Sheen's priorities regarding missionary work would be reordered. Along with his experience as a crusader against communism, Sheen's preparation for this role included his great success in the art of instructing converts, and his ecumenical attitude as an apologist for the Catholic faith. By the end of the time of his service at the Propagation Society in 1966, Sheen would place more emphasis on ecumenical openness, having grown noticeably in the office. These years of transition in the life of Fulton Sheen illustrate his ability to serve as a bridge between the old Church and the new Church, spanning the

---

[27] Sheen's Vita, part of the collection of the Sheen Archives.

[28] Sheen, quoted in *The Catholic Week* (Birmingham), September 23, 1950.

[29] Sheen's Vita.

years of the Second Vatican Council. Reflecting back in his autobiography, Sheen was cognizant of his own spiritual and intellectual odyssey, and the effect that his experiences in serving the poor
of the world had on his life:

> I came into this office at the Society for the Propaga-
> tion of the Faith at just the moment when the Church
> was beginning to sense a conflict between divine salva-
> tion and human liberation, between working for per-
> sonal salvation of those in a parish or in a community
> and having a concern about their social welfare. God
> never intended that individuals and social justice should
> be separated.[30]

At the beginning of his tenure as National Director, Sheen
decided to channel all of his energies toward the single goal of furthering the work of the Church's missions. Many of his old concerns persisted — communism, electronic evangelization, his
prolific writing — but they were all colored by his missionary vision. The task of administering the work of the Society for the
Propagation of the Faith was one of great complexity, and Sheen's
already heavy workload increased significantly. He guided the work
of the individual diocesan offices across the country, and was required to make annual reports in Rome. His personal forums —
radio and then television, and the "Bishop Sheen Writes" columns
— were often given over to promoting the work of the missions.
In addition, Sheen began to write another column — "God Love
You" — syndicated in the Catholic press as a direct appeal for contributions. He also edited two mission publications: *Worldmission*,
a more scholarly journal of opinion containing articles and book
reviews written by leading missionaries, and regular editorials by
Sheen; and the "punched-up" snappy *Mission Magazine*, consisting largely of appeals to the Catholic faithful to make financial
sacrifices for the missions, and photographs from the mission field.

---

[30] Sheen, *Treasure in Clay*, p. 108.

Under Sheen's direction, *Mission* began to win accolades, and was transformed from a losing proposition into a profitable publication, which increased the revenues in the society's coffers.[31] Sheen was assisted in this administrative work by a large staff at his headquarters in New York City, but in many respects, he ran a one-man show as the voice and heart of the missions. Morale in the office was high, owing largely to Sheen's personality and example; he referred to the office workers as missionaries in their own right, and led the entire staff in daily afternoon prayers.[32] Sheen also carried on a personal correspondence with many of the thousands of missionaries in the field around the world, and set aside time in his busy day to meet with the visiting heralds of the gospel, who brought inspiration to his life, and served as the source of stories he incorporated into the "God Loves You" columns.[33] In addition, he logged many miles in his journeys to the far corners of the earth to observe the missionaries at work and to bless their efforts.

Bishop Sheen's mission philosophy evolved gradually during these years as America's most famous home-based missionary, and that evolution can be observed through his numerous public addresses and editorials in the pages of *Worldmission*. His first editorial appeared at the end of 1950 and was entitled "The World Crisis and the Missions"; a slightly rearranged version would comprise the title of the collection of his best editorials, published in book form in 1963: *Missions and the World Crisis*.[34] Just as the crisis mentality prevailed in Sheen's treatment of the communist menace, it arose often in his discussions of the critical importance of the Church's missionary work in the age of international socioeconomic crisis which followed the Second World War. According to Sheen, the purpose of *Worldmission* was to educate and inform its readers about the Church's missions, especially in regards to the future importance of the East:

---

[31] See *Time* (April 14, 1952), "Microphone Missionary," and *The Bishop Sheen Story* by James Conniff, p. 22.

[32] Sheen, *Treasure in Clay*, p. 110.

[33] *Ibid.*, pp. 111-112.

[34] Fulton Sheen, *Missions and the World Crisis* (Milwaukee: The Bruce Publishing Co., 1963).

The Providence of God is beginning to lift the veil which
hung over Eastern civilization, that in this late hour of
history, the Incarnation may display its Power as it did
in the beginning of the Christian Era! It behooves the
West to know what the Eternal Galilean is doing in the
East.... the purpose of the missions is not to unite the
world in one political system or to make other countries
all believe in a particular form of democracy, but to allow them great political diversity with unity in the
spirit.[35]

This concentration on the East was a prevalent and persistent theme in Sheen's ideology. During his tour of the Orient in
1948, Sheen formulated his thoughts on the Eastern mind, and the
best method for the Church's missionaries to employ in their approach to the task of bringing the Gospel to the region. Right from
the beginning, Sheen's approach was an enlightened one, which
would blossom in advance of the Church's official advocacy of ecumenism at the Vatican Council. In Singapore and Bangkok, Sheen
preached a "sermon in French on the possibility of the East being
the new seat of the power of the Gospel"[36] — a possibility that
would become a firm conviction in Sheen's mind. He had been
disturbed by the French missionaries' attitude toward the Buddhists,
and instead advocated a method from his own apologetics: "one
must look for the good in everything, as St. Paul did in Athens."[37]
In Sheen's conversation with Bishop Walsh on the trip, he found
several points of agreement, noting that they shared an interest in
reading Confucius: "We have to know the Chinese way of thinking."[38] And Walsh was "most enthusiastic" about one particular
broadcast of Sheen's, in which he made "Confucius a John the

---

[35] Fulton Sheen, "The World Crisis and the Missions," *Worldmission* I (December, 1950),
pp. 7, 5.

[36] Sheen, 1948 Diary, entry for May 25.

[37] *Ibid.*, entry for June 9.

[38] Sheen, *Treasure in Clay*, p. 146.

Baptist of China."[39] Decades after his youthful resolution to address contemporary issues in the light of Thomistic philosophy, Sheen found an opportunity to apply his philosophy in the Far East: "some day Buddha and Confucius may be to Eastern Catholic theology what Plato and Aristotle were to St. Thomas and St. Augustine."[40] In a lecture entitled "Apologetics in China," Sheen "pleaded that Catholics recognize Chinese culture and give them no more Gothic cathedrals."[41] In light of the current political crisis, he also delivered a broadcast on "China and Communism," suggesting that "God kept China behind a veil all these centuries and allowed it to keep a 5,000 year old culture to one day become a great Christian nation." After the broadcast, Bishop Walsh told Sheen that Pius XI had told him the very same idea years before.[42] Looking back on the insights he gained on that trip, Sheen also concluded that "it might be shortsightedness on our part to impose the Aristotelian philosophy on the Eastern mind.... Confucius is relatively just as good for some minds as Aristotle is for others. Our missionaries... should start with what is good in the religions they find in their countries."[43]

This open-minded attitude which characterized Sheen's focus on the East also had a practical side, given the current political tensions. In the Cold War context, the threat of communism was very real, and when Sheen spoke on the subject of communism, he often talked in terms of crisis. He was convinced that the post-war world crisis involved a shift of gravity from the West to the East, an idea which persisted over the course of many years. At the end of the decade of the fifties, for example, Sheen was still urging the Church to increase its missionary efforts in the East, for the "political, economic, social and military power of the world is moving from West to East, and the future of the Church is moving with

---

[39] Sheen, 1948 Diary, entry for May 29.

[40] Ibid., entry for May 23. This same quotation appears in Sheen's autobiography, p. 137.

[41] *Ibid.*, entry for June 3.

[42] *Ibid.* Also appears in the autobiography, p. 139.

[43] Sheen, *Treasure in Clay*, p. 146.

it."[44] In his very first appeal for support on Mission Sunday in 1950, this crisis mentality was readily apparent. He spoke of the heroism of the missionaries who suffered for their faith at the hands of the communists, and the ultimate contribution that the Catholic Church's missionaries could make to world peace:

> The world's peace is centered in these men. The East-
> ern world is gradually surrendering its ethical systems.
> This is unfortunate, for they kept it cultural and moral
> for centuries. It will lapse into communistic barbarism
> unless the Gospel of the love of God and neighbor is
> preached to them. I am therefore not speaking here
> merely of aid to the missions, but of saving the world.[45]

Although Sheen's fixation on communism was understandable, in the light of world events and the extent of communist persecution of Catholic missionaries behind the iron and bamboo curtains, his views were not really extreme or narrow. He often pointed out that there was another force to be reckoned with as he concentrated on the mission work in the East: Islam. Sheen initially voiced fears that "Communism and Moslemism may unite against Christianity" and urged the missionary to "save the crescent from the hammer and the sickle."[46] He quickly overcame this fear, and his subsequent discussions offered a more favorable opinion on the spiritual potential of the Moslems. In "Moslemism Is Also a World Force," Sheen argued that "historical clashes between Moslemism and Christianity in the past must not impede reconciliation and affection among peoples."[47] Christians were advised to find what was good in the Moslem faith: the common belief in God. Asia, thought to be "wooed by two lovers" — the Soviets and the United

---

[44] Sheen, quoted in the *New York Times*, November 10, 1958.

[45] Sheen, "Text of the Electrical Transcription of the Address of Monsignor Fulton J. Sheen in Preparation for Mission Sunday," typescript in the Sheen Archives collection.

[46] Fulton Sheen, "The Sword, the Hammer, the Sickle and the Cross," *Worldmission* 2 (Winter, 1951), pp. 3, 6.

[47] Sheen, *Missions and the World Crisis*, p. 31.

States — might instead reject both "in favor of a third, forgotten contender, Islamism." Therefore, Christians were exhorted to pray for the Moslems; if peace were to reign, "God must be restored to international life... and the Moslems may hold the key to world order."[48]

This grand quest to restore God to international life was at the heart of Sheen's service as National Director of the Society for the Propagation of the Faith. The recurrent subjects he concerned himself with — communism, Islam, foreign aid — indicate that he was influenced by "the signs of the times," and responsive to contemporary currents of change in the world. He was always careful to remain in step with the official teachings of the Church as well; much in the evolution of Sheen's "mission mind" was rooted in Pius XII's papal encyclical on the missions, issued in 1951. Sheen wrote a lengthy commentary on this encyclical — *Evangelii Praecones* — in *Worldmission*.[49] When viewed from the perspective of hindsight, this commentary, along with the personal contributions he made to the missions over the next decade and a half, demonstrates how these early ideas would germinate and grow under Sheen's direction. Especially revealing was Sheen's introduction, in which he suggested that the purpose of the encyclical was to "reaffirm the pristine glory of missionary and propaganda," for while the term "missionary" had always been associated with religion in the past, it became associated with politics with the rise of the totalitarian powers in the twentieth century. Even worse, the word "propaganda" was presently used in "the pejorative sense of enslaving minds," overlooking the positive and noble connotations of "Propaganda," the "title of an official Roman Congregation since the seventeenth century... which stood for the diffusion of the Faith in Christ."[50]

This tradition of diffusing the faith was proceeding with a renewed zeal in the twentieth century. In fact, on the present sta-

---

[48] *New York Times*, March 10, 1952.

[49] Fulton Sheen, "A Commentary on *Evangelii Praecones*," *Worldmission* 2 (September, 1951), pp. 3-13.

[50] *Ibid.*, p. 3.

tus of the missions, the Holy Father said that "missionary work...
has experienced an impulse, an external growth, an internal vigor
such as perhaps has never before been encountered."[51] Bishop Sheen
had entered the mission field at an historic moment, when "the
blood of martyrs is truly the seed of Christians." During these years,
the missions flourished more "than at any time in the last three
centuries," for it was a "theological principle that spiritual prosperity of the missions is tied up in some way with persecution."[52] At
this time of prosperity for the missions, Pius XII outlined several
principles and norms of missionary activity, and Sheen had taken
them to heart. His respect for native cultures was in the same spirit
as the Pope's insistence that "the missionary's home is a foreign
land." "The missionary may not be a nationalist, or the spiritual sop
to colonial expansion," said Sheen. "He must be as universal as
Christ."[53] Another principle well-suited to Sheen was that which
called for "the initiation of social reforms demanded by justice and
charity,"[54] an idea which had been prominent in Sheen's life for
decades. And the guidelines on "the sanctification of pagan truths"
echoed Sheen's own thoughts during his earlier travels. Restating
them, he said that "European culture is not to be transferred to the
missions; rather, the missionary will give his people those Christian principles which can be fitted into what is good and sound in
the native culture."[55] Thoughts on American culture, and his role
in furthering the work of the U.S. branch of the Society for the
Propagation of the Faith, concluded Sheen's commentary. He acknowledged that over half of the total revenues for the Church's
missions came from the United States, and asked for continued
support, in terms of alms and prayers, for the Lord's work:

---

[51] *Ibid.*

[52] Sheen, quoted in the *New York Times*, June 1, 1953; restating a point he made earlier in
his mission encyclical commentary.

[53] Sheen, "A Commentary on *Evangelii Praecones*," p. 6.

[54] *Ibid.*, p. 7.

[55] *Ibid.*, p. 8. This was an expression of the missionary principle of "adaptation."

America in the economic order is the pantry of the world; in the military realm, it is the arsenal of democracy; in the domain of the spirit, it must become the nursery of the future apostles to lands that are older in culture but still unborn in the faith.[56]

Many of these core ideas in the Holy Father's teachings on the missions were mirrored and developed further in Fulton Sheen's book, *Missions and the World Crisis*. Organized topically, it offers a clear insight into Sheen's views on the subject of the Catholic Church's missionary calling, and what he considered his most important contributions to that effort. Published in 1963, during the Second Vatican Council, the book also highlights the ideological route Sheen traveled to arrive at the Council. As in so many other aspects of his career, Fulton Sheen could be securely in the mainstream of Catholic thought, even as he managed to function as an innovator, helping to shape the Church of the future. Over the span of thirteen years, of course, Sheen's interpretation of the world crisis evolved and changed in emphasis. From an early opinion that dialogue with the communists was impossible, for example, Sheen evolved into a proponent of opening the lines of communication with communists and atheists during the sixties. He became increasingly aware of the opportunities available to missionaries in the social sector, especially regarding the alleviation of poverty. At the Council session in 1964, on the Church's missionary activities, Bishop Sheen's call rang out around the world: "Go out into the world of the poor.... This is Mission! This is Dialogue!"[57]

As reflected in his choice of editorials included in *Missions and the World Crisis*, the topics most associated with the Sheen legacy in the field of mission work include "reserves of missionary power," "spirituality and the missions," and "foreign policy, foreign aid and the missions." Sheen's lasting contribution to the Society

---

[56] *Ibid.*, p. 12.

[57] Fulton Sheen, Vatican II typescript, dated October 15, 1964, on "Missions," Sheen Archives.

for the Propagation of the Faith, above and beyond the millions of dollars he raised, was to educate the Catholic faithful on the realities and vital importance of its work. In addition, Sheen wanted to change and expand the whole concept of "mission" beyond the traditional notion of "religious with feet itching to travel" to pagan lands... "to stress the ecumenical character of the contemporary world."[58] One way of expanding the entire notion of missions was to call upon previously untapped reserves of missionary power, such as the universities and the laity. As a scholar, Sheen was alarmed that the influence of the missions in world affairs "had been ignored by politics, and underplayed in the teaching at Catholic universities in the United States."[59] Arguing that the "great struggle in the present world was not for new colonies, but for minds and souls," he believed that the catholicity and universality of the Church could be demonstrated best by a greater emphasis on the missionary apostolate. Another underused source of mission strength, according to Sheen, was the lay apostolate. Taking his inspiration from the doctrine of "Catholic Action" and the words of Cardinal Suhard,[60] Sheen called upon the laity to assist in the work of saving not only individual souls, but "society in its totality":

> Christian civilization was once considered as "inside" the reservation, and non-Christian civilizations as "outside"; but today the fence has been broken down with the result that the distinction between foreign and Christian, or Christian and pagan, is practically eliminated. It is the world of mass civilization which has to be reconciled to God... the entire world, therefore, is the mission of the Church, and those who think in terms of the world have the "Catholic sense."[61]

---

[58] Sheen, *Missions and the World Crisis*, pp. 69, 76.

[59] *Ibid.*, pp. 67, 69.

[60] "The Christian is not called upon to destroy or vilify the world, but to assume it, to sanctify it, to offer it in homage to God"; these words of Cardinal Suhard are quoted by Sheen in *Missions and the World Crisis*, p. 86.

[61] Sheen, *Missions and the World Crisis*, p. 79.

The Catholic sense of going out into the world, to sanctify the social and economic order, to save society as well as souls, became a concern of the whole community of bishops in the sixties. At Vatican II, social justice became a top priority. From Sheen's perspective, social justice figured prominently in his missionary burden of serving the poor, and he began to pursue new ways of drawing attention to the plight of the majority of poor people in the world who went to bed hungry every night. Often, he stressed the special responsibilities rich and comfortable Americans had to alleviate the suffering of the poor, reminding his followers that America was once a foreign mission. In the past, the Society for the Propagation of the Faith had given large sums of money to the bishops in the United States. Since the "growth of the American Catholic Church owed a great deal to this aid"[62] American Catholics were obligated to come to the aid of other foreign missions. This obligation was being met under Sheen's leadership, when the U.S. contribution increased to "over 60% of the Propagation's revenues."[63] In the international arena, Americans were encouraged to become more mission-minded and more ecumenical, to establish "beachheads as a natural base of operations to introduce the supernatural order"[64] into the world. Rather than approaching non-Christians as "pagans" who possessed no truth, missionaries should see them as potential members of Christ's Mystical Body: "the fullness of truth is a 360 degree circle; every religion has a segment of truth.... Missionaries must complete the segment of truth which is already possessed. Their stress is upon the fullness of truth rather than error."[65] And these non-Christians were in need of practical as well as spiritual assistance; the missionary had a responsibility

---

[62] *Ibid.*, p. 152.

[63] *Ibid.*, p. 156.

[64] *Ibid.*, p. 144.

[65] *Ibid.*, p. 176. Sheen made the same point of the fullness of truth as a complete circle in his autobiography, a lesson learned from "the combination of travel, the study of world religions, and personal encounters with different nationalities and peoples," p. 148.

"to the hungry as well as the unevangelized,"[66] to work to secure social justice in the temporal order.

Social justice at home, within the United States, should also be a concern of the mission-minded members of the Catholic Church. An area which attracted Sheen's interest in this regard was racial justice. Although Sheen had never been an overt spokesman in the field of race relations, he had been personally charitable over the years to blacks in the South. He was responsible, through personal donations, for building the first Negro maternity hospital in the South, the Blessed Martin de Porres Hospital in Mobile, Alabama.[67] As a missionary leader, he wanted to open a general seminary in the U.S. especially for black missionaries to Africa, a profession of the spirit of "Christian witness" advocated by Pius XII.[68] In an editorial encouraging a union of all Christian churches in a cooperative mission effort, emphasizing social fellowship and ignoring doctrinal differences, Sheen asked: "Whence comes the dedication of our age to integration, and for the downtrodden, the underprivileged and the social wrecks of humanity if it be not the leaven of the Church working in the world?"[69] The concepts of spiritual witness and the Church as leaven in the world — for both spiritual and temporal ends — were outlined in "The Apologetics of Sanctity." According to Sheen, certain characteristics of the modern age demanded a rethinking of the missions and the missionary spirit: "the aim of missionary activity is not so much to implant the Church in pagan lands, as it is to reconcile the world to God."[70] He wanted the Vatican Council II Church to "call the world to new techniques, new methods, new spirit, new zeal, new kinds of apologetics, new missionary concepts, and a new outpouring of the

[66] Sheen, *Missions and the World Crisis*, p. 166.
[67] Sheen's personal charities were well known, as was his "deep-seated love of the Negroes" — he gave most of the money he earned through writing and public appearances to charity. See "Missionary with a Microphone," *Time* (April 14, 1952), and Conniff, *The Bishop Sheen Story*, p. 29.
[68] Sheen, *Missions and the World Crisis*, p. 144.
[69] *Ibid.*, p. 180.
[70] *Ibid.*, p. 199.

Spirit of Christ."[71] Among the new methods consistently recommended by Sheen was cooperation between the Church and the government; for the sake of good works, the United States government might consider learning from the Church's example, and making use of the expertise and missionary network in place around the world.

On the general subject of "Missions and Foreign Aid," Sheen was quite outspoken, and sometimes critical of the errors he perceived in the policies of the government. During an interview shortly after taking command of the U.S. Propagation office in 1951, Sheen said: "in this office we learn more of the truth of foreign affairs than any chancellery. But I will never permit an iota of this knowledge to be put to work for political or nationalistic use."[72] He also proposed that the United Nations subsidize the world's underdeveloped areas; this subsidy could then be distributed by "both Roman Catholic and Protestant missionaries, who were experts in languages as well as humanitarian projects." Determined to use every means at his disposal, and to reach beyond traditional methods to explore new ways of aiding the destitute, Sheen was careful to point out that this work would be done "not in the name of any country, but in the name of humanity."[73] It was Sheen's contention that in addition to the U.S.-Soviet rivalry in the underdeveloped areas, a third major influence — the missions — was at work in the contemporary world. Catholic missionaries were meeting the communists "head-on," and it was "a pity that our foreign policy and Point IV programs did not utilize the missionaries… in their social works."[74] If the government would cooperate with missionaries in the poor lands, the United States would benefit and the prospects for world peace would increase. "These Protestant and

---

[71] *Ibid.*, p. 206.
[72] Fulton Sheen, quoted in Gretta Palmer's "Bishop Fulton J. Sheen," *Catholic Digest* 15 (October, 1951), p. 60.
[73] *New York Times*, October 23, 1951.
[74] Sheen, *Missions and the World Crisis*, p. 59.

Catholic missionaries will not sell America, nor will they win military pacts. But America will gain by it in the end."[75]

Though Sheen's suggestions were never put into practice, his influence was recognized and appreciated by some government officials. In "Proselytizing by Foreign Aid," Sheen sought to help the United States by sharing the understanding gained by Catholic missionaries. Just as the Church had appreciated the wisdom of adjusting its tactics, the government should recognize the errors inherent in proselytizing. "America has gone in for proselytizing," said Sheen, "and proselytizing is always bad where people are poor."[76] It was ineffective, and smacked of the tactics employed by the communists:

> Bread to the poor must have no strings attached to it… hot soup cannot be mixed with cold war. It is both an insult to the people who receive it and an undignified gesture on the part of those who offer it… people should be helped by our government, but not to win them to our way of life; rather to let them be free to live their way of life.[77]

Sheen believed that America would win no friends by its present tactics, and that "any good missionary could tell the government of the evils of tying up the gift of food with a requested favor."[78] When the White House held a conference on "Foreign Aspects of U.S. National Security" in 1958, Bishop Sheen was invited, along with leading government figures like Harry Truman, Adlai Stevenson, Vice President Richard Nixon and President Eisenhower himself, to convey the message of "good missionaries." Sheen argued first on religious grounds that it was the moral duty of Americans to aid the underprivileged, for "the superfluities of the rich are the

---

[75] *Ibid.*, p. 64.
[76] *Ibid.*, p. 54.
[77] *Ibid.*, pp. 60, 63.
[78] *Ibid.*, p. 59.

necessities of the poor."[79] In the Parable of the Good Samaritan, Christ had said that "charity begins away from home with people who are not of our race or country."[80] Proceeding along to social and practical arguments — if the United States wanted freedom to triumph over communism — Sheen summed up the "crux of the question of foreign aid":

> The foreign aid of the United States must introduce some factor besides the economic, political and military; one which is the strongest in our national traditions and one which the Soviets not only lack but repudiate... our belief in God, the dignity of the human person... and freedom of conscience.... Our great country must recognize that not by bread alone doth man live.[81]

These remarks were delivered in 1958, the same year that Pius XII died and Pope John XXIII was elected as his successor. It was a major turning point for the Catholic Church; Pope John's decision to call the Second Vatican Council changed the course of Church history. As far as the course of Bishop Sheen's life was concerned, it was a propitious time, for his role at the ecumenical council would revolve around his reputation as American Catholicism's missionary spokesman and self-proclaimed "beggar with a tin cup" for the poor of the world. Sheen arrived at the Council sessions in Rome in a mission frame of mind, shaped by years of service as National Director of the Society for the Propagation of the Faith. In his own words:

> What the appointment as National Director brought to my life was the opportunity to see that Christian salva-

---

[79] Fulton Sheen, "Religious Imperatives and the Foreign Aid Issues," published by the Foundation for Religious Action in the Social and Civil Order: a copy of this address can be found in the collection at the Sheen Archives. Sheen's remarks were also recounted in two articles in the *New York Times*: February 26, 1958 and March 2, 1958.

[80] Sheen, "Religious Imperatives and the Foreign Aid Issue."

[81] *Ibid.*

tion has both an earthly and a historical dimension; that
the conversion of a single soul may not be alienated from
the promotion of human rights as required by the Gospel, and which is central to our ministry; that soul-win-
ning and society-saving are the concave and convex side
of the love of God and love of neighbor; that in addition to begetting children of God through evangelization, we have to give the witness of fraternal love in a
sensitiveness toward humanity's desire for freedom and
justice; ...that earthly liberation is an integral part of
evangelization and that they are united as Creation and
Redemption.[82]

On Christmas Day, 1961, Pope John XXIII issued *Humanae
Salutis*, calling for the Second Vatican Council to begin the following year. In this convocation, the Holy Father declared:

Today the Church is witnessing a crisis underway within
society. While humanity is on the edge of a new era,
tasks of immense gravity and amplitude await the
Church.... we have felt immediately the urgency of the
duty to call our sons together, to give the Church the
possibility to contribute more efficaciously to the solution of the problems of the modern age.[83]

Fulton Sheen's impact on the Council, though not great, grew out
of the interventions he submitted on several subjects, including
ecumenism, religious freedom, education, priestly formation, and,
of course, the *Decree on the Church's Missionary Activity*. And the
Council would have a profound impact on the subsequent course
of Bishop Sheen's life. He described his own presence and part in
the Council as "one of the great blessings the Lord bestowed" on

---

[82] Sheen, *Treasure in Clay*, p. 108.
[83] Pope John XXIII, *Humanae Salutis*, in *The Documents of Vatican Council II*, edited by
Walter Abbott, SJ, pp. 703, 705.

his life.[84] He was named both to the pre-conciliar Catholic Action Commission — which he viewed as domestic missionary activity — and the Conciliar Commission on the Missions.[85] Sheen arrived at the Council with great expectations. As one who appreciated the power of mass communications, he noted that "every advantage of the electronic age was used" to keep the world informed of the Council's work; "all the world came to the Church as the Church prepared to go to the world."[86] For Sheen, the single most important feature of the Second Vatican Council was its sense of "balance": "the Vatican Council was held at that period of history when it was necessary to strike a balance between two extremes in the world and in the Church — individualism and socialism."[87] Establishing, and maintaining, a sense of equilibrium or balance was an essential characteristic of Fulton Sheen's career from beginning to end, and he especially valued the "balanced thinking" that came out of the Council.

This concept of balanced thinking was evident in Sheen's observations submitted on the schema on the *Dogmatic Constitution on the Church*, entitled "On the Locked Doors." Pointing out that the Church was not a "detached traveler through the world," but a Church in the process of formation, Sheen stated that the schema should stress "dialogue" as the best indicator of the spirit of the contemporary Catholic Church. He called for the Church to carry on a dialogue with "the nations of the world, with atheistic, unbelieving people, with the poor and the starving."[88] The closer the Church drew near to the world, Sheen believed, the more the world would give itself in dialogue with the Church, in line with Pope John's spirit of aggiornamento.[89]

---

[84] Sheen, *Treasure in Clay*, p. 281.

[85] *Ibid.*, pp. 283-284.

[86] *Ibid.*, p. 282.

[87] *Ibid.*, p. 289.

[88] Cited in *American Participation in the Second Vatican Council*, edited by Monsignor Vincent A. Yzermans (New York: Sheed and Ward, 1967), p. 44.

[89] *Ibid.*

With reference to the *Pastoral Constitution on the Church in the Modern World*, which he considered the most representative and balanced document to come forth from the Council, Sheen submitted an observation on women's role in the Church,[90] and a lengthy intervention on the socioeconomic order. Applying the lessons he had learned as leader of America's missionary efforts, he urged that Catholics cooperate with Protestants, Jews and all men of good will, because "toleration of other groups in social action should give way to cooperation."[91] Displaying that basic consistency that had been woven into the fabric of his life, he went on to insist that Catholic endeavors in the economic order never descend to being merely anti-communistic,[92] but should always be linked with a concern for social justice. This same thread of consistency was evident in Sheen's statements on "Christian Education," the "Relationship of the Church to Non-Christian Religions," and "Religious Freedom."[93] In all three instances, Sheen offered nothing strikingly new, but rather demonstrated that he was in the mainstream of Catholic thought. In the debate on religious freedom, Sheen argued from the American pluralistic experience, and his knowledge of the Constitution, noting that he was in agreement with the position of John Courtney Murray.[94]

In typical Sheen style, his most noteworthy performance at the Council was given in conjunction with his intervention on the schema on the Church's missionary activity; it was significant because it was the most detailed and longest single intervention submitted by any American.[95] In all, Sheen submitted five written interventions on the subject of the missions, and was the only speaker at the Council allowed to exceed his time limit, perhaps because of his eloquence and the fact that he happened to be the last speaker

[90] *Ibid.*, pp. 202-203.
[91] *Ibid.*, p. 210.
[92] *Ibid.*, p. 211.
[93] *Ibid.*, pp. 548, 580 and 637 respectively.
[94] See Sheen's notes on Vatican Council II in the Sheen Archives, especially a typescript dated January 26, 1965.
[95] Yzermans, p. 530.

on the subject. The National Office of the Society for the Propagation of the Faith printed and distributed an article published in the Chicago *New World* under the banner headline: "Bishop Sheen Delivers Dramatic Council Talk."[96] The article stated that the "bishops of the world awaited the views of the American whose work for the missions has made his name almost universally known," and then heard "an impassioned plea that the whole concept of missionary be enlarged to embrace… the poor throughout the world, especially in Latin America."[97]

It should be noted that Bishop Sheen was a very active member of the Commission on Missions, attending every meeting and traveling back and forth from Rome several times. He felt that the most important work of the commission was "eulogizing the concept of missions beyond territories under the Propagation and making the missions the burden of the whole Church." He felt that the emphasis in the decree that "bishops are consecrated for the salvation of the whole world rather than for a particular diocese" would be one of the most lasting fruits of their efforts.[98] Sheen even suggested that "a new title be attributed to the Congregation of the Propagation of the Faith which would help it to eradicate divisions," seeing "Congregation of Charity" as appropriate; although his advice was not heeded, several years later the name was changed to the "Congregation for the Evangelization of Peoples."[99] He ultimately wanted the schema to be called simply *Concerning the Missionary Church*, and urged the Council to establish a World Council of Missions "to affirm the responsibility of the whole Church for the whole world and to foster the ecumenical spirit."[100]

The best summary of Sheen's mission philosophy was contained in the intervention he delivered on November 9, 1964.

---

[96] The article was written by Placid Jordan, OSB, for the November 13, 1964 issue of the *New World*. A copy of the reprint is found in the collection at the Sheen Archives.
[97] *Ibid.*
[98] Yzermans, p. 525.
[99] *Ibid.*, p. 526. See also Sheen's autobiography, p. 284.
[100] Yzermans, p. 531 (A).

Speaking on a task "with which he was most familiar,"[101] he carefully deliberated over this document, as indicated by the multiple
revisions and versions of the talk he preserved among his Vatican
Council papers.[102] First and foremost, Sheen advocated a new concept of missions, from several perspectives. Perceiving western civilization as being in darkness, Bishop Sheen wanted to move beyond the old, and now false, notion of mission being identified with
white men and European civilization. The old concept of missions
as geographical and colonial, said Sheen, must now give way to an
economic concept; rather than the East-West dichotomy, a more
accurate description of the missions was to be found "above and
below the hunger line on the thirtieth parallel." Missionaries in the
future must therefore focus their energies on Africa, Asia and Latin
America, and the spirit of poverty must be thought of as the fruit
of the Second Vatican Council: the Church would either become
the Church of the poor, or be known as the poor Church. In place
of the theological question, "What are the missions?", Sheen sub-
stituted the question "Where are the missions?" Providing his own
answer, he stated that "wherever there is poverty and a grave lack
of priests, wherever people are burdened by material or spiritual
wants, there are the missions! — it is souls, not territories, which
make the missions."

Reminding the more affluent bishops at the Council that the
greater number of bishops in the world Catholic community lived
in want and in persecution, he asked that every diocese increase its
contribution to the missions, setting aside a portion of its income
for this vital work of evangelization. Repeating his views on the
necessity of the entire Church adopting a spirit of poverty, he
pointed out that it would complement that conciliar spirit of ecumenism: "as ecumenism without poverty can become indifference,
so poverty without ecumenism can lead to ghettoism and segrega-
tion." Finally, he concluded with these ringing words:

101 Sheen, *Treasure in Clay*, p. 294.
102 See Sheen's Vatican II papers at the Sheen Archives, typescripts dated October 15, 1964
     and November 24, 1964. The final version of Sheen's remarks is also reprinted in Vincent
     Yzerman's book, pp. 533-534.

As only a wounded Christ can convert a doubting Thomas, so only a Church wounded by poverty can convert a doubting world. If we show an ecumenical spirit to brothers that are outside the Church, then let us show an ecumenical spirit to brothers who are inside the Church. Let us be charitable about the missions, remembering that the Lord who said "Go teach all nations" is the same Lord who said to the poor and starving: "I have mercy on the multitudes."[103]

Bishop Fulton Sheen returned from Rome to the United States infused with the spirit and zeal of the Second Vatican Council. Although he was not yet aware of it, he would soon be leaving his office at the Society for the Propagation of the Faith in New York City, within a year after the Council closed. Pope Paul VI would appoint Fulton Sheen to succeed the aging Bishop James E. Kearney in the Diocese of Rochester, New York. Sheen would make his way upstate with a new perspective gained from his years as America's missionary spokesman and his experiences at the Council. As he put it, "one cannot spend fifteen or more years serving the underdeveloped nations and the poor of the world by begging for them without developing an entirely new point of view with regard to the world."[104] And over the next three years, in that smaller corner of the world which became his responsibility as a diocesan bishop, he would try to put into practice many of the ideas he had voiced during the Council sessions. His concerns with the wider responsibilities of the Church in the world, and his love of the missions, would continue for the rest of his life. As Sheen perceived it, the fundamental issue of Vatican II was not schism or heresy, but "the Church and the world… it was the Church's mission to affirm a divine intervention in the world."[105]

---

[103] All of the quotations above are taken from the typescripts on Missions in Sheen's Vatican II papers, Sheen Archives.

[104] Sheen, *Treasure in Clay*, p. 151.

[105] *Ibid.*, p. 293.

Asserting his current views on the Church's mission in the world, Sheen collected his thoughts on the developments in the updated Church and published them as a book of "vital words for today's changing world": *Footprints in a Darkened Forest*.[106] Issued in 1967, this book can be read as an ideological bridge spanning Sheen's missionary years and his service as the Bishop of Rochester. It is a compendium of Sheen's reflections on many subjects: Teilhard de Chardin, refined views on psychology and death, and the world's modern saints: Gandhi, John F. Kennedy, Pope John XXIII, and Dag Hammarskjold. The more salient aspects of the book, which illumine the commonality of Sheen's concerns during these two careers of the 1960's, are devoted to the subject of poverty — the war against affluence, and the scandal of the thirtieth parallel — and hopes for world peace, which depended on rectifying the imbalance between rich and poor nations. As always, Sheen was able to combine his more traditional concerns — the saving of individual souls, and simple Christian love and charity — with a more progressive openness to social issues. In Rochester, pressing social issues of poverty and race relations would weigh heavily upon him; he would find himself caught up in a storm of controversy, created partially by the winds of change unleashed by the Council. But in *Footprints in a Darkened Forest*, he wrote in an optimistic vein, a precursor to some of the goals he sought to accomplish and a testimony to his own sincerity:

> Every advance toward racial justice, every move toward the improvement of actual human conditions, every striving of nations to unite in the peaceful settlement of disputes, every picking up of the broken pieces of the world and putting them together again is a heightened form of service which is love. Every move toward dialogue, even with the widest varieties of ideologies, every move to save humanity from nuclear destruction, because one loves his fellow man, is another step in the

---

[106] Fulton Sheen, *Footprints in a Darkened Forest* (New York: Meredith Press, 1967).

amorization of humanity... this love of humanity had its even greater expression in the opening of the doors of the Church to let in the world and also doors to let the Church out.[107]

Sheen's preparation for the opening of the doors proclaimed by the Second Vatican Council had been his sixteen years of work on behalf of the Church's missions. It was an opportunity for him to go out and become acquainted with the entire world through his travels, and his task as missionary and evangelist had been to take the Church out to the far corners of the world. From champion of the poor of the third world as mission leader, the man who awakened the American Catholic conscience to the reality of poverty and suffering in other parts of the world, Sheen moved on to become a champion of the poor at home — the unemployed, slumdwellers, racial minorities — and sought to prod the conscience of Rochestarians to the shame of poverty in their own city. Before taking up that challenge of administering a diocese, however, Sheen finished up his work at the Society for the Propagation of the Faith. Although historical assessments are few, and somewhat premature, some good things can be said of Bishop Sheen's accomplishments as missionary director. Certainly, he was a great source of inspiration, and a successful publicity man for this vital apostolate. In the realm of the speculative, a reporter wrote of Fulton Sheen at the outset of his missionary years: "his largest work today is one whose results he can never see... the alms from America he sends will reap a harvest of souls whose reckoning he will never know. For that is the true significance of the change that has come to Fulton J. Sheen in mid-career."[108] Shortly after Sheen's death in 1979, *Worldmission* offered this eulogy, words of praise as a special memoriam to Sheen for the lasting impression he made on the Society for the Propagation of the Faith:

---

[107] *Ibid.*, pp. 93, 250.

[108] Gretta Palmer, "Bishop Fulton J. Sheen," p. 62.

> With eminent missionary ardor he directed the work,
> awakened new initiatives and worked intensely and
> efficaciously to encourage the faithful to help the mis-
> sions with more generosity. He well understood the
> great and urgent needs of the missions.... Vatican II
> gave fresh impetus to many of the missionary themes
> that Sheen had unfolded and expounded. This foresight
> is one of the great monuments to the sweep and vision
> of this twentieth century missionary apostle.[109]

And in his humble self-assessment of the most unique aspect of
his mission ministry, Sheen gave credit to the Lord for the extra
fiscal prosperity he was able to bring to the Society for the Propagation of the Faith: "Divine Providence indeed opened a way for a
vast increase of aid to the missions."[110] The opportunity to appear
on a weekly television show in the 1950's, for which Sheen was paid
$26,000 a night, made it possible for him to personally give mil-
lions of dollars to the poor. It was a well-known fact that Sheen
gave all of the money he earned on television making "Life Is Worth
Living" to charity, and his favorite charity was the missions. The
height of Sheen's popularity and influence, as a television star, coincided with his missionary apostolate, and the Catholic Church's
missions profited significantly from that fortuitous occurrence.

Like the Church, then, all during the decade of the fifties
Fulton Sheen was preparing a valiant attempt at reconciliation with
the modern world, expressed in the Vatican Council's historic *Pastoral Constitution on the Church in the Modern World*. The spirit
enunciated in this document would have pivotal and far-reaching
consequences.

Addressed not just to Catholics, but to all men of good will,
the *Pastoral Constitution* demonstrated that the Catholic Church
had become "responsible to the world in a quite genuine and im-

---

[109] *Worldmission* 31 (Spring, 1980).
[110] Sheen, *Treasure in Clay*, p. 109.

mediate sense."[111] Sheen was much impressed with one passage: "Let everyone consider it his sacred obligation to esteem and observe social necessities as belonging to the primary duties of modern man."[112] Sheen took that obligation quite seriously in his capacity as National Director of the Society for the Propagation of the Faith, and as Bishop of Rochester. One historian's judgment on the main thrust of the Council rose from this document, "that Catholics should meet the world in a spirit of openness, ministering to its needs and cooperating with all the movements for good at work within it."[113] This assessment offers a fine description of the type of agenda Bishop Sheen tried to follow in Rochester. In his book on the missions, Sheen had made a striking prediction on the outcome of Vatican II:

> Perhaps no single force in the world today may be as important for the betterment of the future as the good that will come from the Second Council of the Vatican.[114]

As time would tell, it was not entirely accurate. For Bishop Sheen in Rochester, and the entire American Catholic Church, the results of the Second Vatican Council would prove to be a mixed blessing; while a certain amount of good would be accomplished, the Council would also provoke a considerable amount of turbulence and tension.

---

[111] Thomas F. O'Dea, *The Catholic Crisis* (Boston: The Beacon Press, 1968), p. 123.

[112] Quoted by Sheen in *Treasure in Clay*, p. 192.

[113] Philip Gleason, "Catholicism and Cultural Change," p. 92.

[114] Sheen, *Missions and the World Crisis*, p. 194.

CHAPTER EIGHT

Bishop in a Diocese:
The "Sound and Fury" of the Rochester Years, 1966–1969

> Write to me, Brother priests and religious whom I love so
> deeply in the Heart of Christ. Tell me how to intensify the pastoral life
> of the parish, the diocese and the community, both in the letter and
> spirit of the Vatican Council. Our sanctification is our apostolate;
> our apostolate is our sanctification. And you, my beloved People of
> God, my lambs and my sheep, write me the assurance of your prayers.
> *Fulton Sheen, Installation Sermon as Sixth Bishop of Rochester*
> *December 15, 1966*

> We shouldn't have been so unprepared. His image may
> have been conservative. But his work for the Society of the
> Propagation, and his wide contacts with people in many walks
> of life, had made him keenly aware of social issues. Vatican II
> had the same effect on him as it did on many other bishops.
> *Times-Union (Rochester), October 25, 1967*

On December 15, 1966, approximately one year after the closing
ceremonies marked the completion of the work of the Second Vatican Council in Rome, Fulton John Sheen was officially installed
as the sixth Bishop of Rochester, New York. It was an auspicious
moment, both in the life of Sheen and in the history of American
Catholicism: "for a brief hour… the spirit of Pope John's aggiornamento — a sense of spiritual renewal and reinvigoration — swept
throughout the American Church."[1] The new Bishop of Rochester's
hour would be especially brief: after a short but highly controver-

---

[1] John Cogley, *Catholic America* (Garden City, NY: Doubleday and Co., 1974), p. 102.

sial reign of just three years, Sheen would resign the post, ending his tenure "on a general note of frustration and disappointment for himself and his flock."[2] When he had first arrived, expectations ran high on both sides. The community of Rochester welcomed the famous celebrity, and looked forward to the prestige and attention that he would bring with him, the spotlight that would shine on their city. And Sheen, who had been very impressed with the future direction charted by the leaders of the Church, envisioned having a hand in creating the good which was destined to come forth from the reforms of the Council. Bishop Sheen saw his diocese as a microcosm of the Church in these promising times, and what would transpire in Rochester was indicative of the turbulence which would occur throughout the American Catholic Church during these revolutionary years. Although Sheen got off to a very good start in upstate New York, making national headlines frequently as a great innovator, things grew increasingly difficult for him. Sheen's life took a new turning at this point in his career, for after the successes came failure, and Fulton Sheen had never had much experience with failure. These years in Rochester would be remembered as ones of "sound and fury," signifying the general sense of upheaval which came to afflict the post-Vatican II Church in the United States.

When the news of Sheen's appointment to fill the vacant see in Rochester was announced in October of 1966, there was a general note of surprise sounded in the national press. After all, with the exception of a year spent as a curate in a small parish in Peoria — St. Patrick's — after the completion of his university studies in 1925, Sheen had no real pastoral or administrative experience in running a diocese. And although he was still vital and in good health, he was seventy-one years old. There was also some rumored speculation that this was some sort of demotion for Sheen, perhaps due to the interventions of the powerful Cardinal Spellman. At the very least, sending Fulton Sheen to Rochester was seen to

---

be a misuse of his talents. For the public record, Sheen dispelled all these notions, consistently saying that he was happy about the appointment and the job that awaited him — taking care of souls in Rochester. In the numerous interviews he gave to the press, Bishop Sheen spoke of his first love, the missions, and declared that his "love and service would always be available to the Propagation"[3], even after he moved to Rochester. He summarized his feelings in speaking of the "privilege of service":

> I'm a soldier. I go where the general sends me... I've been dealing long enough with the circumference of the world. Now it is time to deal with a point within that circumference. I'm overjoyed. Rochester is one of the finest dioceses in the United States... now, at 71, something is here that is new and challenging. I feel up to it... What I'd wish to do would be the task of implementation and putting into action, the decrees of the Ecumenical Council. Today the people come to the Church. Tomorrow the Church must go to the people.[4]

The eagerness to implement the reforms of the Vatican Council was at the heart of Sheen's approach to his new assignment. It was a theme he mentioned repeatedly before he left New York City, and it appeared consistently in all the official documents that came forth from the Bishop's office once he took over in Rochester, the justification for every action he took. Obviously, Sheen took the responsibility of "transporting aggiornamento across the Atlantic to American shores"[5] very seriously. To a *New York Times* reporter, Sheen "pointed out that he was one of the first, if not the first, diocesan bishop named since the enactment of the new Church legislation. He declared himself determined to carry out the reforms

---

[3] *New York Times*, October 27, 1968.

[4] Sheen, in an interview with Bob Considine, "Bishop Sheen's Great Joy — The Privilege to Serve," *World Journal Tribune* (New York), November 8, 1966.

[5] Vincent Yzermans, editor, *American Participation in the Second Vatican Council*, p. 13.

at once in Rochester, in a pastoral administration emphasizing ecumenical and social work." Sheen left the lingering impression that he was "set to remold Rochester into a demonstration diocese of his Church in America."[6]

In making the final preparations to move on to the challenge in Rochester, Sheen wrote several letters to his brother priests and bishops who had sent their congratulations. He spoke of his feelings of "liberation," in the "words of the psalmist: the snare is broken and the bird is free." Welcoming this chance to take up the "sweet burden of pastoral care," Sheen declared that he was happy about the appointment. "I will now have an opportunity to put into practice many of the ideas which I have cherished through the decades."[7] Upon arriving in Rochester on December 14, to a welcoming crowd of over 3,000 people gathered at the Monroe County Airport, Bishop Sheen reiterated these feelings of joy: "I have an ardent desire to spend myself and to be spent, to get my arms around Rochester." Describing himself as an astronaut who had circled the earth for sixteen years, he said he was relieved at this re-entry: "it is a good touchdown."[8] Playing up to the hometown throng, he continued:

> All that ever entered into the service of my priesthood, the research of my professorship, the dedication to the poor of the world, my vulnerability to the missions and lepers, all my prayers, petitions and sacrifices have been lived for this one happy moment: Rochester.[9]

Though he had overstated it, Sheen really did perceive Rochester as his first opportunity to apply his ideas in a concrete situation, having episcopal jurisdiction over his own diocese. As Cardinal

6   *New York Times*, November 8, 1966.
7   Sheen, in a letter to the Most Rev. Cornelius Lucey, Bishop of Cork, November 10, 1966, in the Correspondences Files, Sheen Archives.
8   *New York Times*, December 15, 1966.
9   *Times-Union* (Rochester), December 15, 1966.

Spellman had reminded him when the appointment was first announced: "every bishop dreams of having a diocese of his own."[10] And by exuding such a sense of enthusiasm, Bishop Sheen certainly got off to a promising start in Rochester, convincing his flock that he was totally dedicated to his new assignment.

The character of the installation at Sacred Heart Cathedral, and the other welcoming ceremonies, foreshadowed many of the qualities which would come to define Bishop Sheen's administration. They were marked by a simplicity in style and an ecumenical theme which would become the hallmark of Sheen's pastorate. The new Bishop's mood — "earnest, devout and gracious"[11] — was conveyed in his installation sermon and the addresses he gave at the luncheon and public reception held in his honor. Throughout the day, Bishop Sheen spoke of his plans and dreams for Rochester. He wanted to be a shepherd, feeding the lambs and sheep of his flock.[12] Using a simple simile to address the questions and predictions which surrounded his coming to Rochester, he declared that a new bishop in a diocese was "like a new baby in a family: there is no doubt about the child being loved; the problem is what kind of child will he be?"[13] During the first few hectic months of his administration, he was always careful to state his intentions openly, in an attempt to answer that question. Employing another favorite metaphor, he spoke of the Church as both a river and a rock, and declared that he would adopt the same symbols in his pastoral rule: stability and solidity on the one hand, and freshness and challenge on the other.[14] Extending the paradox from his farewell sermon at St. Patrick's Cathedral in New York City, Bishop Sheen directed his attention to the current contrast in the Catholic Church between liberals and conservatives, and the sense of uneasiness that

[10] *New York Times*, October 27, 1966.

[11] Robert F. McNamara, *The Diocese of Rochester, 1868-1968*, p. 526.

[12] Sheen, Installation Sermon, December 15, 1966; a typescript of this sermon is contained in the collection at the Sheen Archives.

[13] *Ibid.*

[14] The *Catholic Courier-Journal*, December 23, 1966.

prevailed. The seeming tension and contradiction between radicalism and conservatism need not prove destructive, according to
Sheen: "all tends to unity; as the Master Craftsman united the two
sides with a keystone arch, those who wished to serve the Church
must strive for a reconciliation of extremes."[15] Perceiving himself
in the role of reconciler as well, Sheen began his work as Bishop of
Rochester in that spirit.

The Sheen administration's most singular strength was probably its ecumenism, a fact much appreciated by the non-Catholic
community in Rochester. Leaders from the Jewish and Protestant
religions were on hand to welcome the famous Bishop to Rochester, pointing out his reputation as an advocate of the poor, which
they especially admired. The Right Reverend George M. Barrett,
Episcopal Bishop, greeted his fellow bishop in confident hope that
they would share an "apostolic task in an ecumenical age," and described Sheen as a man "who understands modern life... with an
active concern for the hungry and wretched of the earth, who knows
the Church is called not to serve itself but the world."[16] Rabbi
Herbert Bronstein, on behalf of the Jewish community, welcomed
Sheen as "one of the gifted few who have been able meaningfully
to interpret profound spiritual truths to the multitudes." Rochester was in need of that kind of teaching and guidance, and a voice
which would "nag at the conscience of an affluent and comfortable
America." Looking forward to working harmoniously with Bishop
Sheen, Rabbi Bronstein concluded by outlining the massive challenge which confronted all religious leaders: "the conquest of poverty, the resolution of war, and the building of an equitable and
free society both at home and throughout the world."[17] The passage of time would clearly demonstrate Sheen's receptivity to these
messages of good will. The overwhelming impression left by Sheen's
first months in office was that of a man in a hurry, committed to
the reforms of Vatican II, especially in regards to the ecumenical

---

[15] *Ibid.* See also Fr. McNamara's summary in his history of the Diocese of Rochester, p. 526.

[16] *Democrat and Chronicle* (Rochester), December 11, 1966.

[17] *Ibid.*

movement of cooperation and the Church's mission to the inner city. The new Bishop was also determined to set a fine example, in the hopes that his flock would be more likely to follow his lead if they believed in his sincerity. A significant gesture which demonstrated his personal charity was his choice of a residence. After spending his first night in Rochester at St. Bernard's Seminary — a symbolic affirmation of his conviction that the seminary was both the root of the diocese and the most cherished possession of a bishop — Sheen moved into a special apartment at the Columbus Civic Center. He had informed his predecessor, Bishop Kearney, that he wished him to remain living at the episcopal center, a demonstration of his thoughtful good will.[18] With his usual industriousness, Sheen proceeded to set in motion his blueprint plans to make Rochester a "test case" of the post-Vatican II Church, and to travel all around the diocese, becoming acquainted with his flock and preaching. He made special visits to the city jail and the Auburn State Prison, demonstrating his willingness to minister to the poor and unfortunate sinners in the diocese, and strived to make himself accessible, to be close to his priests and people.

According to the historian of the Rochester Diocese, Father Robert F. McNamara:

> The Bishop's pastoral approach to diocesan visitation was another illustration of his policy in action; and as the weeks unfolded, those familiar with the details of the Council's legislation could see in his views on the clergy, the laity, ecumenism, the inner city, the missions, and many other subjects, a strong reflection of the thinking of the recent Council.[19]

One of his first duties as a new Bishop was to choose his advisors and counselors. In a bold, decisive move — the first official act of Bishop Sheen in Rochester — he appointed a young activist priest, Father P. David Finks, to the newly created post of Episco-

[18] McNamara, p. 520.
[19] *Ibid.*, p. 528.

pal Vicar of Urban Ministry. In meeting with his clergy from the
inner city parishes, Sheen had become convinced that an imaginative, precedent-setting stroke was needed to draw attention to the
plight of the urban poor. In the years prior to Sheen's arrival, Rochester, like many other American cities, had been the scene of racial
tensions and violence. Rochester had undergone its trial by fire in
the riots of the summer of 1964. The calm of the city dubbed
"Smugtown, U.S.A." had been rudely shattered, and the entire
community was forced to become painfully aware of the urgency
of the inner city's problems. One civic step towards finding a solution was the formation of FIGHT: "Freedom, Integration, God,
Honor, Today."[20] The FIGHT organization was built through the
intervention of Chicago activist Saul Alinsky, who had been invited by the Inner City Ministry of the Rochester Council of
Churches to set up a grass-roots mechanism to deal with the concerns of the inner city. Some Catholics from the inner city wards
— including Father Finks from Immaculate Conception parish —
soon affiliated with the supporting Friends of FIGHT, and became
embroiled in a struggle with Eastman Kodak Co. over minority
hiring practices. Fulton Sheen arrived in Rochester right in the
midst of this very heated public controversy between FIGHT and
Kodak, and the appointment of Father Finks focused national
media attention on the city, the first of many Sheen episodes which
would result in big headlines and even bigger controversies.

In the official letter Bishop Sheen wrote to Father Finks on
January 3, 1967, he spoke of this first official appointment as "evidence of my own sweet impatience to serve those most in need," as
well as his confidence in Finks as a "worthy priest of Christ."[21] Sheen

---

[20] For details on the social crisis in Rochester, see Fr. McNamara's history, pp. 504-505.
   An especially valuable insider's view can be found in the social autobiography written by
   P. David Finks: "Crisis in Smugtown: A Study of Conflict, Churches and Citizen Orga-
   nizations in Rochester, New York, 1966-1969" (Ph.D. dissertation, Union Graduate
   School of the Union for Experimenting Colleges and Universities, 1975).

[21] Sheen, letter to Rev. P. David Finks, January 3, 1967. This letter is categorized as "Docu-
   ment 3-D" in the "Eight Months Report on the Diocese of Rochester," submitted by
   Bishop Fulton J. Sheen as a progress report, and preserved with Sheen's papers as the
   Sixth Bishop of Rochester in the Sheen Archives.

described his soul as "anguished by this dehumanization of our community... as I look out, I can see Christ weeping over the inner city of Jerusalem."[22] So moved, he proposed to take this "very unusual step" and outlined the following areas of responsibility for the position of Vicar of Urban Ministry in the inner city: "housing, education, employment, health, social justice, equality, and the sharing of the common heritages of American well-being and Christian civilization."[23] By announcing the appointment in terms of this wider "American and Christian heritage," and by preparing a special press release for the national wire services, Sheen was hoping to set an example for other cities to follow, by attracting as much attention as possible to this action. By way of further explanation, he waxed eloquently on the "besieged city" and the "Exodus from the inner city and flight to the suburbs":

> The solution to this problem is not to be found in ignoring personal dignity. Nor is the solution to be found in trying to rally congregations into old boundaries, for stained glass windows are apt to becloud our vision of poverty and distress. Neither is the Church to be an Ivory Tower outside of the Inner City. The Church must be where problems are, where hunger is, where rooms are cold and where difficult decisions have to be made. The mission of the Church is to participate in Christ's suffering in the world, and to have even a kind of lovers quarrel with those members who would not feel the pain of the stripes on the backs of others.[24]

This initial "virtuoso" performance by Sheen, recalled by Finks several years after the fact, cast Sheen as "the epitome of the pastoral bishop envisioned by Vatican II."[25]

---

[22] *Ibid.*
[23] *Ibid.*
[24] *Ibid.*
[25] Finks, "Crisis in Smugtown," p. 178.

Continuing his lively interest in the unrest and suffering in the inner city, the pastoral Bishop Sheen proceeded to initiate a kind of lovers quarrel with the city's powerful business interests, one of the first indications of the increasingly bitter divisions which would come to plague him. As guest speaker at a Chamber of Commerce dinner, Sheen told the gathered members that Rochester was like a beautiful woman — well-dressed, but flawed by an unsightly blemish: inner city poverty. When the rest of the world looked at Rochester, he warned, it saw not industry and commerce, but the "little pimple on our city's face." Lest the business leaders risk seeing their city's image damaged, Bishop Sheen encouraged them to apply "an ointment of humility, love and service" to remove the blemish.[26] And as a sign of his own good faith, Sheen announced plans to impose a tax on all church construction in the diocese, "a percentage graduated according to the expenditure to be given to the poor in this city and diocese and to the poor of the world."[27] The unpredictable Bishop Sheen left quite an impression on his audience, but not entirely favorable. In the words of Father Finks, who gave Sheen credit for noble intentions and good instincts, "he would find many checkbooks closed to him when he went looking for money."[28] Some criticism followed, and conservative members of the flock also voiced objections to the perceived radicalism of Father Finks, but Sheen stayed the course. Convinced that he was morally right, and that perhaps the community needed some shaking up, Sheen continued steadfastly in the same direction. He had never been one to shy away from controversy if the cause was just.[29]

Along more regular lines of his administrative duties in se-

---

[26] Sheen, remarks quoted in the *Courier-Journal*, January 27, 1967.

[27] *Ibid.*

[28] Finks, p. 180. Despite the talk about Sheen having alienated the business community, the Chamber of Commerce awarded the "Salesman of the Year" award to Bishop Sheen in 1968 for his "outstanding job of selling Rochester to the country, the world, and itself"; *Time* (January 12, 1968).

[29] In response to one journalist's question about the opposition to some of his actions, Bishop Sheen replied: "I was sent here to do a job. If some people don't like it, they will like it less as time goes on." Cited by Douglas Roche in *The Catholic Revolution* (New York: David McKay Co., 1968), p. 81.

lecting his advisors, Bishop Sheen proceeded to fill the standard offices. Even in this task, however, he struck a blow for the concepts of collegiality and democracy which had come out of the Vatican Council's deliberations. In a letter addressed to all the priests of the diocese, Sheen asked his "Brothers in Christ," after they had prayed thoughtfully and invoked the "guidance of the Holy Spirit," to submit the names of three priests whom he might "appoint as your leaders." Sheen explained that he operated on the assumption that "if the voice of the people can sometimes be the voice of God, then certainly there are times when the voice of the priesthood can be the voice of Christ."[30] Promising to personally count the ballots, and to be guided by the priests' recommendations in choosing their leaders, Bishop Sheen signed himself as "Your Co-Worker in Christ," underscoring the concept of collegiality.[31] True to his word, Sheen followed the priests' advice and announced the results within a month's time: the Rt. Rev. Msgr. Dennis W. Hickey was appointed Vicar General; Fr. James Moynihan became the new Chancellor; and Fr. Michael Hogan was selected as secretary to Bishop Sheen.[32] In addition, Sheen appointed a Vicar of Pastoral Planning, a Vicar of Religious Education, and two vicars with territorial jurisdiction within the diocese.[33] Extending the guidelines of democracy further into the hierarchical structure, Sheen outlined plans for the creation of a Priests Council in another letter to the diocesan clergy. This idea came directly from the conciliar decree *Christus Dominus*, which called for the creation of a priests senate to be "collaborators of the Bishop in the government of the diocese."[34] In the minutes of one of the meetings of the Priests Council, it was noted that "the Council was formed by Bishop Sheen to implement the spirit of Vatican II, to

---

[30] Sheen, quoted in the *National Catholic Reporter*, February 1, 1967.

[31] Sheen, in a letter to all diocesan priests, December 30, 1966: in the "Pastoral Letters" file of Bishop Sheen, Archives of the Diocese of Rochester.

[32] McNamara, p. 528.

[33] *Ibid.*, pp. 529-530.

[34] Sheen, in a letter dated January 27, 1967, "Pastoral Letters" file.

consult with his priests, to hear their judgments."[35] Other administrative reforms incorporated into the new diocesan structure included a turning over of the financial affairs to a three-man board of laity to oversee the "secular and business side of diocesan administration," leaving Sheen free for the pastoral duties he did best: "teaching, preaching, and visiting the poor."[36] Sheen even changed the name of the Chancery to the "Pastoral Office," to emphasize the "pastoral spirit breathed into the Church by Pope John XXIII… and the transition to a more person-oriented atmosphere," emphasizing the "shepherding" role of the episcopal function.[37]

In his conception of himself as a shepherd, Bishop Sheen had spoken of the two most important duties of a bishop as "the sanctification of the clergy, and the care of the disadvantaged and socially disinherited."[38] Setting his sights on the principal diocesan seminary, St. Bernard's, Sheen decided to direct his attention to a major renovation of that institution, incorporating his Vatican II ideas on the formation of the clergy, ministry to the poor, and ecumenism in a single showcase. To those who hinted that Sheen was interested solely in the spectacular, short-term actions that attracted national publicity, the reforms set in motion at St. Bernard's suggest otherwise. Here, Bishop Sheen's emphasis was on long-term changes of great importance, where he was "quietly laying a foundation on which other bishops in the future would have to build."[39] Sheen's goal was to open up the seminary to the world, by expanding its scope and curriculum; and to bring the world into the seminary, in the form of new professors. Following the conciliar decrees that theology and philosophy should be integrated in the training of priests, Bishop Sheen said that "combining the knowledge of the Christian heritage and the contemporary world will be the aim of

---

[35] Minutes of the Priests Council Meeting, November 27, 1967, in the Archives of the Diocese of Rochester.

[36] *National Catholic Reporter*, February 1, 1967, and Document #2 in Sheen's "Eight Months Report."

[37] Sheen, "Eight Months Report," Document #1; see also McNamara, p. 530.

[38] Sheen, in a letter to the Rev. P. David Finks, January 3, 1967.

[39] Douglas Roche, *The Catholic Revolution*, p. 81.

instruction,"[40] a concept which had guided Sheen since his own days in the seminary, and was in line with the traditional Catholic conviction that the priest should be "in the world but not of it."[41] More startling changes were introduced regarding pastoral training, where Sheen was influenced by his desire to concentrate on the inner city and its problems. Seminarians, in a cooperative field training program with the Colgate-Rochester Divinity School, would be sent out into the slums, to learn by doing. As Sheen described it, he wanted to make theology "come alive in exposure to urbanization, poverty, and... the multitudinous needs for caring, which are most often found outside the rectory."[42] This cooperative venture in social work would be aided by a liaison between the seminary and the inner city ministry around Father Finks, to insure a more intensified apostolate.

To bring the world into the seminary, Bishop Sheen added fourteen professors to the teaching staff at St. Bernard's, all within the first few months of his tenure in office. Father Sebastian Falcone, O.F.M. Cap., had given a series of popular lectures on Holy Scripture, in keeping with Sheen's belief that the seminary should reach out and serve the entire community; Sheen later appointed him to the faculty at St. Bernard's to teach New Testament. Along more unorthodox lines, Sheen invited some professors from Europe to teach at the seminary as well. His first ecumenical appointment to the faculty was the Rev. Michael Bordeaux, a young Anglican priest who had graduated from Oxford and studied at the University of Moscow, and would teach electives on "religion behind the iron curtain."[43] In a more unusual move, Bishop Sheen also asked the ex-Communist editor of the London *Daily Worker*, Dr. Douglas Hyde — a famous crossover communist convert — to teach the techniques of conversion and explore the pos-

---

[40] Sheen, "Eight Months Report."
[41] *Ibid.*
[42] *Ibid.*
[43] Sheen, *Treasure in Clay*, p. 175. See also Bishop Sheen's "Eight Months Report."

sibilities of a Christian-Marxist dialogue.[44] Another ecumenical appointment was the Rev. Conrad Massa, pastor of Rochester's Third Presbyterian Church who would assist in the instruction of seminarians on the art of preaching; Sheen believed that Protestants generally had a better heritage as evangelical preachers to draw upon. Additional reforms on the seminary level included the creation of a board of laymen for the purpose of reviewing candidates for the priesthood, and the psychological testing of seminarians to determine their fitness for service.[45] Stressing the notion that the priest should serve the laity, Bishop Sheen thought that it was only fair that the faithful in the pews should have "some choice about their servants" who "stand in the pulpit and on the other side of the communion rail."[46] The minor seminary, St. Andrew's, was closed after consultation with the clergy, and replaced by "King's Preparatory School," a co-educational high school designed to encourage the formation of a "spiritual elite," and to provide its students with an opportunity to test their "vocation for a dedicated service to God, humanity and the Church."[47]

Perhaps the most ambitious and long-lasting of Bishop Sheen's seminary reforms was a plan initiated during his administration for joint cooperation between the Catholic St. Bernard's Seminary and the Protestant Colgate-Rochester Divinity School, one of America's oldest schools of theology. The idea was to form an ecumenical cluster in Rochester, which would set an example and ideally be duplicated around the nation, in keeping with the spirit of Vatican II. In Sheen's own words:

> The needless multiplication of faculties, the need of dialogue, the recognition of sharing God's work, and the

---

[44] Sheen, *Treasure in Clay*, p. 175. See also Frank J. Prial's "Boat-Rocking Bishop" in the *Wall Street Journal*, September 12, 1967.

[45] See Sheen's "Eight Months Report."

[46] Sheen, quoted in the *National Catholic Reporter*, May 24, 1967.

[47] McNamara, p. 533. Fr. McNamara, Professor of Church History at St. Bernard's Seminary, called this action of Sheen's a "bold attempt to solve a question that many thought insoluble."

common resolve to be spiritual leaven in the mass of society have prompted this move to a coalition.[48]

Many of these dynamic and fast-paced reforms set in motion by Fulton Sheen at the seminary in Rochester resulted in a good deal of favorable publicity for the new bishop and his diocese. The national press also took notice of two of Bishop Sheen's other acts of departure from previously established Church practice: his announcement on gradually deferring the age for administering the sacrament of Confirmation; and his "wide-ranging personal ecumenism."[49] Grounded in Sheen's lifelong interest in the process of Christian, particularly Catholic, education, and based upon his interpretation of the decrees of the recent Council, Sheen proposed a complete restructuring of the preparation process for Confirmation, the "Sacrament of Lay Priesthood."[50] Rather than administering the sacrament to spiritual infants or "babes," Sheen suggested that a delay — until the child was old enough to realize the significance of Confirmation — was in order. Ideally, Confirmation would be conferred when the candidate graduated from high school, in the expectation that with age would come a maturity of conviction and a greater sense of commitment to the Church. To assist that process of maturation, the Church would develop a program of "liturgical and spiritual training for puberty, of two or three years duration."[51] The program, according to Sheen, should consist of three courses: a reverent and prudent sex education; practical charity, emphasizing a concrete love of neighbor and the poor and the social responsibilities of all Christians; and an explanation of the Spirit of Christ in contrast to the spirit of the world, climaxed by a renewal of the candidate's baptismal vows.[52] Initially, Bishop Sheen

---

[48] Sheen, quoted in Roche's *The Catholic Revolution*, p. 84.

[49] Prial, "The Boat-Rocking Bishop."

[50] Sheen, "Eight Months Report"; see also Sheen's report on Confirmation, and his letter dated February 13, 1967.

[51] Sheen, "Eight Months Report." See also the short article, "Awaiting Confirmation," in *Newsweek* (February 27, 1967).

[52] Sheen, "Eight Months Report."

would be left standing all by himself on this matter,[53] but as the reform was followed in dioceses around the nation in subsequent years, Sheen would be remembered as the one who set the precedent.

Setting precedents in more dramatic fashion was Sheen's forte when he returned to the pulpit in Rochester. Not only did he speak in Protestant churches, but he reached out beyond the Christian community to embrace the Jews as well. Although some conservative Rochestarians would be taken aback by their Bishop's appearances in synagogues, for the most part his ecumenical efforts won praise and admiration for Sheen.[54] In January of 1967, shortly after his arrival in Rochester, Sheen was invited to a welcoming reception at Temple B'rith Kodesh, where he delivered an address to a crowd of 2,300 people.[55] Bishop Sheen, saying that he felt like St. Paul at Ephesus, who went to the synagogue to "speak confidently and hold discussions," appealed to Jews because of his social consciousness and concern for the poor. Rabbi Herbert Bronstein, so impressed by Sheen's willingness to speak in the synagogue under such happy and friendly circumstances, said that "to find a precedent for this we must go back deep into our history, beyond the Middle Ages, when St. Jerome consulted with the rabbis of his day."[56] A few days after this performance, Bishop Sheen shared the platform with Rabbi Mark Tannenbaum — the only rabbi to participate in the activities of the Vatican Council — at a colloquium on Catholic-Jewish relationships.[57] Sheen spoke of the common heritage and community of faith between the two reli-

[53] *Newsweek* (February 27, 1967).

[54] Rabbi Philip Bernstein joked that "Catholics tell me that if they want to see their new bishop they have to go to Jewish services"; reported by Frank Prial. Mr. Prial also reported that some of the criticism was harsher; one bitter opponent complained to the Vatican that Sheen was setting the diocese on a course of "wildly heretical universal ecumenism."

[55] See McNamara, p. 535; and Roche, pp. 79-80. Sheen also kept the accounts of his speeches to the Jewish community in the "Eight Months Report."

[56] *Ibid.* Sheen's comments were quoted in the *Courier-Journal*, February 3, 1967.

[57] McNamara, p. 535.

gious groups, and the tendency of both to be at odds with the secular spirit in the world:

> ...neither you Jews, nor us Christians, are at home in the world... we are both revolutionists, uneasy, upstarts, irritants, catalysts, disturbing the moods and philosophies of the world; and why — because we have a vocation from God ...in the face of persecution, we should find unity.[58]

Assuming the role of upstart and disturber in his Sunday sermon at Sacred Heart Cathedral on July 30, 1967, Bishop Sheen used the occasion to issue a striking challenge to the President of the United States. For a man described as "full of surprises" since coming to Rochester, this was the greatest surprise yet, and it caught much of the national press off guard. In response to President Johnson's proclamation of a "National Day for Peace and Reconciliation," Bishop Fulton Sheen asked that all American troops be immediately withdrawn from Vietnam. Linking racial peace with a call to end the war, and disassociating himself from "all those who would carry placards instead of a Cross," Sheen, speaking humbly and "only as a Christian," asked the President to announce:

> In the name of God who bade us love our neighbor... for the sake of reconciliation, I shall withdraw all our forces immediately from Southern Vietnam, so that, in the words of Abraham Lincoln, we "may unite in most humbly offering our prayers and supplications to the Great Lord and ruler of nations, and beseech Him to pardon our national and other sins" ...is this reconciliation to be limited only to our citizens? Could we not also be reconciled with our brothers in Vietnam? May we plead only for a reconciliation between blacks and

---

[58] Sheen, quoted in the *Courier-Journal*, March 3, 1967. This newspaper article is labeled as "Document #4, Ecumenism" in the "Eight Months Report."

whites, and not between blacks and whites and yellows?
…to paraphrase the gospel …go and be reconciled to
your northern Vietnam brother then come back and
offer your prayers.[59]

Because of Fulton Sheen's well-known reputation as an ardent anti-communist, this sermon was reported in the press as if
Bishop Sheen had undergone some type of transformation.
Newsweek, under the headline "Conversion," pointed out that
"Sheen's call for unilateral withdrawal was the first unequivocal
public statement against current U.S. policy by any American
Catholic bishop."[60] It also pointed out that Sheen's stand "directly
countered the hawkish stand" of his former superior, Francis Cardinal Spellman.[61] Another hawk, William F. Buckley, Jr., was
moved to devote his "On the Right" column in the *National Review* to Sheen's plea for a day of reconciliation. Buckley suggested
that President Johnson probably did not expect such a reaction in
the form of Sheen's "political bombshell."[62] And the Protestant
journal *Christian Century* applauded Bishop Sheen's "profound and
significant statement" and his "uncanny and greatly envied ability
to capture and hold the nation's attention."[63]

Capturing the nation's attention was probably what Sheen had
in mind when he made the statement; it was the motivating force
behind much of what he did as Bishop of Rochester. And although
his stand may have been unexpected by many who considered him
a traditional Catholic priest, even somewhat conservative, it was
fully consistent with his earlier views on peace and social justice.
He saw the opportunity, in a time of national tension and turmoil,
to recommend a course of action which would cause Americans to

[59] Bishop Fulton Sheen, News Release, July 30, 1967; "Sermon of Bishop Sheen on President Johnson's Call for a National Day of Prayer"; Document #6, "Eight Months Report."

[60] *Newsweek* (August 16, 1967).

[61] *Ibid.*

[62] *National Review* (September 5, 1967).

[63] *Christian Century* (August 16, 1967).

consider the relationship between peace at home and peace abroad — and he took advantage of it. In explaining himself later, he suggested that he was calling for a thoughtful consideration of our national policy, advocating instead a policy of Christian "restraint."[64] Appearing on the CBS news program "60 Minutes," Bishop Sheen pointed out that his viewpoint was expressed as a moral action, not a political one: "If we are to be the moral leaders of the world, we must give an example, and be the most powerful also. We must show our power by appreciating the weak."[65] In reiterating his idea that there was a relationship between the racial violence in America's inner cities, and the war in Vietnam, the Bishop also declared that the war was costing too much. From a practical, economic point of view, as well as a moral one, Sheen recommended withdrawal, arguing that the money spent on armaments to carry on the war might be put to better use in alleviating the sufferings of the poor.[66]

Within a year of Fulton Sheen's arrival in upstate New York, he was the subject of several extensive evaluations by the media. Certainly, publicity was no stranger to Sheen; the press had followed his activities for decades, and he had always enjoyed the attention. But the national spotlight was new to Rochester, and the angle of vision focused on Sheen was different as well. Essentially, the accounts contrasted the popular Sheen "image" with the reality of the post-conciliar Bishop of Rochester. On the surface, it appeared as though there were a "new" — and in the opinion of some reporters, an "improved" — version of Fulton Sheen creating such excitement in the city of Rochester. Beneath the surface, however, some reports were able to penetrate to the reality behind the story — the underlying truth. The truth was that Sheen's actions in Rochester were a natural progression in his career. The change was not so much in the man as it was in the times; there

---

[64] Sheen, in remarks he made on William F. Buckley's "Firing Line" television program, February 1, 1970. A tape recording of the interview is found in the audio collection of the Sheen Archives.

[65] Sheen, quoted in the *New York Times*, October 29, 1969.

[66] *Ibid.*

was a basic consistency in Bishop Sheen's efforts to respond to the needs of a changing world. Having spent a lifetime rising to meet one new challenge after another, the general consensus was that Fulton Sheen was a success at this new assignment as well.

In August of 1968, Bishop Sheen issued his own in-house progress report — "Eight Months Report on the Diocese of Rochester, New York" — highlighting the same accomplishments that were winning him favorable reviews outside the diocese also. The overriding impression given in this self-evaluation was Sheen's desire to implement the decrees of the Second Vatican Council, particularly in regard to the spirit of poverty and ecumenism.[67] Bishop Sheen had declared that the implementation of the reforms of Vatican II was "one of the primary objectives of his episcopate here,"[68] and he was off to a promising start, thriving on the controversies he had precipitated. One of the local city newspapers, the *Times-Union*, published its own assessment in October, "Bishop Sheen Stirs Up the Winds of Change."[69] Expressing the community's sense of "lingering surprise" that Sheen would advocate "so sharply and ardently the reforms of Vatican II," the article continued: "perhaps we shouldn't have been so unprepared." After all, Sheen had been "keenly aware of social issues" in his capacity as America's missionary spokesman. One liberal Catholic interviewed felt that Bishop Sheen's biggest achievement had "probably been to give the Church a sense of social mission, and an awareness of the needs of the poor."[70] Sheen's influence extended beyond the boundaries of the diocese, for he was "making headlines not because of his famous friends and converts, but because of his advocacy of change." Of all these changes, the "bishop's concern for the poor (his speech to the Chamber of Commerce, his appointment of Fr. Finks) has come through perhaps the strongest."[71] It was clear

---

[67] Sheen, "Eight Months Report."

[68] Sheen, "Pastoral Letter," April 28, 1967; in the Pastoral Letters file, Archives of the Diocese of Rochester.

[69] *Times-Union* (Rochester), October 25, 1967.

[70] *Ibid.*

[71] *Ibid.*

that the city was beginning to look past the image to appreciate their Bishop's substance: "There is no disagreement at all about the saintliness, idealism, and devotion of Sheen."[72] Summing up, the report suggested that Sheen's continued effectiveness was dependent "on the bishop's lines of communications"[73] — a prophecy of what would go wrong for Sheen the following year, when the opinion of the local press changed dramatically.

On the national level, both *Time* magazine and the *Wall Street Journal* sent reporters to Rochester to write reviews of Sheen's new career moves. *Time,* in one of the first notices, spoke of Sheen as one who had "something of a reputation as a churchly conservative," but was now a "highly imaginative innovator."[74] Citing the democratic style of his administration, his concern for the poor, and his appearances in Jewish synagogues, the magazine pronounced Sheen's performance thus far "spectacular," and offered the laudatory opinion that "he may be remembered as the best bishop Rochester ever had."[75] The longer analysis written in the *Wall Street Journal* was more balanced, but sensational in its provocative headline: "Boat-Rocking Bishop: Fulton Sheen Assumes New Role as Innovator in Rochester Diocese."[76] Contrasting Sheen's image as a "dynamic, articulate but conservative cleric" who had just interpreted Catholic doctrine for decades, with his growing reputation as "one of the most innovative bishops in the United States," the reporter said that Bishop Sheen "has left hardly a boat unrocked."[77] Although winning the support of many liberals in the diocese, Sheen had upset some conservatives who thought he was going too far too fast, and already a Catholic backlash was taking shape. But the wider community of Rochester seemed to be welcoming the torrent of change taking place under Sheen's leadership. Richard Hughes, executive

---

[72] *Ibid.*
[73] *Ibid.*
[74] *Time* (February 10, 1967).
[75] *Ibid.*
[76] *The Wall Street Journal*, September 12, 1967.
[77] *Ibid.*

director of the Rochester Council of Churches, expressed his appreciation for the prestige and support Sheen had lent to FIGHT's struggle to improve the quality of life in the inner city neighborhoods. Saying that although he had expected a personable religious conservative, Hughes was delighted to get "a man infused with the whole spirit of Catholic ecumenism; he's an exciting presence in this town."[78] A closer priest friend of Sheen, trying to set the record straight, told the reporter that it was difficult to apply a simple label to such a man. Actually, Sheen had changed little:

> He's always been eloquently anti-communist and anti-Freudian, and these are the marks of a conservative. But his writings on the Mass and the liturgy never were conservative. I'd say that sociologically he's a progressive, on the liturgy he is contemporary, and theologically and philosophically he's, well, a traditionalist.[79]

The essential Fulton Sheen, it seemed, was a man of great complexity.

A Catholic journal, *Ave Maria*, editorialized at the same time that Fulton Sheen was also a man of great energy. At the age of 72, he was laying to rest an old myth: "the idea that vitality, concern, fresh approaches and strong leadership are prerogatives of the young."[80] Contrary to those who dismissed him as an anachronism, he had become an effective leader in Rochester. Assuming an even more glowing tone, the editorial implied that after a "life of scholarship, eloquence and national fund-raising," Sheen was "making his most lasting impact on religion in the U.S. providing a blueprint for decisive leadership as a living example of what the churchman must be in our society."[81]

The churchman as a "den mother of Catholic leftism" was how

---

[78] *Ibid.*

[79] *Ibid.*

[80] *Ave Maria* 106 (September 2, 1967), "Let's Have More Older Bishops, Please."

[81] *Ibid.*

Sheen was described in the most unusual, even bizarre, assessment of the Bishop of Rochester. *Ramparts*, a radical magazine, published a cover story on "Left-Wing Catholics" which featured Fulton Sheen in the company of Fr. Groppi, Fr. William DuBay, and Jesus Christ.[82] Although the article contained several inaccuracies, and impugned the motives of the "theatrical" Sheen, it attracted a good deal of attention — if only from the perspective of the unexpected. Warren Hinckle, editor of *Ramparts* and a self-described former Catholic, saw Sheen as an "old caterpillar who had metamorphosed from a fundamentalist, anti-communist and modernist-baiter to the social butterfly of the renewal movement."[83] This superficial and misguided judgment was qualified, however, by Fr. P. David Finks — Sheen's Vicar for the Poor — who was quoted in the article. According to Finks, Bishop Sheen was an effective force for good in Rochester, playing the role of "churchman as reconciler," who allowed sufficient changes to make it possible for the needed reforms in the Catholic Church to continue.[84] The title "churchman as reconciler" was an accurate one, which Sheen himself would have found flattering, and in line with his self-appraisal of the function of the Catholic Church's leaders in the sixties. Bishop Sheen had spoken often of the need for reconciliation, within the Church and within the nation. His most ambitious, and drastic, attempt to promote that spirit of reconciliation in Rochester's inner city — the donation of a Catholic parish and its property to the U.S. government in order to create housing for the poor — would prove to be the source of Sheen's greatest failure as Rochester's short-term bishop.

All the while that Sheen was basking in the media spotlight, his attention kept returning to the problems of the inner city and the poor. In fulfillment of a promise he had made before the Chamber of Commerce, Sheen announced in May the details of his "spirit of poverty" plan to tax all expenditures for new church construc-

---

[82] *Ramparts* 6 (November, 1967).

[83] *Ibid.*, p. 23.

[84] *Ibid.*, p. 24.

tion in the diocese. The money raised from the tax would be donated to the poor. In a news release issued from the Pastoral Office,
Bishop Sheen announced that the "Diocese of Rochester will share
its prosperity and its progress with the poor of the diocese and the
poor of the world."[85] A graduated tax, ranging from 1.25% to 3%
on all construction, would raise the funds to be distributed to the
poor of the city, and to the missions of the world. The purpose of
the tax, according to Sheen, was "not only to cut down on extrava-
gances in building, but also to make the local Church conscious
that it is part of the Mystical Body throughout the world."[86] Bishop
Sheen had always maintained his wider perspective as he governed
in Rochester, and said that his action was being taken in conso-
nance with the encyclical of Pope Paul VI, *On the Development of
Peoples*. The Holy Father had reminded the faithful that "the advanced nations have a very heavy obligation to help the developing
nations."[87] This proposal was praised as a symbol of Sheen's good
faith and determination to come to the aid of the poor; he hoped
to set an example which would be followed in other dioceses all
around the country. But Bishop Sheen was also becoming preoccupied with the urgent need for housing among the urban poor,
and was setting the wheels in motion for what he saw as his historic gesture — the donation of the entire property holdings of St.
Bridget's Church, a poor parish in Rochester's third ward, to the
federal government. Sheen hoped that the generous donation would
serve as a "beachhead" assault on the problem of housing, and that
the publicity and attention surrounding the announcement would
stir up enthusiasm and an outpouring, on the part of the churches
and the business community, of financial support to alleviate the
critical housing shortage. Instead, the grandstand gesture backfired.
The publicity Sheen wanted materialized, but most of it was negative. In the end, he was forced to rescind the offer, and the reper-

---

[85] Sheen, "Spirit of Poverty - Document #2," "Eight Months Report."
[86] *Ibid.*
[87] *Ibid.*

cussions of the St. Bridget's case ultimately led to Fulton Sheen's decision to resign his office as Bishop of Rochester, less than three years after his arrival. St. Bridget's was the turning point in Sheen's administration; he never fully recovered from the swirl of controversy and criticism which surrounded him after the plan failed. The second half of his term in Rochester was a marked contrast to the first; he withdrew from the spotlight into the shadows, and when he finally left in November of 1969, it was on a note of sadness and frustration.

The whole affair began in earnest in early November, 1967, when Sheen sent a letter to Robert C. Weaver, Secretary of Housing and Urban Development. Sheen offered the "free, total and unqualified gift of one of our parishes in the Inner City."[88] The only provision to the gift was that the government pledge to use the property "to build within the shortest possible time, housing for the poor."[89] In the inimitable Sheen style, he wrote out of the consciousness that he might create an "Inner City Captivity of the Churches" (contrasted with Gibson Winter's "Suburban Captivity of the Churches"):

> The Church must do something like St. Lawrence did centuries ago; he gave away the precious vessels of a church to help the poor. We now want to give away a church. We do this not because we do not need it, nor because we are not finding new expressions of apostolate in a tightly circumstanced environment, nor because it is a burden to our budget, but because the poor are a greater burden on our conscience. We are under the

[88] Sheen to Robert Weaver, letter dated November 8, 1967, and preserved in an extensive file assembled by Rev. Robert F. McNamara, Archivist Emeritus of the Rochester Diocese. This file contains copies of all the official correspondence and newspaper accounts surrounding the "St. Bridget's Affair," as well as oral interviews he conducted in 1970 with some of the principal diocesan participants in the case. (Hereafter referred to as "St. Bridget's Case" file.)

[89] *Ibid.*

Gospel imperative not just to be a Receiving Church,
but a Giving Church, not just a Ministering Church but
a Surrendering Church. We are moved by the Spirit to
do this to crash the "giving barrier" just as technology
has crashed the "sound barrier."... We are giving not just
what we have; we are trying to give what we are: a recognition of our servanthood and self-forgetfulness born
of Him who has "compassion on the multitude."[90]

Over the next several months, Sheen worked diligently behind the scenes, laying the groundwork for a dramatic announcement on Ash Wednesday of the following year. He consulted with
his advisors — chiefly Fr. Finks and Fr. Joseph W. Dailey, Episcopal Vicar for Pastoral Planning — and waited for officials from
the federal government to get the project moving from their end.
Secretary Weaver had replied to Sheen's "interesting proposal" two
weeks after meeting with him in Washington. Favorably impressed
by the offer, Weaver wrote: "We shall look forward to cooperating
with you and your associates in the hope of translating the idea into
reality."[91] Upon mutual agreement, officials from Housing and
Urban Development traveled to Rochester to survey several parish
properties and pick the one they deemed most suitable; Sheen
wanted to avoid any criticism that he had given away an old, use-
less church, and therefore thought it best that the government make
the choice.[92] Both sides also agreed that it would be best to keep
the whole plan secret until all the details had been worked out.
Sheen, meanwhile, consulted with what he considered to be the
proper and necessary authorities: Rome, the Apostolic Delegate,

---

[90] *Ibid.*

[91] Robert C. Weaver to Bishop Sheen, letter dated November 20, 1967, in the "St. Bridget's Case" file.

[92] Sheen offered these recollections and explanations for his actions in an interview on the "Dick Cavett Show," January 30, 1970; a tape recording of the program is contained in the collection at the Sheen Archives. These statements were the first public statements that Sheen made on the St. Bridget's episode after the plan fell through — almost two years after the controversy had occurred.

and local Rochester housing officials.[93] Secretary Weaver wrote a formal letter accepting Sheen's offer of the church and surrounding structures and property of St. Bridget's parish, valued at $680,000, on January 29, 1968. In this letter, Weaver declared Sheen's proposal to be "feasible and most desirable"; deferred to Sheen's judgment regarding the timing of the public announcement; and pledged his cooperation with press communications "so as to achieve the maximum effect" in establishing the Rochester proposal as "a model which could be duplicated in other communities."[94]

The news of the donation of the inner city parish was released to the national press on Ash Wednesday, February 29, 1968 — a dramatic Lenten gesture in Sheen's scheme:

> The Diocese of Rochester has chosen Ash Wednesday as the day on which to make a symbolic and real sacrifice for the poor.... the Diocese of Rochester, its Bishop, its clergy and its people have offered Church property to the propertyless.[95]

Bishop Sheen went on to explain how he had made the offer to the Secretary of Housing and Urban Development "in order that through a sacrificial gift, the Diocese might alleviate the plight of the needy" with one condition: that the land be used to build housing for the poor. Assuring his flock that "the diocese is not leaving the people nor neglecting their needs," and that the Church's pas-

---

[93] There is some contention evident in the recorded recollections of some of the participants. Auxiliary Bishop Dennis Hickey and Father James Moynihan, Chancellor, said that the local urban renewal agency was angry, feeling that HUD had gone over its head, and that the Sheen plan conflicted with their own plans in the inner city. The local officials were not consulted until days before the announcement. See notes of the oral interviews conducted by Fr. McNamara, "St. Bridget's Case" file, Archives of the Diocese of Rochester.

[94] Robert C. Weaver to Bishop Sheen, letter dated January 29, 1968; in the "St. Bridget's Case" file.

[95] News release, February 29, 1968, issued from Bishop Sheen. A copy is contained in the "St. Bridget's Case" file.

toral program for school children, parishioners and neighbors would continue in a more intensified way, Sheen concluded his announcement:

> It is not easy to give up what is already so serviceable and so beloved. It is even harder for the diocese with its ever-increasing need for areas of ministrations. But even more important is the need of the parish, of the diocese and all forces of the community to de-egotize their own interests, that a socially disenfranchised people might have roofs over their heads and enjoy the personal dignity which belongs to them as the children of God.[96]

Just as Sheen had predicted, there was plenty of publicity surrounding this announcement, locally and across the nation. But it was certainly not the reaction that he had expected. Instead of praise for his grand gesture, there was an outcry of dismay, protests, harsh criticisms and enough misunderstanding to confuse and cloud the issue for a long time. Within four days, Sheen had to withdraw the offer, and some of the rifts created between the Bishop and the diocesan clergy, and the Bishop and his flock, never quite healed. The immediate reaction within the community, especially among the parishioners at St. Bridget's, was adverse. Sheen had acted in the name of the clergy and the people, but they were unaware of the plans. Although Bishop Sheen would be given credit for the nobility and sincerity of his gesture, the general consensus was that he had made a mistake. The people of St. Bridget's were shocked to learn in the newspapers that their beloved parish was being taken from them. The pastor of St. Bridget's, the Rev. Francis H. Vogt, asked the Bishop publicly to reconsider his decision. Fr. Vogt had not been consulted, nor informed of the proposed giveaway of his parish, until after the final decision had been made, a few days before the announcement. He spoke openly of the reactions among his parishioners, most of them poor blacks and Puerto Ricans: "the

---

[96] *Ibid.*

church school was the most important thing in the neighborhood. There is enough empty property around without taking down the church and the school."[97] From a broader perspective, criticism was leveled against Bishop Sheen's whole handling of the matter — he seemed to be in violation of his own principles of dialogue and democracy within the administrative structure of the diocese by failing to consult with the clergy and the people.

Soon, news of the protests and friction in the Rochester diocese was appearing in the national press as well. The *New York Times*, under the headline "Sheen is Picketed in Rochester," told of the negative phone calls which poured into the rectory at St. Bridget's, and the Catholic college girls marching in front of the Bishop's headquarters.[98] Even worse, Sheen's priests were beginning to voice their criticisms of their pastoral leader, and some of it was severe. On March 1, twenty-two diocesan clergy signed their names to a letter sent to Bishop Sheen objecting not so much to the "disposal of St. Bridget's as to the manner in which it was done."[99] The tone of the letter, though not hostile, expressed "sheer disappointment and disillusionment."[100] In the letter of protest, the "undersigned priests" stated:

> We… are aware of and share your concern for the people of the inner city, and especially their need for adequate housing. At the same time we feel that… precipitous decisions could fail to achieve the good they intend…. this decision has completely bypassed the principle of collegiality. Neither the lay people affected by nor the priests involved… participated in this decision.… Therefore, we recommend that your decision be withdrawn.[101]

[97] *Times-Union* (Rochester), February 29, 1968, in the "St. Bridget's Case" file.

[98] *New York Times*, March 2, 1968, in the "St. Bridget's Case" file.

[99] Remarks of an "unidentified priest," reported in the *Democrat & Chronicle* (Rochester), March 3, 1968, in the "St. Bridget's Case" file.

[100] *Ibid.*

[101] Letter to Bishop Sheen, signed by 22 diocesan priests, dated March 1, 1968, in the "St. Bridget's Case" file. Later reports would expand the list to "over 100" or "133" dissident priests.

In the face of such criticism, and the growing furor in the press, Sheen backed down. At Sunday Mass on March 3, Fr. Vogt announced to his overjoyed parishioners that "St. Bridget's will not be given away and will continue to serve the people living in the shadow of its tower."[102] Throughout the entire controversy, Bishop Sheen had been unavailable for comment, and "never publicly spoke of reversing the decision or of losing the battle" for the remaining months of his time in Rochester.[103]

In the recriminations and numerous evaluations which followed Sheen's "reversal" or "change of mind," many factors were offered by way of explaining what had turned out to be such a fiasco. The local *Times-Union* editorialized on the "Generous But Misguided Gift," suggesting that there might have been better means to fulfilling Sheen's ends. "To give away to the poor that which already belongs to them — without even consulting them or properly determining the feasibility of the housing envisioned — would not have eased their poverty."[104] *America*, the Jesuit journal of opinion, ran an editorial entitled "Flaw in a Good Deed," agreeing with a statement by Fr. John Reedy, C.S.C., who lamented that so "imaginative and edifying a gesture should issue in a public relations bruise for the experienced Bishop of Rochester":

> In Rochester we witness a classic example of true Christian charity, of welcome involvement of the Church in secular needs, of admirable cooperation between church and state — all marred by a lack of one ingredient: dialogue.[105]

The following week, *America* labeled the St. Bridget's episode a

---

Democrat & Chronicle (Rochester), March 4, 1968.

Fr. Robert McNamara interview with Hickey and Moynihan, conducted on March 7, 1970, "St. Bridget's Case" file. Sheen acknowledged that he was speaking out for the first time when he appeared on the "Dick Cavett Show."

Times-Union (Rochester), March 4, 1968.

America 118 (April 5, 1968).

"brilliant blunder"; Sheen's insight into the needs of the poor had led him to ignore the rights of the parishioners.[106]

Along these same lines, demonstrating that those outside Sheen's diocese could be more forgiving, *Commonweal*, standing alone, supported Bishop Sheen's gesture on the grounds that a greater good would have been accomplished had he "stood his ground."[107] Although the situation had clearly presented a "nice dilemma," *Commonweal* admired Sheen's decision to place the "Church's financial and political security on the line" and his "prophetic witness." Noting that Sheen's "eye for the dramatic had served him well," and that the parish had won a victory for democracy in the Church, the inescapable conclusion was:

> We support Sheen. The needs of the poor in American cities are greater than the needs of Catholics to determine their parochial life. There are times when authority must be prophetic and this may mean acting against the wishes of the people.[108]

Despite the positive nature of this judgment, there is no evidence to suggest that it brought any comfort to Fulton Sheen.

Among the behind the scenes players in the St. Bridget's affair, who looked back on the episode from the valuable perspective of hindsight, there are several notable areas of agreement. The overwhelming significance of the episode was in the change that occurred in Bishop Sheen, who was never the same regarding his actions and feelings in Rochester. Fr. P. David Finks, while acknowledging that he and Bishop Sheen were on a "collision course" due to their divergent styles and methods, and Sheen's "footloose apostles" plan and his failure to respond to Finks' letters and memos,[109] expressed genuine sorrow about how things turned out

---

[106] *America* 118 (April 13, 1968).

[107] *Commonweal* 87 (March 15, 1968).

[108] *Ibid.*

[109] Finks, "Crisis in Smugtown," p. 196. Finks felt that Sheen's plan, to unleash a "band of white priests from the suburbs" in black neighborhoods, would be a "disaster."

for Sheen. Finks had agreed with Sheen's desire to make a historic gesture to the inner city poor; nevertheless, he thought it should have been redirected. Fr. Finks wanted to build a factory on the land, to employ blacks in the ghetto and to be run by the FIGHT organization.[110] As Finks remembered it:

> On Ash Wednesday... it all began to come apart.... his pastoral experiment never regained steam after the St. Bridget's incident. He began to draw back into deepening seclusion, writing rambling jeremiads in the weekly Catholic *Courier-Journal*, sallying forth only for ceremonial occasions.[111]

Father Francis H. Vogt, the priest who would have been most personally affected had the St. Bridget's plan succeeded, always recognized Sheen's sincerity and good intentions. In a letter he sent to his parishioners, in lieu of the parish meeting scheduled to formulate a plan of action to resist the giveaway of their church and school, Father Vogt thanked Bishop Sheen for keeping the parish, and paid "tribute to his zeal and concern for the poor." "Strange as it may seem to some," he said, "after all the excitement of the past week, I think Bishop Sheen's idea was basically a tremendous one."[112] But although Sheen had hoped that his project "would set the country on fire," encouraging other bishops to follow suit, he succeeded only in starting a brushfire of dissent within his own diocese.[113] Of the 100 letters Fr. Vogt had received, "only 2 were favorable: 90% of the antagonistic reaction was not pro-St. Bridget's so much as anti-Sheen," prompted by liberals from outside the parish, in Vogt's opinion. Ironically, it was the local press that was especially upset by Sheen, who had foolishly bypassed them and

---

[110] Finks to Bishop Sheen, memo dated November 10, 1968, in the "St. Bridget's Case" file.

[111] Finks, "Crisis in Smugtown," pp. 183-184.

[112] Letter from Fr. Vogt to the Parishioners, in the "St. Bridget's Case" file.

[113] Fr. McNamara interview with Fr. Francis Vogt, January 22, 1970; "St. Bridget's Case" file.

given the news releases only to the national press. And along the lines of the "if only Sheen had done this" approach, Father Vogt said that had the parish been consulted first, it would probably have gone along.[114]

The closest administrative advisors to Sheen, Vicar General Hickey, Father Moynihan, and the Vicar for Pastoral Planning, Fr. Dailey, had the best insiders' perspective on the entire event and its consequences. All three agreed with Fr. Finks regarding the change in persona and demeanor apparent in Bishop Sheen after the controversy: "He was never the same afterwards, never advanced any more really imaginative proposals — he even looked different."[115] Fr. Dailey, who had had the most to do with the plans and communications with officials from Housing and Urban Development, referred to the episode as an "explosion," and spoke of Sheen's anger, and the "bitter and crude" letters of protest which were sent to him. When the anger died down, "Bishop Sheen lost heart as Bishop of Rochester," for he felt that the priests wouldn't cooperate with him and would no longer be open to his new ideas. The St. Bridget's case was, without a doubt, the "turning point" in Sheen's administration. Within the controversy itself, the turning point came when the priests sent the letter of protest; Bishop Sheen was genuinely hurt. He backed down from his grand gesture under pressure from the priests, who threatened to release their statement of protest to the press if Sheen didn't rescind the gift. After Sheen had already decided to withdraw the offer, the priests' statement was leaked to the press,[116] and Sheen felt betrayed. He had reversed his decision, at the urging of his advisors, to prevent "tearing down the fabric of the diocese."[117] Yet the rent in the diocesan fabric which had already happened, in the final analysis, was never mended. Fulton Sheen had lost his spirit and enthusiasm as Bishop

[114] Fr. McNamara's interview with the Hickey and Moynihan, "St. Bridget's Case" file.
[115] Fr. McNamara interview with Rev. Joseph Dailey, April 23, 1970; "St. Bridget's Case" file.
[116] McNamara interview with Fr. Dailey, "St. Bridget's Case" file.
[117] McNamara interview with Hickey and Moynihan, "St. Bridget's Case" file.

of Rochester. The whole St. Bridget's episode, in retrospect, was more damaging and painful for Sheen, coming as it did on the heels of all the glowing reviews in the national press on his performance. Looking back on some of the upbeat notes sounded then — on how he might be remembered as the best bishop Rochester ever had, or how happy and content he was in Rochester — they can certainly be considered as premature judgments, even ironic. The promising fortunes of Fulton Sheen as the sixth Bishop of Rochester were reversed in a single stroke. When Sheen looked back on these years in his autobiography, he was overwhelmed by a sense of failure:

> It is customary in reviewing a bishop's life in a diocese to do so in terms of the churches built and schools erected.... I would like to dwell on the clay that was found in the treasure, or rather, things that I would like to have done but failed to do.[118]

After the failure of Bishop Sheen's gesture to give away St. Bridget's parish for a noble cause, he retreated from center stage. To many observers, he appeared simply to be going through the motions, having lost his zeal. When he did venture forth to propose a new idea — that the inner city churches be better utilized to help the underprivileged, as dispensaries or depots for food or clothing[119]; that union leaders in the construction trade donate their time and skills to repair houses of and for the poor; that the Catholic Church buy a regular page in the secular press to reach an expanded audience[120] — nothing came of them. Bishop Sheen never gave up on his idea that the Church should divest itself of property to build much needed housing for the poor. In an article entitled "Church and Community: A Prophecy," published in the *Courier-Journal* in July of 1968, Sheen spoke of his hope that the Church might one

---

[118] Sheen, *Treasure in Clay*, p. 177.
[119] *National Catholic Reporter*, July 17, 1968.
[120] Sheen, *Treasure in Clay*, pp. 180-181.

day be a "sign of salvation" in the inner city.[121] But there would be no more grand gestures. Throughout 1969, the Bishop wrote a series of articles in the *Courier-Journal* on such topics as "The Edifice Complex" and the "Theology of Space." His last appearances at meetings of his once cherished Priests Council were noticeably defensive, and he appeared to be weighed down by a heavy burden. At the suggestion of an advisory "Personnel Board" to assist him, Sheen commented that "this is an agony we would be glad to share."[122] At the next month's meeting, he suggested that "no one wants authority these days — those who do are inviting untold difficulties."[123]

Occasionally, Bishop Sheen traveled outside the diocese, maintaining the wider perspective and responsibilities to which he would return full-time after he left Rochester. Pope Paul VI had named him to the Synod of Bishops shortly after his dramatic sermon on the Vietnam war, and he focused on the issue of world peace at Synod meetings. In July of 1968, he went on a trip to Ireland "to recruit priests to help offset a shortage in his diocese."[124] Right after the St. Bridget's case was resolved, in March of 1968, Sheen participated in the pageantry of a consecration ceremony for two auxiliary bishops, Dennis Hickey and John McCafferty. It was the first time in the history of the Diocese of Rochester that it would be served by three bishops. And finally, in October of 1969, in the last surprise to come from Bishop Sheen in Rochester, he announced that he would resign as Bishop of the Rochester Diocese.[125] He had traveled to Rome months before, and asked Pope Paul VI to allow him to resign. Publicly, he offered age as the explanation, saying that he was approaching his seventy-fifth birthday, the age for retirement decreed by the Second Vatican Council. But rumors

[121] *Courier-Journal*, July 5, 1968.
[122] Minutes of the Priests Council Meeting for February 4, 1969; Archives of the Diocese of Rochester.
[123] Minutes of the Priests Council Meeting for March 5, 1969.
[124] *National Catholic Reporter*, July 17, 1968.
[125] *New York Times*, March 15, 1968.

continued to surround him, concentrating on his unhappiness, frustration, and the general sense of disappointment which lingered on in Rochester. By all accounts, Sheen had had a hard time in Rochester, and wanted now to return to New York City: "to teach, do television, and enter into dialogue with unbelievers," a reference to his recent appointment to the Commission for Non-Believers established by the Pope.[126] Now that the end was in sight, and Bishop Joseph Hogan had already been appointed to succeed him, Sheen could stress the positive, insisting that "I am not resigning work. I am not retiring, I am regenerating."[127] In going over his own record in Rochester, Bishop Sheen said that he could recite a "long litany of failures," and a few successes, including his initial consultations with the priests on appointing their leaders, and the purchase of homes for fourteen indigent slum families.[128] When he finally left the city of Rochester on November 29, 1969, he asked his priests in his farewell speech for "forgiveness for the things I said and should have left unsaid, and for the things I left unsaid and should have said; for the times I monologued when I should have dialogued."[129] With a reinvigorated sense of humor, as the party of well-wishers walked to the boarding gate with Sheen, he quipped: "See, they're walking along with me, they're not pushing me."[130]

After Sheen's departure, one last set of reviews circulated in the press. Sheen would be best remembered as an innovator and visionary, who stirred things up and succeeded at focusing attention on the plight of the poor. His greatest shortcomings were his failure to communicate with the people — he sent form letter replies — and his failure, or inability, to follow through on ideas, most of which were good, even brilliant. In many respects, Sheen was perceived as a maverick who had upset conservative Rochester, and was considered, after the fact, ill-suited for the task of administer-

---

[126] *New York Times*, October 16, 1969.
[127] *Ibid.*
[128] *Ibid.*
[129] *New York Times*, November 29, 1969.
[130] *Ibid.*

ing such a conservative diocese. *Time* magazine, in an overly sensationalized "Calvary in Rochester" story,[131] said that it was "no secret that Sheen was restless and unhappy in this out-of-the-way" diocese, and that he had "never seemed an appropriate choice to head the diocese of Rochester"[132] — conveniently overlooking its earlier story which called Sheen "spectacular" and predicted that he would be Rochester's best bishop. The *National Catholic Reporter*, on a more positive note, declared that "Rochester's Loss is T.V.'s Gain."[133]

Quite accurately, however, the *Reporter* pointed out that "his efforts frequently had the opposite effect that he desired"; many of his plans did not materialize or were short-lived — "he was great at getting an idea but not at carrying it through."[134] The *Courier-Journal*, which had served as Bishop Sheen's forum for three years, was kinder still, yet balanced:

> The diocesan history will contain many brilliant chapters about the Bishop's endeavors here… and the major headline will be his concern for the poor…. Sheen's three years as head of the Rochester diocese have been highlighted with drama, against a backdrop of turbulence in a Church witnessing many changes.[135]

In Pope Paul's apostolic letter appointing Fulton J. Sheen as the sixth Bishop of Rochester, New York, the Holy Father spoke of Sheen's past record of success and wished him well in his new assignment:

> Everything that you have so tirelessly accomplished in the past, by deed and by the spoken and written word

---

[131] *Time* (October 24, 1969).
[132] *Ibid.*
[133] *National Catholic Reporter*, October 22, 1969.
[134] *Ibid.*
[135] *Courier-Journal*, October 17, 1969.

to feed the sheep of Christ's flock… has won for you universal acclaim. We now nourish the fond hope that in the future you will vigorously undertake even greater things.[136]

Judged by any standard, Bishop Sheen vigorously undertook great things in Rochester, guided always by the reforms of the Second Vatican Council. Observers generally spoke of Vatican II and the spirit of "aggiornamento" as the source of Sheen's inspiration. The sound and fury of his years in Rochester illustrate how one of traditional Catholicism's most well-known figures forged a new and vibrant image for the Catholic Church in America. In a "first hand report on turmoil and reform in the Catholic Church," written in 1968, journalist Douglas Roche devoted an entire chapter to the "Post-Conciliar Sheen," and offered a very favorable account of Sheen's actions:

The ecumenical movement blessed by Vatican II went forward in Rochester by leaps and bounds…. In every action that he took, Sheen revealed an intense commitment to conciliar thought as formulated in… the Council documents…. the conciliar revolution, launched by Pope John, was brought down to earth and planted in local soil by Fulton Sheen.[137]

And Father P. David Finks, Sheen's high-profile "Vicar to the Poor" who participated in some heated disagreements with his Bishop, nevertheless was "impressed with how deeply the Council years had affected him."[138] The explanation for Sheen's "innovative style as mover and shaker in his golden years," Finks believed, was in "his four years residency in Rome during Vatican II." The bishops from the Third World who traveled to Rome lived below

[136] Cited in the *New York Times*, December 16, 1966.
[137] Roche, pp. 79, 70.
[138] Finks, "Crisis in Smugtown," p. 182.

the poverty line themselves; but the "one bishop they all knew was Fulton Sheen, the missionary's friend, the lover of the poor."[139] Unlike most of the Americans who lived in first class accommodations, Sheen resided near these bishops in a convent during the Council's sessions, and assisted the poor bishops financially, with mission funds, and received in turn a valuable, informal education. Despite all of his faults, then — and Finks found many — Sheen's heart was in the right place, and he was "miles ahead of previous diocesan administrations."[140]

Despite Sheen's promising beginning, however, the acclaim in Rochester was not universal. Though he would "cause many good things to happen, he would also produce many misunderstandings."[141] For the first time in his illustrious career, those misunderstandings would tarnish the Sheen image, and he would lose some of his lustre. Many explanations for Sheen's failures would be offered, by observers and by Sheen himself. In his autobiography, Sheen had spoken of the inevitable "tensions and turbulence" which developed after the Church Councils throughout Catholic history.[142] But he certainly encountered more than he expected in Rochester, and was unprepared to deal with some of the reactions to his controversial actions. After his resignation, he tried to come to terms with his experiences in Rochester, and offered his own justifications, insisting that he had no regrets:

> I was too young for the old ones — too demanding that we introduce now the innovations called for by the Second Vatican Council — and too old for the young ones; they didn't want advanced ideas to come from my generation.[143]

---

[139] *Ibid.*, p. 182.
[140] *Ibid.*, p. 188.
[141] *Ibid.*, p. 170.
[142] Sheen, *Treasure in Clay*, pp. 292-293.
[143] *New York Times*, November 30, 1969.

Many of his public pronouncements were characterized by this sense of sadness — there was something quite tragic about his experience in Rochester. Sheen spoke often of how he had moved too fast: "I'm a little too progressive."[144] Caught up in the climate of the times, he became overzealous, and simply tried too hard. He saw the effect of these years on the entire Church and the world: "The world pouring into the Church and the Church rushing into the world."[145] In Rochester, with the best of intentions and with his instincts pointing in the right direction, Sheen had rushed in too quickly himself, without always giving enough thought to the consequences of his actions. The St. Bridget's case is the prime example of this tendency and this one spectacular failure, in Sheen's own mind, seemed to overshadow all of his accomplishments. Things went tragically awry for Sheen in Rochester after this episode, and one is left looking for an explanation as to why. Most of the immediate evaluations of Bishop Sheen's administration in Rochester, undertaken by those close to the situation, offered words of praise for his genuine spirituality, and many of the good things that he was able to accomplish. Beyond the lingering sense of controversy, Fulton Sheen was often remembered as a man of vision and conviction, perhaps a man who came too soon. Among the projects instituted by Bishop Sheen that proved to be of permanent value are the lay business manager and financial advisory board; the Human Concern projects; the Spanish-speaking mission apostolate; and the Bishop Sheen Housing Fund. Father Finks, writing in 1975, offered this assessment of Sheen's strengths and weaknesses:

> My respect for Bishop Sheen remains. My subsequent experience convinced me that for all his autocratic faults, Sheen honestly tried to meet the problems of the times head-on, and that was a rare occurrence for a Catholic

---

[144] *New York Times*, October 15, 1969. Sheen also called himself "too progressive" when he appeared on the William F. Buckley ("Firing Line") and Dick Cavett talk shows.

[145] Sheen, *Treasure in Clay*, p. 293.

bishop.... Bishop Sheen had no administrative experience.... he thought he could move ahead by preaching
and example.

It is enough that he helped when he did. In a time of
ambiguity, he did some good things. That is not a bad
epitaph, for a man or a bishop.[146]

After Sheen's death, Father Robert F. McNamara, historian and
archivist of the Rochester Diocese, prepared a short piece on Sheen's
time in Rochester to be distributed at the Bishop's funeral. He
agreed with Father Finks, and many other observers, that Sheen's
greatest weakness was the lack of administrative experience, but
remembered him as a force for good:

Fulton J. Sheen was essentially an idea man and a
prophet, and as such he set his diocese in the right direction. If he had had more experience in administration, he would have seen more of his dreams for Rochester come true.[147]

In the final analysis, Fulton Sheen proved to be, and saw himself, as a catalyst — for innovation, experimentation and change.
He performed a service for the Diocese of Rochester and the American Catholic Church simply through his efforts, and attracting attention to the Church's program of renewal and reform when it
was most needed. What transpired in Rochester was a microcosm
of what would happen within the American Church; discord and
disarray would come to characterize the state of the Catholic
Church in the years after the Vatican Council. Church historian
John Tracy Ellis wrote in 1967 that "the Catholic Church finds
herself today in the midst of the gravest crisis she has experienced

---

[146] Finks, "Crisis in Smugtown," p. 210.
[147] McNamara, typescript dated December 10, 1979, in the Archives of the Diocese of Rochester.

since the Protestant Revolt."[148] Certainly, Fulton Sheen found himself in the middle of a crisis and stormy controversy in Rochester over the course of the next few months. And when he left Rochester, he passed the torch to his successor, Bishop Hogan — reminding him and the people of Rochester that they would have to "work out a Christian response to the challenge of the times"[149] — as he returned home to New York City for the final decade in his own odyssey of fashioning Fulton Sheen's American Catholic response to the challenge of the twentieth century.

---

[148] John Tracy Ellis, *Commonweal* 86 (March 10, 1967).
[149] *New York Times*, November 30, 1969.

A "Life Worth Living"

A priest is mysterious, and he is mysterious because he is amphibious:
he lives in two worlds. He is at his best when he leads a "double life," at
once both human and divine. Because of this duality, he functions best
at times of crisis like ours, for his faith began in tragedy when Goodness had only a Cross on which to lean. Like a sailor in a storm at sea,
he is dutifully climbing to the crow's nest, but looking back in fear at
the thought of a fall. No life is more adventurous, for at every moment,
like the trapeze artist, he is swinging between time and eternity.
Fulton Sheen, Those Mysterious Priests (1974)

Archbishop Fulton J. Sheen was born seventy-five years ago… and
became a priest in the Catholic Church just after the first World War.
He is considered by almost everybody a great enigma. Those who like
to disparage his evangelism have a difficult time accounting for his
extraordinary academic record. Those who paint him as a
conservative are continually amazed at his positions on behalf of statist
welfarism. Those who have been inspired by his anti-communist
lectures which began in the early thirties cannot understand
his current calls for withdrawing from Vietnam… he is,
in my opinion, the greatest preacher in English.…
William F. Buckley, Jr. (1970)

When Bishop Fulton Sheen left the Diocese of Rochester behind
him in 1969 to return to New York City, he announced that he
had no intention of retiring. Rather, he saw himself as embarking
upon a period of "regeneration," trusting in the Lord to "open new
doors." For the next ten years — destined to be the final decade of
his life — he continued to lecture and write, and devoted much of
his time to the work he found most satisfying: giving retreats for

priests. After accepting his resignation as Bishop of Rochester, Pope Paul VI appointed Sheen to the honorary position of titular Archbishop of Newport (Wales), in recognition of his fifty years of service as a priest, encompassing so many fields of the Catholic apostolate.

Maintaining his status as a celebrity during these twilight years, Sheen made occasional public appearances as American Catholicism's "living legend." The old Sheen style and charisma were commodities still valued by his Church, but his experience and expertise in the field of communication and spreading the gospel allowed him to contribute something more substantial as well. In May 1978, Archbishop Sheen made a rare appearance at a meeting of the National Conference of Catholic Bishops because the topic under consideration was evangelization. During the fifties, Sheen recalled, he had used an indirect method on television, finding "a common denominator in secular culture that would serve as a springboard to the Christian message." Advising the bishops that America's spiritual climate had changed again, for the better, he added: "Never before have the American people been so disposed to hear about Christ. But we must preach Christ and Him crucified," for that is "the only way to win people."[1]

But America's improved spiritual climate would be the province for a new generation of preachers, for Sheen's earthly journey was drawing to a close. After sixty years devoted to Christ and the Cross, Fulton Sheen was called to his heavenly reward on December 9, 1979. He had confided to friends several years earlier that he prayed to be "taken home" by the time he turned eighty, for he did not want to survive to work below full capacity. But he survived open heart surgery in 1977, and succumbed to heart disease at the age of eighty-four. Another prayer came closer to being answered; it was always Sheen's desire to die in the presence of the Blessed Sacrament on a feast of the Blessed Mother. His death came in his apartment, in the presence of the Blessed Sacrament where

---

[1]   Sheen, cited in the *Chicago Sun-Times*, May 4, 1978: "Archbishop Sheen still shows 'em" by Roy Larson. Newspaper clipping files, Sheen Archives.

he had made a Holy Hour every day of his priesthood. But he died one day after the feast of the Immaculate Conception, the patroness of the American Church.

The news of Fulton Sheen's passing made headlines across the nation, in the form of glowing tributes to the man who had had such an impact on the religious life of the American nation. He was almost unanimously memorialized as the "greatest evangelizer" in the history of the American Catholic Church... one of the "greatest preachers" of the twentieth century... the most "eloquent exponent" and "effective champion" of the Catholic faith in the United States. Sheen was buried in the vault beneath the altar at St. Patrick's Cathedral, a most fitting final resting place for the man who had "so frequently and so uniquely adorned" New York's most prominent pulpit.[2]

The eulogy and homily at Sheen's funeral Mass was delivered by Archbishop Edward T. O'Meara, Sheen's close friend who had succeeded him as the National Director of the Society for the Propagation of the Faith. Stating that there was never a time in his life when Sheen wished that he had pursued a career other than that of a priest, O'Meara paid witness to the unique achievement of his "dear friend" as a spokesman for the American Catholic Church:

> A voice is silent in the midst of the Church and in our land, the like of which will not be heard again in our day. The vocation of Fulton Sheen is consummated; he has responded with one final "yes" to the call of God.[3]

The text of O'Meara's homily was devoted to Sheen's own reflections on his life as a priest. Many of Sheen's thoughts during the

---

[2] See John Tracy Ellis, *Catholic Bishops: A Memoir*, p. 84.

[3] "Bye Now, Fulton Sheen, and God Love You Forever"; homily delivered at St. Patrick's Cathedral on December 13, 1979 by Archbishop O'Meara; printed in pamphlet form by the Society for the Propagation of the Faith. Copies of this pamphlet are located in the collection at the Sheen Archives.

final decade of his life were consumed with those reflections on the nature and meaning of the priesthood. O'Meara surmised, in Sheen's classically simple style, that the "apex" of his career — a career which included outstanding accomplishments as philosopher, teacher, preacher, missionary, pioneer of the electronic gospel and bishop — took place when Pope John Paul II embraced Sheen just two months before his death. Sheen had taken great comfort and satisfaction in the words of the Holy Father on that occasion: "He told me that I had written and spoken well of the Lord Jesus, and that I was a loyal son of the Church."[4] The Pope's description of Sheen as "a loyal son of the Church" is a good place to begin a critical evaluation of Fulton Sheen's role and significance in the history of American Catholicism. Though the assessment is an understatement, it is quite accurate nonetheless. From the day he was ordained in 1919 until the day he died in 1979, Sheen was motivated by one consideration: his priesthood and his desire to serve his Church. There was never a time when he could recall not wishing to be a priest, and he never looked back beyond his vocation. Given the talents with which he was blessed, and the challenging times in which he lived, Fulton Sheen was given more opportunities than most men, and he took full advantage of every one. For six decades, the good Lord opened doors, and Fulton Sheen dutifully walked through them, finding great success on the other side. From professor to popularizer, from the pulpit to the radio and television, from the classroom to the missionary expanse of the globe, Sheen amassed a singular record of achievement, unmatched by any other Catholic prelate of his age. Judged by three standards — popularity, longevity and versatility — he performed an inestimable amount of good work on behalf of the Catholic Church. Without a doubt, he was the most popular and celebrated representative of the American Church. Because of his high profile and visibility, he became *the* image and *the* authentic voice most closely associated with the Church during the middle decades of the twen-

---

4   *Ibid.*

tieth century. The longevity of his career was matched by his productivity and versatility. He reached out to millions of souls through the wonders of the mass media, converting many and comforting more. And he used his personal popularity and image to raise millions of dollars to further the work of the missions, touching the lives of countless more souls. In the opinion of Monsignor John Tracy Ellis, who spoke from personal knowledge and as the dean of American Catholic historians, the contribution of Fulton Sheen to the Catholic Church and the general American public was "incalculable." It is "difficult to exaggerate" what he accomplished. "Anyone who would deny the fact that his contribution was a great one is either unfair, or does not know of what he speaks."[5]

Despite his record of great accomplishments, an accurate and fair evaluation of Fulton Sheen's life must come to grips with his failures as well. A retrospective look leaves one with a sense of irony, even tragedy. That the last chapter of the story of Sheen's official service was written in Rochester was ironic, and it was a tragic account of dashed dreams and failure. Even Sheen's own version in his autobiography is characterized by disappointment and a sense of bewilderment, for he never fully comprehended how it had all gone wrong in Rochester. It was ironic that Sheen was sent to Rochester in the first place, for the administrative needs of the diocese and the talents of Fulton Sheen were clearly mismatched. Once there, he made the best of the situation, viewing it as an opportunity to finally put into practice the ideas he had developed over a lifetime. Devoted to implementing the reforms of the Second Vatican Council, he got off to a promising start, and the initial reviews of his performance were positive. But his weaknesses caught up with him in Rochester; he was betrayed and disappointed by his own vanity and reputation as a star. His best-laid plans were undone by his lack of administrative ability and experience. Disheartened and

---

[5] This summary of Ellis' opinion comes from three sources: his memoirs in *Catholic Bishops*; his remarks in "And now a word with his sponsor" by James Breig in *U.S. Catholic* 45 (February, 1980); and a personal conversation with this writer at the Catholic University of America on February 20, 1987.

profoundly saddened by the St. Bridget's episode, he never fully recovered, and left Rochester with his first real taste of failure.

On the surface, he left Rochester on an upbeat note of "regenerating," saying that one must never become discouraged in the service of God. But he wouldn't have been human if he had been unaffected by the experience. It was obvious that his failures had a profound effect on him. The last decade of his life was by no means unproductive, but he never recaptured the glory of his earlier years; a planned comeback to television never materialized due to lack of interest. But in the long run, some good came out of his experiences in Rochester; he became more introspective and concerned with the real meaning of his priesthood.

In the immediate aftermath of his resignation in 1969, Sheen returned to the bright lights of television, appearing on three national interview shows in the span of three months.[6] He seemed compelled to return to the place where he was most comfortable, the scene of his greatest triumph. Eager to offer his own explanations for what had transpired in Rochester, he also used the opportunity to provide justifications and insights into his entire life's work as the best known Catholic priest in America. Although his words were sometimes guarded — he claimed that he could have risen higher in the Church if he had been willing to pay the price — they reveal a good deal about Sheen's personality. His appearances on these television shows provide an unusual view of Sheen's self-evaluation and justifications for the actions of a long career.

Responding to those who seemed surprised that a man who had a reputation as a conservative should become such an innovator, Sheen denied any suggestions that he had changed. He spoke of an underlying consistency in his multifaceted life, and characterized himself as a follower of the wisdom of Pope John XXIII, who opened the doors and the windows. At the Second Vatican Council, the Church went out and the world came in. But Fulton

---

[6] Sheen appeared on "60 Minutes" on October 28, 1969; on the "Dick Cavett Show" on January 30, 1970; and on William F. Buckley's "Firing Line" on February 1, 1970. The following comments are taken from Sheen's remarks during those interviews.

Sheen had spent decades trying to bridge the gap which separated the Church from the modern world, always clinging to the security of the middle ground. He called himself a "man of ideas" and a "man between generations," similar to the characterizations of others: a visionary, and a man ahead of his times. Sheen said that his major mistake in Rochester was going too fast: "I was too progressive." But his actions were all part of his central mission: to always address himself to the thought of the times, and to discern current trends and move with them when it would help secure a place for the Catholic Church in the American mainstream. Sheen's attempts to Americanize the Church, however, were never undertaken at the expense of the Church's integrity; he would never sacrifice the Church's ideals.

Sheen said that the change was not in him, "the change was in what was outside." Consistent with the goals he had expressed as a young priest, he was interested in assisting the Church to respond to a changing world. All of his life, Sheen seemed overly concerned about the Church and himself being considered irrelevant, or behind the times. He was determined to work out an adaptation of the Church to the world, seeing the wisdom in shaping the inevitable changes rather than resisting them. He admitted that he was traditional in terms of faith and morals, but said with some pride that he had never been accused of using traditional methods. In many respects, the life of Fulton Sheen had emerged as a microcosm of the changes occurring in the American Catholic Church. Perhaps his most telling comment came when he suggested that his critics must allow for a certain amount of growth: "I'm always trying to strike a balance."

Therein lies the key to the essential Fulton Sheen, the man striving for a lifetime to maintain a delicate sense of balance. He was not entirely successful, but on the whole, he maintained his balance well in the service of God and his Church. He occasionally lost his footing, stumbling over the block of vanity, his greatest flaw. Often, he erred on the side of style over substance. His reality fell short of his ideals, and practicality was not his strongest suit. Especially in Rochester, he tossed out ideas which were utterly unrealistic, with no thought as to the implementation or consequences. His inability to follow through on these grand gestures led to his bitter disappointment, his own impulsive style frustrating his dreams. But his earliest and constant dream, to be a good priest, was fulfilled beyond any expectations he might have had as a young man.

Because his life was dedicated to this balancing act, he is often perceived as an ambivalent figure. He was orthodox theologically, and more progressive in social issues. He was the scholar and professor who gave up a promising academic career to become the intellectual popularizer. To many today, Fulton Sheen probably exists as a nostalgic figure, forever frozen in time on the television screen. But, as this study has demonstrated, this is an incomplete picture of Fulton Sheen. He was so much more than the television star of the fifties, and worthy of more serious consideration. Those who cavalierly dismiss him for being a popularizer miss the point of his life entirely: the secret of his fame was precisely the fact that he was such a superb popularizer. There is no separating the man from the style, and there is no reason to, for it would destroy his effectiveness as a major figure in American Catholic history.

The essential Fulton Sheen was the popularizer and the performer, in the best sense of those words. He was more complex than these characterizations indicate, and he possessed other strengths as well. Sheen was a born teacher in his ability to reduce a subject to its essentials, and he used this gift to educate an entire nation. As a preacher, he had few equals; Billy Graham called Sheen one of the greatest preachers of the century. In this age of televised religion, the question is often asked: why can't the Catholics come up with another Bishop Sheen? There have been no successors, and Sheen himself would be considered an anachronism today. He met the needs of yesterday perfectly, but he would be unsuitable for today.

The more private side of Fulton Sheen, attested to by those who knew him well, was his intense spirituality and devotion. His spirituality never wavered, and he credited it as the sustaining source of his strength. The same man who loved the adulation of the crowds and the trappings of celebrity spent an hour every day in quiet prayer and meditation, the hour that made his day. Equally intense was his devotion to the Blessed Virgin, manifest in so many ways. The piety of Fulton Sheen caused him to dedicate every book he wrote to her; to make a pilgrimage to Lourdes or Fatima during every trip to Europe; and to frequently fall back on his favorite Marian poem, Mary Dixon Thayer's "Lovely Lady Dressed in Blue" as a closing for a book or television show.

In the final analysis, the story of Fulton Sheen's life comes down to his spirituality and priesthood. His life came full circle during his final years, which were dedicated to reflections on the priesthood: the sermons, retreats and books which constituted his final words. A series of tape recordings for priests' retreats were made in his old age, when his health was failing. They were entitled "Renewal and Reconciliation," and discussed general topics like the Holy Hour, devotion to Mary, and the Holy Spirit. He talked about priests as "fools for Christ's sake" and in terms of treasure and pots — the nobility of the vocation contrasted with human frailty. These themes of renewal and reconciliation succeeded in Sheen's final years, where his desire to be regenerated fell a bit short. In reflecting on the nature and meaning of the priesthood, Sheen renewed his own sense of vocation and found reconciliation and peace in his final days. The young priest who began his journey in the years following World War I, determined to resist the rapid spread of secularization in the modern world, was still determined in the seventies, talking about the priest working out a reconciliation between the divine and secular worlds. Sheen had been called as a priest to go out into the world, and to penetrate the secularist milieu as an ambassador of Christ's divinity. For over half a century, Sheen performed the same priestly function, protesting against the isolation of the divine from the modern secularist world.

The meaning of Fulton Sheen's long-running performance as a Catholic priest on the American stage was only alluded to during the final decade of his life. He remained the consummate performer, remarking at one point that getting off the stage was the hardest thing to do, for he feared that he did not know the last line.

Unable to draw the final curtain on his life, he did not make the task an easy one for the historian either, taking many of his secrets with him when he died. When the Fulton Sheen Archives were dedicated at St. Bernard's Seminary in Rochester in 1976, Sheen warned of the difficulties inherent in attempting to get at the heart of his life. He stated that there was no complete explanation of Fulton Sheen to be found there, in the books or in the tapes, suggesting that "you have to look for a secret on the outside."[7] He suggested that the only answer to his life was to be found in his faith, and offered the answer of his great mentor, St. Thomas Aquinas, to the effect that a man is better known by his character than by his writings.

The real Fulton Sheen remains an elusive character. He provided a clue in the last book that he wrote, in 1974: *Those Mysterious Priests*. He called a priest a mysterious man, but also said that no life was more adventurous. Certainly, "a mysterious priest" is an unsatisfactory epitaph for the historian looking for the real Fulton Sheen. The man in the spotlight succeeded in keeping himself partially hidden in the shadows. But there is no mystery in the fact that Sheen's "adventure" was an unparalleled one. Fulton J. Sheen will long be remembered for embodying an American Catholic response to the challenge of his times, and for making an enduring contribution to the story of the Catholic Church in the twentieth century.

---

7   "An Address by His Excellency," May, 1978 (Press of the Green Mountain: Rochester, New York), at the dedication of the Fulton J. Sheen Archives at St. Bernard's Seminary.

Bibliography

A. The Sheen Archives (Archives of the Diocese of Rochester, New York)

The Archbishop Fulton John Sheen Archives were formally dedicated at St. Bernard's Seminary in Rochester, New York, on September 27, 1976. At that time, Archbishop Sheen called the Archives established in his honor simply "a collection of a period of Church history," and emphasized the value of the archives as representing "the beginning of the era of the electronic gospel in the United States."

The initial organization of the Sheen collection was undertaken by the Rev. Jasper Pennington; he supervised the expansion of the collection to include Sheen's personal library, books, pamphlets, radio and television tapes by Sheen, and materials transferred to Rochester after Sheen's death in 1979, including some records from his offices in New York City, personal items of Sheen's relatives and friends, and the bulk of Sheen's personal papers. By 1980, the "Special Collections Room" at the Seminary in Rochester had become a memorial to the legacy of Bishop Sheen, and consisted of a vast collection of films, tapes, books, newspaper articles, photographs, memorabilia and manuscripts reflecting all aspects of Sheen's life and ministry.

In May of 1981, the Archives were closed, following the announcement by the Bishop that the diocesan Seminary, St. Bernard's, was being closed. Eventually, the Sheen materials were sent to the Colgate-Rochester Divinity School, when St. Bernard's was resurrected as St. Bernard's Institute. As the first scholar to do extensive research on Sheen's life and his place in the history of American Catholicism, the task of reorganizing the materials fell to me; the Rev. Sebastian Falcone, Dean of the Institute, hired me

to work as a part-time archivist and administrative assistant. Guided
by Fr. Pennington's "Fulton John Sheen: A Chronology and Bibliography," published in *The Sheaf* at St. Bernard's, I fashioned some
rudimentary finding aids, including a "Scope and Content Note"
and a "Series Description/Content Listing."

The Sheen Archives were merged with the Archives of the
Diocese of Rochester and moved yet again in 1995 to the present
location at the Diocesan Pastoral Center. Since my original research
was done, many subsequent scholars have traveled to Rochester to
do research, and the collection remains an essential starting place
for those interested in the life and times of Fulton Sheen.

B. Additional Archival Sources Consulted

Archives of the Diocese of Rochester
    Rochester, New York
Catholic University of America Archives
    Washington, D.C.
University of Notre Dame Archives
    Notre Dame, Indiana

C. Books and Pamphlets of Fulton J. Sheen

The Armor of God (New York: P.J. Kenedy and Sons, 1943).

The Choice: The Sacred and the Profane Life (New York: Dell Publishing
    Co., 1963).

The Church, Communism and Democracy (New York: Dell Publishing
    Co., 1964).

Communism and the Conscience of the West (Indianapolis and New York:
    Bobbs-Merrill Co., 1948).

Communism Answers Questions of a Communist (New York: The Paulist
    Press, 1937).

Crisis in History (St. Paul, MN: The Catechetical Guild and Educa-
    tional Society, 1952).

The Cross and the Beatitudes (Liguori, MO: Liguori Pub., 2000;
    originally published by P.J. Kenedy and Sons, 1937)

The Cross and the Crisis (Manchester, NH: Ayer Co. Pubs. Inc., 1977; originally published in Milwaukee: The Bruce Publishing Co., 1938).

A Declaration of Dependence (Milwaukee: The Bruce Publishing Co., 1941).

The Divine Romance (New York: Alba House, 1982 and 1997; originally published in 1930, this work was re-issued by Garden City Books in 1950).

The Divine Verdict (New York: P.J. Kenedy and Sons, 1943).

The Enrollment of the World (New York: The Paulist Press, 1928).

The Eternal Galilean (New York: Alba House, 1997; originally published in 1934, Garden City Books re-issued the book in 1950).

Footprints in a Darkened Forest (New York: Meredith Press, 1967).

For God and Country (New York: P.J. Kenedy and Sons, 1941).

Freedom Under God (Milwaukee: The Bruce Publishing Co., 1940).

Go to Heaven (New York: The Dell Publishing Co., 1960; originally published in 1949).

God and Intelligence in Modern Philosophy (Garden City, NY: Doubleday and Co., 1958; originally published in 1925 by Longmans, Green and Co., London and New York).

God and War (New York: P.J. Kenedy and Sons, 1942).

God Love You (Garden City, NY: Doubleday and Co., 1955).

Guide to Contentment (New York: Alba House, 1997; Simon and Schuster, 1967).

The Ideological Fallacies of Communism (Washington, DC: U.S. Government Pamphlet 197608, published for the House Committee on Un-American Activities, 1957; with Dr. S. Andhil Fineberg and Dr. Daniel A. Poling).

Liberty, Equality and Fraternity (New York: The Macmillan Co., 1938).

Life Is Worth Living (San Francisco, CA: Ignatius Press, 1999).

Life Is Worth Living - First Series (New York: McGraw-Hill Book Co., 1953).

Life Is Worth Living - Second Series (New York: McGraw-Hill Book Co., 1954).

Life Is Worth Living - Third Series (See *Thinking Life Through*).

Life Is Worth Living - Fourth Series (New York: McGraw-Hill Book Co., 1956).

Life Is Worth Living - Fifth Series (New York: McGraw-Hill Book Co., 1957).

The Life of All Living (New York: Garden City Books, 1951; originally published in 1929).

Life of Christ (New York: Popular Library Edition, 1960; originally published in 1958). An abridged edition has been published in New York by Doubleday/Image books, 1977.

Lift Up Your Heart (Liguori, MO: Liguori/Triumph Books, 1997; New York: Garden City Books, 1952; originally published in 1950).

Love One Another (New York: Garden City Books, 1953; originally published in 1944).

Missions and the World Crisis (Milwaukee: The Bruce Publishing Co., 1963).

Moods and Truths (New York: Appleton-Century Co., 1934).

The Moral Universe: A Preface to Christian Living (Manchester, NH: Ayer Co. Pubs., Inc., 1977; originally published in 1936 by The Bruce Publishing Co., Milwaukee).

The Mystical Body of Christ (New York: Sheed and Ward, 1935).

Old Errors and New Labels (New York: The Century Co., 1931).

Peace of Soul (Liguori, MO: Liguori Press, 1996; Garden City, NY: Doubleday and Co., 1954; originally published in 1949).

Philosophies at War (New York: Charles Scribner's Sons, 1944).

Philosophy of Religion (New York: Appleton-Century-Crofts, Inc., 1948).

Philosophy of Science (Milwaukee: The Bruce Publishing Co., 1934).

The Power of Love (New York: Maco Magazine Corporation, 1964).

Preface to Religion (New York: P.J. Kenedy and Sons, 1946).

The Priest Is Not His Own (London: The Catholic Book Club, 1963).

The Prodigal World (New York: Alba House, 2003; originally published by the National Council of Catholic Men in collaboration with Our Sunday Visitor, 1935-1936).

The Rainbow of Sorrow (New York: P.J. Kenedy and Sons, 1938).

Religion Without God (New York: Garden City Books, 1954; originally published in 1928).

The Rock Plunged Into Eternity (New York: Alba House, 2003; originally published by the National Council of Catholic Men in collaboration with Our Sunday Visitor, 1950).

Science, Psychiatry and Religion (New York: Dell Publishing Co., 1962).

Seven Capital Sins (New York: Alba House, 2001; originally published by the National Council of Catholic Men in collaboration with Our Sunday Visitor, 1939).

The Seven Last Words (New York: Alba House, 1982 and 1996; originally published by the National Council of Catholic Men in collaboration with Our Sunday Visitor in 1940 as part of a series of talks on the "Seven Last Words and the Seven Virtues"; Garden City Books later published the first part in this form in 1952, and it was subsequently re-issued by Alba House).

Seven Pillars of Peace (New York: Charles Scribner's Sons, 1944).

The Seven Virtues (New York: P.J. Kenedy and Sons, 1940).

That Tremendous Love (New York: Harper and Row, 1967).

These Are the Sacraments (as photographed by Yousuf Karsh and described by Sheen; New York: Hawthorn Books, Inc., 1962).

Thinking Life Through (Third Series of Life Is Worth Living; New York: McGraw-Hill Book Co., 1955). It was recently re-issued under the title *Simple Truths: Thinking Life Through with Fulton J. Sheen* (Liguori, MO: Liguori/Triumph, 1998).

This is Rome (a pilgrimage conducted by Sheen, photographed by Yousuf Karsh and described by H.V. Morton; New York: Hawthorn Books, Inc., 1960).

This is the Holy Land (a pilgrimage conducted by Sheen and photographed by Yousuf Karsh; New York: Hawthorn Books, Inc., 1961).

This is the Mass (as celebrated by Sheen, described by Henri Daniel-Rops, and photographed by Yousuf Karsh; New York: Hawthorn Books, Inc., 1959).

Those Mysterious Priests (Garden City, NY: Doubleday and Co., 1974).

Thoughts for Daily Living (New York: Garden City Books, 1956).

Three to Get Married (Princeton, NJ: Scepter Pubs., 1997; New York: Appleton-Century-Crofts, Inc., 1951).

Treasure in Clay: The Autobiography of Fulton J. Sheen (San Francisco, CA: Ignatius Press, 1993; Garden City, NY: Doubleday and Co., 1980).

Victory Over Vice (New York: P.J. Kenedy and Sons, 1939).

Way to Happiness (New York: Alba House, 1997; originally published by Garden City Books in 1954).

Way to Inner Peace (New York: Alba House, 1994; originally published by Garden City Books in 1955).

The Way of the Cross (New York: Appleton-Century-Crofts, Inc., 1932).

Whence Comes War? (New York: Sheed and Ward, 1940).

The World's First Love (San Francisco, CA: Ignatius Press, 1996; New York: McGraw-Hill Book Co., 1952).

You (New York: Alba House, 2003; originally published by the National Council of Catholic Men in collaboration with Our Sunday Visitor, 1944-1945).

D. The Catholic Hour Broadcast Series of Fulton J. Sheen - published by Our Sunday Visitor Press, Huntington, Indiana

"The Divine Romance" (1930).

"Manifestations of Christ" (1931-1932).

"The Hymn of the Conquered" (1933).

"The Eternal Galilean" (1934).

"The Fullness of Christ" (1934-1935).

"The Prodigal World" (1935-1936).

"Our Wounded World" (1937).

"Justice and Charity: the social problem and the Church" (1938).

"Justice and Charity: the individual problem and the Church" (1938).

"Freedom: Parts I and II" (1939).

"Peace: The Fruit of Justice" (1940).

"The Seven Last Words and the Seven Virtues" (1940).

"War and Guilt" (1940-1941).

"Peace" (1941-1942).
"The Crisis in Christendom" (1943).
"One Lord: One World" (1944).
"You" (1944-1945).
"Love On Pilgrimage" (1946).
"Light Your Lamps" (1947).
"The Modern Soul in Search of God" (1948).
"The Love That Waits For You" (1949).
"The Rock Plunged into Eternity" (1950).
"The Woman" (1951).
"The Life of Christ" (1952).

E. Articles by Fulton J. Sheen

"Adaptation at Athens," *Worldmission* 17 (Fall, 1956) 3-9.
"Americans in the Missions," *Worldmission* 15 (Fall, 1964) 3-8.
"Assault on the Missions," *Worldmission* 9 (Spring, 1958) 3-11.
"Assumption and the Modern World," *Thomist* 14 (January, 1951) 31-40.
"Barnes-Storming," *America* 41 (April 27, 1929) 58-59.
"Bishop Fulton J. Sheen Tells the Story of the Birth of Christ," *Collier's* 132 (December 25, 1932) 23-27.
"Catholic Action and the Mystical Body," *The Homiletic and Pastoral Review* 35 (May, 1935) 866-873.
"Catholic Social Program," *Commerce and Finance* 27 (November, 1938) 18-19, 22.
"Changed Concepts of a Missionary," *Worldmission* 15 (Spring, 1964) 3-12.
"A Changed Outlook on Social Work," *The Catholic Charities Review* 20 (March, 1936) 69-75.
"The Christ Life of the Church," *Sign* 14 (February, 1935) 393-395.
"Christ Was There First," *Worldmission* 17 (Summer, 1966) 3-17.
"The City and the World," *Worldmission* 15 (Summer, 1964) 3-11.
"A Commentary on *Evangelii Praecones*," *Worldmission* 2 (September, 1951) 3-13.

"Communism: The Opium of the People," *The Franciscan* 17 (January, February, 1937) 6-10; 8-11, 24.

"Communism's Double Face," *Sign* 17 (March, 1937) 463-466.

"The Conqueror of Death," *Commonweal* 17 (February, 1931) 432-434.

"Contemporary Concepts of Religion," *Proceedings of the American Catholic Philosophical Association* 2 (December, 1927) 66-79.

"Conversion in the Mission World," *Worldmission* 15 (Winter, 1964-65) 3-7.

"The Coronation of Pope John XXIII," *Worldmission* 9 (Winter, 1958) 3-6.

"Cosmic Gods," *Commonweal* 21 (November 30, 1934) 137-138.

"Delusions of Atheism," *Catholic Mind* 33 (July 22, 1935) 271-273.

"Do You Know What Communism Is?", *Catholic Digest* 9 (July, 1947) 76-81.

"Educating for a Catholic Renaissance," *National Catholic Educational Association Bulletin* 25 (August, 1929) 6-15.

"Education in America," *National Catholic Educational Association Bulletin* 51 (August, 1954) 50-56.

"God and Country," *Christian Education* 20 (February, 1937) 166-170.

"God in Evolution," *Thought* 1 (March, 1927) 575-587.

"Going Back Into Council," *Worldmission* 14 (Summer, 1963) 3-8.

"Guest Editorial: Twenty-Fifth Anniversary," *Worldmission* 25 (Fall, 1974) 2-3.

"Heywood Broun: Biography of a Soul," *Catholic Mind* 38 (March 22, 1940) 115-120.

"How To Arouse Missionary Fire," *Worldmission* 16 (Summer, 1965) 3-9.

"How to Convert the Moslems," *Worldmission* 8 (Fall, 1957) 3-11.

"Ideals of Catholic Social Work," *Catholic Action* 20 (June, 1938) 27.

"Intolerance in the Coming Order," *America* 55 (July 4, 1939) 293-294.

"Lenten Reading List," *Catholic Mind* 47 (March, 1949) 168-172.

"Liberty Under Communism," *Sign* 16 (February, 1937) 393-397.

"Making the Stork a Bootlegger," *America* 41 (June 1, 1929) 179-180.

"Man, The Image of God," *Proceedings of the American Catholic Philosophical Association* 17 (1941) 65-66.

"Mary and the Russians," *Our Lady's Digest* 10 (November, 1955) 163-166.

"Mercier and Thomism," *Commonweal* 3 (February 10, 1926) 372-373.

"The Metaphysics of Character Training," *National Catholic Educational Association Bulletin* 26 (1929-1930) 569-573.

"Mission of the Society of St. Vincent de Paul," *Catholic Charities Review* 29 (November, 1945) 234-236.

"Missionaries: Give Us a New Theology," *Worldmission* 16 (Fall, 1965) 3-8.

"Missionary Reflections on the Council," *Worldmission* 14 (Spring, 1963) 3-8.

"The Missions and Nationalism," *Worldmission* 8 (Spring, 1957) 3-11.

"The Missions Are Catholic," *Worldmission* 9 (Summer, 1959) 3-10.

"Missions in a Planetary World," *Worldmission* 17 (Winter, 1966-1967) 3-7.

"Morticians of a Conciliar Decree," *Worldmission* 17 (Spring, 1966) 3-17.

"Moscow Makes Confusion for Reds and for Nations," *America* 62 (October 28, 1939) 60-61.

"Moscow: The Second Munich?", *Sign* 23 (November, 1943) 197-202.

"A New First," *Worldmission* 13 (Fall, 1962) 12-22.

"New Physics and New Scholasticism," *New Scholasticism* 3 (July, 1929) 241-252.

"A New Theology of Missions," *Worldmission* 22 (Fall, 1971) 20-25.

"Organic Fields of Study," *Catholic Educational Review* 28 (March, 1930) 201-207.

"The Papacy's Mission to the Nations," *Worldmission* 16 (Winter, 1965-1966) 3-12.

"Paul VI - Pope for Our Time," *Worldmission* 14 (Winter, 1963-1964) 3-5.

"Peace, What Shall It Be?", *PIC* (May 27, 1941) 8-9; (with Rabbi Stephen Wise and Bishop G. Bromley Oxnam).

"Philosophy and Order in Thought and Action: Radio Broadcast Symposium," *Proceedings of the American Catholic Philosophical Association* 17 (1941) 167-172; (with C.A. Hart and Mary Hohm).

"Philosophy and Science," *New Scholasticism* 7 (April, 1933) 109-133.

"A Plan for the Missions: The Need of Making Every Day Mission Day," *Worldmission* 14 (Fall, 1963) 3-12.

"The Pope As I Saw Him," *Catholic Digest* 19 (October, 1955) 62-64.

"The Priest and the Missions," *American Ecclesiastical Review* 126 (February, 1952) 81-86.

"Professor Arnold Toynbee and the Religions of the Mission World," *Worldmission* 7 (Winter, 1956) 387-394.

"Professor Whitehead and the Making of Religion," *New Scholasticism* 1 (April, 1927) 147-162.

"Religion and Values," *New Scholasticism* 2 (January, 1928) 29-50.

"Reply to *Izvestia*," *Catholic World* 158 (March, 1944) 589-591.

"The Signs of the Times," *Columbia* 50 (November, 1970) 16-19.

"Soviet Russia May Be Helped, But Russia Must Be Reformed," *America* 66 (October 18, 1941) 33-35.

"Spain Through Red Tinted Glasses," *The Irish Monthly* 67 (March, 1939) 169-180.

"The Spirit Is Now Moving East," *Worldmission* 8 (Summer, 1957) 24-28.

"Storm Over Communism," *The Irish Monthly* 65 (April, 1937) 222-232.

"The Sword, the Hammer, the Sickle and the Cross," *Worldmission* 2 (Winter, 1951) 3-6.

"The Tactics of Communism," *Sign* (November, 1936) 201-204.

"These Are the Sacraments," *Sign* 41 (April, 1962) 36-43.

"They Who Are Christ's," *Catholic Mission Digest* 7 (July-August, 1949) 1-5.

"The United States and the Missions," *Worldmission* 11 (Summer, 1960) 3-9.

"War, Freedom and Justice," *New Irish Monthly* 69 (April, 1941) 208-212.

"What Are We Fighting For," *Scribner's Commentator*, 10 (May, 1941) 83-85.

"What Kind of Person Was Christ?", *Look* 20 (April 3, 1956) 77-84.

"When Stalin Kissed Hitler the Communists Blushed Red," *America* 62 (October 21, 1939) 32-33.

"Witnesses to Christ," *Worldmission* 2 (February, 1951) 3-6.

"The World Crisis and the Missions," *Worldmission* 1 (December, 1950) 3-7.

F. Periodicals and Magazines

America

American Catholic Philosophical Association Proceedings

American Ecclesiastical Review

Ave Maria

Catholic Action

Catholic Charities Review

Catholic Digest

Catholic Educational Review

Catholic Mind

Catholic World

Christian Century

Commonweal

Homiletic and Pastoral Review

Mission

National Catholic Educational Association Bulletin

Newsweek

New Scholasticism

Ramparts

St. Anthony's Messenger

Sign

Social Justice Review

Thomist

Thought

Time

U.S. Catholic

Worldmission

G. Secondary Works: Books and Pamphlets

Abbott, Walter, SJ (ed.). *The Documents of Vatican II* (London: Geoffrey Chapman, 1966).

Abell, Aaron (ed.). *American Catholic Thought on Social Questions* (Indianapolis and New York: Bobbs-Merrill Co., 1968).

Abell, Aaron. *American Catholicism and Social Action: A Search for Social Justice, 1865-1950* (Notre Dame: University of Notre Dame Press, 1960).

Ahlstrom, Sydney E. *A Religious History of the American People* (New Haven: Yale University Press, 1972).

Alexander, Charles. *Holding the Line: The Eisenhower Era, 1952-1961* (Bloomington: Indiana University Press, 1975).

Barres, Oliver. *World Mission Windows* (Staten Island, NY: St. Paul Publications, 1963).

Betten, Neil. *Catholic Activism and the Industrial Worker* (Gainesville: University Presses of Florida, 1976).

Binchy, D.A. *Church and State in Fascist Italy* (New York and London: Oxford University Press, 1941).

Blanshard, Paul. *American Freedom and Catholic Power* (Boston: The Beacon Press, 1949).

_____. *Communism, Democracy and Catholic Power* (Boston: The Beacon Press, 1951).

Blantz, Thomas E., CSC. *A Priest in Public Service: Francis J. Haas and the New Deal* (Notre Dame: University of Notre Dame Press, 1982).

Brinkley, Alan. *Voices of Protest: Huey Long, Father Coughlin and the Great Depression* (New York: Alfred A. Knopf, 1982).

Broderick, Francis. *Right Reverend New Dealer: John A. Ryan* (New York: The Macmillan Co., 1963).

Brooks, Tim and Earle Marsh. *The Complete Directory to Prime Time Network T.V. Shows, 1946-Present* (New York: Ballantine Books, 1979).

Brown, Les. *The New York Times Encyclopedia of Television* (New York: The New York Times Book Co., 1977).

Brown, Robert McAfee and Gustave Weigel, SJ. *An American Dialogue* (Garden City, NY: Doubleday and Co., 1960).

Budenz, Louis Francis. *This Is My Story* (New York: Whittlesey House, The McGraw-Hill Book Co., 1947).

Callahan, Daniel. *The Mind of the Catholic Layman* (New York: Charles Scribner's Sons, 1963).

Campbell, Robert E., MM (ed.). *The Church in Mission* (Maryknoll, NY: Maryknoll Publications, 1965).

Carter, Paul. *Another Part of the Fifties* (New York: Columbia University Press, 1983).

Catholicism in America: A Series of Articles from the Commonweal (New York: Harcourt, Brace and Co., 1953).

Caute, David. *The Great Fear: The Anti-Communist Purge Under Truman and Eisenhower* (New York: Simon and Schuster, 1978).

Christ, Frank L. and Gerald E. Sherry (eds.). *American Catholicism and the Intellectual Ideal* (New York: Appleton-Century-Crofts, Inc., 1961).

Cogley, John. *Catholic America* (Garden City, NY: Doubleday and Co., 1974).

_____. *Religion in America: Original Essays on Religion in a Free Society* (New York: Meridian Books, Inc., 1958).

Cohalan, Florence D. *A Popular History of the Archdiocese of New York* (Yonkers, NY: U.S. Catholic Historical Society, 1983).

Colaianni, James. *The Catholic Left: The Crisis of Radicalism Within the Church* (Philadelphia: Chilton Book Co., 1968).

Conniff, James C.G. *The Bishop Sheen Story* (Greenwich, CT: Fawcett Publications, Inc., 1953).

Considine, John J., MM (ed.). *The Missionary's Role in Socio-Economic Betterment* (Maryknoll, NY: Newman Press, 1960).

Cooney, John. *The American Pope: The Life and Times of Francis Cardinal Spellman* (New York: Times Books, 1984).

Couturier, Charles, SJ. *The Mission of the Church* (Baltimore: Helicon Press, 1957).

Cowan, Wane H. (ed.). *Facing Protestant-Roman Catholic Tensions* (New York: Association Press, 1960).

Crosby, Donald F., SJ. *God, Church and Flag: Senator Joseph R. McCarthy and the Catholic Church, 1950-1957* (Chapel Hill:

The University of North Carolina Press, 1978).

Curran, Charles E. *American Catholic Social Ethics: Twentieth Century Approaches* (Notre Dame: University of Notre Dame Press, 1982).

Curran, Charles and Richard McCormick, SJ (eds.). *Readings in Moral Theology #5: Official Catholic Social Teaching* (New York: The Paulist Press, 1986).

Curry, Lerond. *Protestant-Catholic Relations in America: World War I Through Vatican II* (Lexington: The University Press of Kentucky, 1972).

Cushing, Richard J. *The Missions in War and Peace* (Boston: The Society for the Propagation of the Faith, 1944).

Delaney, John J. *Dictionary of American Catholic Biography* (Garden City, NY: Doubleday and Co., 1984).

Delaney, John J. (ed.) *Why Catholic?* (New York: Doubleday and Co., 1979).

Diggins, John P. *Mussolini and Fascism: The View From America* (Princeton: Princeton University Press, 1972).

Dohen, Dorothy. *Nationalism and American Catholicism* (New York: Sheed and Ward, 1967).

Dolan, Jay P. *The American Catholic Experience* (Garden City, NY: Doubleday and Co., 1985).

Dulles, Avery. *A History of Apologetics* (Hutchinson of London, Corpus of New York, 1971).

Ellens, J. Harold. *Models of Religious Broadcasting* (Grand Rapids: William B. Eerdmans Publishing Co., 1974).

Ellis, John Tracy. *American Catholicism,* 2nd ed. (Chicago: University of Chicago Press, 1969).

_____. *American Catholics and the Intellectual Life* (Chicago: The Heritage Foundation, Inc., 1956).

_____. *Catholic Bishops: A Memoir* (Wilmington: Michael Glazier, Inc., 1983).

_____. (ed.), *The Catholic Priest in the United States: Historical Investigations* (Collegeville: St. John's University Press, 1971).

Elvy, Peter. *Buying Time: The Foundations of the Electronic Church* (Mystic, CT: Twenty-Third Publications, 1987).

Flynn, George Q. *American Catholics: The Roosevelt Presidency* (Lexington: University of Ketucky Press, 1968).

_____. *Roosevelt and Romanism: Catholics and American Diplomacy, 1937-1945* (Westport, CT: Greenwood Press, 1976).

Flynn, John T. *The Road Ahead: America's Creeping Revolution* (New York: Devin-Adair, Co., 1949).

Fogarty, Gerald P., SJ. *The Vatican and the American Hierarchy from 1870-1965* (Stuttgart: Antonin Hiersemann, 1982).

Fracchia, Charles A. *Second Spring: The Coming of Age of U.S. Catholicism* (New York: Harper and Row, 1980).

Frady, Marshall. *Billy Graham: A Parable of American Righteousness* (Boston: Little, Brown and Co., 1979).

Gannon, Robert I., SJ. *The Cardinal Spellman Story* (Garden City, NY: Doubleday and Co., 1963).

Gleason, Philip (ed.). *Contemporary Catholicism in the United States* (Notre Dame: University of Notre Dame Press, 1969).

_____. *Keeping the Faith: American Catholicism Past and Present* (Notre Dame: University of Notre Dame Press, 1987).

Greeley, Andrew. *The Catholic Experience: An Interpretation of the History of American Catholicism* (Garden City, NY: Doubleday and Co., 1967).

Hadden, Jeffrey K. and Charles E. Swann. *Prime-Time Preachers: The Rising Power of Televangelism* (Reading, MA: Addison-Wesley Publishing Co., 1981).

Halsey, William D. *The Survival of American Innocence: Catholicism in an Era of Disillusionment, 1920-1940* (Notre Dame: University of Notre Dame Press, 1980).

Hastings, Adrian. *The Church's #1 Problem* (Glen Rock, NJ: The Paulist Press, 1965).

Hennesey, James, SJ. *American Catholics: A History of the Roman Catholic Community in the United States* (New York: Oxford University Press, 1981).

Herberg, Will. *Protestant-Catholic-Jew* (Garden City, NY: Doubleday and Co., 1960).

Hillman, Eugene, CSSp. *The Church in Mission* (New York: Herder and Herder, 1965).

Hitchcock, James. *The Decline and Fall of Radical Catholicism* (New York: Herder and Herder, 1971).

Horsefield, Peter. *Religious Television: The American Experience* (New York: Longman, 1984).

Hudson, Winthrop. *Religion In America* (New York: Charles Scribner's Sons, 1973).

Isserman, Maurice. *Which Side Were You On? The American Communist Party During the Second World War* (Middletown, CT: Wesleyan University Press, 1982).

Kaiser, Robert Blair. *Pope, Council and World: The Story of Vatican II* (New York: The Macmillan Co., 1963).

Kane, John J. *Catholic-Protestant Conflicts in America* (Chicago: Henry Regnery Co., 1955).

Kauffmann, Christopher. *Faith and Fraternalism: The History of the Knights of Columbus, 1882-1982* (New York: Harper and Row, 1982).

Klehr, Harvey. *The Heyday of American Communism* (New York: Basic Books, Inc., 1984).

Kossmann, Patricia (ed.). *From the Angel's Blackboard: The Best of Fulton J. Sheen, A Centennial Celebration* (Liguori, MO: Triumph Books, 1995).

Ladd, Gregory. *Archbishop Fulton J. Sheen: A Man for All Seasons* (San Francisco: Ignatius Press, 2001).

Levering, Ralph B. *American Opinion and the Russian Alliance, 1939-1945* (Chapel Hill: The University of North Carolina Press, 1976).

Lynch, Christopher. *Selling Catholicism: Bishop Sheen and the Power of Television* (Lexington: The University Press of Kentucky, 1998).

McAvoy, Thomas T., CSC. *A History of the Catholic Church in the United States* (Notre Dame: University of Notre Dame Press, 1969).

McAvoy, Thomas T., CSC (ed.). *Roman Catholicism and the American Way of Life* (Notre Dame: University of Notre Dame Press, 1960).

McGuire, Frederick A., CM (ed.). *The New Missionary Church* (Baltimore: Helicon Press, 1964).

McGurn, Barrett. *A Reporter Looks at American Catholicism* (New York: Hawthorn Books, 1967).

McLoughlin, William G. Jr. *Billy Graham: Revivalist in a Secular Age* (New York: The Ronald Press Co., 1960).

_____. *Revivals, Awakenings and Reform: An Essay On Religion and Social Change in America, 1607-1977* (Chicago: University of Chicago Press, 1979).

McNamara, Robert F. *The Diocese of Rochester, 1868-1968* (Rochester: The Diocese of Rochester, 1968).

_____. *The Diocese of Rochester in America, 1868-1993* (Rochester: The Roman Catholic Diocese of Rochester, New York, 1998).

McShane, Joseph M., SJ. *Sufficiently Radical: Catholicism, Progressivism and the Bishops Program of 1919* (Washington, DC: Catholic University of America Press, 1987).

Manchester, William. *The Glory and the Dream: A Narrative History of America, 1932-1972* (Boston: Little, Brown and Co., 1973).

Marty, Martin. *An Invitation to American Catholic History* (Chicago: The Thomas More Press, 1986).

_____. *Modern American Religion, Volume 3: Under God, Indivisible, 1941-1960* (Chicago: The University of Chicago Press, 1996).

_____. *Pilgrims in Their Own Land* (Boston: Little, Brown and Co., 1984).

Massa, Mark J. *Catholics and American Culture: Fulton Sheen, Dorothy Day and the Notre Dame Football Team* (New York: The Crossroad Publishing Co., 1999).

Maynard, Theodore. *The Story of American Catholicism* (New York: The Macmillan Co., 1941).

Meyer, Donald. *The Positive Thinkers: Religion as Pop Psychology From Mary Baker Eddy to Oral Roberts* (New York: Pantheon Books, 1980).

Miller, Douglas T. and Marion Nowak. *The Fifties: The Way We Were* (Garden City, NY: Doubleday and Co., 1977).

Miller, William D. *A Harsh and Dreadful Love: Dorothy Day and the Catholic Worker Movement* (New York: Liveright, 1973).

Millot, Rene P. *Missions in the World Today* (New York: Hawthorn Books, Inc., 1961).

Moore, R. Laurence. *Religious Outsiders and the Making of Americans* (New York: Oxford University Press, 1986).

Morris, Charles R. *American Catholic: The Saints and Sinners Who Built America's Most Powerful Church* (New York: Times Books/ Random House, 1997).

Murphy, Edward L., SJ. *Teach All Ye Nations: The Principles of Catholic Missionary Work* (New York: Benziger Brothers, Inc., 1957).

Murray, John Courtney, SJ. *We Hold These Truths: Catholic Reflections on the American Proposition* (New York: Sheed and Ward, 1960).

Nash, Gary H. Th*e Conservative Intellectual Movement in America: Since 1945* (New York: Basic Books, Inc., 1976).

Nolan, Hugh (ed.). *The Pastoral Letters of the American Hierarchy, 1792-1970* (Washington, DC: United States Catholic Conference, 1984).

Noonan, Daniel P. *Missionary With A Mike* (New York: Pageant Press, 1968).

_____. *The Passion of Fulton Sheen* (New York: Dodd, Mead and Co., 1972).

Novak, Michael. *Freedom With Justice: Catholic Social Thought and Liberal Institutions* (San Francisco: Harper and Row, 1984).

Oakley, J. Ronald. *God's Country: America in the Fifties* (New York: Dembner Books, 1986).

O'Brien, David J. *American Catholics and Social Reform: The New Deal Years* (New York: Oxford University Press, 1968).

_____. *The Renewal of American Catholicism* (New York: The Paulist Press, 1972).

O'Brien, John A. (ed.). *The Road to Damascus* (Notre Dame: University of Notre Dame Press, 1949).

_____. (ed.). *Winning Converts* (Notre Dame: University of Notre Dame Press, 1957).

O'Brien, Sister Mary Consilia. *Christian Social Principles*, with an Introduction by Fulton J. Sheen (New York: P.J. Kenedy and Sons, 1941).

O'Dea, Thomas F. *American Catholic Dilemma: An Inquiry into the Intellectual Life* (New York: Sheed and Ward, 1958).

_____. *The Catholic Crisis* (Boston: The Beacon Press, 1968).

Ogden, August Raymond, FSC. *The Dies Committee: A Study of the Special House Committee for the Investigation of Un-American Activities, 1938-1944* (Washington, DC: Catholic University of America Press, 1945).

O'Neill, James M. *Catholics and American Freedom* (New York: Harper and Brothers, 1952).

Ong, Walter J., SJ. *Frontiers in American Catholicism* (New York: The Macmillan Co., 1957).

Piehl, Mel. *Breaking Bread: The Catholic Worker and the Origin of Catholic Radicalism in America* (Philadelphia: Temple University Press, 1982).

Poggi, Gianfranco. *Catholic Action in Italy: The Sociology of a Sponsored Organization* (Stanford: Stanford University Press, 1967).

Powers, J.F. *Prince of Darkness and Other Stories* (New York: Doubleday and Co., 1958).

Purcell, Edward. *The Crisis of Democratic Theory: Scientific Naturalism and the Problem of Value* (Lexington: The University Press of Kentucky, 1973).

Reeves, Thomas C. *America's Bishop: The Life and Times of Fulton J. Sheen* (San Francisco: Encounter Books, 2001).

_____. *The Life and Times of Joe McCarthy* (London: Blond and Briggs, 1982).

Retif, Louis and Andre. *The Catholic Mission in the World* (New York: Hawthorn Books, Inc., 1962).

Ribuffo, Leo P. *The Old Christian Right: The Protestant Far Right from the Great Depression to the Cold War* (Philadelphia: Temple University Press, 1983).

Richardson, William J., MM (ed.). *The Modern Mission Apostolate: A Symposium* (Maryknoll, NY: Maryknoll Publications, 1965).

Roche, Douglas J. *The Catholic Revolution* (New York: David McKay Co., 1968).

Roy, Ralph Lord. *Apostles of Discord: A Study of Organized Bigotry and*

Disruption on the Fringes of Protestantism (Boston: The Beacon Press, 1955).

_____. *Communism and the Churches* (New York: Harcourt, Brace and Co., 1960).

Rumble, Leslie and Charles Carty (eds.). *Radio Replies*, with an Introduction by Fulton J. Sheen (St. Paul, MN: Radio Replies Press, 3 volumes, 1938, 1940, 1942).

Rynne, Xavier. *Letters From Vatican City* (New York: Farrar, Straus, Giroux, 1963).

_____. *The Second Session* (New York: Farrar, Straus, Giroux, 1964).

_____. *The Third Session* (New York: Farrar, Straus, Giroux, 1965).

Schneider, Louis and Sanford Dunbusch. *Popular Religion: Inspiration Books in America* (Chicago: University of Chicago Press, 1958).

Seldes, George. *The Catholic Crisis* (New York: Julian Messner, Inc., 1939).

Shannon, William. *The American Irish* (New York: Collier Books, 1963).

Sheed, Frank. *Communism and Man* (New York: Sheed and Ward, 1938).

Sheed, Wilfrid. *Clare Boothe Luce* (New York: E.P. Dutton, 1982).

_____. *Frank and Maisie: A Memoir of Parents* (New York: Simon and Schuster, 1985).

Shuster, George. *The Catholic Spirit in America* (New York: Dial Press, 1927).

Tull, Charles J. *Father Coughlin and the New Deal* (Syracuse: Syracuse University Press, 1965).

Underwood, Kenneth. *Protestant and Catholic: Religion and Social Interaction in an Industrial Community* (Boston: The Beacon Press, 1957).

Wakin, Edward and Joseph Scheur. *The De-Romanization of the American Catholic Church* (New York: The Macmillan Co., 1966).

Walsh, Bishop James E. *The Church's World-Wide Mission* (New York: Benziger Brothers, 1948).

Wills, Garry. *Bare Ruined Choirs: Doubt, Prophecy and Radical Religion* (New York: Dell Publishing Co., 1971).

Woodward, Kenneth. *Making Saints: How the Catholic Church Determines Who Becomes a Saint, Who Doesn't and Why* (New York: Simon and Schuster, 1990).

Yzermans, Vincent A. *American Participation in the Second Vatican Council* (New York: Sheed and Ward, 1967).

H. Secondary Sources: Articles

Adler, Les K. and Thomas G. Paterson. "Red Fascism: The Merger of Nazi Germany and Soviet Russia in the American Image of Totalitarianism, 1930's-1950's," *American Historical Review* 75 (April 1970) 1046-1064.

Attwater, Donald. "Passing the Buck," *Commonweal* 24 (October 2, 1936) 517-518.

Bates, Ernest Sutherland. "A Champion of Reason," *Commonweal* 3 (January 13, 1926) 264-265.

Breig, James. "Fulton J. Sheen: And Now a Word With His Sponsor," *U.S. Catholic* 45 (February, 1980) 24-28.

Brophy, Liam. "Catholic Action Confronts Communist Action," *Social Justice Review* 40 (September, 1947) 147-149.

Budenz, Louis. "Know Your Enemy," *Sign* 4 (March, 1955) 21-24.

Burnham, Philip. "Russia As An Ally," *Commonweal* 35 (February 6, 1942) 381-383.

Carey, Patrick W. "American Catholic Religious Thought: An Historical Overview," *U.S. Catholic Historian* 4 (1985) 123-142.

Cogley, John. "The Failure of Anti-Communism," *Commonweal* 52 (July 21, 1950) 357-358.

_____. "The Unspoken Ism," *Commonweal* 54 (May 18, 1951) 144-146.

Colby, Frances Sedgwick. "Monsignor Sheen and Mrs. Luce," *American Scholar* 17 (Winter, 1947-1948) 35-44.

Conniff, James C.G. "Women Listen to Bishop Sheen," *Catholic Digest* 19 (December, 1954) 115-118.

Cox, Ignatius. "Pillars of Peace," *Thought* 20 (June, 1945) 197-201.

Curran, Charles. "American and Catholic: American Catholic Social Ethics, 1880-1965," *Thought* 52 (March, 1977) 5074.

Daly, John Jay. "The Man Behind the Mike," *Sign* 24 (May 10, 1945) 509-512.

Dawson, Christopher. "The Threat to the West," *Commonweal* 31 (February 2, 1940) 317-318.

Day, Dorothy. "The Diabolic Plot," *America* 49 (April 29, 1933) 82-83.

Diggins, John P. "American Catholics and Italian Fascism," *The Journal of Contemporary History* 2 (October, 1967) 51-68.

Dolan, Jay P. "American Catholicism and Modernity," *Cross Currents* 31 (Summer, 1981) 150-162.

Draper, Theodore. "American Communism Revisited," *The New York Review* 32 (May 9, 1985) 32-33 ff.

_____. "The Popular Front Revisited," *The New York Review* 32 (May 30, 1985) 44-45 ff.

Eckhardt, A. Roy. "The Christ Child and Bishop Sheen," *Christian Century* 71 (January, 1954) 78-80.

Egan, Alcuin, S.A. "Propagation Headquarters," *Missionary Digest* 25 (August, 1954) 15-16.

Ellis, John Tracy. "American Catholicism in 1960: An Historical Perspective," *American Benedictine Review* 11 (March-June, 1960) 1-20.

_____. "American Catholicism, 1953-1979: A Notable Change," *Thought* 54 (June, 1979) 113-131.

_____. "The Catholic University of America, 1927-1979: A Personal Memoir," *Social Thought* 5 (Spring, 1979) 35-62.

_____. "Changing Concerns of the American Bishops, 1792-1970," *Catholic Historical Review* 58 (October, 1972) 388-393.

Fogarty, Gerald P., SJ. "Public Patriotism and Private Politics: The Tradition of American Catholicism," *U.S. Catholic Historian* 4 (1984) 1-48.

Frazier, George. "Fulton J. Sheen: Unprofitable Servant," *Catholic Digest* 14 (October, 1950) 20-26.

Gillis, James, CSP. "Open Letter to Anti-Catholic Agitators," *Catholic World* 170 (March, 1950) 406-407.

Gleason, Philip. "Americans All: World War II and the Shaping of American Identity," *Review of Politics* 43 (October, 1981) 483-518.

———. "American Identity and Americanization" in Stephan Thernstrom et al., *Harvard Encyclopedia of American Ethnic Groups* (Cambridge: Harvard University Press, 1980) 31-58.

———. "The Bicentennial and Oher Milestones: Anniversary Assessments of American Catholicism," *Communio* 3 (Summer, 1976) 115-135.

———. "Catholicism and Cultural Change in the 1960s" in Ronald Weber's *America In Change* (Notre Dame: University of Notre Dame Press, 1972) 91-107.

———. "Identifying Identity: A Semantic History," *Journal of American History* 69 (March, 1983) 910-931.

———. "In Search of Unity: American Catholic Thought, 1920-1960," *Catholic Historical Review* 65 (April, 1979) 185-205.

———. "Pluralism, Democracy and Catholicism in the Era of World War II," *Review of Politics* 49 (Spring, 1987) 208-230.

Goldstein, David. "Come Into My Parlor Prays the Communist Spider," *America* 59 (June 25, 1938) 274.

Gurian, Waldemar. "Soviet Foreign Policy," *Commonweal* 52 (September 1, 1950) 503-505.

Hayes, John S. "Fulton J. Sheen: Shepherd," *Homiletic and Pastoral Review* 81 (February, 1981) 63-66.

Heffron, Edward. "Contemporary Catholic Authors: Monsignor Fulton Sheen, Theologian, Philosopher and Orator," *Catholic Library World* 12-13 (1940-1941) 203-207.

———. "McCarthy: The Case for Him," *Commonweal* 57 (October 31, 1952) 87-90.

Herberg, Will. "A Jew Looks at Catholics," *Commonweal* 58 (May 22, 1953) 174-177.

Hettinger, Herman S. "Broadcasting in the United States," *Annals of the American Academy of Political and Social Science* 177 (January, 1935) 1-14.

High, Stanley. "Catholic Converts," *Current History and Forum* 52 (September, 1940) 29-31.

Hinckle, Warren. "Left-Wing Catholics," *Ramparts* 6 (November, 1967) 14-26.

Hoffman, Paul. "Bishop Sheen in Rochester," *Catholic Digest* 32 (December, 1967) 19-21.

Hughes, Lawrence M. "Bishop Sheen's Sponsor," *Catholic Digest* 20 (May, 1956) 17-21.

Hyde, Douglas. "I Was A Communist," *Sign* 27 (May, 1948) 9-11.

Johnson, Dr. George. "Social Justice and Communism," *Catholic Action* 19 (June, 1937) 16-19, 27.

Jones, Stacy V. "Monsignor Fulton J. Sheen," *Catholic Digest* 10 (September, 1946) 79-84.

Kantowicz, Edward R. "Cardinal Mundelein of Chicago and the Shaping of Twentieth Century American Catholicism," *Journal of American History* 68 (June, 1981) 52-68.

Keating, John J., CSP. "Bishop Sheen: Purple Passage to the Church," *Catholic World* 179 (April, 1954) 6-11.

Kiniery, Paul. "The Catholic Answer to Communism," *Catholic World* 14 (March, 1937) 652-660.

_____. "Equals in Evil: Communism and Fascism," *Catholic World* 145 (August, 1937) 524-531.

Kselman, Thomas A. and Steven Avella. "Marian Piety and the Cold War in the United States," *Catholic Historical Review* 63 (July, 1986) 403-424.

Kucharsky, David, "Bottom-Line Theology: An Interview with Fulton J. Sheen," *Christianity Today* 21 (June 3, 1977) 8-11.

LaFarge, John, SJ. "Can We Cooperate With Communists?", *America* 53 (August 24, 1935).

_____. "The Catholic Press and Communism," *America* 55 (May 30, 1936) 177-178.

_____. "The Catholic Reply to Communism," *America* 54 (November 23; November 30; December 14, 1935) 150-152; 175-177; 225-227.

_____. "Causes and Communism," *America* 52 (February, 1935) 421-423.

_____, "Fascism and Communism: Which Is the Greater Danger?", *America* 56 (October 10, 1936) 4-5.

_____. "Shall We Recognize Russia?", *America* 48 (February 18, 1933) 472-473.

Lally, Francis J. "State of the Catholic Press," *Commonweal* 57 (February 6, 1953) 444-445.

Luce, Clare Boothe. "The Real Reason," *McCall's Magazine* 74 (February, March, April, 1947) 16, 117-135; 16, 156-176; 26, 76-90.

McAvoy, Thomas T., CSC. "American Catholics and the Second World War," *Review of Politics* 6 (April, 1944) 131-150.

McCoy, Charles N. "Dialectics of Freedom," *Commonweal* 22 (October 25, 1935) 626-627.

Marciniak, Edward A. "Catholics and Social Reform," *Commonweal* 58 (September 11, 1953) 557-560.

Maynard, Theodore. "Catholics and the Nazis," *American Mercury* 53 (October, 1941) 391-400.

Meyer, H. Gregory. "Going for the Church's Highest Rating/ From Prime Time to a Patron Saint?" *Chicago Tribune,* 3 November, 2002.

Miller, Spencer, Jr. "Radio and Religion," *Annals of the Academy of Political and Social Science* 177 (January, 1935) 135-140.

Minsky, Louis. "Dilemma of the Secularist," *Commonweal* 26 (June 18, 1937) 201-202.

_____. "The United Front," *Commonweal* 25 (February 19, 1937) 457-458.

_____. "You're A Fascist! You're A Communist!", *America* 56 (March 27, 1937) 581-582.

Miscamble, Wilson D. "Catholics and American Foreign Policy from McKinley to McCarthy," *Diplomatic History* 4 (Summer, 1982) 223-240.

Moody, Joseph N. "Catholic Defense Against Communism," *America* 56 (December 12, 1936) 223-225.

Morrison, Charles. "Religion Reaches Out," *Look* 18 (December 14, 1954) 41-45.

Murray, John Courtney. "Paul Blanshard and the New Nativism," *The Month* 5 (New Series) (April, 1951) 214-225.

Newman, Larry. "Bishop Sheen and the T.V. Camera," *Catholic Digest* 16 (May, 1952) 115-117.

O'Brien, John A. "Fighting for Social Justice," *Commonweal* 26 (June 11, 1937) 179-180.

O'Brien, John C. "Monsignor Sheen Will Preach," *Extension* 40 (February, 1946) 8-9.

O'Gara, James. "McCarthy: The Case Against Him,"*Commonweal* 57 (October 31, 1952) 91-95.

Palmer, Gretta J. "Bishop Sheen on Television," *Catholic Digest* 17 (February, 1953) 75-80.

_____. "Bishop Fulton J. Sheen," *Catholic Digest* 15 (October, 1951) 55-62.

_____. "Southern Catholics Fight Race Hatred," *Look* 14 (March 28, 1950) 99-100.

Parsons, Wilfrid. "Fascist-Communist Dilemma," *Commonweal* 25 (February 12, 1937) 429-431.

_____. "Popular Front and Catholicism," *Commonweal* 25 (February 19, 1937) 465-466.

Patterson, Lawrence Kent, SJ, "The Communist Common Front," *America* 55 (May 23, 1936) 155-157.

_____. "What Shall We Do About Communism?", *America* 54 (November 16, 1935) 126-127.

Prial, Frank J. "Boat Rocking Bishop," *Wall Street Journal* (September 12, 1967) 1ff.

Reeves, Monica. "The Man No One Suspected," *St. Anthony Messenger* 75 (December, 1967) 12-14.

Rice, Fr. Charles Owen. "Debating the Outstretched Hand," *Commonweal* 29 (January 20, 1939) 351-353.

Riley (Fields), Kathleen L. "A Life of Mystery and Adventure: Fulton Sheen's Reflections on the Priesthood," *U.S. Catholic Historian* 11:1 (1993) 63-82.

Roddy, Joseph. "A Talk With Bishop Sheen," *Look* 17 (January 27, 1953) 35-41.

Saunders, D.A. "Liberals and Catholic Action," *Christian Century* 54 (October 20, 1937) 1293-1295.

Shine, Donald, SJ. "Bishop Sheen's Threshold Apologetics," *American Ecclesiastical Review* 125 (October, 1951) 274-279.

Shuster, George N. "Three Encyclicals," *Commonweal* 27 (November 12, 1937) 163-164.

_____. "The World's Cardinal," *Commonweal* 3 (February 3, 1926) 344-345.

Sisk, John P. "On Heavenly Mr. Budenz," *Commonweal* 50 (July 22, 1949) 360-363.

Skillin, Edward J. "A Note on Anti-Communism," *Commonweal* 45 (February 28, 1947) 489-491.

Smith, William J. "Behold the American Reds So Double-Crossed by Stalin," *America* 61 (September 30, 1934) 586-587.

_____. "Marx Versus Aquinas, Lenin Versus the Popes," *America* 52 (December 2, 1939) 200-201.

_____. "Soviet-Nazi Compact Strips the Party in U.S.A.," *America* 61 (September 23, 1939) 562-563.

Soares, Aileen. "The Catholic Hour," *Radio Varieties* (January, 1940).

Stewart, Kenneth. "An Interview With America's Outstanding Roman Catholic Proselytizer and Philosopher," *P.M. Magazine* 6 (June 16, 1946).

Sturzo, Lynn. "Communism and Fascism," *Commonweal* 25 (April 16, 1937) 686-688.

Talbot, Francis X. "The Communist Is No Longer Sacred," *America* 52 (November 4, 1939) 93-94.

Taylor, Tim. "Fulton Sheen: Verities on Television," *Cue* 22 (November, 1952) 14-20.

Thorning, Joseph F., SJ. "Another Trojan Horse: The United Front," *America* 54 (October 19, 1935) 33-34.

_____. "Communism in the United States," *America* 53 (September 21, 1935) 559-560.

Valaik, J. David. "American Catholic Dissenters and the Spanish Civil War," *Catholic Historical Review* 53 (January, 1968) 537-555.

_____. "Catholics, Neutrality and the Spanish Embargo, 1937-1939," *Journal of American History* 54 (June, 1967) 73-85.

Walsh, Edmund, SJ. "The Basic Issue in Recognition of Soviet Russia," *Catholic Mind* 31 (May 22, 1933) 192-200.

Walsh, William Thomas. "Is Communism Dangerous?", *Commonweal* 22 (February 8, 1935) 420-422.

Watt, Lewis, SJ. "Communism and the Catholic Social Program," *Catholic Mind* 32 (March 8, 1934) 81-94.

Wentz, F.K. "American Catholic Periodicals React to Nazism," *Church History* 31 (December, 1962) 400-420.

Westfield, J. Edgar. "Communist Effrontery Designs New Trojan Horse," *America* 59 (September 17, 1938) 560-561.

Williams, George H., Waldo Beach and H. Richard Niebuhr. "Issues Between Catholics and Protestants at Mid-Century," *Religion in Life* 23 (Spring, 1954) 163-205.

Wiltbye, John. "Pinks, Reds and Other Pests," *America* 43 (August 2, 1930) 402-403.

Wintz, Jack, OFM. "American Catholics' John Powell, SJ: No Clone of Bishop Sheen" (An Interview), *St. Anthony Messenger* 89 (September, 1981) 22.

I. Unpublished Sources

Aschettino, Richard F. "Fulton John Sheen: The Good Man Speaking Well" (M.A. thesis, University of Kansas, 1973).

Carpenter, Joel A. "The Renewal of American Fundamentalism: 1930-1945" (Ph.D. dissertation, Johns Hopkins University, 1984).

Finks, P. David. "Crisis in Smugtown: A Study of Conflict, Churches and Citizen Organizations in Rochester, New York, 1964-1969" (Ph.D. dissertation, Union Graduate School of the Union for Experimenting Colleges and Universities, 1975).

Hanford, William James. "A Rhetorical Study of the Radio and Television Speaking of Bishop Fulton J. Sheen" (Ph.D. dissertation, Wayne State University, 1965).

Valaik, J. David. "American Catholics and the Spanish Civil War, 1931-1939" (Ph.D. dissertation, University of Rochester, 1964).

Willis, H. Warren. "The Reorganization of the Catholic University of

America During the Rectorship of James H. Ryan, 1928-1935" (Ph.D. dissertation, Catholic University of America, 1972).

Yablonsky, Mary Jude. "A Rhetorical Analysis of Selected Television Speeches of Archbishop Fulton J. Sheen on Communism, 1952-1956" (Ph.D. dissertation, Ohio State University, 1974).

J. Encyclopediae/Reference Works

New Catholic Encyclopedia (New York: McGraw Hill, 1967; and second edition, Washington, DC: Thomson Gale, for the Catholic University of America Press, 2002).

The Papal Encyclicals (Wilmington, NC: McGrath Publishing Co., A Consortium Book, 1981).

Seven Great Encyclicals (Glen Rock, NJ: Paulist Press, 1963).

K. Interviews/Telephone Conversations

Dr. Joel A. Carpenter, Jr. February 24, 1987 Billy Graham Archives, Wheaton College, Wheaton, Illinois.

Rev. Robert F. McNamara. September 4, 1986 Rochester, New York.

Monsignor John Tracy Ellis. February 20, 1987 Catholic University of America, Washington, DC.

INDEX

A

Abell, Aaron 54
Adelphi Theatre 219
Admiral Corporation 221
Aeterni Patris 5, 30, 31
Alexander, Samuel 9
Alinsky, Saul 276
America 9, 133, 298
American Catholic Philosophical
  Association 18
American Freedom and Catholic Power
  208-210
American Legion 189
American Scholar, The 81
anti-Catholicism 57, 61, 68, 70, 81-83,
  116, 126, 141, 186, 206-215
anti-communism x, 42, 55, 61, 75, 98,
  104, 109, 111, 127-186, 191, 192, 209,
  231, 286, 290, 291, 311
anti-Semitism 39, 87, 88, 91, 92, 112, 127
apologetics 16, 17, 22, 23, 36, 58, 88,
  201, 204, 205, 207, 208, 247, 254, 255
Aristotle 5, 247
Augustine, St. 96, 97, 218
Australia 240, 241
Avella, Steven 171
Ayer, William Ward 82, 83

B

Barrett, Bishop George M. 274
Bates, Ernest Sutherland 9, 110
Becker, Frank J. 229, 230
Bell, Bernard Iddings 167
Berdyaev, Nicholas 168
Bergan, Fr. William J. 3
Bergson, Henri 9
Berle, Milton 219
Bishop Sheen Story, The 3, 219, 224, 225,
  245, 254
birth control 36, 209
Bishops' Program of Social Reconstruction
  31-33, 92, 93
Blanshard, Paul 208-210, 213, 214
Blessed Martin de Porres Hospital 221,
  254
Blessed Mother 76, 312
Blessed Sacrament 312
Bordeaux, Rev. Michael 281

Bourne, Francis Cardinal 7
Brennan, Fr. Robert E. 204, 205
Brinkley, Alan 61
Brockmann, Fr. Lambert V. 14, 15
Bronstein, Rabbi Herbert 274, 284
Brooklyn Tablet 133
Brothers of Mary 2
Broun, Heywood 74, 80
Browder, Earl 135, 143-146, 151
Buckley, William F. 286, 287, 308, 311,
  316
Buddha 247
Budenz, Louis F. 74, 75, 76, 80, 135, 143,
  149-154, 158
Bukharin, Nikolai 147
Butler, Nicholas Murray 7

C

Calvary Baptist Church 82
Calvary Episcopal Church 58
capitalism 46-50, 54, 123, 140, 166
Cardinal Mercier Prize 8
Carpenter, Joel A. 59
Carroll, Bishop John 94
Catholic Action 34, 39-42, 87, 88, 103,
  252, 259
Catholic Action 45, 63-67, 69, 71, 154,
  155
Catholic Hour Broadcast Series (published
  transcripts) 36, 47, 85, 92, 94, 99, 121,
  140
"Catholic Hour" radio broadcasts 6, 19, 35,
  36, 38, 47, 52, 56, 57, 62-74, 84-86, 88,
  96, 97, 100, 113, 118, 121, 124, 126,
  140, 196, 210, 213
Catholic Renaissance 21, 196
Catholic Review 69
Catholic School 45
Catholic University of America ix, xvi, 1-5,
  8, 11-19, 22, 24, 25, 31, 33, 57, 74, 78,
  80, 145, 150, 179, 189, 210, 221, 234,
  315
Catholic World 204
Cavett, Dick 294, 298, 308, 316
CBS television 287
Chesterton, G.K. 10, 23, 79
China 240, 242, 246, 247

351

Index   *353*

ST PAULS

This book was produced by St. Pauls/Alba House, the Society of St. Paul, an international religious congregation of priests and brothers dedicated to serving the Church through the communications media.

For information regarding this and associated ministries of the Pauline Family of Congregations, write to the Vocation Director, Society of St. Paul, P.O. Box 189, 9531 Akron-Canfield Road, Canfield, Ohio 44406-0189. Phone (330) 702-0359; or E-mail: spvocationoffice@aol.com or check our internet site, www.albahouse.org